Mountain Masters, Slavery, and the Sectional Crisis in Western North Carolina

THE UNIVERSITY OF TENNESSEE PRESS / KNOXVILLE

Mountain Masters, Slavery, and the Sectional Crisis in Western North Carolina

John C. Inscoe

The author wishes to thank the *North Carolina Historical Review,
South Atlantic Quarterly, Civil War History, Slavery and Abolition,*
and Appalachian Consortium Press for permission to reprint
portions of this book that first appeared as articles in their
pages.

All maps produced by University of Georgia
Cartographic Services.

Frontispiece: The French Broad Valley in Bancombe County.
North Carolina Division of Archives and History, Western
Branch.

Library of Congress Cataloging in Publication Data

Inscoe, John C., 1951-
    Mountain masters, slavery, and the sectional crisis in western
    North Carolina / John C. Inscoe. — 1st ed.
    p.   cm.
    Bibliography: p.
    Includes index.
    ISBN 0-87049-597-6 (cloth: alk. paper)
    1. Slavery—North Carolina—History—19th century.
    2. Slaveholders—North Carolina—History—19th century.
    3. Slavery—Appalachian Region, Southern—History—19th
    century.   4. Slaveholders—Appalachian Region, Southern—
    History—19th century.   5. North Carolina—History—1775–
    1865.   6. Secession.
I. Title.
E445.N8I57   1989
975.6'00496—dc19   88-26172   CIP

To Jane

Contents

Illustrations

Preface

In 1833 Henry Barnard, a young law student in Pennsylvania, took time out from his studies to tour Virginia and the Carolinas. Upon moving into the western part of North Carolina, he wrote to his brother from Burke County: "This county and that of Bunkcome [sic] are situated amidst the Blue Ridge and the inhabitants are a set of cutthroats and savages, with some exceptions."[1] It is those "exceptions" in Burke, Buncombe, and surrounding counties during the decades before the Civil War that are the focus of this book. More specifically, this study relates how western North Carolina, a portion of the "other South," reacted to the crisis precipitated by that most distinctly southern institution—slavery.

Southern Appalachia has always been the most easily delineated and recognizable of the "other Souths," using that term both, as Carl Degler did to refer to those white nineteenth-century southerners who opposed or simply did not share the prevailing views and values of their region; and, in a far broader context, to designate a southern area not characterized by a plantation society or a cotton economy.[2] But just as the South was never the social, political, or economic monolith its regional designation has often suggested, so too were its highland areas not nearly as homogeneous as generalizations about them often imply. Nor were these latter areas nearly so out of tune with the rest of the South during the mid-nineteenth century as has often been assumed. Certainly most western Carolinians were not the cutthroats or savages that Henry Barnard suggested were predominant in that part of the state, though his misrepresentation of southern highlanders [xiii] was neither the first nor the last of such distortions. But those non-cutthroats and nonsavages who made up the vast majority of Carolina highlanders—Barnard's "exceptions"—were indeed exceptional in several ways. Their response to slavery, either as labor system or as political issue, and to the sectional crisis was more attuned to the low-land South than to other sections of Appalachia. In many respects, the very fact that the "otherness" of western North Carolina was less pronounced that that of other mountain areas was what rendered its situation unique.

Much in the Carolina highland experience during those tension-filled late antebellum years sheds light on southerners' commitments to their rights, to their multi-leveled identities and allegiances, and perhaps most of all, to their "peculiar institution." While western Carolinians' responses were often familiar and even predictable, the reasons behind those responses were often very different from those of others in the South, whether highlander or lowlander.

The conclusions drawn in this study could hardly differ more from the set of assumptions with which I began it. My original intention was to examine the impact of the Civil War on a part of the South largely isolated and alienated from the rest of the region, an area that had remained for the most part unencumbered by the slave labor system it ultimately was forced to defend. I now cringe rereading the opening sentence of my dissertation prospectus, which proclaimed: "There were probably few groups of southerners to whom the issues that led to secession and the Civil War were more irrelevant or for whom the war's outcome had lower stakes than the inhabitants of the Southern Appalachians." For as I moved from the secondary literature, much of which suggests just such a conclusion, to the evidence that antebellum mountain residents themselves left in their correspondence, journals, business and farm records, newspapers, political speeches, and voting returns, it very quickly became apparent that those issues which divided North and South were by no means irrelevant to these highlanders. Not only did they fully recognize their stakes in the sectional crisis from its beginning, but they reacted to the perceived threats to the South with fully as much interest, concern, and commitment as did any other group of southerners.

I am much indebted to William Barney for his valuable guidance, creative thinking, and sound judgment in overseeing this project as a dissertation at the University of North Carolina. Harry Watson and

Joel Williamson were equally helpful in the questions they raised and the issues they urged me to confront. I profited considerably from the wisdom of William Powell, George Tindall, and Peter Walker as well.

In its transformation from dissertation to book, the manuscript benefitted immensely from thorough and perceptive readings by Gordon McKinney, Daniel Crofts, Martin Crawford, James Klotter, John Barrett, and particularly Jane Censer, whose insights as a critic were matched by her skills as a copyeditor. The input of each of these scholars to my work was even more gratifying because of my high regard for and considerable use of their work. For sharing with me, or pointing me toward, valuable sources that have much enhanced my final product, I thank Loyal Jones, Ed Cabbell, Bill Auman, Alice Mathews, Ralph Mann, Tom Jeffrey, Richard Shrader, Marie Moore, Mattie Russell, Eric Walther, Tyler Blethen, and Curtis Woods.

Although (much to my regret) I began this study only after his death, I owe a great deal to the work of a fellow Morgantonian, Edward W. Phifer, Jr. Dr. Phifer was a local surgeon who, in his extensive writings on Burke County's past, endowed its residents with a historical legacy as thorough and varied, particularly on the antebellum period, as that of any North Carolina or even southern county. Dr. Phifer's insights into the nature of slavery and the character of slaveholders in our home county served both as a major inspiration for my own pursuit of this topic and as a valuable resource once my work was under way.

I am grateful to the staffs of the North Carolina Collection at Chapel Hill; the North Carolina State Archives; the Duke University Manuscript Collection; the Appalachian Collection in Boone, North Carolina; Western Carolina University's Special Collections; and the Pack Memorial Library in Asheville, for their guidance and service. I am particularly indebted to good friends and colleagues at the Southern Historical Collection, University of North Carolina, for their interest and support and for all that they taught me over six years as both a researcher and a fellow worker.

I owe much to my colleagues in the history department at the University of Georgia, and particularly to Lester Stephens, for constant support and encouragement as I have pursued this project here. I am especially appreciative of the skill, efficiency, and good humor with which Jennell Hutchins and Kathy Coley produced and reproduced the manuscript in its various manifestations.

I am grateful for the early interest of Mavis Bryant at the University of Tennessee Press in my work, and even more so for that of her successor, Cynthia Maude-Gembler, whose dogged persistence and infinite patience have had much to do with getting this manuscript into print.

I owe an enormous debt to Mike Martin, Tom Dyer, and John David Smith, three good friends with whom or for whom I have been privileged to work on other projects, for their sound advice and encouragement at various stages in this project's development. Each has been a great teacher and partner to me and I will always be thankful for their faith in me, for the opportunities they have provided me, and for all that I have learned from them.

Finally, very special thanks go to my parents, my parents-in-law, and my wonderful wife for all of their help and support throughout this endeavor and for much, much more.

Mountain Masters, Slavery, and the Sectional Crisis in Western North Carolina

Introduction

In *Absalom, Absalom!*, William Faulkner provided his only description of antebellum Appalachian society. Probing the background of Mississippi planter Thomas Sutpen, in an effort to explain his volatile behavior and ruthless sense of purpose as an adult, Faulkner focused on Sutpen's childhood move with his family from the mountains of what would become West Virginia to the plantation society of the Tidewater. An incident in which a black house servant refused Sutpen entry at a planter's front door, ordering him to the back door instead, served as the mountain youth's sudden realization of his own poor white status within this strange new society. In explaining why this rebuff so traumatized Sutpen, Faulkner contrasted it with the mountain life from which the boy had come. "Sutpen's trouble was innocence," Faulkner wrote, though it was an innocence of region as well as of youth. He elaborated:

> —he was born where what few other people he knew lived in log cabins with children like the one he was born in—men and grown boys who hunted or lay before the fire on the floor while the women and older girls stepped back and forth across them to reach the fire to cook, where the only colored people were Indians and you only looked down at them over your rifle sights . . . where he lived the land belonged to anybody and everybody and . . . only a crazy man would go to the trouble to take or even want more than he could eat or swap for powder or whiskey. . . . So he didn't even know there was a country all divided and fixed and neat with a people living on it all divided and fixed and neat because of what color their skins happened to be and what they happened to own, and where a certain few men not only had the power of life and death and barter and

[1]

sale over others, but they had living men to perform the endless repetitive personal offices . . . that all men have had to do for themselves since time began. . . . So he had hardly heard of such a world until he fell into it.[1]

It was only on leaving this egalitarian, nonmaterialistic, almost utopian communal highland existence that Sutpen was exposed to the evils bred by race and class. He soon learned that there was a difference "not only between white men and black ones, but . . . between white men and white men" as well.[2]

These passages from Faulkner's 1936 novel both reflected and perpetuated two long-standing, deeply engrained myths regarding antebellum Southern Appalachia: first, that its people had no slaves and thus no familiarity with either the institution of slavery or with black people; and second, that given the region's poverty and lack of opportunity (and, not coincidentally, its lack of slaves), it had insufficient economic or social variation to allow for the distinguishable class hierarchy that characterized the rest of the South.

These misconceptions began to emerge not long after the Civil War, as the distinctive culture of the Southern Appalachians was "discovered" by those outside the region. From Reconstruction through the first two decades of the twentieth century, the region held a particular fascination for travelers, local-color writers, missionaries, educators, and social workers, all described "a strange land and peculiar people."[3] The appeal of these mountains and mountaineers was based on what outsiders presumed to be their isolation and insulation from the outside world. The nation's vast progress in industry, transportation, and communication since the mid-nineteenth century seemed to have passed the southern highlands by. In characterizing its residents as poor, ignorant, and eccentric, outside observers assumed that, for Appalachia, time had stood still. They took the mountain society they saw to be virtually the same as that of the pioneers who had originally settled the region.

Turn-of-the-century accounts described southern mountaineers as "our contemporary ancestors," "the laggards of the original American stock," and "exponents of an arrested civilization."[4] In 1899, William Frost, the president of Berea College and observer of Appalachian life, stated his purpose in documenting mountain residents. They are an anachronism, he explained, "who are living for all intents and purposes in the conditions of the colonial times . . . these eighteenth century neighbors and fellow countrymen of ours are in need of a friendly interpreter." A journalist speculated three years earlier that if George

Washington had returned to life in Gilded Age America, only in Appalachia could he say, "At last here I find a part of the world as I left it."[5]

John Fox, in an extended analysis, placed southern highlanders within a universal sociological pattern which made backwardness endemic to highland life. In 1901 he wrote, "Arcadia held primitive the primitive inhabitants of Greece. . . . The Pyrenees kept unconquered and strikingly unchanged the Basques—sole remnants perhaps of western Europe's aboriginees . . . just as the Rocky Mountains protest the American Indian in primitive barbarism and not wholly subdued to-day." By the same token, Fox concluded, the Appalachians had kept the southern mountaineer restricted "to the backwoods civilization of the revolution." As late as 1924, a chronicler of the region wrote, "While the rest of the nation has grown far from our revolutionary ancestors, the Mountain People have been marooned on an island of mountains, and have remained very much the same as they were at that time."[6]

Such commentators on the region usually took as their central themes the negative effects of this economic and cultural stagnation. But in addition to emphasizing the present poverty and ignorance of those they encountered, many also saw admirable traits stemming from the "otherness" of Appalachia. Ulrich B. Phillips's somewhat backhanded tribute typified the ambivalence of many such assessments. "The mountains," he observed in 1929, "denied ambition . . . and the mountaineers acquiesced with a sturdy, self-respecting simplicity." Though often condescending in tone, observers recognized the pioneering spirit, the fortitude, the independence, and even the strong moral fiber of the mountain people. Residents themselves, from the earliest settlers on, claimed a special sense of virtue for their physically elevated locales. After several years' residence in the mountains of western Virginia, a Colonel John Stuart commented in 1798, "I here hazard a conjecture that has often occurred to me since I inhabited this place, that nature has designed this part of the world [as] a peaceable retreat for some of her favorite children, where pure morals will be preserved by separating them from other societies at so respectful a distance by ridges of mountains." Later writers usually attributed these virtues to the heritage of that first generation of settlers in those "forsaken hinterlands."[7]

In an influential 1980 article, James Klotter posed a provocative explanation for the sudden "discovery" of Appalachia in the late nineteenth century. Southern highlanders, he argued, presented an alternative target for the regionally focused philanthropists and reformers whose earlier efforts on behalf of southern freedmen had been frustrated by the failure of Reconstruction and increased racism in both the North and the South. They thus turned from southern blacks to southern mountaineers, who offered a special advantage— they were all white.[8]

The appeal of mountain "whiteness," though unstated and perhaps even unconscious, derived from yet another widely held assumption regarding highland virtue—that mountaineers had never owned slaves. It was not merely that most mountain residents could not afford or had no use for slaves. Writers often interpreted this demographic fact in highly idealistic terms. Those in Appalachia, according to one account, "cherish liberty as a priceless heritage. They would never hold slaves and we may almost say they will never be enslaved. They are true democrats, holding all men to be equals in human society, as they are taught that all of us are before God." An even more general account stressed the incompatibility of bondage and high altitudes: "Freedom has always loved the air of mountains. Slavery, like malaria, desolates the low alluvials of the globe. The sky-piercing peaks of the continents are bulwarks against oppression: and from mountain valleys has often swept most fearful retribution to tyrants."[9]

Others believed that the southern highlanders' physical separation from the bulk of the South's slave population kept them from sympathizing with the institution. "The feeling of toleration and justification of slavery," according to one such version, "with all the subtleties of states rights and 'South against North' which grew up after the Revolution, did not penetrate the mountains." Some credited the settlement of the mountains to the fact that poor whites were forced into the hills from the lowland South by the slave labor system that denied them "every avenue of honest employment." Slavery, in effect, "penned them up in their mountains . . . with no market for their skill and strength."[10] Thus the mountaineers' resentment of the slave system was based on their own exclusion, not only from the slaveholding class but from the areas dominated by that class as well. As an early twentieth-century missionary to the mountains concluded, "The aristocratic slaveholder from his river-bottom plantation looked with scorn on the slaveless dweller among the hills; while the highlander repaid his scorn with high disdain and even hate."[11]

In such accounts, this alienation from the slaveholding South meant that "when the Civil War came there was a great surprise for both the North and the South. Appalachia America clave to the old flag."[12] Mountain residents were thought to have remained aloof from the sectional controversies of the 1850s, and it was assumed that, when forced to take sides when war broke out, "the great majority of the Mountain People, like Lincoln himself, were on the side of the Union."[13]

Closely related to these misconceptions is the myth of the "rugged individualism" of the southern mountaineer. The decisive role of western Carolinians in defeating the British at King's Mountain in 1780 achieved almost legendary status and became a requisite reference in any portrayal of the highlander, by himself or by others, as the epitome of an independent and self-reliant spirit upon which America was built. "That glorious October day when the "Mountain Men" swept up the heights of King's Mountain, turned the tide of the Revolution and fixed the destiny of a Continent" runs a rendering of that highly valued victory typical in tone and in content.[14] Both John Campbell and Horace Kephart, the two most influential standardizers of the mountaineer image, reaffirmed the dominance of the traits of independence and self-reliance in mountain residents. Campbell devoted an entire chapter of his 1921 book, *The Southern Highlander and His Homeland*, to developing the idea that "heredity and environment have conspired to make [the mountaineer] an extreme individualist." (Campbell even attempted to depict yet another almost sacred part of the Carolina revolutionary tradition—the Mecklenburg Declaration of Independence—as a manifestation of highlanders' love of freedom, even though Mecklenburg County, where that 1775 precursor to Jefferson's document was drawn up, hardly qualifies as the "Carolina foothills" he claims it to be, much less as mountain territory.)[15]

A few years earlier, Horace Kephart explained the basis of this "fiery individualism" in his major study of mountain life, *Our Southern Highlanders* (1913):

Our highlanders have neither memory nor tradition of ever having been herded together, lorded over, persecuted or denied the privilege of freemen. So, even within their clans, there is no servility nor any headship by right of birth. . . . In this respect, there is no analogy whatever to the clan

system of ancient Scotland, to which the loose social structure of our own
highlanders has been compared.

Thus, Kephart concluded, even in his own time, "mountaineers are
unsocial. . . . they recognize no social compact. Each one is suspicious of the other. Except as kinsmen or partisans they cannot pull together." Even in the mid-1960s, Jack Weller echoed these conclusions
in his aptly titled *Yesterday's People*, where he noted that mountain people "have no community life as such or life outside their very limited
family group."[17]

Perhaps because there is a certain logic to these conclusions, and
because later mountain residents themselves perpetuated these stereotypical views of their fathers and grandfathers, these simplified and
somewhat romanticized depictions of Appalachia have persisted to
some degree up to our own time.[18] Indeed, for some sections of the
southern highlands and for some later periods in its history, such
characterizations are valid. But as generalizations about the region as
a whole prior to the Civil War, these views contain more fallacies than
grains of truth. This study is in part an attempt to refute such assumptions for at least one section of Southern Appalachia, the westernmost counties of North Carolina. An analysis of the antebellum
social and economic life of Carolina highlanders indicates that these
people were far from being the deprived, isolated, self-centered mountaineers depicted in later accounts. On the eve of the Civil War, their
society was a vigorous, complex, and growing one in which slavery
played a small but very basic part. The negative conditions that later
set the Appalachians apart as a region passed over by time and progress reflected not a perpetuation of conditions long inherent in mountain life, but rather a regression based on a variety of factors both
during and after the war.

Western North Carolina during the 1840s and 1850s was very much
a region of communities, and its development during that period was
characterized by a subtle interplay of its residents' identities as parts of
larger wholes. In social, economic, and particularly political terms,
they came to see themselves as citizens of towns and/or counties
within their mountain district, as westerners within North Carolina,
as North Carolinians within the South, and as southerners within the
nation. Through a growing awareness of their vested interests in all of
these roles, they shaped their responses to the sectional crisis at mid-
century.

It is in this context of community and regional interaction that the Carolina highland experience speaks to much broader and more significant concerns than the mere debunking of stereotypes about mountain society and its past. For, except for their eloquent rendering by William Faulkner, the stereotypical concepts outlined above have been limited primarily to chroniclers of Appalachia. Just as such regionalists have neither examined nor analyzed the attitudes and motivations of their subjects during the sectional crisis, so historians of the sectional crisis and secession have failed to examine this particular region. Yet the character and dynamics of mountain society, and in particular its leadership, suggest important insights into the nature of class and racial structures in the antebellum South. These insights in turn enhance our appreciation of the complexity and diversity of factors that shaped reactions to threats posed to the continued existence of those structures.

Western North Carolinians were a set of southerners far removed from the planter class of the cotton-, rice-, and sugar-producing South. Prohibited by terrain and climate from opportunities for such large-scale one-crop production, the economic and political elite of North Carolina's mountains consisted, for the most part, of a prosperous, ambitious, and progressive middle class of business and professional men. Most of them were also landholders who, like the small subsistence farmers making up the vast majority of the region's residents, engaged in a widely diversified agriculture. This entrepreneurial elite exemplifies that aspect of southern society increasingly recognized by scholars of the Old South—the strong capitalist propensities among its upper classes. Such characteristics have been stressed by those who believe that the similarities between antebellum North and South were at least as important as their differences. Edward Pessen, in his 1980 synthesis of these theories, argued that, like their counterparts above the Mason-Dixon line, "Southern planters depended heavily on outside trade, participated enthusiastically in a money economy, and sought continuously to expand their operations and their capital."[19] In his even more recent *Southerners All*, Nash Boney builds a strong case for the essentially bourgeois nature of most southerners. "They worked hard at their jobs—or callings—which usually but not always was agriculture, and they wheeled and dealed like expectant capitalists in a credit-fueled, free-enterprise, profit-oriented economy." This aggressive materialism, he claims, was as evident in the rural countryside as it was in urban settings.[20] Likewise, Robert Wiebe's incisive interpretation of the economic, social, and political trends toward democratization between the 1790s and 1860s stresses the commonality of these developments for all Americans—to the extent that they institutionalized and nationalized American society by the mid-nineteenth century—even though inherent in those trends were the impetuses for the ultimate breakdown of national unity through secession and civil war.[21]

Others treat the commercial tendencies of the planter class primarily as evidence of continuity between Old and New Souths.[22] Both Dwight Billings, in his study of postwar North Carolina, and Jonathan Wiener, covering much the same period in Alabama, focus on the mercantile and/or manufacturing interests of antebellum leaders as antecedents of the new social order of Reconstruction and beyond.[23] Even more apt is Paul Escott's analysis of North Carolina class distinctions in the latter half of the nineteenth century. Escott, noting that commercial concerns provided the economic foundation for many of the state's wealthiest families, states that far more of those gentry fortunes were due to entrepreneurial than to seigneurial pursuits.[24]

Nowhere do these trends seem more apparent than among the economic and political leaders of western North Carolina. Simply because landholding and agricultural production alone were not viable options for accruing wealth, almost all of the most affluent mountain residents were merchants, hotel or resort owners, land speculators, manufacturers, bankers, lawyers, doctors, or some combination thereof. As such, they were active promoters of their region's economic development and participated in trade networks that reached well beyond their own highland region. Indeed, in their activities, values, and goals, they had much in common with their commercial-agrarian counterparts in the North.

The affluent mountaineers themselves never recognized such similarities, however, because of two other, far more significant features that shaped and defined their power and influence at home and fully set them apart from their nonsouthern peers. First of all, they were, almost without exception, slaveholders; and second, as businessmen they had established strong commercial links with and intraregional dependence on the Lower South. Geography made the plantation markets of South Carolina and Georgia far more accessible than the eastern and even much of the piedmont sections of their own state. That, plus the tourism from those states to their area, gave western North Carolinians far closer ties with the Lower South than most of the Upper South ever established—a situation that in itself had important political, as well as economic, repercussions.

But perhaps the most significant aspect of antebellum Appalachian life is what it reveals about slavery on the South's periphery. The facts that less than ten percent of the Carolina mountain populace consisted of slaves and that ninety percent of white western Carolinians owned no slaves had important implications for the variations imposed on the "peculiar institution"—on how it shaped, or failed to shape, a class-consciousness among those few who did own black property; on how it functioned as a labor system in a nonplantation rural economy; on how it affected the quality of life for those slaves owned by mountain masters; and finally, on how it infused slavery as an issue into the political consciousness of the region's residents. In many ways, the majority of citizens and their leaders were very much within the mainstream of southern sentiment throughout the sectional crisis. Their reactions to events such as Nat Turner's rebellion, John Brown's raid on Harpers Ferry, Lincoln's election, Fort Sumter, and their own state's secession were often indistinguishable from those common throughout at least the Upper South. Even the more radical views of the Lower South were voiced by some western Carolinians who enjoyed the consistent support of their fellow mountaineers.

The course of mountain politics in the 1850s particularly demonstrates that the strength of the proslavery ideology within the South was by no means limited to those areas most dependent on it economically or most immersed in it demographically. For western Carolinians, slavery, as an abstract and symbolic concept, took on a life of its own, with an importance and a centrality in political rhetoric far out of proportion to any commitment which the extent of slave ownership alone would have justified. At the same time, strong support for southern rights and even southern nationalism was based on much more than a defense of slavery alone. The sectional crisis of the late antebellum period helped to shape a southern identity and a regional loyalty in the mountains of North Carolina (as elsewhere in the South) that rose above the tangible self-interest of either the area as a whole or its citizens as individuals. Throughout the developments that culminated with secession, the range of feelings, attitudes, and degree of commitment to the South among western North Carolinians ran the gamut from extreme unionism to equally extreme secessionism. But far more than has generally been recognized for at least this one major segment of Appalachia, the latter sentiments not only outweighed the former, but both sides cast their arguments in terms of which course would best ensure the survival and safety of slavery.

The "innocence" of Faulkner's mountain characters was certainly far removed from the energetic, entrepreneurial, slaveholding western Carolinians who, with their eyes open wide, led those in their small corner of the South toward secession and the Civil War. The typical and the unique aspects of these leaders' situation, and how they shaped and were shaped by that situation, raise important questions about the nature and multiplicity of southern societies, about the dynamics of slavery as both a political and an economic force, about the interplay of local and regional identities, and about how all these factors contributed to the flow of events that drove the South out of the Union in 1860 and 1861.

Chapter 1

Mountain Agriculture:

"Yielding in abundance and variety"

In the first issue of *Mountain Life and Work* in 1925, the journal's co-founder, Olive Dame Campbell, wrote, "There is no fundamental reason for separating mountain people from lowland people, nor are mountain problems so different at bottom from those of other rural areas in the United States."[1] This was an extraordinary statement at a time when social consciousness of the poverty, ignorance, and isolation of the people of the Southern Appalachians was at its peak. While stereotypes and caricatures of mountaineers were rapidly establishing themselves in American minds, Mrs. Campbell's attitude was refreshing, although its applicability to mountain life in the early twentieth century is debatable. But if her statement is applied to the same area in an earlier era, the years before the Civil War, it takes on new significance and becomes far more accurate as an assessment of highland society.

Only slowly and reluctantly have historians recognized that antebellum society in the Southern Appalachians shared much in common with the rest of the South.[2] By the 1840s and 1850s, with trade and transportation advancing elsewhere in the South, the topographical disadvantages of the highlands began to be recognized as possible hindrances to its residents' full participation in the economic development around them. At the same time, settlers were beginning to push back into the more secluded highland coves and hollows that would sooner or later cut off much of their contact with the outer world. But most mountain residents saw such trends as little more than temporary phases which, as in other frontier situations, would

[11]

give way to the inevitable march of progress and civilization. They did not view themselves as part of a separate region with special problems distinguishing them from the rest of the South. Any distinctiveness in their geographic or demographic situation they saw as a minor aberration soon to be overcome, and foresaw nothing to prevent their eventual integration into an economic network that would allow them to share even more fully in the rest of the South's prosperity and development.

Thus, on the eve of the Civil War, western North Carolina was far from the backward, isolated area it was later seen to be. The variety of situations and the diversity of its populace equaled if not surpassed those of any other rural section of the antebellum South. The judgment of a western Carolinian that "probably no section of the State contains a population so widely diversified in politics, wealth, morals, and general intelligence" is an exaggeration.[3] But his suggestion that mountain society was far more complex and varied than was usually recognized is a valid one. The region did retain and perpetuate some of the cruder aspects of its frontier origins, and a trend toward increased isolation, with resulting alienation, was apparent in some of its remoter sections. But as this chapter and the next demonstrate, the antebellum populace of North Carolina's mountains in many respects constituted a thriving, productive, and even a progressive society which looked forward with confidence to a promising economic future. James Patton, one of the region's earliest and most prominent residents, observed in 1837 that when he settled in the Carolina mountains, it was "the poorest part of the country I ever saw to make property." But he went on to say, "I do not entertain the same opinion now. Changes and improvements have convinced me that there are few sections of country superior to the western part of North Carolina."[4]

From the revolutionary era on, the broad fertile valleys of North Carolina's mountain region offered strong inducements to those seeking accessible, productive farm land. French botanist Francois Michaux explored the region in 1802 and noted, "These mountains begin to be populated rapidly. The salubrity of the air, the excellence of the water, and more especially the pasturage of these wild peas for the cattle, are so many causes that induce new inhabitants to settle there."[5] The early patterns of settlement in the western part of the state were based largely on those valley contours. East of the Blue Ridge, the rich bottomland of the Catawba and Yadkin rivers attracted a steady influx of settlers from the mid-eighteenth century on. Soon after the Revolution, settlement expanded across the Blue Ridge Mountains, and the French Broad, Swannanoa, Toe, and New rivers offered equally attractive opportunities for productive farming. Much later, as Cherokee lands were made available to white landholders, the Nantahala and Tuckaseigee valleys were the sites first claimed.

The earliest settlers in western North Carolina were able to acquire large tracts of flat, fertile, well-irrigated bottomland. This, plus access to trade routes and markets, made these first landholders so successful in both raising and selling crops that by the late antebellum period they were the area's best established residents and its social, economic, and political leaders. Once the best land of these major valleys was occupied, settlers began to push along smaller rivers or creeks or up to wide gaps above these valleys. Although topography there dictated smaller farms, those who settled these areas did not have to isolate themselves from either the larger valleys or the world beyond. A prime consideration for most settlers was proximity to others. That, along with accessibility and soil fertility, in most cases led them first to occupy the land along the mouths of creeks and streams. Only gradually did settlers move up their lengths unless particularly good tracts of land farther upstream forced them to choose between accessibility and fertility.[6]

In a study of settlement patterns in the northern part of the Blue Ridge in Virginia, Gene Wilhelm has demonstrated the logical progression of settlement by topographical setting, moving chronologically from the flattest and most accessible valleys to gaps and hollows and finally to more remote coves and upper ridges. Even in the Virginia mountains, where settlement preceded that in western North Carolina by as much as fifty years, very few settlements had developed by the 1850s in areas remote enough to isolate its residents from access to or influence by other mountain or piedmont communities.[7] The same is even more true for the North Carolina mountains, where, because of Cherokee occupation of much of the region, settlement began much later but then proceeded more rapidly.

The agricultural output of the mountain counties reflected both the diversity and the productivity of the settlements. As in the rest of the South, farming was the mainstay of western North Carolina's economy, and most mountain residents were engaged to some extent in agricultural pursuits. But without the predominance of any single cash crop, the range of crops grown was as wide as or wider than that in any other part of the state or of the South. Despite a cooler climate and thus a shorter growing season than the surrounding "lowlands," the mountain counties more than held their own in the variety and quantity of their output.

Table 1.1 indicates those agricultural products and byproducts that were grown in larger quantities in the mountains than elsewhere in North Carolina, as shown by the rankings of the fifteen westernmost counties among counties statewide, according to 1850 and 1860 census data. Table 1.2 consists of those products in which the proportion of mountain production within the state was greater than the mountain counties' share of the population; in other words, where per capita production in the region exceeded that in the state.[8] As both tables reveal, mountain counties led the state in production of grains such as buckwheat and rye, and of farm-manufactured by-products such as cheese, butter, and molasses. Mountain apples made up a substantial part of the state's output, but they were only the most prevalent of fruits grown in the mountains, with peaches and grapes just as common in some areas. One observer in Henderson County noted that all the farms he passed were making apple cider, and many made apple or peach brandy as well. He also saw many waterwheels utilized in crushing sorghum to make sugar and molasses.[9] In market value of garden produce, too, the totals for western counties far exceeded those of counties elsewhere in the state.[10] But perhaps the most significant statistic revealed by these charts, other than the sheer diversity of mountain agriculture, is that those products in which the region most excelled within the state were by no means the dominant crops within the region. Corn was the one crop grown by all farmers, usually making up at least half of a farmer's total output.[11] Tobacco too was raised in significant quantities in most mountain counties.[12]

More than any crop produced, livestock dominated mountain agriculture, even though its per capita production rate was only slightly higher than the statewide rate (see table 1.2). Professor Elisha Mitchell, the noted geologist at the University of North Carolina, once compared the Carolina mountains to "ancient Arcadia—the country of herdsmen and shepherds." He predicted that "it is to the raising of cattle and sheep and the making of butter and cheese for the counties below the ridge, that it may be expected there will be a tendency in the industry of the mountain region for many years."[13] The various prob-

Table 1.1. Ranking of Crop Production in North Carolina Mountain Counties, 1850 and 1860

County	Buckwheat	Rye	Flax	Irish Potatoes	Value of Orchards	Molasses**	Honey	Cheese	Butter	Wool
	(1850/1860)									
Ashe*	1/1	1/1	6/4		5/	1/	4/	2/1	7/	1/5
Buncombe	5/5			/1	/4	/1	6/	7/3	1/5	3/4
Caldwell	8/						/9			
Cherokee		3/		/5		/2			10/	/10
Haywood	/4				/8					
Henderson		6/2		/4						
Macon	9/									
Madison	/6						10/	/2	/1	
Watauga	2/2	/7	/1		4/		1/1	/8	6/6	7/7
Wilkes	7/	2/10	1/2	2/	/3		5/8	/9		8/
Yancey	3/3	/3	/3	3/3	2/7	2/				

*1860 ranking represents Ashe and Alleghany counties combined.

**1850 figures for molasses are incomplete.

Note: This table includes only those crops for which at least one mountain county was among the top 10 producers in the state in 1850 or 1860. Also, it includes only those counties which ranked in the top 10 producers of at least one crop (11 of the 15 mountain counties in 1860). Computed from Table 9, North Carolina, in *Seventh Census of the U.S.: 1850* (Washington, D.C.: Robert Armstrong, 1853), 318–24; and *Agriculture in the U.S. in 1860: Compiled from the Original Returns of the Eighth Census* (Washington, D.C.: Government Printing Office, 1864), 104–11.

Table 1.2. *Percentage of Agricultural Production of Mountain Region within North Carolina, 1850 and 1860*

Product	1850		
	NC Total	WNC Total	WNC%
Buckwheat (bushels)	16,704	15,281	91.5
Rye (bushels)	229,006	98,006	42.7
Hay (tons)	145,653	21,634	14.9
Flax (pounds)	593,796	128,322	21.6
Irish Potatoes (bushels)	620,318	82,037	13.2
Orchards ($ value of)	34,348	14,355	41.7
Molasses* (gallons)	704	497	70.6
Honey (pounds)	512,564	156,564	30.5
Hogs (swine)	1,812,813	218,421	12.0
Sheep	595,249	107,534	18.0
Cattle**	471,711	72,497	15.4
Milk Cows	221,799	32,306	14.6
Cheese (pounds)	95,921	34,313	35.7
Butter (pounds)	4,146,290	836,723	20.2
Wool (pounds)	970,738	19,829	19.9

*Figures for molasses are incomplete for 1850.
**Includes combined totals for oxen and other cattle.

Note: This table includes all products in which more than 10% of the state total in 1850 and 12% in 1860 was produced in western North Carolina. Computed from Table 9, North Carolina, in *Seventh Census of the U.S.: 1850* (Washington, D.C.: Robert Armstrong, 1853), 318–24: and *Agriculture in the U.S. in 1860: Compiled from the Original Returns of the English Census* (Washington, D.C.: Government Printing Office, 1864), 104–11.

lems that hampered Lower South livestock production—from the physiological strain of its hot, humid climate to parasitic diseases and poor forage yields—may also have added to an awareness of how much more hospitable highland conditions were to animal husbandry.[14] The minimal manpower required to tend flocks and herds, their adaptability to the variations of the mountain topography, and ready access to major markets made the raising of cattle, sheep, and particularly hogs (inexplicably overlooked by Mitchell) an integral part of almost every mountain farm, regardless of its size. As such, they demanded not only the majority of a farmer's land, but also much of his grain crop.

Table 1.2., Continued

Product	1860		
	NC Total	WNC Total	WNC%
Buckwheat (bushels)	35,924	34,926	96.4
Rye (bushels)	436,856	157,445	36.0
Hay (tons)	181,365	23,730	13.1
Flax (pounds)	216,490	88,641	40.9
Irish Potatoes (bushels)	830,565	176,575	21.3
Orchards ($ value of)	643,688	160,926	25.0
Molasses* (gallons)	263,475	173,848	66.0
Honey (pounds)	2,005,969	321,688	16.0
Hogs (swine)	1,883,214	259,862	13.7
Sheep	546,749	100,563	18.4
Cattle**	465,187	65,380	14.1
Milk Cows	228,623	32,689	14.3
Cheese (pounds)	51,119	24,244	47.4
Butter (pounds)	4,735,495	1,412,391	29.8
Wool (pounds)	883,473	192,158	21.8

The availability of what Mitchell called "luxuriant meadows of the most valuable grasses" provided ample grazing land, as did the natural balds in the state's far western highlands. A number of the more affluent farmers along the Catawba and Yadkin valleys east of the Blue Ridge bought these higher pasturelands to their west and sent their cattle and/or sheep there for the summer months. Raising hogs demanded even less effort. Usually they were allowed to forage freely on nuts and mast in the woods for much of the year and were rounded up in the fall for final fattening on corn before being slaughtered or sold. As with crop production, for the average mountain farmer there was very little specialization in raising livestock. Most raised at least two types of animals, which, in addition to cattle, sheep and hogs included horses, mules, milk cows, goats, and poultry.[15]

Diversity, then, was the key to mountain agriculture. The variety of crops grown was exceeded only by the variations with which they were combined from one farm to another. A sample of the output of twelve farmers in 1850 (one from each of the mountain counties in ex-

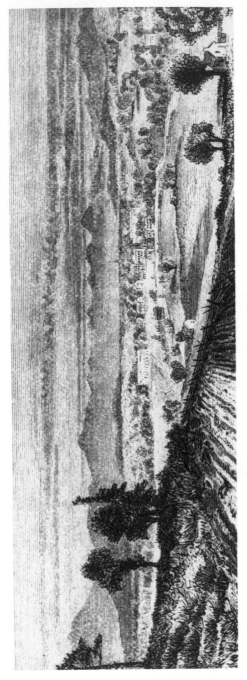

Figure 1. The French Broad Valley in Buncombe County. North Carolina Division of Archives and History, Western Branch.

istence at that time) reflects that range. Their improved landholdings ranged from sixty to seven hundred acres, with unimproved acreage from three to five times larger. Corn was the only crop raised by all twelve men, and it made up at least half of the total crop production of each. Nine of the twelve also grew oats, seven produced Irish and/or sweet potatoes, and five raised either flax, hay, or both. Three grew tobacco. Five of the men harvested a substantial apple crop, and five produced large amounts of honey and/or molasses. All twelve owned swine, ranging from 30 to 110 in number. All but two raised either cattle, sheep, or both, though their hogs almost always outnumbered either.[16]

Visitors were impressed and residents seemed to appreciate the relative quality and productivity of mountain farms. After a discussion of the malarial climate of South Carolina and Georgia, George Swain, one of Asheville's earliest and most prominent citizens, wrote of the advantages of the "healthy climate" that originally brought him to Buncombe County and of the added bounties that led him to settle there. "I would not now," he declared, "exchange our salubrious air, pure Mountain water, Excellent Pork, Beef, Butter, Cheese, Poultry, Mutton, or Vension to say nothing of the best of Cabbages and Irish Potatoes, for all the advantages of stagnant putrid Air, puddle water . . . and rancid Beef & Butter."[17] An early visitor to Ashe County described it as "mountaineous and Hilley," but went on to say that "the soil is extremely rich yielding in abundance wheat Rye oats Barley & Buck wheat and every other vegetable equal to any cold country on Earth. It is a fine County for pasture and Meadows from which Great numbers of cattle and sheep are raised which brings much wealth to the farmer."[18]

Other travelers marveled at the Yadkin, Oconaluftee, Swannanoa, and Tuckaseigee valleys as they passed through them, equally impressd with their appearance, output, and climate.[19] The French Broad Valley, which ran through both Henderson and Buncombe counties, was described as one of the richest sections of agricultural wealth in the country. One journalist characterized the river as being "as calm and smooth as any lowland stream. Its course is through broad, fertile valleys, famed for their beauty and richness of soil."[20] A British visitor to Henderson County, William W. Malet, was particularly impressed with the fruit produced there. After commenting on the size and flavor of the peach crop, he said of the apples he saw, "they are as superior, the best tasting weighing up to one pound each; strawberries and grapes, of great size and flavour, abound also."[21]

A number of progressive agriculturalists, among both mountain residents and outside observers, recognized the special qualities of climate and terrain in western North Carolina and sought to adapt farming products and methods to them. Nicholas and John Woodfin, the latter an associate editor of the state's agricultural journal, the *North Carolina Planter*, made their extensive holdings in Buncombe County models of crop and livestock productivity. The quantity of corn grown per acre, the variety of grasses, and the quality of their cattle were all noted throughout the region and, in the words of one visitor, "demonstrated that the mountain lands of Buncombe . . . may be made renumerative."[22] The wealth of transplanted South Carolinians and Georgians in Henderson County was often invested in such "model farms." "Their improvements and mode of farming," one observer noted with approval, "together with their improved breeds of stock of all kinds, are attracting much attention, and are quite instructive to our people."[23]

Though not a native of the region, Professor Elisha Mitchell was a frequent visitor and close friend of many mountain residents. He was very much concerned with their fulfilling what he saw as the extraordinary productive capacity of their natural resources. After a trip through Ashe County in 1828 he wrote, "It is a favorite theory of mine that Ashe has greater facilities for maintaining its soil in a state of productiveness . . . than any other part of North Carolina, [and] that all the forests will hereafter be cut down and converted into extensive pastures on which will be fed vast herds of cattle and flocks of sheep."[24] He advised western North Carolinians to study New England to see how an area similar in soil and climate had utilized its resources, particularly its grazing lands, to best advantage. What had been accomplished in two centuries there, he said, should inspire mountain residents to follow that northeastern example and to "fix upon many spots that are now in great measure neglected, but which a patient industry will in the course of a few years render the most productive and valuable."[25]

Mitchell's former student (but later rival), Congressman Thomas L. Clingman of Asheville, also took an active interest in the agricultural potential of his native region. He corresponded regularly with experts all over the country, seeking and supplying information on the cli-

Figure 2. Elisha Mitchell. North Carolina Division of Archives and History.

mate, topography, geology, and horticulture of the area. His efforts before the Civil War concentrated on promoting projects to increase the
production and marketability of dairy products, sheep, and even
wine.[26]

Others sought to do more than merely suggest means of improvement. A Pennsylvanian proposed that the North Carolina legislature
provide three thousand acres of mountain land for testing how well
Merino sheep could be raised in that area. As a result, he informed the
state's lawmakers, "resources that are now worthless in your State"

would, in five years, "place your State in the front-rank of wool-grow-
ing states."[27] Certainly the most accomplished horticulturist in the region was Silas McDowell of Macon County. A regular contributor to
the *North Carolina Planter* and other southern agricultural journals, he
was recognized as the state's leading apple producer, or pomologist,
and western North Carolina's most active botanist. His successful
grafting experiments introduced new and heartier varieties of winter
apples to the region that encouraged others to devote more of their
land to orchards. By the late antebellum years, apples had become one
of the region's most marketable commodities.[28] In 1858 McDowell reported that he had been told by Georgia merchants that their market
was regularly supplied with fruit from Cherokee County, which they
found superior to that previously obtained from the northern states.
McDowell was also enthusiastic about grape production, for which he
found the North Carolina mountains particularly well suited, calling
them "the favourite home of the Vine."[29]

Despite the many advantages and great potential they offered, the
mountains, in both real and personal wealth, remained the poorest
section of the state. In 1860 the cash value of western farms averaged
$1,354, less than two-thirds of the state-wide average.[30] Such compar-
isons are misleading, however, for they obscure the peculiarities of
mountain farming. The valley settings of most western North Carolina
farms meant that landholdings usually consisted of a section of relatively flat bottomland and even larger sections of forested hills or
mountainsides. Thus the ratio of improved to unimproved acreage in
the mountain counties was, in 1860, roughly one to five, compared
with a statewide ratio of 1 to 2.6.[31] But such a large proportion of un-
cleared property was not a reflection of waste or negligence. Given the
terrain and the predominance of animal over crop production throughout the region, such land utilization was both practical and cost-effec-
tive, since livestock could graze or forage in wooded areas with
virtually no expense or labor required of their owner for much of the
year. As a result, it was the unimproved acreage, even more than the
improved, on which the most prolific and marketable of highland
products were raised.[32]

The improved acreage of western Carolina farms in 1860 averaged
sixty-eight acres per farm, though it varied greatly from one county to
another, ranging from a median of almost one hundred acres under
cultivation in Burke and Alleghany counties to about fifty acres in Wa-

Table 1.3. Distribution of Farm Size in Mountain Counties, 1860

County	Total No. of Farms	Under 20 Acres		Under 50 Acres		Over 50 Acres		Over 100 Acres	
		No.	Percent	No.	Percent	No.	Percent	No.	Percent
Alleghany	347	23	6	118	34	229	66	125	36
Ashe	818	120	15	433	53	385	47	177	22
Buncombe	924	91	10	379	41	545	59	268	28
Burke	495	19	4	242	49	253	51	99	20
Caldwell	566	57	10	235	42	331	58	148	26
Cherokee	959	167	15	631	66	328	34	106	11
Haywood	441	54	12	213	48	228	52	106	24
Henderson	724	72	10	370	51	354	49	122	17
Jackson	493	116	23	321	65	172	35	46	9
Macon	632	128	20	372	59	260	41	77	12
Madison	493	91	18	273	55	220	44	96	20
McDowell	423	11	2	168	40	255	60	89	21
Watauga	598	145	24	428	72	170	28	60	10
Wilkes	1,324	119	9	730	55	594	45	219	16
Yancey	1,050	277	26	721	69	329	31	110	10
WNC Total	10,287	1,480	14	5,634	55	4,653	45	1,848	18
NC Total	67,022	6,929	10	27,811	41	39,211	59	20,715	31

Source: Computed from *Agriculture of the U.S. in 1860*, 210.

tauga and Yancey.[33] As table 1.3 indicates, in eight of the fifteen westernmost counties in 1860, at least a fifth of the landholders had over a hundred acres under cultivation, led by Alleghany and Buncombe counties, where 36 and 28 percent of farmers, respectively, fell into this largest landholding classification. In all of the mountain counties but one (Jackson), at least a tenth of the landholders farmed a hundred acres or more. Mountain counties varied somewhat more in their percentages of small farmers. In four counties, fewer than 10 percent of their landholders worked under twenty acres, while in only two counties, did more than a fourth of the farmers do so (see table 1.3). Though all of these figures seem small compared with the statewide averages, it should also be remembered that the statewide figures were considerably inflated by the inclusion of numerous large eastern plantations. Large farms were very much a part of mountain agricultural operations, but even the small and medium-sized holdings that predominated in the area were ample in size and productivity to support their human and animal occupants and to allow for often substantial surpluses of some products as well.

The relevance of all of this to the study at hand lies in those surpluses. Although such marketable extras were often only a small proportion of the output of this region presumably characterized by small farm self-sufficiency, even that limited commercial potential proved to be of vital significance in establishing links between western North Carolina and the rest of the South—links which greatly influenced the character and identity of mountain residents. The impact of both the markets for, and the marketability of, this highland productivity is the focus of the following chapter.

Chapter 2

Mountain Community and Commerce:

"Where the world got out . . .
and where the world got in"

In *The Hills Beyond*, Thomas Wolfe's fictionalized account of his native region's history, he described antebellum Asheville as "the place, not only where the world got out, but also where the world got in."[1] Asheville was indeed the hub of western North Carolina's trade and commerce throughout the nineteenth century, but to varying degrees, Wolfe's description was applicable to other highland towns and villages as well. Their origins were often inauspicious, and some early settled areas were slow in developing any concentrated community center. By the early antebellum period, however, these highland towns had become, and remained, as integral to the character of mountain society as were its farms. Whether they developed as county seats, commercial centers, or tourist resorts, these more concentrated communities generated much of the area's progress, diversity, and entrepreneurial spirit. As such, they not only shared much with other southern communities but also served as the region's primary links to those communities. Though many remained quite small and crude even by the standards of the rural South, these mountain towns became their region's strongest bulwarks against any tendencies toward isolation or alienation from the outside world. Very few mountaineers were so secluded that they did not have access to, or make use of, some such community, and such commercial connections, as much as any other factor, shaped the mountaineers' identities as southerners with a vested interest in slavery's survival.

Western North Carolina's earliest settlers, whose primary goals were simply to acquire land and make it as productive as possible, [25]

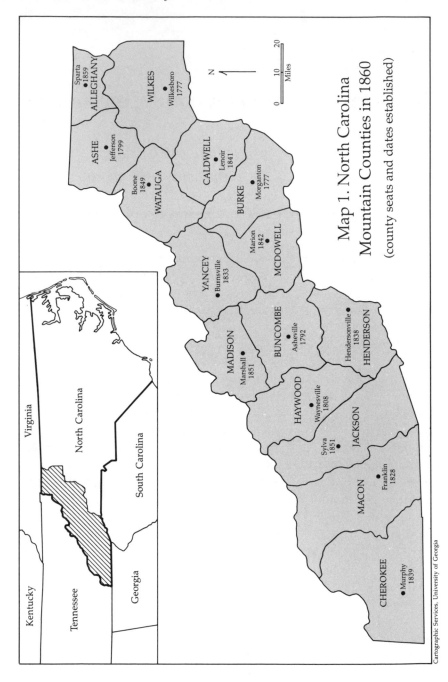

Map 1. North Carolina
Mountain Counties in 1860
(county seats and dates established)

Cartographic Services, University of Georgia

seem to have had no pressing need for towns or the services they offered. In most of the region, it was only the formation of new counties
and the need of a seat for newly-organized local governments that led
to any effort at establishing nonrural community centers. Morganton,
the earliest town in the western part of the state, was established only
when the legislative act creating Burke County in 1777 also stipulated
that a commission fix the location for a courthouse, prison, and stocks.
Even then, it was seven years later, when the creation of the Morgan
Judicial District gave some urgency to the need for a courthouse, before a site was selected and a town plan drawn up.[2]

Between 1835 and 1860, nine new western counties were created.
Despite the fact that several of them had had substantial populations
well established for several decades at least, they often had no community or commercial center to designate as a county seat. Thus Marion in McDowell County, Webster in Jackson County, Sparta in
Alleghany, Waynesville in Haywood, Burnsville in Yancey, and Wilkesboro in Wilkes were established only when the need for a county seat
arose, and in locations chosen strictly for their accessibility, topo-
graphic suitability, and/or their central position within the new county
boundaries.[3]

In other instances, the presence of a store or trading post was the
determining factor in the selection of a site. James Harper had operated a large store, tannery, blacksmith shop, and harness shop for a
full decade before the site of these enterprises was chosen in 1841 for
Lenoir, the county seat of newly-formed Caldwell County.[4] Likewise,
Jordan Councill's mercantile operation became such a focal point for
trade and communication in his area that it, with the new name of
Boone, was designated as Watauga County's seat in 1850.[5] Cherokee
County was created from Indian territory soon after the 1838 removal
of the Indians, and its county seat, Huntersville (later called Murphy),
was established on the site of an earlier trading post from which Col.
Archibald Hunter had maintained a brisk business with the Cherokees.[6] Macon County was also part of former Indian territory, and its
county seat, Franklin, grew from the foundations of what had once
been a sacred Cherokee village.[7]

County residents fully recognized the potential economic and political significance of these seats of local government, and bitter disputes sometimes broke out between communities or sections of a
county as to which would reap those benefits. In several cases, the

Figure 3. View of Asheville, North Carolina, 1851. North Carolina Division of Archives and History.

more obvious choices were passed over in favor of smaller communities or even relatively unsettled locations as the result of hard-fought contests between rival factions. Buncombe Courthouse, later called Morristown and finally Asheville, was built on a plateau where a wagon road forked at "the big branch between the Indian graves." Such an obscure locale was a compromise choice between the county's most concentrated settlements at Reems Creek and Swannanoa. But even that so-called midpoint was considered a victory for the northern section of Buncombe and a loss for those to the south, whose selection committee refused to sign the final report.[8]

With Madison County's formation in 1851, the small but lively village of Jewell Hill, site of the area's militia muster and court sessions, was assumed to be the logical choice for the county seat except by the few but influential citizens of Lapland, a smaller settlement farther up the French Broad River. Zebulon Vance, who had grown up in Lapland, donated fifty acres there for the county government facilities and was so confident that his action would settle the matter that he wrote to his fiancée, Harriett Espy: "You may expect to see, next time you pass that place, a flourishing and romantic village."[9] His influence, along with that of his uncle Adolphus E. Baird, who had long operated a tavern and inn there, and Samuel Chunn, whose stock-stand was equally well established, finally won the day for the Lapland site in 1855, though by only a single vote of the selection committee.[10] Lapland's name was promptly changed to Marshall, yet another four years elapsed before the court began to meet there instead of at Jewell Hill.

The most heated contest was in Henderson County. After the county was created in 1838, a three-year controversy raged over the location of its seat, Hendersonville, whose name at least had already been determined. Advocates for a site on the French Broad River were opposed by those favoring one along Buncombe Turnpike. "River" and "road" factions, as they came to be called, remained so adamant that it took three appeals to the state supreme court and a referendum election throwing the decision to the county's voters before the "road" location was finally agreed upon.[11] In this as in the other disputes, commercial interests were at least as decisive as political factors in the choices made. Both the French Broad and the turnpike offered potential for substantial trade between their region and South Carolina and Georgia, and the final decision was based largely on the judgment of county residents that the latter offered the greater potential as a trade route and so was the one to which their new seat of local government should be most accessible.

Not all mountain towns owed their origins to demands for commercial centers or county government bases. Tourism contributed to the early growth of several communities. Hotels, inns, or seasonal private residences often formed the cores of what grew into fully operational, multi-functional towns and villages. Though many of western North Carolina's most successful and best-known resorts did not emerge until late in the nineteenth century, Warm Springs in Madison County, Flat Rock in Henderson County, and White Sulphur Springs and others in Haywood County were all fully established and thriving by the 1830s and 1840s.[12]

Despite dubious and often long-delayed origins, the functions and services of these mountain communities, once established, became indispensible to the farmers they served. The towns attracted enterprising men of varied training and backgrounds, whose skills and services did much to move most parts of the region beyond the frontier stage of development and to add diversity and complexity to a largely agricultural economy and farming populace. The governmental function of the county seats, along with the judicial function of their county and circuit courts, made lawyers, judges, clerks, and other officeholders prominent among the earliest residents and most frequent visitors. They and their families created the need for other professionals such as doctors, ministers, and teachers, who soon followed in their wake, either as permanent or seasonal residents or as circuit riders who served several communities in an area. Merchants, artisans, tavern- and innkeepers, and land speculators recognized the business opportunities offered by these emerging towns; by moving there early, they were often able to engage simultaneously in several types of commercial ventures, with profitable results.[13]

Despite certain features shared by all mountain communities, there were also significant differences in their characters and patterns of development. Western Carolina towns can be divided into three distinctive groupings, based on their geographic locations, their dates of origin, their growth rates, their appeal to outsiders, and the abilities and ambitions of their citizens during the antebellum period. One such group consisted of the older, more established towns in the foothills east of the Blue Ridge. Morganton, Lenoir, Wilkesboro, and, to a lesser degree, Marion, developed a thriving commerce which, along with their functions as county seats, gave them as diverse and as affluent a populace and an economy as any small town in the nine-teenth-century South. Situated in broad fertile valleys formed by streams and rivers converging from the mountain slopes just to the west, these communities catered to, and were to a large extent built by, the affluent landholding families nearby who had been the area's ear-liest settlers. Even more vital to their sustained growth was their func-tion of providing an accessible outlet to the piedmont to meet the market needs of farmers further west. At the same time, these towns served as gateways for traffic moving up into the mountains from the rest of the state. The mere appearance of these towns reflected their relative prosperity and earlier roots. Of Morganton, "the oldest village in the mountain district," one visitor noted "its pleasing avenues and inviting residences" and concluded that "from a society point of view, the town sustains its ancient reputation for polish and cleverness."[14]

Almost sixty miles west and across the ridge, Asheville was the most prominent of a second group of communities—those along the French Broad Valley, an accessible, well-traveled north-south corridor that was in many ways the region's social and economic lifeline. In 1795, soon after the selection of Buncombe Courthouse's site, two en-terprising brothers, Bedent and Zebulon Baird, recognized its profit-able real estate potential and bought all of the land designated for the county seat. After donating a central lot as the site of the courthouse, they laid out streets and lots which they sold to families and busi-nesses as they moved into the area. From this promising start, the town prospered and grew. Thanks to its accessible scenic location at the intersection of the wide valleys of the French Broad and Swanna-noa rivers, it became a natural crossroads for most trade and travel west of the Blue Ridge. As Thomas Wolfe much later described the set-ting of his hometown and its significance, "It was, indeed, of all that mountain district of the west, 'the place.' It was a natural confluence of the hills, the junction of the four directions of the map—the ap-pointed, the inevitable, place."[15] By the late antebellum period, its res-idents included many of the region's ablest and most ambitious citizens, who had built and supported over twenty stores or busi-nesses, a courthouse, a jail, three churches, three large hotels, several schools, and a female college.[16]

Due to the Carolina highlands' scenic settings and cool, pure air, summer tourism played a major role in the economic and social vitality

Figure 4. James W. Patton's Eagle Hotel, Asheville, North Carolina. Pack Memorial Library, Asheville.

of Asheville and other mountain communities. Local residents quickly sought to capitalize on this influx of visitors from May to October every year. Among the most successful and influential citizens of Asheville were its hotel owners. James Patton's Eagle Hotel and James M. Smith's Buck Hotel were among the town's largest buildings and were so often filled to capacity that nearby homes profited by accommodating their overflow.[17] Like the Walton House in Morganton, which in 1859 advertised that it was "supplied regularly with Fresh Fish from Norfolk and Newbern, in fact with every delicacy usually found at First Class Hotels," these establishments prided themselves on the quality of their accommodations and service.[18] Among their most basic services were the various forms of transportation they provided. The Eagle Hotel, for instance, declared that it was "in readiness at all times to convey passengers to any part of our beautiful Mountain Country." In addition to daily or every-other-day stagecoach service to Greenville and Spartanburg, South Carolina, Greenville, Tennessee, and Morganton, Salisbury, and Charlotte, North Carolina, its livery stable offered "superior saddle and harness horses and a lot of entirely NEW Vehicles: consisting of Hacks, Carriages, Buggies etc., which are safe and comfortable."[19]

In addition to the commercial boom brought about by the "summer people," as they were referred to by mountain residents, tourists also did much to enhance those communities to which they flocked. An Asheville native boasted that the town was "adorned with many beautiful residences, the result of cultivated taste among its inhabitants, or the summer residences of citizens of South Carolina." He went on to praise his fellow residents, "who, in spirit of improvement, a love for the beautiful, and a taste for the refined, make gardens of waste places, and turn the barren hillsides into blooming undulations."[20] A young female visitor wrote of a ride she took on the outskirts of Asheville along the Swannanoa River. "It was," she exclaimed, "quite a merry drive indeed; [I] saw a great many fine farms and residences and a good many people riding out—in buggies and some on horseback in riding costumes, looking quite like city folks and city life."[21] Western Carolinians elsewhere viewed Asheville as a cultural center and seemed to admire the relative sophistication of its residents and its social life. Despite the less than serious tone of her letter to a cousin, that admiration is reflected in a Macon County girl's 1847 description of the community, seventy miles east of her home, where she was in boarding school: "Well as you are aware I am settled in for the present in the notable city of Asheville, a place unsurpassed in the known world for the intelligence, refinement, correct taste, generosity and hospitality of its inhabitants."[22]

Even more impressive to travelers were the adjacent Henderson County communities of Hendersonville and Flat Rock. In 1827, Charles Baring, a prominent Charleston rice planter, sought relief from the ill effects of the swampy coastal climate on his wife's health and built a lavish estate at Flat Rock. Others from South Carolina and Georgia soon followed him, and both Flat Rock and Hendersonville quickly gained reputations throughout the South as "charming refuges from the hot plains of the lowlands."[23] There the affluence and taste of its transplanted South Carolinians and Georgians was apparent in the fashionable clientele of their hotels and even more so in the "baronial style" of their estates. To a New York traveler, they "rivaled in elegance and taste any villa or mansion on the Hudson," and an aristocratic British visitor said that they reminded him "more of England than anything we had seen in America."[24] Just as Baring had led many of his fellow Charlestonians into the area, his plantation, with its magnificent columned home, beautifully landscaped lawns and gardens, private chapel and rectory, complex of stables and slave quarters, and vast private park for deer hunting, served as a model that inspired others to imitate or even outdo it.[25] The social activities in these communities were fully in keeping with the lavish settings in which they took place. As summarized by a Hendersonville woman, they included "quadrilles danced under candled chandeliers, gracious conversations over three o'clock dinners in silver-laden banquet rooms, morning gatherings on latticed porches, carriage drives over Little River Road . . . and picnics on the mountian ridges."[26]

The mineral springs resorts catered to an equally affluent clientele in much the same manner, if on a smaller scale. In addition to its healthful waters, Warm Springs, some thirty miles north of Asheville near the Tennessee border, was the best-known and best-attended of these spas. Though even grander resorts were already well established in western Virginia, local promoters proclaimed that their Madison County operation "presented more attractions to the seeker of pleasure than probably any watering-place in the South." Elaborating on those attractions, Charles Lanman, an 1849 visitor, wrote that "music, dancing, flirting, wine-drinking, riding, bathing, fishing, scenery-hunting, bowling, and reading are all practiced here to an unlimited extent."[27]

Finally, a third category of more typical mountain communities consisted of county seats both northeast and farther west of the French Broad group. In sharp contrast to the thriving resorts, most of these villages were established later and remained small, crude, frontier-like settlements. Most visitors describing them tactfully chose to extol their magnificent, "romantic" physical settings. But Augustus S. Merrimon, a young Asheville attorney who practiced in various superior and county courts throughout western North Carolina in the early 1850s, was more openly contemptuous of them and their residents. Of the state's westernmost town, Murphy, he wrote that it "is a small place and poorly improved. There are several small stores here that seem to do a small business. All of them together would not make one good one."[28] Waynesville, despite the presence of several fashionable resorts

Figure 5. Warm Springs Hotel, Madison County.
Harper's New Monthly Magazine L (April 1875).

in the vicinity, was no more appealing to Merrimon, who found it "a dirty small village and there is no place of entertainment in it fit to stay at. One would suppose it to be a large negro quarter to see it from a distance." Its buildings, he wrote, were already dilapidated and decayed, including the courthouse which had been built only a few years earlier.[29]

But it was Jewell Hill (where Madison County's court still met despite the selection of Marshall as its county seat) that Merrimon found most offensive. Its men were generally drunk, as were its women, whom he described as "dirty, filthy strumpets." He wrote with disgust, "I do not know any rival for this place in regard to drunkenness, ignorance, superstition and the most brutal debauchery."[30] British geologist George Featherstonhaugh echoed these statements in recording his impressions of Franklin. "What a dreadful state of things! Here was a village most beautifully situated . . . that might become an earthly Paradise, if education, religion, and manners prevailed . . . But I could not learn that there was a man of education in the place disposed to set an example of the value of sobriety to the community."

He revealed his own national bias by concluding that the town served as a "perfect specimen of that kind of equality which democratic institutions often lead to."[31]

But in their emphasis on the backwardness of these westernmost communities, contemporary observers failed to acknowledge their commercial and social vitality. For example, Boone, Watauga County's seat, was described by one visitor as "nothing but a few dwellings clustered around the Court-house," while another called it "a bad place, abounding in grog shops, street fights, and bad weather." But by 1860, Boone actually consisted of six stores, two tanneries, two hotels, several boarding houses, a blacksmith shop, and only one saloon. The demand for lumber to keep up with the pace of construction in the community was great enough to make three sawmills among the town's most successful enterprises in the 1850s.[32]

Regardless of their rate of growth or the degree of sophistication of their citizens, all of these mountain towns exerted an influence far in excess of their size. Community studies have provided a number of models by which these towns may be categorized in terms of function and relationship to the dispersed populace of their region. As links between their own county's residents and the "outer world," almost all of these mountain communities are best described by models emphasizing the contacts and accessibility they provided.

In a study of twentieth-century Appalachian communities, for example, Art Gallaher, Jr., has categorized five types of communities on a continuum from the most extreme cases of social and geographic isolation through progessively more complex and sophisticated communities to the region's few urban centers. The fourth level of community development along his scale is that of county seat community, in which political and trade functions provide "systematic links to the greater society which exist in more variety and in more institutional areas" than in the three preceding levels. Almost all of western North Carolina's antebellum towns and villages met the criteria for Gallaher's county-seat model, whether they were indeed county seats or only tourist resorts or commercial centers.[33] Darrett B. Rutman has distinguished between the horizontal (commonality within a community) and the vertical (links by external associations to larger social units) as dimensions of community life. By his criteria, most North Carolina mountain communities fell well within the normal range of nineteenth-century community development along both dimensions.[34]

The government and judicial functions of the actual county seats entailed regular contacts by its residents with agencies and individuals outside the region and brought frequent visits from various officials and other professionals. The impact of tourists and seasonal residents on those in and around the resort communities was even greater. But on the majority of mountain residents—farmers and their families beyond the bounds of these communities—these particular types of outside influences had minimal effect. Travelers only occasionally veered from their well-beaten paths, and when they did so their encounters with the more remote local residents were sporadic and superficial. Likewise, county officials came in contact with their county's rural citizens only when the latter bought or sold land or paid their taxes.

It was as commercial centers that almost all of these towns, from Asheville and Morganton to Franklin and Murphy, exerted their most pervasive influence on their region. The functional cores of these communities were the merchants, and it was through them that rural mountaineers maintained their most substantial and immediate links with the world beyond their own. Just as stores and trading posts were often the nuclei around which communities grew, so too did merchants remain vital to the further prosperity of both town and county residents. Many businessmen provided various services as well as merchandise, so that a "store" was often only one of several operations conducted by a single owner. Jordan Councill of Boone, William McKesson of Morganton, Jesse Siler of Franklin, and James Harper of Lenoir are only four examples of merchants who operated tanneries, blacksmith shops, and mills in addition to their mercantile businesses, and each of them was among the most prominent and influential leaders in his community. By meeting multiple needs of their areas, they and their counterparts in other mountain towns served as the primary, and often the only, contact many western Carolinians had with the outside world. Residents' dependence on these men, based on personal contact as well as economic need, made the influence of those businessmen considerable. A Buncombe County resident recalled that "old settlers in the country each had his merchant in Asheville, not only to supply his wants, but in whom he confided as a trusted friend."[35]

In addition to supplying local residents with a wide variety of manufactured goods and imported food staples, highland store owners provided an equally vital service as an outlet for surplus goods that those same customers wished to sell. The scarcity of cash often necessitated a barter system. Its flexibility and localized nature provided a readily available means by which mountain farmers could, and often did, move beyond mere subsistence farming and enter the market economy, if only in a limited way. Mountain merchants encouraged these transactions. An Asheville store, advertising a variety of new goods available, reminded its customers that "country produce will be taken at the usual rate in discount." Burnsville merchant J.W. McElroy announced in a newspaper, "I am determined to sell [my merchandise] for cash and country produce, such as feathers, ginseng, wool, Beeswax &c, lower than goods have ever been sold in the county of Yancy [sic] . . . Now you need not carry your cash and best produce out of your own county to get good bargains." Some stores were more specific in the type of produce they sought. A.T. Summey and Company, an Asheville dry goods operation, ran a notice that "BACON! BACON!! will be taken in payment of debts due us at its market value."[36]

While farm produce and meat from slaughtered livestock were the most basic of local goods bartered, the inventory of several mountain stores indicates that a wide variety of distinctively mountain products was also common in these transactions. A British woman visiting Asheville seemed somewhat offended by the diversity of goods carried in shops there. Merely to buy "a bit of ribbon," she had to face "horrible raw hides . . . masses of mica . . . and every imaginable thing for sale."[37] In his store on the present site of Brevard, Leander Gash stocked "hams, venison, hides, and feathers, chestnuts, chestnut bark, apples, cabbages, wild honey and mountain herbs."[38]

Several merchants specialized as dealers in ginseng, the root of a small plant native to the North Carolina mountains, which was sold to China, where its medicinal qualities were in great demand. Calvin Cowles of Wilkesboro bought it, along with other roots and herbs, from mountain residents who gathered it in the forests of the state's northwest corner and brought it down to his store. Bacchus Smith and Nimrod Jarrett of Yancey County found the ginseng, or "sang," business so profitable in the 1830s that they ran three factories at which over 86,000 pounds of the freshly-dug green root were steamed, dried, and prepared for the Chinese market.[39] The great variety of goods exchanged is but one indication of how widespread such mercantile transactions were among all levels of mountain society. The gathering of ginseng was an enterprise usually undertaken by the poorest residents, those who owned little or no land.[40] They too were those most likely to supply stores with many of the forest products stocked, from roots, herbs, and wild honey to bear meat and venison. A combination of merchant account books and census data reveals that the farmers who traded in produce they had raised fell within the fairly wide range of landholders with from twenty to one hundred improved acres, though similar transactions with even smaller farmers were not uncommon.[41] The active trade maintained by mountain merchants in both farm-produced and forest-gathered goods thus meant that there were few families, if any, in the region without some opportunity for commercial transactions of some sort.

There was a close correlation between the unusually large quantities of apples, garden produce, dairy products, and molasses produced on mountain farms (see table 1.2) and the inventories of either local stores or wagons heading for market. This suggests that these were not merely small surpluses left over after the demand for home consumption had been met. Rather they seem to have been produced, on farms of all sizes, specifically for their marketability. These mountain farmers produced cash or barter crops that remained secondary to their far more substantial grain and livestock production, which similarly may or may not have been raised primarily for their own use. These trends illustrate just how thin the line was between self-sufficient and commercial agriculture in western North Carolina. Certainly by any usual standard the majority of farms there would have been classified as basically subsistence rather than commercial operations; and yet the majority of farmers, small as well as large, had some stake in the market economy of their region.[42]

This commercial character of mountain agriculture did not develop only after years of a basically subsistence economy. From its earliest settlement on, Southern Appalachia attracted both farmers and tradesmen who recognized the market potential of the region. In his groundbreaking study of Virginia's Shenandoah Valley, *Commercialism and Frontier*, Robert Mitchell maintained that commercial tendencies were "the most dynamic element in the emerging pioneer economy." As early as 1730, Shenandoah settlers sold up to a tenth of their total production to distant markets. After its first generation or so, the valley's residents became "larger, more occupationally varied and credit-dependent," and "the proportion of goods for sale increased typically from one-third to one-half or more of total output." Though never to so vast an extent, that trend characterized the economic development of the North Carolina mountains as well. There is ample evidence that early settlers there shared in what Paul Salstrom has called "an ambitious and speculative disposition among the pioneers who pushed down the Great Appalachian Valley in the eighteenth century and . . . early nineteenth century."[43]

Since merchants were among those initial inhabitants, from the beginning their transactions with local producers provided the latter with access to commercial outlets well beyond their own region. As early as 1802, Francois André Michaux described the trade pattern he observed in passing through Morganton:

> One warehouse only, supported by a commercial house at Charleston, is established in this little town, where the inhabitants, for twenty miles round, come and purchase mercenery and jewellery goods from England, or give in exchange a part of their produce which consists chiefly of dried hams, butter, tallow, bear and stag skins, and ginseng, which they bring from the mountains.[44]

This pattern was typical and continued in most mountain communities throughout the antebellum period.

James Patton's career serves as a good example of how early the commercial potential of North Carolina's mountain region was recognized and successfully exploited. Born in Ireland in 1756, Patton was among the many post-Revolutionary Scotch-Irish immigrants to Pennsylvania. His failure as a farmer made him, like many of his fellow Ulstermen, an itinerant merchant. Moving down the Great Wagon Road into Virginia in 1789, he encountered another such salesman who advised him that there was money to be made in the area around Morganton, North Carolina. Following that lead, Patton soon established for himself a trade network that entailed the purchase of a variety of mountain products—from livestock and bearskins to ginseng and snake root—from backcountry communities in North Carolina and Virginia for resale in mid-Atlantic urban markets. His business dealings with western Carolina farmers in particular proved so successful that he moved with his family to Wilkesboro in 1791. There he formed a partnership with Andrew Erwin that encompassed a general store, an inn, and his continuing trade with Philadelphia, Lancaster, and Washington. Erwin moved on to Asheville in 1803, and Patton followed four years later. There he opened a store, a tanyard, and the Eagle Hotel. Over the next thirty years, these enterprises and others made him one of that area's most successful and influential businessmen.[45]

Some merchants, particularly those in the northern corner of North Carolina's mountain region, followed Patton's trade pattern by looking north for their primary business contacts. As early as 1794, cattle drives from Wilkes County joined those from western Virginia that proceeded to Baltimore and other Chesapeake markets. Calvin Cowles, also of Wilkes County, made annual trips to Washington, Philadelphia, New York and Boston, where he found ready markets for his ginseng and other roots and herbs. These he sold for cash, which he then used to purchase the merchandise with which he stocked his Wilkesboro stores for the coming year. James Harper of Lenoir sold deer and other animal skins and furs to markets in Baltimore and Philadelphia and obtained much of his merchandise from mercantile suppliers there.[46]

But just as James Patton shifted his sights from north to south, these men, along with the majority of western North Carolina merchants, also participated in the far more established trade network to the southeast. As commercial cotton production came to dominate the agriculture of the Lower South, planters became more dependent on the importation of basic food supplies from the Upper South and beyond. This trend encouraged residents of those "hinterlands" such as North Carolina's mountains to take advantage of the increased demand for their surplus crops.[47] These plantation markets became increasingly profitable and accessible outlets for mountain produce, and the mountain merchant, as the means through which those opportunities were realized, took on new significance to his local clientele.

Charleston and Columbia in South Carolina and Augusta, Athens, and Savannah in Georgia were regular trade centers for these businessmen. Trips to one or more of these towns at least once a year, along with regular correspondence and shipment of goods throughout the year, were routine for most of them. Joseph Cathey, a postmaster and storeowner at Forks of the Pigeon (now Canton) in Haywood County, planned his trips after consultation with agents in South Carolina and Georgia as to the prices on "the bacon, lard, and feather markets." He then headed south, usually in February, with wagonloads of smoked meat, tanned hides, feathers (in demand for beds), and apples. He was accompanied by varying sized herds of livestock, all of which he had bought from or traded with farmers from all over

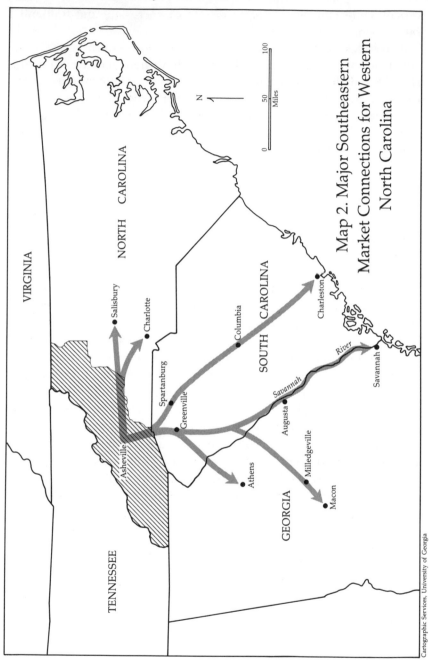

Map 2. Major Southeastern Market Connections for Western North Carolina

Cartographic Services, University of Georgia

the county. In 1854 he sold "40 cattle and 69 sheep" for $1,386 in Augusta. He used the cash to purchase saddles, bridles, and tools from a "hardware importer," and various supplies from a druggist before moving on to Charleston, where he bought coffee, sugar, candy, salt, and rifle powder from a wholesale grocer, and paint, oil, and glass from a "staple and fancy dry goods" establishment.[48]

William Holland Thomas operated a mercantile business at Quallatown in Cherokee County, which catered as much to Indian customers as to whites. He too stocked his store through regular trips to the southern markets, particularly Augusta and Athens, Georgia. He faced competition in the sale of goods to the Indians. At least one other businessman recognized the Cherokees' buying power, particularly after periodic compensatory fees were awarded them by the federal government. In an 1852 letter, Nimrod Jarrett of nearby Franklin wrote that he was on his way to Charleston. "I have sent on a lot of fat cattle and expect to overtake them before they reach there. I expect to purchase some goods myself," he wrote, explaining that "another man is selling goods to the Indians in this country. They had had a large payment made them a few weeks back amounting to over one hundred thousand dollars. Everybody in the country is trying to set some trap for it and me among the rest."[49]

Though all mountain merchants were dependent on the southern markets to maintain their operations, not all took part in these trading excursions themselves. Some either worked through agents or combined forces with other businessmen making the trips. Some merely hired wagoners to make the trips for them. Johnson W. King, a Murphy resident and at one time a partner of Thomas's, recorded in his diary in the mid-1840s that he had hired a wagoner named Hogan to get a load of iron from two local ironworks and "go on to Athens and barter it for such things as is stated in a bill I left." He noted that he would "pay him according to number of miles he has to go, according to Athens rate for hauling." He later recorded that he had "paid Hogan for hauling off iron and for taking cattle to market." Eli Sharpe, also of Franklin, might have qualified as such a "hauler." He reported to his brother John in 1854 that despite a recent trip to Athens, he was planning to return "to haul a load of goods for the merchants in the town of Franklin. I expect to drive 6 horses and mules as I done before." He concluded that "wagoning is a pore business but I have some hawling of my own" that made it worthwhile.[50]

Just as not all merchants made these trips themselves, so neither was it only merchants who made them. In Yancey County, several families shared the expense of hiring a wagon (for four dollars) to carry as much as a hundred pounds of beeswax, cured venison, honey, dried fruits, and animal pelts to southern markets.[51] Many farmers produced livestock and/or produce of sufficient quantity to dispense with the services of mercantile middlemen and either drove those goods south or hired their own drivers to do so. Isaac Avery, for example, a Burke County planter, considered business trips to South Carolina a basic part of his son Waightstill's education. In 1829, he sent the thirteen-year-old boy to Columbia to bargain for supplies. On his return, his father wrote proudly that he had "traded about as well as anybody I could have picked up here." Waightstill was sent back the next year with wagonloads of produce to sell and was soon driving his father's livestock to markets in Raleigh and Charleston.[52]

An 1858 dispute between western North Carolinians and South Carolinians reflects not only the close commercial ties between the mountain region and other parts of the South, but also the mountain residents' increased independence and self-confidence in their role as suppliers. Mountain residents claimed that the Greenville and Columbia Railroad refused to accept their money at its full value, and that this practice had also led South Carolina "merchants, traders, and hotel-keepers [to] take it only at a heavy discount." Western Carolinians were highly offended and quick to point out that South Carolina needed their trade more than they needed South Carolina's. "Greenville enterprise and sagacity," it was said, "proposed to kill the goose that lays the golden eggs."[53] The *Asheville News* proposed that its readers take their business from Greenville, South Carolina, and give it to Greenville, Tennessee. The latter was the same distance (sixty miles) north of Asheville as the former was south, and by the late 1850s, it too provided a railroad connection. Thus, the newspaper's editor declared:

> Now Western North Carolina, while she may have "apples" and "cabbages," which the northern Greenville may not want, will exercise her own discretion in the matter; and the southern Greenville can buy the aforementioned "apples" and "cabbages" or go without, as she may elect. It is certain that goods can be brought here from New York or New Orleans, via Greenville, Tenn., quicker and at less cost than by the old route. One of our

mercantile houses has already made the experiment and others will follow suit. Men will trade where they are best treated, and if the short sighted policy of our South Carolina neighbors should lose them the trade of this section, they can say "we did it."[54]

Livestock production was the most substantial form of commercial agriculture practiced in the mountains and the primary means of exchange used by merchants and those they dealt with locally and out-of-state. The movement of those animals through the mountain counties to South Carolina and Georgia also provided many mountain residents with their most direct access and exposure to the southern market economy. As early as 1800, cattle and hogs were being driven from the North Carolina highlands to markets in Charleston, Savannah, Norfolk, and Philadelphia.[55] After the War of 1812, these drives aimed more and more exclusively at the Lower South, as the rapidly expanding cotton market made it more profitable for Deep South farmers to divert more of their labor and land to its production and rely on the noncotton areas of the Upper South for their meat supply. With this increased demand, Kentucky and Tennessee soon entered the livestock market in full force and utilized the same new routes through western North Carolina.

By the early 1820s, George Swain of Asheville kept a precise record of the number of animals passing through town. In November 1822 he reported that "the hogs crowd the road continually. In fact they exceed last years considerably for the time of year; 19,406 have already passed by. The whole number last year did not exceed 20,000." Only a week later, he wrote, "My list now contains 25,594 . . . since that 2 other droves containing 617 has come forward."[56]

Though hogs made up the vast majority of self-propelled produce that moved through the area, other livestock was also common. An 1845 account by the operator of a small inn in Henderson County for livestock and drovers indicates the diversity of his four-footed clientele. Eli Sharpe wrote to his brother that "thear has passed through the Turnpike gate more horses and mulles than has passed any one year for som years past. Thear has passed a greate number of the bes[t] hoges I ever saw and good many Kentucky and Tennessee fat cattle and among all the cattle drivers has a lot of shotes and sheep with them."[57] Ducks and turkeys also made the trek across the mountains, often headed for slaughterhouses in Spartanburg, South Carolina, from which they were shipped by rail to other markets. A traveler near Warm Springs in 1857 reported passing 373 head of Kentucky cattle followed by a drove of some 400 ducks.[58]

Asheville was already established as the region's center for the livestock trade, but it became even more important with the completion in 1828 of western North Carolina's first major thoroughfare, the Buncombe Turnpike, which greatly increased the road capacity for herds on the hoof as well as for wagon travel. Charles Lanman, who traveled it in 1849, noted that "an immense number of cattle, horses, and hog are annually driven over it to the seaboard markets. Over this road also quite a large amount of merchandise is constantly transported for the merchants of the interior, so that mammoth wagons with their eight and ten horses, are as plenty as blackberries and afford a romantic variety to the stranger."[59]

Running along the already well-traveled French Broad Valley from Tennessee directly south through Madison, Buncombe, and Henderson counties into South Carolina, where it joined highways to Charleston and Augusta, this turnpike brought a commercial boom in its path. As its major junction with other routes, Asheville served as a central point of convergence and thus profited most by the traffic. By the late antebellum years, 140,000 to 160,000 animals were estimated to have passed through the town every year, with a value ranging between two and three million dollars.[60] Some butchering was done in Asheville, with cured meat, bacon, and lard either sold locally or held for later trips south. But the vast majority of animals merely continued toward their destinations under their own steam.

The Carolina highlands were as important a supplier to this lively livestock trade as they were a way station for it. Mountain farmers added significantly to this passing traffic by selling their animals to drovers already en route. For those not located near one of the major turnpikes, this often entailed driving their own herds to the nearest or most accessible point at which the southbound traffic could be met. For many in the northwest counties, this was Boone or Wilkesboro, and for even more in the southwest counties, it was Asheville. Again, many farmers of sufficient means or with marketable herds large enough to justify the time and expense made the trip themselves. Lanman made the acquaintance, for example, of a Nantahala Valley resident who was "by profession a grazing farmer." "He raised a goodly number of cattles as well as horses and mules," Lanman wrote, "and

Figure 6. A hog drive through the mountains. North Carolina Division of Archives and History, Western Branch.

his principal markets for them are Charleston and Savannah, to which cities he performs a pilgrimage in the autumn of every year."[61]

Because these animals, particularly hogs, moved so slowly, averaging no more than eight to ten miles a day, a string of inns, or "drovers' stands," were soon established at frequent intervals along the turnpike and on other routes to accommodate both the herds and the men who drove them. James Patton's success with his Asheville stand led him to purchase and develop Warm Springs as both a tourist resort and a livestock way station. By the late antebellum period, there were fifteen such stands in operation along the fifty-five-mile section of the turnpike north of Asheville. These stands, probably more than any other enterprise in the mountains, served as the most direct—as well as the liveliest—commercial link between mountain residents and the rest of the South. Even more than conventional mercantile operations, these combination store-inn-stable complexes provided mountain farmers with a ready means of social and economic intercourse.

The business handled by each stand from October through December was often staggering. "I have known ten to twelve droves," recalled an Asheville resident of the 1850s, "containing from 300 to one or two thousand stop overnight and feed at one of these stands or hotels."[62] In 1849, William A. Lenoir spent the night at Alexander's Inn north of Asheville, where he reported the presence of "Five Thousands Hogs and seventy-five people."[63] His wife was one of several who noted the strange incongruity of those sites that doubled as drovers' stands and fashionable resorts. She complained that what she'd hoped would be a quiet restful week at Warm Springs was spoiled by the incessant noise of the hogs and hog drovers who daily passed through that elegant hotel's grounds."[64] David Vance claimed that he had fed 90,000 hogs in one month at his stand at Marshall, but Hezekiah Barnard boasted that he had topped Vance's total for the same month by feeding 110,000 at his stand several miles north.[65]

The demand for feeding animals on that scale was enormous, especially since drovers had to compensate for the weight loss of their stock brought on by the long and rigorous journey. But it was a demand to which local farmers readily responded. The large amounts of corn produced on mountain farms not only fed their own livestock before it was sold, but also constituted the one cash crop almost always grown in excess of a farm's own needs.

Before this flood of livestock provided such a convenient market, corn's most lucrative form for mountain farmers was liquid. Most of the surplus grain converted into liquor and fruit turned into brandy was destined for home, or at least local, consumption. But these distilled by-products also proved to be the only practical and profitable means of transporting those crops to distant markets. A turn-of-the-century mountain resident's explanation would have been equally applicable several generations earlier. "The only farm produce we-uns can sell is corn," he said. "You see for yourself that corn can't be shipped outen hyar. . . . Corn *juice* is about all we can tote around over the country and git cash money for."[66]

In 1810, Burke County already boasted 106 distilleries which produced over 20,000 gallons of whiskey and brandy annually. One of Burke's largest planters and most prominent citizens, Isaac T. Avery, testified to the financial advantages such enterprises offered him and many other farmers, when in 1824 he informed his brother-in-law that he had "made enough corn to do me, perhaps can make whisky to pay for my salt, sugar, and coffee and perhaps pay my taxes, but money is as scarce as I ever knew it."[67] As drovers and their herds increased the demand for ground corn from farmers along their route, less of the excess crop was converted into whiskey, though the latter remained a profitable commodity for those in mountain areas farther from that flow of hoofed traffic.[68] In 1859 a Yancey County resident stated that he had sold 1,200 gallons of corn whiskey in Shelby, Charlotte, and South Carolina, though he went on to say that local demand still required the greater part of the amount distilled.[69]

The hog traffic dramatically increased the amount of corn produced. The contrast between the amount raised per farm in the three counties through which the vast majority of livestock passed and the other mountain counties provides the best indication that hog traffic encouraged the production of corn as a cash crop. The Buncombe Turnpike ran through Madison, Buncombe, and Henderson counties. As table 2.1 illustrates, the corn grown in those counties was over one-and-a-half times the per-farm average for western North Carolina as a whole and slightly greater than that for the entire state. Since the number of hogs and other livestock actually raised in those three counties was no greater than that of the other mountain counties, one can only assume that farmers there produced the large amounts of surplus corn because of the large and very accessible markets for it in their immediate vicinities.

Those farmers fortunate enough to own land along drovers' routes often sold corn directly to them. But most sold it to the stand owners, often as payment for goods they had already acquired through these innkeepers who also served as merchants.[70] Just prior to the autumn rush, stand operators frequently advertised that on certain days they would receive corn either as cash sales or as credit on "store accounts." According to the late-nineteenth-century reminiscences of

Table 2.1. *Corn Production Per Farm in the Buncombe Turnpike Counties, 1860*

	No. of Farms	Average Improved Acres Per Farm	No. of Hogs	Hogs Per Farm	Bushels of Corn Produced	Bushels of Corn Per Hog	Bushels of Corn Per Farm
Buncombe	924	78.7	23,270	25.2	463,190	19.9	501.3
Henderson	724	60.0	15,761	21.8	326,110	20.7	450.4
Madison	493	66.1	14,582	29.6	235,276	16.3	477.2
Western North Carolina Total	10,287	66.0	259,862	25.2	3,332,354	12.8	323.9
North Carolina Total	67,258	97.2	1,883,214	28.1	30,078,564	15.9	448.8

Source: Computed from *Agriculture of the U.S. in 1860* (Washington, D.C.: Government Printing Office, 1864), 104–107.

one mountain resident, farmers "would commence delivering frequently by daylight and continue until midnight. I have seen these corn wagons strung out for a mile and as thick as they could be wedged. They were more anxious to pay accounts then than some of us are now; but it was pay or no credit for next year."[71] The price paid for corn fluctuated from fifty cents to one dollar per bushel, according to both the size of the crop and the anticipated number of passing livestock consuming it. Stand owners generally charged drovers twenty to thirty cents more per bushel than they had bought it for, though the size of an average drive, from four hundred to six hundred animals, often necessitated sales by the wagonload.[72]

Even with the large amounts of corn for sale by the western North Carolina farmers, the supply was not always enough to meet the demands of both local consumers and passing droves. In 1854, an Asheville resident reported that due to an unseasonably cold spring season, "everything is nearly eat up and many persons have to go to McDowell and Rutherford counties for corn—it is hard times in Buncombe as there is a good many more people in and passing through the county that the farms did not make corn and oats enough last year to supply the wants, but we hope to get through safe."[73]

Drovers usually waited until their return trips, after the sale of their livestock, to settle their accounts for food and accommodation. They paid the innkeepers in either cash or in merchandise requested, and they in turn paid those farmers from whom they had bought corn, if the latter had chosen to wait for payment rather than take credit on goods earlier. These transactions, combined with those of mountain merchants and large farmers who dealt directly with the southern markets, constituted a complex trade network that either directly or indirectly provided a market economy vital to the mountain region. Through local merchants, stand keepers, passing drovers, or direct contact with South Carolina or Georgia cities, most western North Carolinians had a readily available outlet for whatever surplus crops, livestock, or forest products they chose to sell. Even though a greater influx of Kentucky and Tennessee cattle and hogs in the early 1850s drove down the price for North Carolina livestock joining the southbound stream of traffic, mountain farmers continued to raise more and more animals for market. They recognized the advantages of their product over that of their competition to the northwest. As Thomas Clingman explained it:

Most of this stock comes from Kentucky and Ohio, and when it has reached
Asheville, it has traveled half of its journey to the most distant parts of the
Southern market, viz: Charleston and Savannah. The citizens of my district, therefore can get their livestock into the planting states south of us at
one-half the expense which those of Kentucky and Ohio are obliged to oc-
cur. Not only sheep but hogs, horses, mules, and horned cattle can be produced in many portions of my district, as cheaply as in those two States.[74]

And, though stock prices declined, the heavier traffic led to greater demand and thus higher prices for corn, so that most mountain farmers
welcomed the increase in southbound herds and profitted by them.

The major factor determining the demand for these and other
mountain goods further south was the fluctuation in the overall southern economy, which in turn was based almost entirely on the cotton
market. Whether sales were made directly to large plantations, or, as
was more often the case, to established markets in Columbia, Augusta, Athens, Charleston, or Savannah, the price paid for hogs and
cattle was directly tied to that of cotton. These markets consistently
paid per pound of pork half of what had been received per pound of
cotton.[75] This rate in turn determined how much the farmers, innkeepers, and merchants who made the trip themselves, as well as
those waiting to settle accounts with drovers, received. A Macon
County farmer reflected western Carolinians' awareness of their economic interdependence with the rest of the South when he wrote that
"money is scarce in all of this county and is not hopes of being much
plentier as cotton has been down in the southern market and that rules
all other things in our county."[76] During the Panic of 1857, an Asheville
businessman expressed his confidence that the mountain region
would not be greatly affected by it. Nicholas Woodfin wrote, "I do not
think that our people are greatly indebted & their livestock still brings
[good] prices & as cotton is still doing well & the producers of it are
our customers & are generally free from debt I am compelled to believe
that if we had stock enough to sell we need not feel greatly alarmed."[77]

Through one means or another, then, most western North Carolinians were involved in this complex trade network. Though the degree
of contact varied greatly, from those subsistence farmers who merely
bartered occasionally with local merchants for tools, supplies, or staple foods, to those larger farmers and businessmen who maintained
close regular ties with their counterparts in South Carolina and Georgia, that dependence on southern markets was pervasive throughout
the mountain counties.

Not all mountain residents participated in this market economy, however. Though greatly exaggerated and less true of the antebellum period than of later years, images of the isolation and seclusion of mountain families were not entirely false. In describing the division of western North Carolina society, Rutherford County resident Randolph Shotwell wrote just after the Civil War that the lowest class was made up of "rude mountaineers," who were "neither intelligent nor particularly respectable." They either owned a little land and survived by subsistence farming, or they lived "by fishing, by occasional days' work in the gold mines, by illicit distilling [and] roguery of all sorts."[78] Though his assessment may have been a little harsh and more than a little condescending, by the late antebellum period a growing number of western North Carolinians found themselves outside or on the edge of the mainstream of mountain life. As available land in the larger valleys and more accessible gaps became increasingly scarce, later settlers were forced to move farther up the hillsides and creekbeds into hollows and coves. By their distance and terrain, these locales tended to separate those who settled there from much of what went on beyond them. In other instances, areas that had been fairly accessible and well traveled at the time of settlement became more isolated as trade routes changed and migration dwindled. Some communities were bypassed by traffic that earlier had provided their primary contacts with the outside world.[79] But such detrimental effects took place gradually and began only during the late 1840s and 1850s, so that their full impact was not apparent until the decades after the Civil War.

Far more of the seclusion of mountain residents during the antebellum period seems to have been the result of conscious choice. The major priorities for most settlers moving into the North Carolina mountains were flat fertile land with easy access to either major trade routes or to local markets. But a substantial number of newcomers held more limited goals and were willing to settle for just enough land to support a family, and an adequate supply of water, wild game, and timber or stone for building. To these people the coves and hollows were just as attractive as the larger river valleys.[80] Such families often maintained a pioneering lifestyle of subsistence farming with only minimal contact with anyone other than neighbors, the closest of whom were sometimes several miles away.

In some instances, several families lived together in insulated, self-contained units. One such settlement was Madison County's Shelton

Laurel community. In the 1790s, brothers David and Martin Shelton staked claims in a small Blue Ridge valley, so remote that it was only after almost twenty years that their holdings were ever recorded. They were eventually joined in the valley by three or four other families, but the Sheltons never looked beyond their immediate family and those few neighbors for their social and economic needs.[81] In other cases, groups of relatives or neighbors moved together into the mountains and established communities with only minimal contact with others in the region. In order to maintain their strong Lutheran traditions, several German families moved from the state's piedmont into the secluded Plum Tree Creek area of Watauga County in the mid-1830s. They were led by John Moretz, who served as "farmer, carpenter, and the postmaster," in addition to operating a gristmill.[82]

Almost every mountain county had certain "hermits" whose eccentric lifestyles, misanthropic characters, criminal pasts, or frustrated love-lives had driven them into seclusion and made them well known and much discussed by others in their area. Big Tom Wilson, for example, was a bear hunter and guide, whose discovery of Elisha Mitchell's body on the mountain later named for the professor gained Wilson instant fame and almost legendary status among Yancey County residents. Frankie Silvers lived in a lonely cabin on the Toe River until her gruesome murder of her husband in 1831 led to her sensationalized trial, escape, recapture, and hanging in Morganton. David Greer was the sole resident of Bald Mountain on the Tennessee border. His belligerence toward any and all intruders resulted in several murders, including his own. A failed romance allegedly led Culgee Watson to retreat from society to a cabin over the Linville Gorge where he raised peacocks and refused to speak to anyone who passed his way.[83] The very celebrity or notoriety of these local "characters" suggests that their seclusion was far more the exception than the rule among mountain residents, most of whom viewed the hermits' odd behavior with fascination and curiosity.

For most other antebellum mountain dwellers who lived in relative isolation, limited physical and social contacts did not, as so often has been assumed, automatically entail either ignorance or poverty. Most families, regardless of how secluded their homes were, lived comfortable lives that more than satisfied their basic needs. Despite dwellings that were often viewed as crude and overcrowded, visitors were impressed by the abundance and variety of food they were offered as guests. During his tour of the southern states in 1853 and 1854, Frederick Law Olmsted noted that he saw far fewer instances of real poverty in the mountains than elsewhere in the South.[84] In fact, it was the prospect of prosperity that led some to venture into uninhabited areas. Merchants were among the earliest settlers in the mountains, since being first into an area was a significant incentive for moving. They anticipated that their self-imposed isolation would be only temporary and that they themselves would encourage further settlement in their vicinities. Thus, businessmen John Burton and Jordan Councill were among the first permanent residents of what would become Buncombe and Watauga counties, respectively.[85] Likewise, William Waugh and William Holland Thomas established trading posts in the virtually uninhabited Cherokee country soon after it was opened to white settlement.[86]

For those interested in large-scale agriculture, it was the quantity and quality of available land that led them into remoter areas. Elisha Mitchell described a beautiful Ashe County farm owned by a father and his three sons. It was located along "a brawling mountain stream" at a point where "the mountains instead of coming up close to it recede so as to leave a handsome plantation of level land along its banks." With its abundant peach and apple orchards, it was, according to Mitchell, "as pleasant a spot but for its situation as is to be found in the country. But the only access to it is by a trail or footpath leading over a mountain ridge. 'Tis . . . the place for a person to retire to, who has been ill treated by the world and is disgusted with it."[87]

Olmsted visited a family in a one-room cabin with a loft and a separate kitchen. His highland host told the Connecticut journalist that he owned over a thousand acres of rich tillable land, along with a considerable stock of cattle and large crops of grain. He owned smaller tracts of land and a gristmill elsewhere, all of which he rented out. "He must be considered," concluded Olmsted, "a very respectable capitalist for a mountaineer." And yet, by his own efforts, he kept himself and his family secluded. He used his profits from the sale of his cattle to buy more and more of the mountain range surrounding his cove, to keep squatters as far away as possible.[88]

In the late 1840s Charles Lanman noted several such large farms, situated miles apart from each other in the Nantahala Valley, not long after the area had been opened for white settlement by the removal of the Cherokee Indians. One of those was so noted for its productivity

Figure 7. A mountain farm in Ashe County. Frontispiece, Zeigler and Grosscup, *The Heart of the Alleghanies* (Raleigh, 1883).

and rich soil that its owner had been offered $25,000 for it. Yet Lanman was amazed that this "wealthy man" lived in a "miserable log hovel, a decayed and windowless one, which a respectable member of the swine family would hardly deign to occupy."[89]

The agricultural abundance of these farms, despite their secluded locations, meant that their owners often participated in the market economy of the mountains. Another of the farmers Lanman encountered along the Nantahala was "the only one the traveller meets within going a distance of twenty miles." He was a "grazing farmer" with over five thousand acres, who made trips to Charleston and Savannah every year with "a goodly number of cattle, as well as horses and mules."[90] Despite its relative inaccessibility and lack of transportation, a settlement in Rocky Creek Hollow in Yancey County managed to acquire medicines, coffee, salt, and sugar through regular contacts with South Carolina and Georgia markets.[91] Even an eccentric man in Watauga County, who lived with four women in an isolated location high on the Blue Ridge, sold as many as eighty hogs each year, presumably to drovers passing through Boone.[92]

Only a relatively small part of western North Carolina's population, then, was to some degree set apart from other mountain residents. Most of them saw their situation as either temporary, only natural in an area in its frontier stage of development, or as self-imposed, for the economic advantages offered by more remote sites. Observers of these situations noted, often with surprise, that neither such locations nor the relatively crude living conditions they found there actually indicated financial hardship or deprivation for the individuals or families involved.

Likewise, ignorance—either in the form of illiteracy or in lack of knowledge of the outside world—was by no means characteristic of the more isolated settlers. One mountain resident, who grew up in a cabin in the Cherokee country situated closer to Indians than any other whites, noted that the illiteracy rate in the mountains prior to the Civil War was much lower than it was in the generations following it. He recalled the importance of frequent and active correspondence with family and friends elsewhere for those with few other means of social contact. The weekly visit by the mail carrier who traveled between Franklin and Robbinsville was eagerly awaited by his family, particularly his mother, "who regarded him as our best friend because he brought letters from the old home across the sea."[93] This determination to maintain ties with loved ones and acquaintances elsewhere was probably typical of mountain settlers, especially during the antebellum period when many of them were not more than a single generation removed from families and communities in nonmountain locales. Visitors often noted that Bibles and other reading materials were almost always present in the mountain homes in which they stayed, regardless of how simple or rough they were. Even Olmsted, who never failed to play up any geographical or political misconceptions held by the mountaineers he encountered, noted that "books are more common than even in the houses of the slaveowners of the planting districts" he had visited and that mountain families enjoyed reading aloud to each other.[94]

By the 1850s, there were signs of the "backwardness" and poverty that increasingly would isolate and alienate the region from the outside world later in the nineteenth century. But such situations existed only on the fringe of what was, in the antebellum years, a vigorous and multi-faceted society. Living in an area made up of affluent resort communities, small, rough, but lively commercial centers and county seats, and productive, comfortable farms, very few if any of its residents would have characterized western North Carolina as plagued by serious economic or social problems. If they considered their area in any way distinctive, it was more in terms of its physical attributes—its scenic beauty, cool healthy climate, and abundance of land, mineral, and forest resources.

The towns and villages of western North Carolina, for all their differences in size and character, provided the means by which most area residents could participate in either local or more extended aspects of the market economy, thus tying their own interests, and those of the mountain region, to other parts of the South. Far from foreseeing a bleak future of poverty and ignorance for their region, Carolina highlanders had ample reason for optimism on the eve of the Civil War: the growing reputation and popularity of their tourist resorts; the discovery and promotion of new products and farming methods to improve an already diversified and abundant agricultural output; the extraordinary livestock trade that moved through the heart of the Carolina highlands, bringing direct and indirect benefits to those on or near its path; and, perhaps most important, the imminent prospect of railroad construction through the region, which would have the effect of drawing it even closer to the rest of the state and the rest of the South.

Chapter 3

Mountain Masters:

"Chiefly professional men, shop-keepers,
and men in office"

It has long been a common assumption that slavery played little part in the society or economy of antebellum Appalachia. The labor system based on black bondage was considered profitable only when applied to large-scale, cash-crop agriculture in areas with a long growing season and accessible markets. Because of the rugged terrain and cool climate of the Southern Highlands, regional analysts have reasoned, slavery was not economically feasible, and thus there were few slaves or slaveholders in the mountains. In 1921 John Campbell wrote in his landmark book on the Southern Appalachians that "there were few Negroes in the Highlands in early times . . . they have never been a factor in rural mountain life." More than fifty years later Ora Blackmun repeated this assumption in her history of western North Carolina. "The Negro population of the mountains was . . . almost negligible," she wrote. "The economy of the mountains generated no need or desire for slaves."[1] Even native son Thomas Wolfe stated categorically that his region's antebellum residents were "backwoods folk" who had never been wealthy, had never owned slaves, and hated blacks. Wolfe's most recent biographer seems to have bought those assumptions himself. David Donald described Asheville, Wolfe's hometown, as "a city with few links to the antebellum slavery era," and thus "not especially southern."[2]

Perhaps because the relative scarcity of slaves in the mountains is an established demographic fact, these and other scholars have concluded that the "peculiar institution" did not affect the region, and they have felt no need for examining it further.[3] As a result, no one has [59]

Table 3.1.   *Slaves as Percentages of Population of Western North Carolina*
             Counties, 1850 and 1860

County	Total Population	Slave Population	Percent of County Population	Free Black Population
		1850		
Alleghany	—	—	—	—
Ashe	8,777	595	6.7	86
Buncombe	13,425	1,717	12.8	107
Burke	7,772	2,132	27.4	163
Caldwell	6,317	1,203	19.0	109
Cherokee	3,385	337	10.0	109
Haywood	7,074	418	5.9	15
Henderson	6,853	912	13.3	37
Jackson	—	—	—	—
Macon	6,389	549	8.6	106
Madison	—	—	—	—
McDowell	6,246	1,262	20.2	213
Watauga	3,400	129	3.7	29
Wilkes	12,079	1,142	9.4	224
Yancey	8,205	346	4.2	50

Source: *Seventh and Eighth U.S. Censuses:* 1850, table 1; 1860, tables 1 and 2.

closely explored either the nature of slavery in that atypical setting or the ways in which the institution was shaped by that setting. But the black presence, though relatively small, cannot be shrugged off as having been merely peripheral or incidental to the structure, attitudes, and values of antebellum Appalachian society. An examination of slaveholders and their black property in western North Carolina provides ample evidence that slaves possessed a far greater economic and political impact on that area and its people, both slaveholders and non-slaveholders, than the numerical proportion of slaves would suggest.

In many ways, mountainous North Carolina, which includes some of the ruggedest terrain in eastern America, was an unusual environment for southern slavery. Unlike most parts of the South, black labor there was the exception rather than the rule. The region's economy was far less dependent on the labor slaves provided, and its social sta-

Table 3.1., Continued

County	Total Population	Slave Population	Percent of County Population	Free Black Population
			1860	
Alleghany	3,590	206	5.7	33
Ashe	7,956	391	4.9	142
Buncombe	12,654	1,933	15.3	111
Burke	9,237	2,371	31.6	221
Caldwell	7,497	1,088	14.5	114
Cherokee	9,166	520	5.6	38
Haywood	5,801	313	5.4	14
Henderson	10,448	1,382	13.2	85
Jackson	5,501	268	4.8	6
Macon	6,004	519	8.6	115
Madison	5,908	213	3.6	17
McDowell	7,120	1,305	18.3	273
Watauga	4,957	104	2.0	81
Wilkes	14,749	1,208	8.2	261
Yancey	8,655	362	4.2	67

bility was less dependent on the hierarchy that slavery defined. Yet the slave labor system not only existed in the mountains; it also proved profitable for those who utilized it.

The most basic misconception in need of correction is the demographic generalization that the number of slaves in the western part of the state was "almost negligible." The distribution of slaves in North Carolina's mountain counties was far more varied than such statements imply. Slaves made up over a fourth of the population of Burke County in 1860 and about a fifth of that of its adjoining counties, Caldwell and McDowell, in 1850—ratios higher than those for several piedmont counties to the east[4] (see table 3.1 and map 4.) Though Buncombe and Henderson counties, just across the Blue Ridge, had official slave proportions of 13 and 15 percent, respectively, their black populations swelled to far greater numbers during the summer months when slaveholders and their property from South Carolina and Georgia moved up to these mountain resort areas. At the other extreme were Madison and Watauga counties, where in 1860 slaves made up only 3.6 and 2 percent, respectively, of their populations. Some areas within those and other counties had no black residents at all.[5] Slaveholding in the remaining mountain counties fell somewhere within this relatively wide range, so that the average percentage of slaves in the population of North Carolina's fifteen westernmost counties in 1860 was 10.2 percent.[6] But this figure and other statistical summaries of highland slavery as a whole fail to acknowledge the major differences between areas within the region and particularly tend to obscure those areas with heavier concentrations of black bondsmen.

Because agriculture in the mountains was characterized by relatively small landholdings, the demands of farm production alone never could have justified the labor force of even the small number of slaves who lived in the mountains. Nor did the output of those farms prove sufficient to support, much less earn profits from, those slaves. Thus the means needed to acquire even a few slaves was usually dependent on capital derived from nonagricultural sources, so that the characteristic that probably most distinguished mountain slaveholders from their counterparts elsewhere in the South was the diversity of their economic activity. Olmsted recognized this distinction on his 1854 trip through the Southern Appalachians. "Of the people who get their living entirely by agriculture," he observed, "few own negroes; the slaveholders being chiefly professional men, shop-keepers, and men in office, who are also land owners, and give a divided attention to farming."[7] This astute observation was an accurate description of the kind of mountain residents not only able to acquire black property, but whose situations called for its labor. With few exceptions, the largest slaveholders in western North Carolina derived significant amounts of income from nonagricultural enterprises. The economic activities of the ten largest slaveholders in each of five sample counties in 1860 can be categorized as follows: professional, 32 percent; mercantile or commercial, 68 percent; real estate and/or mining, 24 percent; hotel management or other aspects of the tourist trade, 12 percent; and agriculture alone, only 3 percent.[8]

Almost a third of all mountain masters were either doctors or lawyers, those slaveholding professionals James Oakes has called "the single most influential class in the antebellum South." Many of western North Carolina's most prominent slaveholding families, such as the Averys of Burke County, the Loves of Haywood, the Pattons of

Map 3.
North Carolina Slave Population by County, 1860

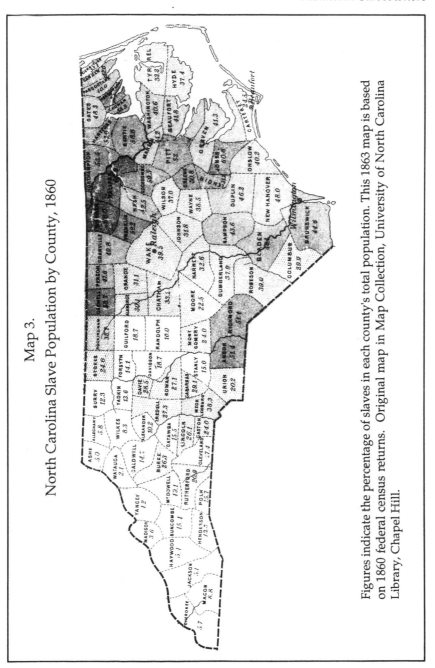

Figures indicate the percentage of slaves in each county's total population. This 1863 map is based on 1860 federal census returns. Original map in Map Collection, University of North Carolina Library, Chapel Hill.

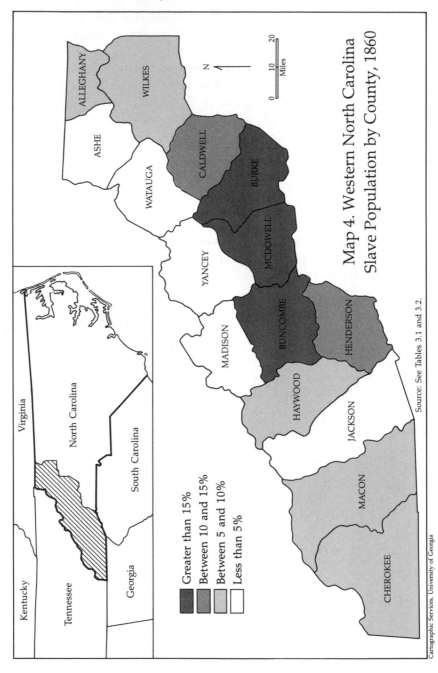

Map 4. Western North Carolina Slave Population by County, 1860

Greater than 15%

Between 10 and 15%

Between 5 and 10%

Less than 5%

Source: See Tables 3.1 and 3.2.

Cartographic Services, University of Georgia

Buncombe, and the Carsons of McDowell, included several active at-
torneys or court officials. Other prominent examples included Nicholas W. Woodfin, the Asheville lawyer and legislator who was the
region's second largest slaveholder in 1860; W.W. Erwin, Burke County's superior court clerk for more than forty years, who owned over
ninety slaves by the time he died in 1837; and future governors Tod R.
Caldwell and Zebulon Vance, who acquired modest slaveholdings during their early legal careers in Morganton and Asheville respectively.[9]
Most of these men shared the entrepreneurial spirit that made so
many mountain residents successful, and their legal careers did not
hinder them from participating actively in various business ventures,
which in turn increased their capacity for purchasing slaves.

Many of the region's doctors were slaveholders as well. One of early
Asheville's most prominent citizens and largest slaveholders, George
Swain, was a merchant, postmaster, and hat maker as well as one of
the area's busiest medical practitioners in the 1820s and 1830s.[10] Morganton physician John Happoldt managed both a store and a hotel in
addition to his medical practice, and by 1850 he had used the profits
from all three enterprises to invest in twelve slaves. Dr. Mitchell King's
thirty-four slaves made him Henderson County's fourth largest slaveholder in 1860. Three of the four physicians listed in the Cherokee census of 1860 were slaveholders, though their holdings—from three to
seven slaves—were modest.[11]

Such professionals were by no means the only mountain masters
with business interests. Well over half of the area's largest slaveholders
were involved in commercial ventures of some type. The variety of
projects that attracted the most successful entrepreneurs suggests a
strong correlation between business diversification and large slaveholdings. George Bower ran a store, a post office, and a hotel from his
large brick home in Ashe County, and throughout the antebellum period he maintained the distinction of being the only man in that county
with more than thirty slaves. Watauga County's largest slaveholder
was Jordan Councill, whose store was the nucleus around which the
town of Boone developed. Jesse R. Siler's store, tannery, and blacksmith shop in Franklin enabled him to acquire the second largest slave
force in Macon County.[12] In Wilkes County, James Gwyn and his partner Lytle Hickerson used the profits from their several stores to make
a number of substantial purchases of slave families and individuals
during the 1840s. By 1850, Gwyn's twenty-two slaves and Hickerson's

thirty-one were among the county's largest holdings. The thirty-six slaves of Burnsville merchant Milton Penland made him by far the largest slaveholder in Yancey County in 1860.[13]

Perhaps the careers of William F. McKesson and William Holland Thomas provide the best examples of how slaveholdings combined with, and resulted from, a wide range of financial pursuits. With 174 slaves, McKesson, a Burke County resident, was the largest slave-holder in western North Carolina in 1860. He was also the area's quintessential businessman. He successfully operated several stores throughout the county as well as a sawmill on his Linville River farm. During the 1840s he tried his hand at mining, and by 1850 he owned and operated the region's most productive gold mine, with a capital investment of $35,000. He had acquired over a hundred slaves by this time and used many of them in his mines. In 1858 he was granted a large part of the construction contract for the Western North Carolina Railroad, and soon after the Civil War began, he took over the entire project.[14]

Farther west in Cherokee County, Thomas was equally versatile. In addition to his effective work as government agent for the Cherokee Indians, he had established what his partner James W. Terrell described as "the largest and most varied business anywhere west of Asheville, consisting of store, tanyard, boot and shoe shop, blacksmithing and wagonmaking." He began to accumulate slaves in the mid-1840s and owned over fifty by the early 1860s, which made him one of the largest slave owners in the southwest section of the state.[15]

Hotel management provided both another means by which mountain residents gained the capital to acquire substantial slaveholdings. As noted earlier, the attractions of the North Carolina mountains for affluent planters from the Lower South made the seasonal tourist trade quite profitable to many western Carolinians. As hotel and resort owners prospered, their slaveholdings expanded. By 1850, James R. Love, owner of the White Sulphur Springs Resort near Waynesville, was Haywood County's largest slaveholder, with eighty-five slaves. James W. Patton operated the Eagle Hotel in the center of Asheville and, with his brother John, the Patton Hotel at Warm Springs some thirty-five miles north of Asheville. By 1860 Patton owned more slaves than anyone in Buncombe County except Nicholas Woodfin. His holdings of seventy-eight slaves were matched by the seventy-five slaves of James McConnell Smith, who operated the Buck Hotel in Asheville and was

Patton's strongest competitor.[16] Though their hotels were only one of many business pursuits of these men, the money spent by wealthy planters and their families contributed substantially to the slave-buying capacity of their mountain hosts.

Land speculation was yet another business venture engaged in by many mountain slave owners. Though the process had begun much earlier, the removal of the Cherokees in 1838 provided a major impetus for land sales that continued through the rest of the antebellum period. The availability of vast tracts at low prices and the fact that land, like slaves, provided one of the few available outlets for surplus capital in the western part of the state made real estate investments very popular with local residents.

Col. William Waugh of Wilkes County was among the first to tap the economic potential of the newly opened Cherokee lands. Convinced that he would "become prosperous dealing in buying and selling land," he moved to Valleytown in Cherokee County in the late 1830s, staying just long enough to stake a large claim and establish a trading post. Though he soon returned to Wilkes County, his real estate and mercantile ventures in the Indian country continued to be so successful that by 1850 the thirty-five slaves he had acquired with his profits made him Wilkes County's largest slaveholder.[17] Though he owned fewer slaves, Calvin J. Cowles, another Wilkes County merchant, was one of the most active and aggressive promoters of mountain real estate. He accumulated fourteen thousand acres of land scattered across the western part of the state through grants or tax sales, when they could be purchased cheaply. He corresponded with many out-of-state connections and even ran advertisements of land for sale in newspapers around the country, in which he extolled the value of his mountain property for mining, timber, grazing, and railroad development. In 1856, he convinced several Caldwell County men to join him in the purchase and operation of a gold and copper mine in Ashe County.[18]

Not only business and professional men took advantage of this promising opportunity to acquire land; so too did farmers who saw land not as a commodity to be passed on for a profit, but as a long-term investment to be utilized for its own resources. Indeed, some of the wealthiest families east of the Blue Ridge supplemented their landholdings at home with unimproved mountain acreage to their west, which they used either as grazing land for livestock or for its timber.

Thomas Lenoir of Caldwell County first acquired mountain property as a gift from his father-in-law. As a young man he left his father's Fort Defiance plantation and moved up to his Haywood County holdings with his wife, children, and several slaves. After a decade of trying to "eke out a living in the cold mountains," he returned home to manage the family estate. But the difficulties and loneliness of life in the highland wilderness did not discourage him from continuing to acquire land there. By the late 1840s, his properties "on top of the Blue Ridge" greatly exceeded his holdings at home in the Yadkin Valley.[19] Another prominent slaveholding family, the Averys of Burke County, also invested heavily in land. In 1821 Isaac Avery inherited 50,000 acres of grazing land in the mountains of Watauga County along with the family's Swan Pond plantation of only 850 improved acres.[20] Similarly, three Burke County slaveholders in 1854 became partners in purchasing "Eagle's Cliff," a tract of bald meadows in Yancey County, "for the sole purpose of raising stock and improving said place."[21]

The diversity of economic activity among mountain masters should not obscure the fact that the North Carolina mountains were primarily rural with an economy firmly rooted in agriculture. Most slaveholders, including those described above, were farmers in addition to their business or professional pursuits. This further diversification of their interests and activities suggests that their slaves probably performed more types of work than slaves in most areas of the South. Again Olmsted's writings provide confirmation. He observed that the slaves in the Southern Appalachians were more like "ordinary free laborers" than were most southern slaves in that their work was "directed to a greater variety of employments and they exercise more responsibility."[22]

The sheer diversity and self-sufficiency of mountain agriculture called for a greater variety of activity than was likely the case in commercial-crop plantation operations elsewhere in the South. Presumably slave labor was utilized in all aspects of crop production and livestock management. Thus masters often sent slaves to spend the warmer months tending the grazing cattle and sheep in their masters' highland pastures. This was particularly true for the larger slaveholders of the foothill counties such as Isaac Avery, Thomas Lenoir, and Samuel Fleming, who usually reported on census or tax records slaveholdings in the higher counties to their west in addition to their far larger holdings at home.[23] Hogs were usually allowed to roam freely to forage in the woods, but slaves were sent to round them up and bring them home in order to fatten them on corn before sending them along with thousands of other hogs on the drovers' routes to the plantation markets farther south.[24] Except for short periods of the year, the care of livestock probably required relatively little manpower.

Likewise, crop production would hardly amount to enough work to occupy a slave labor force all year around. Perhaps the best indication that it did not is the lack of any correlation between the number of slaves and the number of improved acres owned by mountain residents. Despite their many differences in production, the random sample of twelve farmers used in chapter 1 to illustrate the wide variations in mountain farming shared a significant common denominator. Each owned between ten and twelve slaves in 1850.[25] Yet their cultivated landholdings ranged from 60 to 700 acres, with a yield in quantity and type just as varied. Inversely, four landholders with approximately the same acreage (200 to 250 acres) each owned thirty-two, twenty, twelve and seven slaves.[26] Two sets of brothers provide further evidence of this lack of correlation. Abram Harshaw had fifty slaves but only 150 improved acres in Cherokee County in 1850, while his brother Joshua had almost half as many slaves (twenty-eight) but over twice the cultivated land (350 acres). In Madison County ten years later, James Pain had 40 improved acres and ten slaves, while his brother Robert had 60 acres but only three slaves.[27] Thus, farms the same size and with much the same output varied greatly in the number of slaves that worked them, just as black work forces of similar size worked farms of vastly different acreages.

These statistics at first might suggest gross inefficiency in the use made of slave labor. If seven or twelve slaves were adequate for a two hundred-acre farm, then twenty or thirty-two slaves performing the same amount of labor suggests poor management and considerable waste.[28] At least one slaveholder acknowledged that, to a certain extent, this was the case. Thomas Lenoir, tired and frustrated at the strain of managing his father's many slaves, complained that their number was excessive for the amount of work they performed and that they were "eating up all the profits" made from plantation production.[29] But there are two alternatives to the conclusion that this attitude was prevalent among Lenoir's counterparts in the region. One is that slaveholders found enough other types of work for the surplus time and manpower not applied to crop production to make their investment profitable. The other is that the inherent value of slave property, either as a stable investment for surplus capital or as a source of liquid capital derived from hiring them out, encouraged the accumulation of black property in excess of actual labor demands. There is substantial evidence that both of these rationales motivated western Carolina slaveholders.

In many cases, the business ventures of slaveowners provided outlets for slave labor in addition to, or in place of, more routine work in the fields. Hotel keepers employed much of their black work force during the busy summer months in providing for the care and comfort of their guests. Visitors made occasional references to the duties of black servants, which included waiting on tables, providing room service, attending bathers at the various mineral springs, tending the stables, and even leading the dogs on deer or bear hunts organized for guests. James Buckingham, a British visitor to Asheville in 1840, complained that too much responsibility was placed on the slaves of hotel owners. "The business of the inn," he wrote, "is left mostly to the black servants to manage as they see fit." Some of their work was shared with the slaves of the travelers themselves, who often accompanied their masters and their families to their highland retreats. George Featherstonhaugh, another British tourist, described his Asheville hotel as "filled with Southern people and their black servants."[30]

Those masters involved in manufacturing or mercantile enterprises were also able to draw on the manpower of their slaveholdings. Besides assisting in the general maintenance of their owners' stores, slaves often produced some of the merchandise sold. William Holland Thomas put his slaves to work in his brickyard and in "hauling off iron" from various Cherokee County ironworks by wagon to Athens, Georgia, to barter for general merchandise for his Quallatown store. An 1860 letter from his partner James Terrell reported on other activities of Thomas's slaves. Two were engaged in "putting up" various goods just received, "chains and cutlery mostly and one box of guns." One slave, Dick, was to have set out with a wagonload of supplies, but was reluctant to leave because of severe winter weather. "Powers," Terrell wrote, "is working at rails, fences, getting wood, &c &c, and Alfred would have been all the time shoemaking but the rhumatism prevented his crooking his knee—he is now doing such light jobs about the store and house as he is able."[31]

The wife of Ashe County merchant David Worth set up a cloth-

Figure 8. Slave labor used in gold mining. From copy in North Carolina Collection, UNC Library, Chapel Hill.

making business and trained several of their seven slaves to sew men's and boys' clothing, which she then sold in her husband's store. Profits from that source led the Worths to establish a carriage and furniture factory in which their own slaves, along with several persons hired locally, were employed.[32] Calvin S. Brown's six slaves divided their labor among his Morganton blacksmith shop, wagon-repair shop, and boot- and shoe-making operation. Richard V. Michaux's thirty-seven slaves both grew tobacco and processed it in one of Burke County's two plug tobacco factories.[33] Asheville merchant and postmaster George Swain employed several of his male and female slaves in making wool hats. Of a recently recovered runaway, the elder Swain wrote that in the six days since the slave's return "he has bored 5 wool hats instead of 4 and done them better than he ever did his work before, so that if he continues as faithful six weeks he will compensate for all our losses."[34] Governor Swain's nephew, William Coleman, established his own hat factory in Asheville and by the early 1840s had thirteen slaves working in it. But he believed that it would yet require two more slaves to keep his shop well stocked with hats. The value of these slaves to their owner in manufacturing was revealed when financial difficulties forced Coleman to consider the sale of either his land or his slaves. "If I could get clear to the farm," he wrote, "I could make them earn something in the shop."[35]

Mining was the nonagricultural activity that involved the largest number of slaves most profitably. In 1828, the discovery of gold along various streams in the South Mountains of Burke and Rutherford counties led to a gold rush in western North Carolina that lasted for about five years. Mining towns quickly sprang up as slave owners from eastern North Carolina and Virginia joined local masters in sending their slaves to mine gold in the shafts and along the streams. According to Burke County slaveholder Isaac Avery, some of the "more intelligent, wealthy and enterprising citizens of the State, after personal examination, are withdrawing their slaves entirely from the cultivation of cotton and tobacco, and removing them to the deposit mines of this county." Blacks and whites worked side by side "without any race difficulties, and many even shared the close quarters of hastily erected cabins."[36] An observer at a Rutherford County mine saw slaves employed primarily in "washing." He described them as very submissive but noted that they were "watched closely to prevent their secreting any pieces of gold they might find."[37]

Despite a reluctance on the part of slaveholders in other regions to risk their property in dangerous mining operations, the financial advantages of that utilization of slave labor in the North Carolina mountains often overcame owners' doubts.[38] James Scott wrote to his brother from the mining camp of Brackettown that "there is a general prejudice against letting [slave] hands work in the mines, but it is without foundation, my hands are very healthy and well satisfied." So apparently was Scott himself, since he was doing well enough to urge his brother in Salisbury to hire out some of his slaves for this profitable venture.[39] The combination of gold mining and slave labor proved to be so successful that by 1833 Burke County alone was reported to have had five thousand slaves—more than twice its normal slave population—employed in mining operations.[40]

But by the end of that year most of the miners from outside the area had taken their slaves and moved on, either to try newly discovered mines in northern Georgia or to return to their own tobacco and cotton plantations. Several local residents, however, continued to use at least some of their slaves in mining operations throughout the antebellum period. W.W. Avery and Company hired the slaves of sixteen Burke County owners from January through November 1844 and paid almost three thousand dollars for their services. William F. McKesson employed forty-five of his slaves, half men and half women, in the region's most productive mine until well into the 1850s. Calvin Cowles used six of his own slaves and hired others to work two veins of gold in his Ashe County mine as late as 1856.[41]

A number of western North Carolina slaveholders were even among those who, with their slaves, joined the gold rush to California. By early 1854, it was estimated that there were two hundred slaves in that westernmost free state from Burke and McDowell counties alone.[42] Hamilton Erwin and Thomas Lenoir Avery (Isaac Avery's son) headed west in 1851 with "several able-bodied negro men." When Avery died of cholera the next year (along with some of the slaves), his father, as the owner of several of the slaves surviving in California, worried that controlling them might prove difficult, particularly should they come in contact with the all too numerous abolitionists there. But Erwin assured him that "they are safe from the influence of abolitionists" and said that he planned "to divide them in small companies and try to have an honest one in each and locate them near him." Avery was much relieved when, despite the slaves' period of residence on free soil, they chose to return home with Erwin in 1852.[43] Another Burke County owner, Robert McElrath, sent his son-in-law with four slaves to California to find enough gold to pay his debts. The slaves were led by "Uncle Jim," an expert placer miner, and they were allowed one day a week to mine for themselves. Like Avery's slaves, they were extolled for their fidelity and devotion to their master, in that they too chose to return home after the death of their guardian, even though a circuitous route through New York exposed them to abolitionists who urged them to remain there.[44] Of course, in both cases it is far more likely that loyalty to their own loved ones, rather than to a master, brought these slaves back to Burke County.

On the other hand, the uncertainties of slavery's status in California did generate problems for other western Carolinians, who had to cope with losses by death or "theft," as well as a new laxity in slaves' submissiveness. J.M. Neal of McDowell County lost three of the six slaves who accompanied him when abolitionists in San Francisco used writs of habeas corpus to remove them from the ship on which Neal was embarking for home.[45] Isaac Theodore Avery (a cousin of the Averys mentioned above), wrote to his father from Woods Diggings, California, of the problems not only of keeping one's slaves, but of humoring them as well. "Negroes in California," he wrote, "are not the same that they are at home by a long gap." He explained that "you must give them every Saturday or they would think it was a bad case," though he assured his father that his own slave, Will, "does tolerable well, about as good as any one here." He reported on the losses suffered by fellow western Carolinians: "Col. Wm. Smyth's negro boy Thany died some time back. Wm. Hicks who tended to them is very low. I understand one of R. Perkins boys has left him, also one of Ramseurs took for boss, one of Tom Parks and Licurgus Scotts."[46]

These, to be sure, were exceptional problems induced by exceptional circumstances. Even the labor of those far more numerous slaves who remained on Carolina highland farms was not necessarily all, or even primarily, agricultural in nature, however. Many of the larger farms remained largely self-sufficient, and slave labor provided for the various wants and needs of both blacks and whites. A visitor to Walter Blake's Henderson County plantation marveled at the "baronial style" in which he lived. "He has his own mills and tanyards, curriers and shoemakers," all of which claimed a good portion of his thirty-six slaves' time and energy.[47]

Even William Lenoir must have kept his slaves busy, despite his son's opinion that their number was "excessive." He operated a sawmill and a gristmill on his plantation, as well as a blacksmith shop. His slaves produced more pig iron products there than could be sold locally, and he sent the surplus to Kentucky for sale. His son Thomas made even fuller use of those slaves he inherited. He employed nine female slaves, including some children, in producing most, if not all, of the cloth used on his Fort Defiance plantation. In 1849 he recorded their output as 259 yards of "fine Cloth" for the family's use, 32 yards of coarse cloth for bagging, 23 yards for carpeting, and the remainder, 625 yards, for Negroes' clothes. His male slaves were often employed in building and keeping up the roads connecting his widely scattered highland properties.[48]

Perhaps the best evidence of the division of slave labor on a typical large western North Carolina farm is provided by McDowell County slaveowner James Harvey Greenlee, who had no real business interests other than the management of his farm. His meticulously kept diary of the late 1840s and early 1850s makes it possible to determine ap-

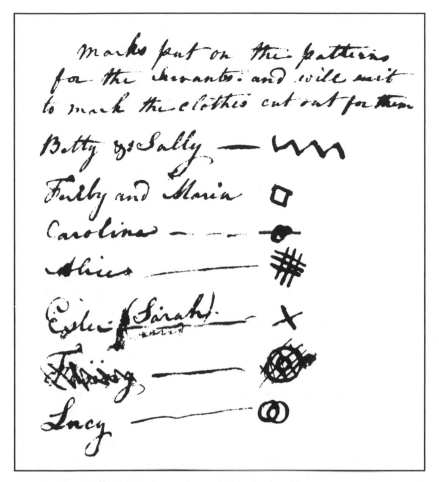

Figure 9. Memorandum concerning cloth produced by Lenoir family slaves at Fort Defiance. Manuscript Department, Duke University.

proximately the amounts and types of work performed by his thirty-odd slaves. The daily entries for two random years (1847 and 1852) indicate that almost 60 percent of their labor was devoted to a wide variety of nonagricultural tasks (in addition to those of a strictly agricultural nature), including making bricks, shingles, and shoes, and working in Greenlee's blacksmith shop, tanyard, and house. His black workers spent almost a fourth of their time in construction work, ranging from building roads, fences, and a dam, to erecting their own slave quarters. Several of his slaves spent much of the year hired out for mining, road work, or quarrying rock.[49] Yet even with such a wide range of activities, Greenlee's slaves probably performed fewer types of work than others belonging to local masters of comparable land and slave holdings, whose businesses often utilized black manpower.

While keeping slaves active performing such a variety of jobs probably required a great deal of planning and management, as well as constant supervision, such burdens did not mean that slave labor was less efficient or productive than labor in large cash-crop operations elsewhere in the South. One means of insuring the flexibility and profitability of slavery in the mountains was the opportunity to purchase and sell slaves' temporary labor. The financial benefits of the latter option were considerable, particularly for those slaveowners involved in pursuits other than fulltime farming. The dependence of E.J. Erwin, a Morganton banker, on such benefits was probably characteristic of others in the region. "Of the hire of my negroes," he informed his son, "I have had to pay my railroad stock, $475, & pay for your mother's buggy. If you will use economy I shall be able to continue your education. I make very little off my farm. I have not a negro that labours as hard as I do."[50]

Because many mountain masters could utilize their slaves most profitably by hiring them out, such transactions probably involved many more of the region's slaves than the 5 to 10 percent Eugene Genovese estimates were hired out annually throughout the South during the late antebellum period.[51] Almost all of those with substantial slaveholdings hired out slaves at some point, and most sometimes supplemented their own work force by hiring slaves themselves. Probably 90 percent or more of such transactions involved two slave owners.

The casual exchange of black labor between family members was common in the region, particularly since so many second and even third generations of slaveholding families remained in the same area and maintained close ties. Greenlee's diary indicates that he occasionally borrowed slaves from his father and brother for particular jobs; even more often, he loaned his own slaves to his uncle and his father-in-law. Sometimes such exchanges within families were arranged more formally. Dr. John Carson in Burke County paid relatives in McDowell County for the use of five slaves to supplement his own work force of six.[52] James Scott's proposal to hire from his brother "one or two half-grown boys and one or two stout young women" to work with his own in mining gold was a financial proposition, implying that profits were to be shared with his brother. In some cases, family ties seem to have had little bearing at all on a deal. Calvin Cowles hoped to hire "two boys" from his uncle but supposed he would have to settle for one "as Uncle R. talked about not hiring at the same price as others got for 'lame negroes.' "[53]

Slaves were often hired for the particular skills they had to offer. William Lenoir hired a neighbor's slave for a month to operate his newly built sawmill while teaching at least one of his own slaves to run it. Samuel McDowell of Franklin hoped that he could continue to keep David L. Swain's slave Cherry and her daughter to cook for his family, because he feared that it would be almost impossible to find a replacement for her in the area. Calvin Cowles paid eight dollars a month or six dollars plus clothing for slaves to work in his store. He assured their owners that they would not work in his mines or in bad weather.[54] In 1835, William Holland Thomas hired one of John B. Love's slaves as a blacksmith for nine months. He agreed to pay Love with "three hundred bushels of corn and $37.50 for said negroes board, washing, lodging & in smithwork or store goods." Thomas later hired out a slave mother and daughter he owned to cook for a family in Asheville who were so pleased with them that their one-year contract was extended, despite Mrs. Thomas's objections.[55]

Occasionally, western Carolinians gave in to more distant opportunities to hire out their slaves. But the very distance from home gave those slaves a sense of autonomy that may or may not have presented their masters with later problems in exerting their own authority. William C. Walker of Cherokee County allowed his slave Elyos to share in the profits earned by hiring out his labor among several employers across the state line in Tennessee. Elyos took an active, even dominant, role in negotiating the rates for his services and seems to have been entrusted by all of the parties involved to handle the financial transactions between them.[56] In other instances, such independence led to less satisfactory consequences. Hamilton Brown of Caldwell County, for instance, sent a slave blacksmith to work for an employer in Hot Springs, Virginia. At the end of his term, the slave dictated a letter to his master requesting permission to remain there and open his own shop. He proposed sharing his profits with Brown and pointed out that such an arrangement would earn him far more than could be made by hiring him out. There is no record of Brown's response, but the sense of independence instilled in this slave well may have led to tensions if he ever did return home.[57]

Sometimes it was the problem of controlling the hirer rather than the hired that made long-distance arrangements risky. David L. Swain, the Asheville native who served as North Carolina's governor and then as president of the University of North Carolina, long after he had moved east continued to keep most of his slave property in Buncombe and Macon counties under the management of his nephew. In 1841, a planter from Shelbyville, Tennessee, hired several of Swain's slaves but was reluctant to give them up at the end of their contracted year, citing his harvest schedule, the pregnancy of one of the slaves, and other reasons why they could not return to North Carolina. Despite Swain's firm rejections of an extention, only when his nephew was sent to retrieve them—almost a year after the end of their contracted term—did he regain his property. Apparently this did not greatly discourage him, for he continued to hire out more and more of his slaves. In 1855, another Shelbyville farmer hired ten of Swain's slaves; by 1861, he was paying for the use of twenty-one.[58]

Various public works projects provided opportunities for more substantial income from slave labor than the hiring out of one or two slaves at a time. James Greenlee sent several of his slaves to McDowell County to help build and maintain roads. Cherokee County paid five thousand dollars to Johnson W. King, at one time William Holland Thomas's business partner, for the use of his slaves for several weeks in building its courthouse.[59] Likewise, the courthouses for Watauga, Macon, and Henderson counties were constructed largely by slaves hired by or loaned to those counties by prominent local citizens. The first churches in Jefferson, Franklin, and other mountain communities were also built with the slave labor of one or more of the members.[60]

By far the largest outlets for hired slave labor in the western part of the state were mines and railroad construction. The gold rush of the early 1830s was exceptional in the high demands it placed on slave labor in the area, and many slaveholders who did not succumb to the mining fever themselves reaped considerable profit by hiring out their slaves to those who did. Hiring slaves also proved advantageous to local nonslaveholding miners, since this was the only means by which they could hope to compete with the manpower imported by large slaveholders from eastern North Carolina and Virginia.[61]

These opportunities did not end after the "rush" subsided in 1833.

Until the late 1850s, gold or copper mining both in western Carolina and across the state line in southeastern Tennessee continued to provide the most profitable outlets in the mountains for hired slave labor. Thomas G. Forney hired slave men and boys to work in his Wilkes County mines until well into the 1840s. In 1844, brothers Hamilton and E. Jones Erwin received $875 and James H. Wilson $600 for eleven months of their slaves' labor in W.W. Avery's Burke County mines. A Mr. Weaver paid James Greenlee $142 for the use of eight of his male slaves to work his mines for about three months in 1847. This seems to have been an annual transaction until complaints from his slaves of harsh treatment led Greenlee to discontinue his dealings with Weaver in 1851. As late as 1858, Calvin Cowles was paying $4 a week for each of six slaves "to draw water night and day" at his Gap Creek gold mine in Ashe County, and a year later, the Cherokee County slave Elyos, mentioned above, was working in the mines of Copper Hill, Tennessee.[63]

By that time, however, plans were under way for the Western North Carolina Railroad to cut through the mountains from Morganton to Asheville and beyond, and the demand for slave labor became as intense as it had been during the gold rush almost thirty years earlier. Slave men were hired to work alongside white laborers digging track beds and laying track, and both male and female slaves cooked and washed for those workers. William F. McKesson, the region's largest slaveholder, became one of the major contractors for railroad construction. Buncombe County's largest slave owners, Nicholas W. Woodfin and James W. Patton, were also actively involved in the construction of an independent section of railroad through Asheville. These men all hired other slaves and some white labor to supplement their own black labor force on these projects. (Patton had four hundred hands, black and white, working for him in 1861.)[64] It was those contractors who came from outside the area, however, who provided local masters with the best opportunities for hiring out their slaves. Charles Fisher of Salisbury, president of the North Carolina Railroad, hired sixty-one Burke County slaves to work, along with fifty-two slaves of his own on the section east of Morganton. John A. Hunt, a Massachusetts surveyor and contractor, moved to Morganton and hired thirty-one young black men to work for him.[65]

Even after the Civil War began, demand continued to rise. The Western North Carolina Railroad ran advertisements across the state

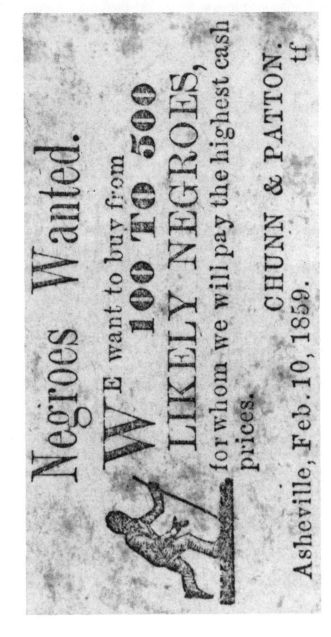

Figure 10. Advertisement soliciting slaves for railroad construction. Duke University Newspaper and Microform Department, Perkins Library. *Asheville News.*

for "100 able-bodied negroes" in December 1861 and for fifty more in mid-1862.[66] As in the earlier gold rush, manpower on this scale was far more than western North Carolinians could supply, as their own labor needs always took precedence over the use of their slaves by others. Despite the considerable financial gains to be had from sending large numbers of one's slave force to work for the railroad, indications are that most masters hiring out slaves only parted with a small percentage of them and that many owners never succumbed to the temptation at all. As a result, much of the black labor used on the railroad had to be imported from other parts of the state.[67]

Such considerations raise the question of slavery's profitability in the North Carolina mountains. The fact that local slaveholders did not respond more fully in either the early 1830s or the late 1850s and early 1860s to what could have been tremendous opportunities to salvage an unprofitable investment suggests that they did not see that investment or their use of it as either unprofitable or in need of salvaging. This is but one of many indications that, while slaves constituted a smaller proportion of the population than in most areas of the South, the institution of slavery was fully entrenched and economically quite healthy in the North Carolina mountains.

Mountain masters were very much aware of the value of their black property. Account books, journals, and correspondence between owners reveal considerable interest in slave prices. Though much of this interest was from a buyer's rather than from a seller's perspective, a number of owners made periodic inventories of their holdings and the increase in their slaves' worth.[68] Olmsted was often told by mountain residents that slaves were profitable only "as they increase and improve in saleable value." Two farmers, explaining their sources of income to him, spoke of the sale of blacks in comparison with that of their livestock. "'A nigger,' said one of them, 'that wouldn't bring over $300 seven years ago, will fetch $1000, cash, quick, this year; but now hogs, they ain't worth so much as they used to be.'" John Hall, a Macon County farmer, was even more emphatic that slavery was the area's sole profitable investment, and thus the only one in demand. In 1842 he declared that "cattle, hogs, sheep, corn, oats, or small tracts of land, they are in no demand at all—negroes are the only property that is wanted." Thomas Lenoir came to the same conclusion two years later. He wrote his brother that he had some cattle he wanted to sell, "but the prospect of getting cash at even a reduced price is bad, and I have no property, but Negroes, that will command money."[69]

As these statements suggest, slaveholders had good reason to be optimistic about slave property they had already acquired, for slave prices in western North Carolina, though not quite as high as the South generally, were rising more rapidly there. Based on accounts, bills of sale, and auction records from the area, the average price for slaves of all ages and both sexes sold in the mountain counties rose 108 percent during the 1850s, compared with a 72 percent rise in slave prices across the South. In 1850, slaves in western North Carolina sold for an average price of $400 each. By the end of the decade, the average price was $835.[70]

Despite Olmsted's observation, there is little evidence that most slaveholders viewed the sale of their property as a primary means of profiting on their investment. The majority of those selling, in transactions for which the reasons can be determined, seem to have sold reluctantly or even as a last resort. Most slaves were sold only in estate settlements after a master's death.[71] There are several instances in which slaves were traded for land or other property or even for other slaves, often in order to bring slave families together.[72] Some owners sold their slaves to pay off debts or to provide cash in financial emergencies. An often-cited incident concerning the 1856 establishment of Mars Hill College a few miles north of Asheville involved a slave, owned by one of the founding trustees, who was taken and held by the building contractors until the debt on the construction of the college's first building was paid.[73]

A Macon County situation in the late 1840s also indicates the way in which slaves were used as financial pawns and the lengths to which both creditors and debtors went to acquire and retain black property. As a result of several large debts owed to various businessmen in Franklin, Eli McKee was required to grant a lien on his slave property. He resisted giving his slaves up, despite persistent efforts by his creditors to take possession of them and even though "every man that could sue me . . . had done so." McKee wrote defiantly, "There is not 10 men in Macon County who shall have the pleasure of owning one negrow I have or ever had in my lifetime. I have had a most cruel time of it and I think it was caused by my having some valuable slave property and some 20 or 30 men wanted the same." By stalling for time with the financial assistance of relatives elsewhere in North Carolina,

McKee was able to keep his slaves, "much to the disappointment of those who have sought [his] ruin."[74]

The only evidence even suggesting that a mountain slaveholder made his primary profits from his black property by selling it comes from the testimony a former slave. According to Mary Barbour, her master, Jefferson Mitchell of McDowell County, sold almost all of his slaves when they reached the age of three, including at least twelve of her brothers and sisters.[75] Most records indicate that young children were sold with their mothers, but there are several examples of single purchases (or acquisitions through gift or legacies) of very young slaves. Because young slaves were seen as long-term investments, slaveholders often found that the lower purchasing prices for them more than compensated for the lack of any real utility for several years. William Lenoir stated that he preferred to acquire slaves at an early age for their low cost and easy trainability.[76] Accounts of other large slaveholders also record purchases of individual slaves, ranging in age from two to ten, without their mothers. In several estate settlements in which the distribution of slaves was left to the heirs' discretion, early requests were made specifically for the slave children inherited, with or without their parents.[77]

The most obvious indication of the wide extent to which young slave children were acquired alone is the remarkably high proportion of single-slave owners whose only slave was a child. Fully a fourth (96 of 375) of all single-owned slaves in the mountain counties in 1860 were ten years old or younger.[78] Since personal records of these small slaveholders are rare, it is difficult to tell whether they, like Lenoir and other large owners, were prepared to wait several years for their investments to pay off in labor or whether, in view of rapidly rising prices, they saw these youthful purchases merely as short-term investments whose resale would earn them substantial profits.

The most striking aspect of these sales is that almost all were made within the area and between western North Carolinians. Though the more acquisitive slaveholders in the region sometimes had to go to markets elsewhere to buy slaves, those selling slaves, even in large numbers (for example, at estate auctions), had no trouble finding buyers among local or nearby residents.[79] Professional slave traders made occasional appearances in the mountain counties, but they were more likely to sell slaves to local residents that to buy slaves from them. A few mountain slaveholders did sell to traders, however. Former slave

Table 3.2. *Western North Carolina Slaveholders and the Distribution of Slaves, 1850 and 1860*

Counties	Total No. of Slaveholders		Percentage of Total Heads of Households	
	1850	1860	1850	1860
Alleghany	—	56	—	10.0
Ashe	132*	85	9.3	6.0
Buncombe	248	293	12.7	15.9
Burke	233	204	23.6	16.6
Caldwell	173	177	18.6	15.1
Cherokee	61	97	5.9	6.7
Haywood	54	61	4.7	6.2
Henderson	159	211	17.0	13.7
Jackson	—	47	—	4.7
Macon	101	62	10.3	6.5
Madison	—	47	—	4.9
McDowell	190	219	22.1	21.5
Watauga	39	31	6.8	3.5
Wilkes	181	232	8.8	9.4
Yancey	77	55	5.5	3.8
Total	1,648	1,877	11.6	10.3

Percentage of WNC Slaveholders, 1860
Percentage of Southern Slaveholders, 1860

*1850 figures for Ashe County include those for Alleghany as well.
Source: Computed from *Seventh and Eighth U.S. Censuses*, 1850, table 1; 1860, tables 1 and 2.

Sarah Gudger recalled the visits of a "specalator" to an Old Fort plantation near her own. He and "Old Marse" would pick out a slave from the field and then "dey slaps de han'cuffs on him an tak him away to de cotton country."[80] But such sales to outsiders, particularly to slave traders, were frowned upon by most mountain masters, who saw them as both inhumane and poor business. Evidence indicates that few violated the community norm of selling slaves only locally.[81] In the novel *Sapphira and the Slave Girl*, Willa Cather's heroine, a slaveholding wife in Virginia's Blue Ridge Mountains, enunciated a moral code regarding slave sales that seems to have been prevalent among North

Table 3.2., Continued

1–2 Slaves		3–9 Slaves		10–19 Slaves		20 or more Slaves	
Distribution of Slaves Owned							
1850	*1860*	*1850*	*1860*	*1850*	*1860*	*1850*	*1860*
—	33	—	18	—	4	—	3
65	38	82	36	14	9	3	2
98	114	94	124	36	40	20	15
75	46	94	101	38	32	24	25
65	74	70	80	23	13	15	10
25	32	27	58	7	3	2	4
21	30	24	25	3	4	6	2
48	73	90	101	14	21	7	16
—	23	—	17	—	5	—	2
46	25	43	25	9	10	3	2
—	23	—	20	—	2	—	1
71	91	85	89	21	24	13	15
23	9	14	20	2	2	0	0
73	94	109	107	29	25	7	6
33	10	33	19	9	25	2	1
	715		840		220		102
	38%		44.7%		11.7%		5.4%
	26%		41%		20%		14%

Carolina's mountain masters as well. "Of course we don't sell our people," she stated in response to a neighbor's offer to buy a "handy girl." "Certainly we would never *offer* any for sale. But to oblige friends is a different matter."[82]

Demographic statistics seem to confirm that this ethical code guided the behavior of highland slave owners. In the 1850s, the rate of natural increase among mountain slaves (34.9 percent) was only slightly higher than that for the state of North Carolina as a whole (33.1 percent).[83] But the increase in slave population overall was significantly greater in the western counties than for the rest of the state. North Carolina's slave population grew 32.1 percent between 1840 and 1860, compared to a growth rate of 46.2 percent in the mountain counties.[84] Thus, far fewer mountain slaves were leaving the area in which they were born (either with their masters or through sales) than was the case for the eastern four-fifths of the state.

Despite the fact that 90 percent of the white residents of western North Carolina never owned slaves, then, the "peculiar institution" was as firmly entrenched there as anywhere in the South. Its future looked particularly bright on the eve of the Civil War, as railroad construction brought a dramatic increase in the demand for slave labor and the line's completion promised to draw the area more fully into the expanding market economy of the rest of the South. The number of slaveholders increased by 13.9 percent in the 1850s, and the fact that many old and new slave owners were investing in slave children reflected their confidence in slavery's future security and growing profitability.[85]

Chapter 4

Mountain Slaves:

"More elevated in soul and intellect"?

One of the most striking incidents in the annals of southern master-slave relationships occurred in western North Carolina early in its development. In the early 1790s, William Walton, Jr., moved to Morganton where he opened a mercantile business with his brother. One aspect of that business came to be the importation of slaves for sale to fellow Burke County residents, a pursuit that proved so lucrative that Walton moved to Charleston for several years in order to buy African labor directly from the ships importing them. He then sent his purchases up to his 600-acre Burke County plantation, which he had acquired specifically to serve as a training ground where his imported laborers learned English and local farming methods from other slaves prior to their local resale. (Walton himself returned home only in 1808, when the congressional ban on further slave importation took effect.)[1]

According to a story recounted later by both his nephew, Thomas Walton, and a descendant of the slave involved, one of Walton's African acquisitions was revealed to have been a tribal leader named Tamishan, who was "of a nobler race than the Guinea negro." That, plus the fact that he could read and write Arabic, much impressed the Burke County residents who came to know him, including Waightstill Avery, who purchased him from Walton. This African prince was unhappy as a slave, however, and around 1800, he made a bargain with his new master to allow him to return to his native land and send four blacks to take his place. Avery agreed, but instead of subjecting others to lives of bondage in America, Tamishan sent him $400 in gold dust, a very fair price for four men at that time.[2]

[87]

Figure 11. Creekside, the Burke County plantation of Thomas George Walton. North Carolina Division of Archives and History.

The accuracy of this extraordinary story may be somewhat suspect and, even if it is true, Avery's motives may have been less than humanitarian. But it was only the first of a great many such incidents in the Carolina mountains which suggest that the quality of life for slaves there was affected by the region's peculiar demographic, geographic, and economic characteristics . How these slaves' lives differed from those of their counterparts elsewhere in the South and how their relative scarcity and more flexible workload affected relationships with owners are more elusive questions, and answers must be grounded on less concrete or quantifiable foundations than those dealing with slavery's economic functions. Still, evidence suggests that antebellum conditions in the Southern Appalachians were indeed conducive to a more satisfying situation for both slaves and masters than those elsewhere in the South.

Mountain slaves generally enjoyed less restricted lives and more relaxed relationships with white residents. Visitors to the area were struck by this contrast. George Featherstonhaugh's first impression of the slaves he encountered in Asheville was that they seemed so happy—"more merry, and noisy, and impudent than any servants I had ever seen."[3] Olmsted, after observing slavery in the southern highlands, wrote that its "moral evils . . . are less, even less proportionately to the number of slaves." As noted earlier, he viewed mountain slaves as more like free laborers than like slaves in the Deep South. They were "less closely superintended," he explained. "They exercise more responsibility, and both in soul and intellect they are more elevated."[4] Charles Lanman, who visited the region only a few years before Olmsted, expressed the same idea even more emphatically. In his somewhat overstated opinion, "the slaves residing among the mountains are the happiest and most independent portion of the population; and I have had many a one pilot me over the mountains who would not have exchanged places even with his master."[5]

To those outside observers, perhaps the most obvious indication of the better treatment of mountain slaves was the freedom of movement which many masters allowed their charges. Lanman, as just noted, was impressed by the independence of those slaves he encountered. Rev. William Malet was also struck by this unrestricted mobility of blacks in the region. A slave woman traveling alone to Flat Rock from South Carolina in a stagecoach with him was proof to him that slaves in that area had even greater freedom than blacks in the North, "where she would not have been tolerated."[6] The fact that slaves often served as guides to visitors touring the mountains not only indicates that they were allowed to travel freely with strangers but also suggests a familiarity with the region that could have come only from considerable movement through it. Hunting trips and other expeditions for resort guests were frequently guided by slaves. Lanman described a deer hunt organized at Warm Springs, in which a slave on horseback was sent about three miles off into the mountains to release dogs to find and chase a deer back toward the waiting hunters. He later told of an expedition up Black Mountain (later renamed Mount Mitchell) that was guided by "an old negro."[7] During the Civil War, slaves often led deserters or escaped prisoners across the mountains as they tried to reach friendlier territory in East Tennessee or above the Mason-Dixon Line.[8]

The variety of jobs blacks performed both at home and as hired labor elsewhere often required masters give certain slaves special responsibilities. As noted in the preceding chapter, those slaves hired for jobs far from home often exercised considerable autonomy. Both

Charles White, Hamilton Brown's slave blacksmith in Virginia and Elyos, William Walker's "free agent" in Tennessee, exhibited strong streaks of independence and self-esteem; yet they enjoyed their privileged status only after and only as long as they earned their masters' confidence through proven loyalty and continued deference. Such cases were by no means unique. William Holland Thomas apparently entrusted several of his slaves with tasks that allowed them considerable mobility. One named Cudjo often traveled around the area carrying messages and deliveries for his master. On at least one occasion, he was sent to Tennessee to make a delivery of $350. Another of Thomas's slaves, appropriately named Wagoner Dick, traveled with a mule-drawn wagon to South Carolina and Georgia to purchase and sell supplies for Thomas's store.[9]

James Greenlee's slaves also frequently moved about on their own. He often sent them individually or as a group to perform work away from his farm. Those whom he hired out traveled with no supervision to and from the mine where they worked.[10] Slaves of eastern Blue Ridge owners who spent their summers tending livestock in the western highlands enjoyed a similar independence. Though an overseer usually superintended these operations, slaves were often on their own while moving between these properties and while rounding up and driving animals to market.[11] Though these black workers, too, obviously had earned such responsibilities through past performance, such trust was but one indication of the accuracy of Lanman's observation that mountain slaveholders "are in the habit of treating [their slaves] as intelligent beings and in the most kindly manner."[12]

Another such indication of mountain masters' greater consideration toward their charges was their widespread reluctance either to sell their slaves outside the area or to professional slave traders, or to split up slave families through purchases, sales, or bequests. William Lenoir, for instance, was strongly opposed to selling his black property, since he was convinced that he could support his "slave family" better than anyone else.[13] At his death, his children sold very few of the slaves they inherited, and those few were sold only "to friends who would be humanitarian, no husbands and wives separated." His son Thomas passed his father's convictions on to his own son-in-law in Alabama, when he urged him not to sell his slaves unless families were kept together and were willing to be sold. He, too, strongly advised that slaves be sold to friends rather than strangers whenever possible.[14] Henry Hardin of Ashe County assigned specific slave families and individuals to his wife and children in his 1846 will, and seemed particularly concerned that at least two pairs of his slaves—an elderly man and wife and a mother and daughter—remain together and be cared for by his children.[15]

Other slaveholders in the region made financial sacrifices in their efforts to respect black family ties. Abraham Wiggins of Macon County was forced to sell a family of seven slaves to pay his debts. He did not want them permanently separated, but did want to retain four for his own use. In order to assure that the family would remain intact, his friend William Holland Thomas agreed to take the mother and two of her children then and to buy the rest from Wiggins' heirs after his death, though such an arrangement could hardly have been of any financial advantage to Thomas.[16] An Asheville slaveholder under serious financial pressure refused to sell a "very valuable negro man" he owned until he could "find a good kind man that will buy him and keep him near his wife who lives in the neighborhood."[17] Nicholas Woodfin wrote approvingly of another Asheville slaveholder who, forced by debts to sell his black property, "very properly directed that a woman and her four children be sold together for $600 even though they could have brought as much as $1000 sold separately."[18] Woodfin himself lost the opportunity to pay $1,000 for a male slave whom a Buncombe County widow was forced by financial pressure to sell. In order to keep him in her family, she sold him to her son for $700, sacrificing at least $300 that she certainly could have used. (Of course, loyalty to her son may have been a more important motivating factor than concern for the slave.)[19]

As in the latter instance, it seems that women often were less likely to give in to financial or other pressures when the welfare of their slaves was at stake. In response to increased mental strain, Priscilla Dowell of Caldwell County turned over control of her "dear negros" to a trustee, with instructions that he could hire them out only to "prudent and kind masters nearby." The only sale she approved was that of a male slave to his wife's master, and she gladly accepted far less than his market value in order to bring the couple together. By passing the responsibility for her slaves on to a trusted friend, she alleviated her fear that she would be declared incompetent to manage her own affairs and that an appointed guardian "would get possession of her negroes [a mother and her two children] and scatter them."[20]

The most dramatic instance (perhaps questionable in its detail) of a slaveholder's sentimental attachment to her property involved a bond not between slave relatives, but between a slave woman and a white child. Margaret Baird Vance, mother of the future governor from Buncombe County, was forced to sell most of her husband's slaves after his death. When her children's nurse, "Mammy Venus," was put on the auction block still holding the youngest of her white charges in her arms, Mrs. Vance was so moved that she quickly paid a dollar to buy her back before the bidding could begin, a move than won hearty approval from the assembled crowd.[21]

The wishes of slaves themselves sometimes dictated whether and to whom they were sold or hired. Jane McDowell of Buncombe County refused to hire out a male slave in an area he disapproved. "Jim does not like Yancey [County]," she wrote, "and I will let him trye some other countery and he wants to go to Buncombe and he Shall goe if I onley get half price." The desire of a slave boy to be reunited with his mother led Thomas Lenoir to sell him, at a considerable loss, to the Caldwell County planter who owned her. He explained that he did so "as I wished for the blacks as well as the whites to be accommodated in their feeling."[22]

The lack of control over how their slaves were treated by those hiring them was often a source of worry to mountain masters and mistresses. William Gwyn informed his father-in-law Hamilton Brown in 1836 that concern for the health of Brown's slaves, Larkin and Sarah, had led him to place them in the care of a Methodist minister, so "that they may have some one to protect them and see that they are not abused." James Greenlee discontinued his annual practice of sending eight slaves to work in nearby gold mines when they complained of harsh treatment there.[23]

The correspondence of the McKee family in Buncombe and Macon counties reveals both the McKees' great sensitivity to the potential for harsh treatment by hirers and their considerable regard for the welfare and wishes of their slaves, a mother and her son. Adaline and young Thomas were owned by John McKee of piedmont Iredell County, who loaned them to his recently widowed sister-in-law Polly in Asheville. After several months, she had no further need of them, but refused to hire them out, as their owner John had suggested, "for fear that she or her child might be abused or not taken care of." She was also reluctant to send them back to Iredell, since Adaline herself had no desire to return.[24] Polly's feelings are revealing, not only because she took a slave's wishes so seriously, but also because the slave Adaline seems to have preferred her new life in the mountains over that on a piedmont plantation. John McKee finally agreed that Adaline and her son could remain in Asheville, but only in the care of a family friend, Colonel Lowry, who would "keep her and pay for her hire." Polly McKee submitted to this arrangement, but only reluctantly, since she would have preferred to care for the two personally to insure against their mistreatment.[25]

Six months later, when another brother, Eli McKee, the sheriff of Macon County, needed an extra servant, it was agreed that he would take charge of Adaline and Thomas. He traveled to Asheville to pick them up from the Lowry family, and was relieved that Mrs. Lowry allowed them to leave "without a murmur or a frown," even though she informed Eli that they had become as close to her as her own children. Once settled back in Macon County, Eli assured his brother that "Adaline appears to be very well satisfied," although he conceded that it would be an adjustment for her, since "we are all strange to her as yet."[26] When Eli planned a visit to his Iredell relatives, Adaline "insisted" on accompanying him for a final visit. He readily assented, though again she made it clear that she preferred her situation in the mountains over any permanent return to her original owners. And no wonder. The concern of this western branch of the McKee family for her was in sharp contrast to that of their lowland relatives. When Colonel Lowry later suggested that Eli rent Adaline out and split the profits among his brothers and sisters, the mountain McKees agreed that "maybe she would be abused and they would rather do without the hire."[27]

The relationship between Adaline and the McKees was, needless to say, an exceptional one. Though they passed her and her son from one guardian to another, those in charge of her took great pains to assure the rest of the family that each change in arrangements was agreeable to her and that each move was actually in her best interest. Subsequent letters consistently contained either inquiries or reports about her and Thomas, who was "a very weakly boy" and thus a cause for further concern among the family.[28] Certainly no family members or acquaintances of the McKees ever received as much discussion as did the health and happiness of these two slaves.[29]

These examples of profits sacrificed for ethical considerations reflect a somewhat heightened sense of duty on the part of mountain slave-holders toward their slaves, whether in daily relationships or in concern for the slaves' long-range welfare. Among the benevolent forms of paternalism manifested by some western Carolinans was religious training of their slaves. A number of mountain masters or mistresses, including the wife of one of the region's largest slaveholders, Isaac T. Avery, provided their black charges with regular Bible readings.[30] This sense of obligation was most explicitly expressed by James Greenlee of McDowell County. A devout Christian himself, he gathered his slaves on Sunday mornings for Biblical instruction, cathechism recitation, and prayer. In a remarkable diary entry in 1848, he explained why he considered this such an important task:

> May we who have the charge of them feel it our indispensable duty to in-struct them tho they are in a degraded and dependent condition. We are no less accountable but more so—as they are under our controll, we cannot plead as an excuse their situation for dereliction of duty on our parte, for the great God of all will hold us to a strict account for the manner we have discharged the various duties we owe to them – even bearing in mind that their souls are as precious in the sight of him with whome we have to do, as tho they were as free as we are, or as white as the fairest son of Adam . . . . Let them have the Bible with the prayers of Gods people, and suitable instruction & they will make better servants—a changed race in a moral & religious point of view, and take a stand more deserving a human being— And should emancipation be found wise for this nation, which I trust it may be, they then can go to their own native Land—as lights to their long-benighted brethren and in civalizing & Christianize them and place them under the guidance of the great author of all things among the Christians of the world.[31]

Greenlee's liberal attitude was exceptional even among his fellow mountain slaveholders. Yet, amid the strong ethical convictions shared by so many of them, his views were less unusual there than they would have been elsewhere in the South. His musings on the inevitable eventual emancipation of his slaves, as well as his uneasiness about the morality of slave ownership, reflect feelings shared by a number of his fellow mountain masters. In relating an incident in which a slave he owned was caught breaking into a store in Caldwell County in 1858, Walter W. Lenoir held that the institution rather than the individual slave was responsible for his misconduct, and that his own guilt outweighed any blame he placed on his black servant. Lenoir confided to his brother:

I feel determined at present never to own another slave. Both Nealy [Mrs. Lenior] and I have concluded after our limited experience with slaves, that the evil of being a master and mistress of slaves is greater than we are willing to bear unless imposed upon us by some sterner necessity belonging to our lot than we know of. Our present feeling is that we will eventually make our home in a free state.[32]

Others went beyond the concerned reflections of Greenlee and Lenoir and actually liberated some or all of their slaves, even though manumission laws provided them with the added burden of establishing new lives for their former property outside of the state. Colonel Stevenson of Macon County, for instance,in his will, provided for his slaves' freedom after his wife's death, and arranged for their transport to Savannah "to take shipping for Liberia."[33] In 1854, Maria Gordon of Wilkes County made provisions for experts in the field to provide the same opportunity for her slaves. In her will she declared, "I give all my other negro slaves to the American Colonization Society, provided the said negroes are willing to go to Liberia, and provided the Colonization Society is willing to receive them and send them to Liberia," stipulations to which, in fact, both parties agreed.[34]

The California gold rush provided yet another outlet through which mountain slaveowners manumitted their black charges. In 1852, William Coleman wrote of his intention, as old age approached, to let his slave property simultaneously earn their freedom and reestablish themselves in the newest of the free states. As with similar owners, such action on behalf of those he owned meant financial sacrifice to himself. "My plan," he wrote to his uncle, David L. Swain, "would be to set them [my young negroes] free at a certain age, but this is out of my power if I keep them in this country. My plan therefore is to send two or three of them to California, and to do this I must borrow $1500 or $2000 . . . and let them go to work and as soon as they can make the borrowed money pay it over so that in a few years they will all be able to get there."[35] Such an arrangement implied a great deal of trust in his slaves, since neither he nor his son planned to accompany them on their westward trek. Samuel McDowell, already in California with his own slaves, had assured him "there is no danger of negroes claiming their freedom," and Coleman reasoned that "as mine are young I would not be afraid to risk them." In asking Swain's opinion of such a proposition, his nephew explained that practicality was not his primary concern. "The reason why I would rather borrow money than sell young negroes is that I would rather pave the way for their freedom."[36]

James Avery of Burke County provided a similar opportunity to Will, an elderly slave esteemed by all the Avery family. Will had joined James's son, Isaac, on his venture to the gold-laden streams of the West Coast, where he was allowed one day a week to pan gold for himself. Will's profits were to be applied to the purchase of himself and his wife Nancy at a considerably reduced price, apparently determined by James Avery before his son and slaves left home. Because this slave was special and because of his family ties to those still in Burke County, Avery instructed his son to tell Will that "he must bring home $400 and I am to give him $50 and you must take $450 for him and I will apply to the Legislature to let him live in N. Car. on account of his kind treatment to you and meritorious services . . . in our state."[37]

Beyond the moral obligations mountain masters felt toward their slaves, genuine affection and intimacy often existed between individual blacks and their owners. Several masters included their slaves along with relatives in referring to "family" matters, and often made no distinction between the two in discussing births, deaths, or illness. George Swain, for example, reported that "the family are well with the exception of Ben and Elias," both of whom were slaves. He wrote of Elias' recovery, "I have real cause for thankfulness to our kind preserver for peculiarly distinguishing mercy in this and ten thousand other instances," a sentiment that could just as easily have been applied to his wife or son.[38] James Gudger wrote with equal fondness of a slave with whom he was raised in Buncombe County. "Butler," he stated, "was my companion, playmate, bodyguard and friend, and the affection that grew between us in our boyhood, has grown with our years and will remain to the end."[39]

A Burke County master, forced by debt to sell a slave, allowed that slave, named Rodman, to choose his new master (in itself, an indication of exceptional benevolence). The slave asked Isaac Avery to purchase him. Avery not only granted his request but soon made him his overseer as well. The attachment between Rodman and the Avery family became so strong that when Avery was killed in 1864, the slave took charge of the affairs of Mrs. Avery and her daughters and even used his own savings to maintain their house and farm.[40] William Holland Thomas seems to have shared a special relationship with his slave

Figure 12. Isaac T. Avery. North Carolina Division of Archives and History.

Cudjo, mentioned earlier as his trusted messenger. In addition to the freedom of movement that position brought, Cudjo was also allowed his own account at Thomas's store, which he used to purchase his own clothing, food, and tobacco. This too implies a privileged status just short of complete emancipation. Cudjo was the only one of Thomas's slaves to accompany his master and his legion throughout the Civil War.[41]

Finally, the sentiments of James Gwyn of Lenoir on the death of an old slave named Mason convey real affection toward the man he owned and a genuine sense of personal loss. Gwyn wrote,"I don't think I ever regretted to part from a friend or relation more than I did to part from him. He was so good, honest, truthful and so careful and attentive to the stock and to everything about the plantation, and so very kind to the children; everybody loved Uncle Mason and they had good reason to do so . . . He has no equal of his color in this part of the country."[42] He added that it was extra work done by the elderly slave, despite his master's efforts to make him rest and care for himself, that deprived him of another eight or ten years of life.

Such testimonials to slaves' devotion to their work and to those who worked them, though often quite sincere, also served a more subtle function. For men of conscience, such as Gwyn and some of his slaveholding neighbors, such reciprocal benefits as the system offered may well have alleviated doubts that plagued them. The story of William Walton's African prince and the surprising means by which he repaid his master's ultimate expression of good faith, like the accounts of the Avery and McElrath slave forces returning home to their masters from California with gold in hand, either without or with minimal supervision, were well known and often repeated among western Carolinians, who were quick to see in them proof of what Walton's nephew himself described as "the uprightness, rectitude, and fidelity of the negro."[43] Though such views may have been self-serving and self-deceptive, they could not help contributing to healthier relations between owner and owned by eliminating much of the suspicion and tension that characterized race relations elsewhere.

This is not to imply, of course, that the situation was so idyllic that there were no racial tensions or discipline problems in the region. Several months after Nat Turner's rebellion in 1831, a white man was arrested in Burke County "under charge of exciting the negroes to insurrection." Little came of either that charge or the subsequent arrest and trial of two slaves for conspiracy. Both were acquitted in a jury trial, a demonstration of the restraint and lack of paranoia within the local community that in itself provides an interesting contrast to the mood of other parts of North Carolina in the aftermath of the bloody massacre in adjacent Southampton County, Virginia. An Ashe County slave murdered his mistress in 1854, the same year in which a free black man in neighboring Wilkes County was hanged for refusing to serve in the army. There even occurred what might be termed a minor insurrection along Ashe County's Virginia border in 1851. Apparently under the instigation of a southwest Virginia abolitionist, at least four slaves rose up and killed Sam Bartlett, the brother of the Ashe County sheriff, and wounded several other local residents.[44] But such incidents seem to have neither attracted the widespread publicity nor inspired the general panic that they probably would have elsewhere; instead, they remained fairly isolated and certainly unusual occurrences for the western district.

Slave patrols were maintained on a regular basis at least in the more populous counties east of the Blue Ridge. They were particularly evident in situations in which large numbers of slaves were brought in from elsewhere, as during the gold rush in Burke and Rutherford counties or the summer seasons for South Carolinians in Henderson and Buncombe counties. This disruption of the status quo and the fear of "outside agitation" led to tighter precautions and controls than was usually the case elsewhere in the mountains.[45]

Runaways were not uncommon among mountain slaves, though the flights of many, if not most, were only temporary ventures from which they voluntarily returned. In 1822, George Swain of Asheville provided his son David, then a student at the University of North Carolina, with a detailed report of such an incident involving a slave of his. Daniel had been punished for being "impertinent" and "very neglectful in his business" by having his weekend pass cut short, so that he had to return home by Sunday night instead of Monday morning. After failing to get the pass extended, "he waited till preaching was over on Sunday evening and then started off . . . without any." In explaining Daniel's behavior, Swain conveyed an attitude of patronizing but bemused tolerance. "I had discovered a long time ago," he wrote, "that finery made a perfect fool of him, and instead of giving him more cloathing was obliged to take away what he had." But Daniel

managed to acquire from various sources an assortment of fancy sec-
ond-hand clothes and accessories. To his master, the effect of this new
wardrobe was that

> like all other Dandies who measure their importance by their dress he had
> entirely forgotten who he was, or what grade and station he ought to fill.
> Nothing but the thoughts of his clothes, I think, had deranged his mind the
> preceding week; but now that he was actually invested in all this splendor
> [it] was more than his tiny soul could bear with calmness or the least de-
> gree of equanimity . . . though really an object of pity, our thoughtless
> waggs were amused with his self important airs while he strutted with his
> hat on one side of his head, his akimbo blowing into the higher regions of
> the air the rich effluvia of a Spanish Segar.

Daniel's "finery was so felicitous" that an early curfew came as a
serious blow and "he could not bear the bereavement of his pleasure,"
and ran away. Swain listed the various plantations that the slave visited and stated the he went "as far along that road as he could possibly
find black audiences to exhibit his finery to." He continued making his
rounds until Tuesday night when "the grease and smoke of nigro huts
and rubing against wet bushes had so effaced the splendor of his robes
as to lesson his importance and partly restore his reason; though not
entirely." Swain explained that although Daniel had begun to think of
home and returned to within sight of it, he went instead to a nearby
clearing where two of his fellow slaves were working and spent the day

> in boasting of his great performances and future intentions . . . Still, how-
> ever, tho his greatness was in measure eclipsed, he lay back like a cautious
> General determined to surrender on conditions truely honorable. But alas,
> while he and Elias [another of Swain's slaves] was negotiating as he thought
> to the best advantage, Messrs. Perry and Evans Brown unluckily rushed
> upon him and made him surrender on their terms. . . . Even then [Swain
> concluded], like Milton's Devil he bore an aspect of majesty until divested
> of the mighty cause.[46]

Considering the laxity of control and the freedom of movement allowed many mountain slaves, it is perhaps more worthy of note that
more did not take advantage of the opportunities for escape than that
a few did. The rugged terrain and general sparseness of the population attracted quite a few runaways from other parts of the South who
sought refuge in North Carolina's mountains. Though they did not
often find much sympathy from white residents of the area, these fu-
gitives often benefitted from the region's general apathy toward their
capture and return.[47]

Other disciplinary problems among western North Carolina slaves were, for the most part, minor. They most frequently entailed drunkenness, the theft of food or other materials, often then sold to whites or other slaves, or fighting with other slaves.[48] But the most striking aspect of these and other cases is the leniency with which masters dealt with offending slaves. Despite occasional instances of whipping or other physical abuse, slaveholders in the mountains often inflicted little or no punishment on their guilty charges. In the case of George Swain's slave Daniel, for instance, his original punishment, a curtailed curfew, seems very mild, and the price he paid for his week-long escapade was even less. According to Swain, Daniel appeared "very humble," so that "I gave him his choice either to choose Wiley for his master, take a good whipping and go to work, or else walk off into the world where he pleased and never plague me any more. He begged to be excused from either and promised if I would only try him once more I should never have any trouble with him."[49] Apparently Swain complied and Daniel was, in effect, forgiven with no disciplinary action considered necessary.

Even more serious offenses were often treated lightly. Slaves were suspected of having set hotel fires in both Asheville and Warm Springs, with no apparent effort ever made to identify or to punish the culprits.[50] David, a slave belonging to William and Margaret Walker of Cherokee County, once assaulted his mistress in their smokehouse. She was forced to stab him in the arm to free herself from his grasp. No physical harm was done to her, and the couple took no punitive action for this most dreaded violation of racial taboos. They did sell David back to William's father, who had given them the slave, but with no mention made of what he had done.[51]

This general permissiveness itself may have caused disciplinary problems that slaveholders were unable to deal with effectively. William Holland Thomas and his wife were plagued by a male slave who often refused to obey orders and could not get along with their other slaves, but they continued to tolerate him much as parents would a spoiled child.[52] A Burke County woman complained that "the servants will not obey me. John ran away 6 weeks since. Last week he returned and says he intends to leave me again whenever he pleases . . . . I have not a single servant at my command."[53]

There were only occasional instances of whipping or other physical abuse by owners in the region. Practically the only (non-court-documented) evidence of such harsh treatment comes from an ex-slave, Sarah Gudger, who recalled that her master was strict and whipped slaves often.[54] Most mountain masters, however, frowned on such physical cruelty and sometimes demonstrated their disapproval in court. County records indicate several cases in which juries convicted owners of assault on their slaves. In 1856, a Wilkes County man was hanged for a particularly brutal beating that had resulted in the death of a sixty-year-old slave of his.[55]

On balance, though, there seems to have been a substantive difference in the treatment of mountain slaves and that of their counterparts elsewhere in the South. It is dangerous to generalize about the relationships between masters and slaves since such feelings, on both sides, were shaped by many personality variables and since much of the relevant evidence is, by its very nature, subjective and impressionistic. But the evidence related here suggests that there was indeed a qualitative, as well as quantitative, difference in mountain slavery. While western Carolinians certainly had no monopoly on kindness, concern, or leniency toward their slaves, the sheer number of instances and the pervasiveness of such attitudes in that region suggests that such treatment was far more likely to have been the norm there than elsewhere.

Comparisons with more general assessments of slaveholders' behavior across the South underscore the contrast. Slave manumission, for example, by the late antebellum period was less and less of an option for slaveholders. Inspired largely by fears of a growing free black presence as subversive to the entire slave system, state after state either prohibited masters from freeing their black property or stipulated that slaves thus freed be banished from the state. By the 1850s, manumission of black property was no longer, to quote Ira Berlin, merely "a wrong-headed act by a soft-hearted master," but rather "outright sedition."[56] Yet, as indicated above, it was during that very decade that a significant number of mountain masters and mistresses, seriously contemplated, discussed, and even carried out the freeing of their slaves, with no evident signs of disapproval from their fellow slaveholding or nonslaveholding neighbors.

There is ample evidence that throughout the South whipping remained the most widely applied and acceptable form of punishment inflicted on slaves. From the 1830s on, southerners paid sporadic lip service to humanitarian reforms in the treatment of slaves, and by mid-century, such barbaric punishments as live burnings, branding, ear-cropping, and other forms of mutilation were only rarely applied. But the use of the lash—resorted to sparingly, if at all, by western Carolina slaveholders—remained "the disciplinary centerpiece of plantation slavery" elsewhere. According to Kenneth Stampp, whipping was inflicted by nearly every slaveholder, and few grown slaves escaped it entirely.[57]

The generally recognized contrast between the Upper and the Lower Souths in the treatment of slaves is not sufficient to account for such differences. Even within the Upper South, sharp distinctions between the behavior and standards of highland and lowland masters are readily apparent. A slaveowner in northeastern Virginia, for instance, was made fully aware of fellow slaveholders' disapproval of his leniency toward his slaves and soon succumbed to the community norm of harsher treatment. In explaining this attitude—so different from that of western Carolinians—one of his slaves later wrote, "The more tyrannical a master is, the more will he be favorably regarded by his neighboring planters, and from the day he acquires the reputation of a kind and indulgent master, he is looked upon with suspicion."[58]

Even within North Carolina, owner behavior seems to have been far more rigid and impersonal in the eastern three-fourths of the state than in the mountain counties. In her recent study of North Carolina planters, Jane Censer concluded that their treatment of their slaves varied greatly, but that negligence and brutal cruelty were not at all uncommon. She reported that these large slaveholders consistently resorted to "severe chastisement," often inflicting "hard and sometimes unmerited punishment" on their unruly charges. She found few signs of owners' affection for or personal interest in their black servants.[59]

Perhaps most strikingly at variance with the practices of mountain masters was the barrier, identified by Censer and others, erected by the fact that masters saw their slaves first and foremost as property. This attitude allowed little regard for either the family ties or the personal feelings of those they owned. In one of the few instances in which statistical data can be applied to a comparative measure of owner attitudes, Censer's findings regarding the dispersal of slaves in estate settlements across the state provide a sharp contrast to that practice in the western counties. She reported that only 9 percent of the planters she dealt with (8 out of 92) made any provision in their wills or through their executors for keeping slaves families intact.[60] In contrast, almost 83 percent (15 out of 18) of the wills, instructions to, or actions by executors of western Carolina slaveholders reflect a concern for preserving or even reestablishing family units among their slaves.[61] This concern, in addition to evidence presented earlier attesting to widespread commitment by mountain masters to the contentment and welfare of those they owned, indicates that their relationships with their slaves were indeed more humane than those elsewhere in the state or in the South.

The reasons behind these qualitative distinctions are even more difficult to pinpoint than are the differences themselves. The most logical explanations lie in the very economic and demographic factors that also set slavery in that region apart from that in the lowland South. The types of economic activity to which masters applied their slaves certainly account for much of the trust and independence those slaves enjoyed. Many of those diverse pursuits involved slaves in nontraditional and nonagricultural forms of labor that often called for more than usual ability and responsibility, and in turn elicited more respect than most slaves elsewhere could expect to command.

The demography of slavery in North Carolina's western counties was also a key factor in the more favorable situations of their black populace. The most obvious conclusion—that smaller slaveholdings led to more intimacy and greater personal regard between owner and owned—is not necessarily the most important one, however. Certainly Censer's conclusions about the harsh treatment and detached nature of master-slave relations among her subjects reflect the fact that she deals with only the state's largest slaveholders.[62] Nevertheless, despite one slave's observation that "de more slaves a man had, de wusser he wus to slaves," it was often the largest of western North Carolina's slaveholders who exhibited the most conscientious concern for their black property.[63] William Holland Thomas, James Greenlee, Nicholas Woodfin, and the Avery and Lenoir families held slaveholdings that were among the region's most substantial. Yet all of them figure prominently in the evidence presented above of masters' permissiveness, kindness, and sense of moral duty. It is revealing that Rodman, the slave who was given the opportunity to choose his own master, chose to become the property of one of the largest slaveholders in all of western North Carolina. Conversely, the Wilkes County slaveholder hanged for the brutal murder of his slave owned only three.[64]

Rather than the size of individual slaveholdings, the more crucial factor in the good treatment those slaves enjoyed seems to be the fact that the region's proportion of slaves in the population was lower than that of most of the South. As such a small minority of the area's population, slaves posed far less of a threat, real or imagined, to the security of both slaveholding and nonslaveholding mountain whites. This sense of relative safety, along with the general lack of restrictions in the movement and activity of many slaves necessitated by their flexible workload under their own masters and the economic necessity of hiring out their labor elsewhere, resulted in a much more relaxed racial atmosphere in most mountain communities. Similarly, that demographic situation made slaveowners themselves a much smaller minority within their communities than elsewhere. Consciousness of their unusual position seems to have led many mountain masters to believe that because their treatment of their human property was conspicuous, their actions would be judged by the vast majority of nonslaveholders in whose midst they lived. Thus, for different reasons, the relatively small numbers of both slaves and slaveholders seem to have resulted in stronger community norms of decency and respect toward slaves by which almost all owners in the area came to abide.

Perhaps even more difficult to assess than the quality of master-slave relationships in the mountains are the racial attitudes of those who made up the vast majority of the populace there, the nonslaveholders. On no other aspect of Appalachian culture do opinions conflict more than on this question of how mountaineers regarded blacks. On the one hand, some have concluded that the lack of contact meant a lack of prejudice as well. Carter G. Woodson, the first scholar—and still one of the few—to have dealt seriously with the subject of race in the Southern Appalachians, maintained that there was more social harmony between the races in the mountains than elsewhere in the South. "There was more prejudice against the slaveholder than against the Negro," he wrote, and "with so many sympathizers with the oppressed in the back country, the South had much difficulty in holding the mountaineer in line to force upon the whole nation their policies," namely, the continuation of slavery.[65] John C. Campbell agreed, stating that "large sections of the Highland South were in sympathy with the North on the Negro question."[66] Far more recently, Loyal Jones, an eminent Appalachian scholar, stated that the "Appalachians have not been saddled with the same prejudices about black people that people of the deep South have."[67] Such statements seem to credit mountain residents with a sort of moral superiority, as if being somewhat removed from the harsher realities of the institution enabled them to view it more objectively and to see the slaves' plight more sympathetically.

At the other extreme are those who believed that the lack of contact with blacks by many white mountain residents resulted in even more intense hostility toward black people than that felt by whites in areas with more substantial black populations. This view owes much of its popularity to the often-quoted statement of W.J. Cash in *The Mind of the South:* "The mountaineer had acquired a hatred and contempt for the Negro even more virulent than that of the common white of the lowlands; a dislike so rabid that it was worth a black man's life to venture into many mountain sections."[68] Some of the more secluded pockets of settlement in western North Carolina did have (and even continue to have) reputations for their vehement opposition to black presence. A resident, explaining the lack of blacks, free or slave, in the Rock Creek section of Mitchell County, stated that "colored people have a well-founded belief that if they venture up there they might not come back alive."[69] Though for more conventional reasons of security, even Asheville citizens, who lived with the mountains' highest concentration of slaves, strongly opposed the presence of free blacks in their area. In 1824, they petitioned the state legislature for a high capitation tax on all free blacks in the state as a means of discouraging "the constant influx of free negroes of every character & description into the western part of the state."[70]

These extreme points of view suggest that the degree of racism among antebellum mountain residents ran the full gamut. Most of the statements above, however, are from twentieth-century secondary sources and largely constitute conjectures about how southern mountain whites would view a race with whom they had had little or no contact. If generalizations must be made, it seems far more reasonable to assume that racism and attitudes toward slavery among nonslaveholding western North Carolinians were no more and no less enlightened than elsewhere in the South. The morality of black bondage never seems to have been an issue in that part of the state. There is no evidence that anyone from the mountain counties was ever a member of North Carolina's Manumission Society, nor was there a local chapter of the American Colonization Society anywhere west of Caldwell County, despite the prevalence of both organizations just to the east in the piedmont and just to the west in East Tennessee.[71] Few mountaineers seemed particularly sympathetic to the many runaway slaves who often fled into their region seeking refuge from lowland masters. According to one western Carolinian, fear of the penalty for aiding a fugitive far outweighed any impulse to help.[72]

The variations in mountain attitudes toward slavery appear to have been linked to attitudes toward slaveholders, which in turn were based largely on residents' physical proximity to the system. Frederick Law Olmsted has provided us with virtually the only contemporary evidence we have on the opinions of mountain nonslaveholders toward slaveholders. Because his observations are so central a source for this information, it seems appropriate to examine the context within which he provided them.

Though it was through his second career, as a landscape architect, environmentalist, and urban planner that Olmsted is most widely remembered, his much briefer stint as a journalist and social critic in the 1850s is equally significant.[73] Commissioned by two New York newspapers as a roving correspondent, Olmsted spent a total of almost fourteen months between 1852 and 1854 traveling throughout the South. Though he, like many of his fellow New Englanders by then, firmly opposed slavery, he was even more offended by the hyperbole and pious posturing of what he felt were overwrought and ill-informed abolitionists. Thus he saw his southern mission as an opportunity to provide a more objective appraisal of slavery based entirely on first-hand observation. "Very little candid, truthful, and unprejudiced public discussion," he wrote, "has yet been had on the vexed subject of slavery."[74] He maintained that the true nature of southern life, both white and black, had thus far proven more inpenetrable to outsiders, and thus more subject to misconception, than the nature of life in most foreign countries.[75]

Once he had begun his travels, Olmsted found the physical treatment and quality of life of slaves somewhat better than he had anticipated.[76] Thus, his central indictment was not so much of the slave system's cruelties and injustices to those enslaved, but rather of the economic and cultural detriments slavery inflicted on southern whites—both slaveholders and nonslaveholders. As a labor force, slaves proved grossly inefficient (due in part to too much indulgence on the part of owners and taskmasters). Olmsted concluded that, because of their lack of incentive and their inherent shortcomings as a race, slaves worked slowly and poorly. Even worse, they lowered the expectations for white labor output as well and thus locked southern agriculture into crude, backward methods that kept the region from achieving the progress and productivity that characterized American farming elsewhere.[77]

Still more serious in Olmsted's eyes were the cultural and social stagnation the system of slave labor imposed upon the region. Slavery prevented southern yeomen from adopting the Calvinist work ethic and eliminated incentive for self-improvement, material or otherwise. Most original, Olmsted believed that his description of the yeoman class—"the non-slaveholders are unambitious, indolent, degraded and illiterate; are a dead peasantry so far as they affect the industrial position of the South"[78]—applied almost equally to the ruling class. Slavery inhibited intellectual activity and interest, and perpetuated among the planter elite, primitive living conditions usually seen only in frontier societies.[79]

It was in the southern highlands, during his tour of the "backcountry" in summer of 1854, that Olmsted found both exceptions to the deplorable conditions of the plantation South and evidence confirming his explanations of those conditions. From late June through late July, Olmsted traveled through the mountainous regions of northern Georgia, eastern Tennessee, and western North Carolina and Virginia.[80] His ten days in western North Carolina were spent primarily in the less developed, remoter areas near the Tennessee border. He visited the region's smallest county seats—Murphy, Waynesville, Burnsville, and Bakersville—and stopped briefly in its bustling hub, Asheville.

As noted earlier, Olmsted was quick to spot the distinctive socio-economic makeup of the area's largest slaveholders, as well as the better treatment mountain slaves enjoyed. In aspects of the highland society he encountered, he found much to support his larger argument. He noted much improved temperaments of those in areas little touched by slavery. "Compared with the slaveholders," he wrote in language similar to that used later by Faulkner,[81] "these people are more cheerful, more amiable, more sociable, and more liberal. Compared with the non-slaveholders of the slaveholding districts, they are also more hopeful, more ambitious, more intelligent, more provident, and more comfortable." Even the material conditions of mountain life were an improvement over those of plantation society, according to Olmsted.[83] In the southern highlands, then, this Connecticut Yankee

Figure 13. Frederick Law Olmsted, about 1859. National Park Service, Frederick Law Olmsted NHS.

discovered interesting variations on his theme that the negative effects of a slaveholding society extend well beyond the impact on its black victims.

Olmsted's interviews with highland yeomen, alone among contemporary sources, gave voice to this ordinarily inarticulate and rarely quoted group. Among those residents with whom he discussed the topic of slavery, most seemed to have equal contempt for slaves, their masters, and the system itself. Whatever objections they had concerning the institution in their own area, however, they objected much more to it in the lowland South. One mountaineer summed up the viewpoint held to varying degrees by almost all whom Olmsted interviewed. "He'd always wished there had n't been any niggers here . . . but he would n't like to have them free. As they had got them here, he did n't think there was any better way of getting along with them than that they had." Another of Olmsted's mountain hosts stated that "slavery is a great cuss [curse] . . . the greatest there is in these United States." But in explaining why, he mentioned only the fact that it allowed eastern planters to dominate state government at the expense of westerners.[84] In an observation echoing Olmsted's own opinion, still another mountaineer objected to the system's moral effect on slaveholders: "He was afraid that there was many a man who had gone to the bad world, who wouldn't have gone there if he hadn't had any slaves. He had been down in the nigger counties a good deal, and he had seen how it worked on the white people. It made the rich people, who owned the niggers, passionate, and proud and ugly, and it made the poor people mean." Olmsted went on to note that that particular highlander even owned a copy of *Uncle Tom's Cabin* and said that he "thought well of its depiction of slavery and its message."[85]

Despite their objections to the system, however, none of the mountain people Olmsted encountered advocated abolition. For some, this was merely because they feared the prospect of free blacks. A mountain woman in Tennessee, on learning that Olmsted was from New York and that blacks there were all free, stated "with disgust and indignation on her face" that "I would n't want to live where niggers are free, they are bad enough when they are slaves . . . If they was to think themselves equal to we, I do n't think white folks could abide it—they're such vile saucey things."[86]

More often, it was belief in the rights of property owners that led most mountain residents to stop their condemnation of the institution short of advocating its abolition. To be deprived of one's possessions, human or otherwise, was an injustice with which they could and did identify. As one highland slaveowner reminded his nonslaveholding neighbors: "If they can take our niggers away from us they can take our cows and hosses, and everything else we've got!"[87] Whatever distaste they may have felt for slavery or slaveholders, most mountain yeomen readily bought this argument. The "peculiar institution" remained considerably less offensive to them than did outside interference with either property rights or any other aspect of their or their fellow southerners' ways of life.[88]

The backgrounds of these small mountain farmers contributed to their attitudes toward slavery. Some observers concluded that the region's poorer residents bore a strong grudge against slavery because their inability to compete with it as free laborers had forced them from their seaboard or piedmont homes up into the mountains. There, the argument followed, they were insulated from the slave system but quickly found themselves also shut off from the economic opportunities the outside world offered, a fact which added to their resentment.[89] As explained by one advocate of this theory, southern mountaineers "were penned up in their mountains because slavery shut out white labor and left them no market for their skill and strength . . . it denied those that looked down from their mountain crags upon the realm of King Cotton a chance to expand, circulate, and mingle with the progressive elements at work elsewhere in the republic."[90] This sense of displacement, whether real or imagined, may have contributed to the animosity toward the lowland planter class that was indeed apparent among the more secluded highlanders. Far more widespread and deeply ingrained in the cultural baggage that western Carolinians brought from the lowlands to the mountains, however, was an intense racism and a concomitant belief in the institution of slavery, regardless of their feelings toward its most prosperous beneficiaries.[91]

Despite the abundant first-hand material Olmsted provides, one must be wary of accepting the comments of those he interviewed as typical of the region as a whole. After all, he used the narratives of his southern tours to confirm his already well-established view of slavery as uneconomical and impractical and thus quoted heavily those with negative feelings toward the institution. Because he, like other outside observers of mountain life, was intrigued by those who maintained an isolated, rustic existence, the encounters he described were only with those in remote areas of the mountains where slavery was all but nonexistent. As revealing as those interviews are, most of the people with whom he talked were only on the fringes of the more vital, more dominant mountain society; therefore, their views cannot be passed off as typical of western Carolinians' beliefs. Much of the strength of Olmsted's overall commentary on the South is based on his determination to understand the region at the grassroots level. But as a result of his failure to contact (or at least to quote) any of the region's business or political leaders (and thus its large slaveholders), or even those nonslaveholders in more settled areas with higher slave concentrations, Olmsted's readers were left with a somewhat one-sided picture of racial attitudes, despite the diversity of opinions expressed by those obscure mountaineers whose views he did utilize. Olmsted's neglect of residents of Buncombe or Henderson counties (despite a day's visit in Asheville) or from those on the eastern side of the Blue Ridge is unfortunate, for they were far more representative of western North Carolina's antebellum population than were those few isolated farmers of the westernmost counties which he did tour.[92] Most mountain residents shared the same fears of free blacks and the same respect for property that led their remoter counterparts so reluctantly to support the system. But unlike those who had virtually no contact with slavery, the majority of mountain farmers seem to have had very little explicit contempt for or disapproval of either slaveholders or slavery. Their complicity, like that of their nonslaveholding counterparts throughout the South, is apparent, though the reasons for it are subject to debate.

The contention of the Owsley school—that most yeomen bore no animosity toward either slavery or slaveholders because they themselves aspired to own slaves—is a reasonable assumption to apply to the small mountain farmers of North Carolina.[93] While slave prices were rising even more rapidly in the western counties than in the South as a whole, it is also true that nonslaveholders there were joining the slaveholding ranks at a higher rate than elsewhere in North Carolina at least.[94] They usually made this transition on a very modest scale, either through a gift or bequest from a relative or through modest purchases of single slaves, frequently very young ones. A general awareness of these trends or even mere acquaintance with specific beneficiaries of it certainly would have contributed toward an implicit acceptance of slavery by many others who foresaw such a possibility in their own futures.

Robert Starobin, among others, has suggested that nonslaveholders acquiesced in the system because of their own easy access to black labor through the hiring out of slaves.[95] As has been demonstrated in the preceding chapter, such temporary transactions in slave labor were indeed common among western Carolinians. In theory, this additional potential for direct benefits from the system might have appealed to those without black property of their own. Yet, in practice, the overwhelming majority of such arrangements in the region were between two slaveholders.[96]

Another major factor defusing class resentments was the unusual nature of the mountain society's ruling class itself. As the following chapter will show, the western Carolina elite, though unquestionably and recognizably a powerful and privileged group, was not a true planter class. Nor were plantations the central structural element of the region's society or economy. Unlike their lowland counterparts, mountain masters did not live on vast plantations insulated physically and socially from the majority of their area's populace. The variety of business and professional pursuits in which these masters were engaged meant that they were more actively and integrally a part of the communities over which they presided.

Perhaps the predominant factor in shaping western North Carolinians' favorable attitudes toward slavery was the obvious connection between slaveholders outside their region and their own region's prosperity. The vast majority of highland agricultural and livestock exports were directed to and dependent on plantation markets in South Carolina and Georgia. The growing reputation of several mountain communities as healthy, fashionable summer resorts which stimulated profitable business opportunities and permanent growth was also directly attributable to the wealth of low country planters. Such visitors' presence, along with that of their slaves, gave many western Carolinians frequent direct contact with individuals from areas characterized far more by slavery on a large scale, and even more mountain residents enjoyed indirect benefits from such contacts.

It seems, then, that the majority of Carolina highlanders, whether they themselves owned slaves or not, had some stake in the institution and thus, to varying degrees, accepted it. Alden B. Pearson, Jr., describing the attitude of a typical "middle-class, non-slaveholding, border-state Christian," wrote that he was "disapproving [of slavery] in principle, wishing to see it disappear, but accepting it in practice as part of the lifestyle of his time and region. . . . Aware of its ills, he feared an even greater evil—abolition, with its threat to disrupt the whole fabric of the South."[97] Much of this description could apply to North Carolina's nonslaveholding mountaineers, but only with qualifications. No real evidence exists to indicate that yeomen in the mainstream of mountain society either disapproved of slavery in principle or were aware of its ills. Even those on the periphery of that society showed little concern for the moral issues involved in humans owning other humans or of the cruelty inflicted on the victims of the system.[98] As indicated here, except for a few isolated incidents, there was very little cruelty or mistreatment for them to see.

Perhaps a more accurate description of western Carolinians' attitudes would be the observation of East Tennessee residents made by historian E. Merton Coulter. "Though entirely different from the Lower South in topography and largely in occupation," he wrote, "it was not an enemy territory alien in sympathy. On the all-absorbing Southern institution, it was harmonious with the rest of the South." The central moral issue for the mountaineer was respect for property rights. Any aversion to slavery was outweighed by an even greater aversion to blacks, so that if the latter's presence had to be tolerated, it was essential that they be kept in bondage. The southern mountaineer, wrote Coulter, "was just as eager to maintain slavery for his protection as the Southern planter was for profit."[99] Thus, on this subject too, Mrs. Campbell's statement that the Southern Appalachians had much in common with the South in general seems particularly apt for the antebellum area.

Chapter 5

Privilege, Power, and Politics:

"Little coteries . . . all-powerful"

In January 1832, an Alabama lawyer told Alexis de Tocqueville that the idea that "the people can do everything [and are] capable of ruling almost directly" was an "erroneous opinion." He complained to the French observer that southern politics as he knew them consisted of "little coteries and little, local intrigues [that] are all-powerful." Over twenty years later, Frederick Law Olmsted echoed that conclusion. "With the slaveholding class there is a pride of birth and social position, much more than in any class in the North. This affects the character and conduct of individuals . . . [and] the whole community."[1] For much if not most of the South, those descriptions remained apt throughout the antebellum period, and western North Carolina proved no exception. As elsewhere, the "little coteries" in the mountain counties consisted of their slaveholding elite, and their influence did indeed shape the character and conduct of their region as a whole.

These slaveholders were mountain "masters" in many more ways than their black property holdings alone implied. Through their wealth, family connections, business interests, and governmental power, they dominated highland society to a degree that would have made them the envy of planter "oligarchies" or "slaveocracies" elsewhere in the South. The ways in which that wealth, influence, and power determined the political course of western North Carolina through the late antebellum period are the concerns of this chapter and much of the rest of this book. Despite assumptions that the Old North State, unlike its neighbors north and south, lacked an aristocratic gentry or that the southern highlands had bred a classless so- [115]

ciety, North Carolina's mountain masters formed an influential and remarkably stable elite that exercised considerable control over the society, the economy, and the politics of both their communities and their region.[2]

The commercial and landed gentry of western North Carolina was a relatively small and unusually close-knit group whose status was usually based on deep roots within the area. There was a strong correlation between when a family settled in western North Carolina and its eventual status within mountain society. In his extensive study of Burke County, Edward Phifer demonstrated the extent to which the county's largest slaveholding families were those whose ancestors had staked the earliest land claims in the county, with the choice property they thus acquired—usually along rivers and streams—often providing the base for their continued prosperity and influence. It was no coincidence that Averys, McDowells and Erwins, all dominant in county and regional affairs during the late antebellum period, had held land titles and settled in the area well before the Revolutionary War.[3]

Martin Crawford has traced similar connections in Ashe County. Capt. John Cox, a Revolutionary War veteran, became one of the first settlers in the state's northwest corner when he moved into Ashe from just across the state line in Virginia. Though he died in 1818, twelve of the county's eighty-two slaveowners in 1860 were his direct descendants. Two other early settlers, Aquila Greer and John McMillan (a Scottish immigrant), left sons who were among Ashe's largest slaveholders and most influential citizens on the eve of the Civil War.[4] Likewise, the Baird and the Patton brothers, instrumental in the founding and early settlement of Asheville; Jordan Councill, who established Boone; and Robert and Thomas Love, founders of Waynesville and Haywood County, all became themselves, and made their offspring, wealthy slaveowners and prominent politicians within the region. Three sons of the two Loves—James, John, and Dillard—in 1860 were by far the largest slaveholders in Haywood, Jackson, and Macon counties, respectively.[5]

The largest land purchases made in the newly opened Cherokee country were made in an 1838 auction by substantial slaveholders from elsewhere in the region. Those who actually moved with their slaves onto the tracts they bought (as opposed to those who made purchases merely as distant investments) quickly became, and remained until the

Civil War, the political and civic leaders of the southwestern corner of the state.[6] Cherokee County's four largest and earliest slaveholders in the 1850s were two pairs of brothers, the Suddereths and the Harshaws. Each set had either fathers or other brothers who ranked among Burke County's wealthiest slaveholders. Even Zebulon Vance, a relative latecomer into western North Carolina politics, could claim roots among the deepest in Buncombe County. His grandfathers were David Vance, one of the first people to settle west of the Blue Ridge when he moved to the Reems Creek Valley in the early 1780s, and Zebulon Baird, one of Asheville's founders.[7]

Such family ties were obviously the most basic factor in assuring the continuity of wealth and power established by the mountain region's founding fathers. Equally significant, those early families tied themselves to each other through intermarriage and thus fortified their positions within both the region and the state. Intermarriage among members of the planter elite was common throughout the South, as indeed it always has been in any society's upper class. But the implications of those kinship networks have received new and more sophisticated analysis in recent work on North Carolinians by Jane Censer, Paul Escott, Martin Crawford, and Robert Kenzer.[8]

Although part of a much broader cultural pattern, the extent of kinship ties among western Carolina slaveholding families remains striking. These families were hardly guilty of the degree of inbreeding attributed to later generations of highlanders who, according to stereotype, "married back and forth and crossways and upside down until every man is his own grandmother."[9] But the number of families and generations that intersected each other throughout the region often resulted in the formation of complex networks.

As elsewhere, the majority of such marriages occurred between families in the same or in adjacent counties.[10] The sister of George Bower, Ashe County's largest slaveholder, married Jordan Councill, the founding father and also largest slaveholder of neighboring Watauga County. The marriage of James McDonnell Smith (generally acknowledged to have been the first white child born west of the Blue Ridge) to Polly Patton linked the families of two of Asheville's wealthiest and most successful merchants. By taking David Vance's daughter, Elizabeth, as his wife, William Davidson of Haywood County made cousins of two of the next generation's leading politicians, Zebulon Vance and Allen T. Davidson. William W. Erwin, who presided over

Figure 14. Fort Defiance, William Lenoir's Caldwell County plantation.
North Carolina Division of Archives and History.

"Belvidere," one of Burke County's earliest and most extensive plantations, fathered sixteen children, and became the father-in-law of
several of the county's most prominent civic and political leaders, including Isaac T. Avery, James H. McDowell, Burgess Gaither and his
brother Alfred, and Dr. J.H.E. Hardy.[11]

Two of Gen. William Lenoir's sons married two daughters of
Waightstill Avery, providing a double link between the largest slaveholding families of Caldwell and Burke counties respectively. The Lenoirs, in fact, probably held the record for the number of distinguished
in-laws they accumulated within the area. The general's daughter Ann
married Caldwell County planter Edmund Jones, and their daughter
became the wife of Samuel Finley Patterson, one of Wilkes County's
most prominent citizens. That network, including the Avery connection, thus encompassed four of the wealthiest and most influential
families along the eastern slopes of the Blue Ridge.[12]

Most of these matches must have pleased parents, who may or may not have had an active hand in arranging them. Making matches that would maintain or enhance family social and economic status was so important that the failure of children to do so could mean ostracism, even within a family. In 1796, Polly Mira Avery, another of Waightstill's daughters, defied her parents' wishes by secretly marrying a yeoman farmer, Caleb Poor, whose name all too clearly suggested why the Averys might have objected to the match. She was denied a dowry but eventually was allowed to live on one of the family's Burke County plantations, where her husband was employed in its tannery. The marriage, which may well have suffered due to the couple's class differences, ended in a bitter divorce in 1813. Yet Polly's descendants would eventually recoup her family position. Her granddaughter married Leander Gash, merchant, slaveholder, and politician, in 1841, thus linking the Averys with one of Henderson County's leading families.[13]

Equally significant were kinship links which western North Carolinians established with prominent leaders elsewhere in the state. The marriage of an early Asheville merchant, George Swain, and Caroline Lane, the sister of one of Raleigh's founding fathers, produced a son who later occupied the governor's mansion. (Her nephew Joseph Lane, also from Buncombe County, went on to become the first United States senator from Oregon and John C. Breckinridge's vice-presidential running mate in the 1860 presidential election.)[14] Two mountain masters, Waightstill W. Avery and Rufus Lenoir Patterson, married daughters of Gov. John Motley Morehead. After his wife's death, Patterson made Mary Fries, of an equally influential piedmont industrial family, his second wife. James Graham, who long represented the mountain district in Congress, was the older brother of a North Carolina governor and United States senator, William A. Graham. The man who replaced James Graham in Washington, Thomas Clingman, was the brother-in-law of his congressional colleague Richard Puryear. Calvin Cowles of Wilkes County greatly enhanced his stature within his county and the state when he became the son-in-law of William W. Holden.[15]

The effect of these various matches is apparent from the existing correspondence of the Carolina highland's major families. Their letters, often to each other, accentuate the extent to which they established and maintained active social contacts to equal their commercial ties (documented in chapter 2) throughout their neighborhoods, region, state, and other parts of the South. Cowles's papers, for instance, indicate that his correspondents made him fully familiar with local happenings in Asheville, Morganton, Salisbury, and Raleigh, just as he did all he could to make them aware of developments in Wilkesboro and elsewhere in the northwest corner of the state.[16] Likewise, the correspondence of the Davidsons, the Erwins, the Loves, William Holland Thomas, and others reflect their thorough grasp of affairs both within and beyond their own communities, as social and political acquaintances as well as transient offspring provided them with fully as much fact and opinion as any journalistic source could have.

The papers of various families in the Happy Valley communities of Wilkes and Caldwell counties provide an unusually revealing portrait of an elite remarkably well connected, informed, and traveled. The bonds among relatives and acquaintances of the Lenoirs, Pattersons, Joneses, Finleys, and Gwyns reinforced and enlarged the social networks of each family, as well as of the community as a whole. Their letters and diaries reflect a vigorous social life, with frequent visiting and hosting of friends and family members. All had visitors and correspondents from across the state—most regularly from Chapel Hill, Hillsboro, Wilmington, and Rockingham. Both the Lenoirs and the Gwyns heard regularly from and were more infrequently visited by siblings and/or offspring who had moved to Alabama and Mississippi in the 1830s and early 1840s.[17]

Several Happy Valley residents made extensive trips themselves, which they reported in detail to those at home. In 1835, Augustus Finley traveled due west to Missouri and then circled back home through Illinois, Indiana, and Ohio.[18] Walter Lenoir and his wife were on a trip down the Atlantic coast to Florida in 1859 when she died suddenly in Charleston. In spite of, or perhaps because of, his grief, he undertook an extensive westward trek the following year that included several weeks in Saint Louis and several in Minnesota. Lenoir's observations on the trans-Mississippi life he encountered reflect something of his view of the western Carolina society of which he was a part. Though impressed with "the immense fertility and agricultural resources of the west and northwest," he expressed disappointment "in the social aspect of the people. Cultivated society seems to abandon the country for the town." Only in the latter was there any "display of public spirit," but even there, "the men and women seemed to be neglecting the cultivation of *themselves*," displaying instead a "love of gain and outside display . . . quite ungenial to my tastes and antecedents." Such sentiments from a Carolina mountaineer could just as well have been those of a planter representative of Tidewater Virginia, Charleston, or Savannah. They indicate the extent to which western North Carolina's elite saw itself as very much within the mainstream of southern planter culture and values, sharing fully in the assumption of social superiority so basic to both. It is thus hardly surprising that in a further critique of "the foreign element in western society," Lenoir found that "it is fanatical, miserably so, on the slavery question."[19]

While social assumptions and familial ties did much to bond western Carolina's large slaveholders together and to define for them and their fellow mountain residents their distinctions as a class, economic status provided an equally solid basis for the hegemonic power they exercised over the region. As table 5.1 indicates, western Carolina's slaveholding families, who in 1860 made up only a tenth of the region's population, held over a third of its landed wealth. The distribution of wealth among slaveowners was equally top-heavy. The fifty with the largest number of slaves, a mere 2.7 percent of all slaveholders, held over a fifth of the group's total slaves and land, and a little less than a fifth of its personal wealth.

This vast concentration of regional wealth was by no means a distinction enjoyed only by mountain masters. Similarly skewed economic distributions typified the antebellum South, as even contemporary observers recognized. In the midst of his southern tour, Olmsted noted that "the wealth class is the commanding class in most districts of the South. . . . Wealth is less distributed and is more retained in families in the South than in the North."[20] Though made before Olmsted moved into the Carolina highlands, his generalization was fully applicable to its slaveholding elite. The twenty-four mountain owners who owned fifty or more slaves (see appendix 1) formed a proportion of all slaveholders in the region (one-tenth of a percent) equal to that of their peers within the whole South.[21] Gavin Wright, in the most sophisticated analysis yet made of southern wealth and its distribution, has demonstrated that slaveholding families in the cotton South, a fourth of all families, held a staggering 93.1 percent of the region's aggregate wealth in 1860.[22] The comparable holdings of western Carolina slaveholders amounted to only 59.1 percent of the region's real and personal estate values, but only a tenth of the populace controlled that hefty majority of the wealth. The western

Table 5.1. *Distribution of Wealth in Western North Carolina, 1860*

	Families		Slaves Owned		Value of Real Wealth		Value of Personal Wealth	
	No.	Percent of Total	No.	Percent of Total	Dollars	Percent of Total	Dollars	Percent of Total
All Slaveholders	1,877	9.9	12,051	100	7,118,520	34.8	17,582,320	76.3
Fifty Largest Slaveholders	50	.26	2,645	21.9	1,433,905	7.0	3,137,583	13.0
[% among slaveholders]		[2.66]				[20.1]		[17.8]
Nonslaveholders	16,975	90.0			13,305,214	65.2	8,449,811	36.6
Total	18,852				20,423,734		23,032,131	

Source: Computed from *Eighth U.S. Census, 1860*, tables 1 and 2. See appendix for further elaboration.

Carolina slaveholders had a grasp on their region's economic benefits fully equivalent to that enjoyed by their southern counterparts
elsewhere.[23]

There seem to be infinite variations on how the apportionment of
slave property can be, and has been, both calculated and interpreted.[24]
The statistical distinctions hindsight now provides are less significant
than the ways in which that wealth, both real and perceived, was actually parlayed into prestige and power. For the mountains' largest
slaveholders, affluence translated directly into political power. Despite
the egalitarian impulses Jacksonianism had set in motion and the increasingly participatory political culture that characterized state and
federal election campaigns throughout the South, as elsewhere in the
nation, deferential politics assured the elite's continued hold on their
traditional roles as government officials and regional representatives.

The mass of correspondence of antebellum western Carolina leaders
both among themselves and with their counterparts elsewhere in the
state reveals the extent to which they were preoccupied with state and
national politics and with the voting behavior of their constituencies.
Their letters (quoted throughout the rest of this and subsequent chapters) exude great confidence, for the most part, in their ability not only
to predict the positions their fellow mountain residents would take toward both candidates and issues, but also to control and utilize those
attitudes for their own ends.

The various contacts in nonpolitical arenas between many members
of that elite and their constituents enhanced both their knowledge of
yeomen concerns and their control over them. William Lenoir, one of
the wealthiest of the region's ruling class, recorded in his diary in 1851
the details of a confrontation with those over whom he "ruled" that reveals much about how mountain masters exerted their considerable
influence upon their nonslaveholding neighbors. State law required
that citizens provide an allocated amount of time on county road projects annually. As a particularly enthusiastic advocate of internal improvements for his own Caldwell County and western North Carolina,
Lenoir was supervising a group of about a hundred men in construct-
ing a new road linking his county seat, also named Lenoir, with Tay-
lorsville to its east. Some of those workers resented this forced labor
requirement and focused their frustration on Lenoir himself, in a confrontation that culminated in abusive language, threats on his life, and
an apparent refusal to cooperate. Ultimately, though, deference to

their slaveholding supervisor and, according to his account, respect for his reasoning soon restored order:

> I worked hard among them, spoke mildly but with firmness and convinced many by various reasons of the importance of the work, showed them some of my correspondence with citizens in Ten. and different parts of our own State upon the subject of a Rail Road through this section—which might be promoted by first making a fine common road.

As a result of these shared confidences, Lenoir won his listeners over. He wrote that "about 12 out of 60 hands at the lower end appeared the first day to work, over 20 the 2nd, etc." His success was much greater, he maintained, when he was able to apply even more fully his powers of persuasion. At the road's upper end, "where I had had more opertunities [sic] of exerting my influence made a tolerable turn out the first day and became much more in the spirit of working as they progressed."[25]

Neither his patronizing approach nor his shared confidences would likely have been necessary in an earlier era. But Lenoir's willingness to lay out his case so patiently to these workers and his ability to maintain full control over them by convincing them that their work was in their own best interest illustrates quite succinctly one means by which mountain masters retained their political hegemony throughout the region.

Continued ability to command yeoman allegiance depended on reinforcement of the mountain masters' own ranks, and it was in that respect that the group's ever-expanding social and kinship networks proved so vital. Lenoir's son-in-law, Edmund Jones, well entrenched in that network through his own marriage as well as that of his daughter to Samuel F. Patterson, confided to the latter that he would call on "our connection" in the county for help in his bid for a seat in the state legislature in 1840.[26] Faith in those connections remained intact throughout the antebellum era and continued to provide highland slaveholders with stability and assurance as the political "masters" of their region.

The degree to which the slaveholders maintained that hold is indicated most strikingly by the fact that the vast majority of elected officials from the westernmost counties were the most substantial slaveholders. Despite the fact that only 10 percent of the region's white families owned slaves, a higher percentage of the men they sent to the state legislature were slaveholders than was true for the state as a

*Table 5.2. Percentage of State Legislators
Who Were Slaveholders, 1850 and 1860*

State Legislators from:	1850	1860
Western North Carolina	88.2	93.7
North Carolina	51.5	85.8
Upper South States	52.3	62.2
Lower South States	59.9	68.0
All Slaveholding States	56.5	65.1

Source: Statewide figures and those for the Upper South
taken from Wooster, *Politicians, Planters, and Plain Folk,* 40.
Those for the Lower South states taken from Wooster, *The
People in Power,* table 6, p. 41. Figures for western North
Carolina legislators were computed from slave schedules in
1840, 1850, and 1860 U.S. Censuses.

whole. Of ninety-two men who represented the mountain counties between 1840 and 1860, seventy-nine, or 87.1 percent, owned slaves.[27] Comparing these figures with those for the legislature as a whole in each of two years is even more revealing.

As table 5.2 above indicates, while just over half of North Carolina's legislators in 1850 owned slaves, fifteen of the seventeen men representing mountain counties were slaveholders. By 1860, the proportion of slaveholders in the General Assembly as a whole had increased dramatically, but the comparable figure for its westernmost members alone still exceeded it, with all but one owning slaves.[28]

Not only were more slaveholders elected to office by the largest non-slaveholding electorate in the state, but the average number of slaves owned by those men exceeded that for North Carolina's slaveholding legislators as a whole. In 1850, the total membership of the state's General Assembly owned more slaves than did their counterparts in any upper South state, with an average of twelve slaves for representatives and twenty for senators in 1850.[29] But western Carolina legislators topped both figures. The median number of slaves for the eleven representatives in 1850 was 13.3, while the four state senators from the mountains owned an average of thirty-one slaves.[30]

An even more striking comparison is that between Carolina mountain legislators and their counterparts throughout the South. No southern state was represented by a group with as large a percentage of slaveholders as were the mountain counties of North Carolina. Even

South Carolinians, whose legislators were 80 percent slaveholders in 1850 and 81 percent in 1860, had fewer slaveholding representatives than Carolina highlanders in those years. In terms of the median number of slaves held, state senators from the lower South outranked those from western North Carolina. (South Carolina's owned a median of fifty-two slaves, compared with the four mountain senators' average of thirty-one.) But the margin between comparable figures for lower house members was much slighter. South Carolinians, again with the South's highest figures, averaged only sixteen slaves each, compared with a little over thirteen held on average by mountain-master-legislators.[31]

Despite the political deference and electoral security which mountain masters continued to enjoy, they did have to make certain concessions to new trends in mass political culture introduced by the Jacksonian era. They were, and recognized themselves to be, what James Oakes has dubbed "democratic oligarchs."[32] The rallies, barbecues, and public debates that quickly emerged as the most visible manifestations of the new democratization were as common in mountain communities as they were elsewhere and served to create stronger mutual awareness of and contacts between the region's leaders and their constituencies.[33]

One of those most aware of, and most outspoken on, the increased need for such concessions (in style if not in substance) to one's constituency was the man who represented the mountain district in Congress through most of the 1830s and early 1840s, James Graham of Rutherford County. As political mentor and frequent correspondent of his younger brother, William—who would ultimately surpass him in prominence in state and national politics—Graham offered advice that made up a virtual manual on the art of political campaigning in the aftermath of the Jacksonian revolution. When William considered a bid for office in Orange County in 1842, James instructed him to "begin in time . . . mix freely with the people, be merry with the young men & attentive to the old." In explaining his own success, he maintained that "I have always accommodated by *habit* and *Dress* to the People when electioneering . . . I have always dressed chiefly in *Home spun* when among the people." He elaborated in telling detail:

> [W]hen a gentleman is addressed in fin[e] broad cloth and silk and stops to stay all night with a plain poor working man, he often renders the man and all his family unhappy, because they think they cannot entertain him in the

same stile he lives at home. I have actually some times felt my self a *sort of Nuisance* when too well dressed in obscure sections. But if a Candidate be dressed Farmerlike he is well received and kindly remembered by the inmates of the Log Cabin, and there is no sensation among the children or the *chickens*.[34]

The extent to which most of the region's political leaders (not to mention his own brother) embraced Graham's techniques is unknown, but the factors that made him so sensitive to voters' impressions were certainly apparent to his political peers.

It was not only local leaders who found themselves catering to their electorates in new ways. An equally important advance in participatory politics for western Carolinians was the advent of appearances by gubernatorial candidates and other state officials from outside the region. In 1840, John Motley Morehead broke new ground in his first bid for governor by undertaking a statewide tour that included stops in Rutherfordton, Morganton, and Asheville.[35] In doing so, he set a precedent maintained by almost all subsequent candidates for the job, with opposing candidates sometimes traveling together and engaging in public debates at each stop. As the state's public leaders came to see the extent to which the mountain counties could prove decisive in a state characterized by partisan balance elsewhere, a disproportionate amount of campaign effort was focused on the region. In 1860, for example, Governor John Ellis and challenger John Pool spent over a third of their tour (fifteen of forty-three stops) in the mountain counties.[26]

One might assume that the effect of such direct contact between state leaders and mountain voters would have been to undermine the control local leaders maintained over their constituents. But such visits actually seem to have strengthened the positions of mountain masters in both local and state political circles. For in their often very visible roles as hosts, sponsors, and organizers of the local appearances by those roving campaigners, they not only reinforced their own positions as intermediaries between voters and higher officials, but in the process made personal connections and often accumulated political debts that translated into at least potentially greater influence and bargaining power in Raleigh.

Even as political campaigns became more public and candidates made themselves more accessible to western voters, campaign strategy and party policy decisions remained the exclusive prerogatives of county committees, or on occasion, of regional or multi-county caucuses, which the slaveholding elite held firmly within its grasp throughout the era. Even in the resolutions and petitions issued from the public meetings that became more frequent in highland communities as elsewhere once the secession crisis intensified, there is no indication that the traditional local leadership ever had to compromise or concede its own priorities or values in the views expressed or the decisions made.[37] The very names attached to those documents attest to the continuity of political power in the hands of mountain masters.

Newspapers within the region, ostensibly another concession to participatory politics, in reality merely fortified regional control by the mountain elite. Though stagecoach deliveries had made the two Raleigh papers, Whig and Democratic, available to mountain subscribers from the mid-1830s on, prior to 1840 Rutherfordton was the only community within the region to publish a paper. In that year, Asheville's *Highland Messenger* became the first journalistic enterprise west of the Blue Ridge. It, like the Rutherford County paper, was a Whig mouthpiece, as was its successor, the *Asheville Spectator*, published from 1853 on. In 1849, Democrats countered with the *Asheville News*, owned and edited by Marcus Erwin, a member of one of the region's oldest families and himself an influential political representative of Buncombe County.[38] Most of these papers were brief, often no more than four pages in length, and much of their space was consumed by material reproduced from papers in Raleigh or elsewhere in the state. Their very *raison d'etre* as partisan organs kept their focus on state and national issues, which contributed to a heightened political awareness among Carolina highlanders. The papers also served as outlets for local leaders to argue their positions, promote their causes, and thus shape the political thinking of their constituents far more pervasively than their public appearances had ever been able to do.

Again, it was James Graham who seemed most sensitive to the need to shape political journalism to the tastes and interests of the electorate. "The Press," he stressed, "disseminates knowledge through the Country, and influences and *forms* public opinion." Recognized by his colleagues as one whose few journalistic efforts were "peculiarly adapted to the rank and file," Graham felt that Whig newspapers could broaden their appeal and increase their readerships by providing more entertaining material for mass consumption. "Short, pithy articles only will do for the crowd," he wrote in 1840.

"Wit, Pleasantry & Anecdotes are the weapons of execution. Arguments like cannon will not do for every day fighting."[39]

While subscription lists for the Asheville papers indicate relatively low circulation in most of the mountain counties, public readings and prominent postings in many communities suggest not only that readers far outnumbered subscribers but also that the papers' contents were discussed more openly and often than might otherwise have been the case.[40] Supplementing and perhaps overshadowing newspapers' influence were the circulars, broadsides, and pamphlets that had long been a staple of American politics. James Graham, Thomas Clingman, Zebulon Vance, and other prominent western leaders utilized these as more thorough and expedient means of communicating with the widest number of their constituents. Anonymous or committee-generated circulars became more and more prevalent throughout the district as tensions mounted and the need to communicate with voters became more urgent in the months before the Civil War broke out.

But it was hardly these concessions in style or method that assured mountain masters of their continued political hegemony throughout the prewar decades. Two factors proved far more vital to the allegiance they commanded: first, their close contacts with their constituents in nonpolitical relationships, and second, the fact that their political causes reflected far more regional than class interests. In his recent analysis of Tennessee's Civil War veterans' questionnaires, Fred Bailey notes that social discontent, or "class ill will," was much less in evidence in mountainous East Tennessee than in any other section of that state.[41] That observation would have been equally applicable to western North Carolina, where, despite the solidarity of the mountain elite just demonstrated, there was also remarkably little evidence of resentment directed against that privileged group from below.

A long-standing debate among historians of the Old South exists as to which was the more prevalent feature of its social structure—class distinctions and animosity based on slave ownership, or white solidarity based on shared racism, agrarian experience, republican values, and/or political democratization.[42] As acknowledged in the previous chapter, there was evidence of "Herrenvolk democracy"—the contention that consensus among white classes was based primarily on a commitment to white supremacy—among western Carolinians. The other common values or shared experiences were also evident to some degree within mountain society.

Other explanations of the absence of class-provoked tensions in the mountains, however, are far more central, and perhaps unique. One is that slaveholders there, even the largest, never made up a real planter class. Unlike lowland planters, very few lived on vast plantations that insulated them physically and socially from the majority of their area's populace. Mountain masters, with their varied business and professional pursuits, played active and vital roles in a society that was far more integrated socially and economically than was true for most of the South. Their commercial endeavors or professional careers depended on their nonslaveholding neighbors' demand for their goods and services. Likewise the yeomen, as customers or clients, depended on what these slaveholders had to offer. These mutual needs and the direct contacts they usually entailed created close, healthy relationships between those who owned black property and those who did not.

In an even larger sense, mountain masters contributed to their own and their neighbors' economic well-being through their efforts on behalf of their region, in roles ranging from civic boosters to state lobbyists. Their achievements in stimulating trade, promoting tourism, pushing for internal improvements, and attracting new business and agricultural development into their region were all measures that benefitted the majority of mountain residents, regardless of their economic or social status.

Finally, as the following chapters will demonstrate, the region's slaveholders were quick, firm, and consistent in championing western interests in North Carolina's political battles over more equitable distribution of property taxes, voting rights, and state allocations for internal improvements. In so doing, they put regional concerns before class interests and demonstrated a loyalty to place that surely served to defuse any potential resentment by their nonslaveholding neighbors. The extent to which both the lives and the priorities of mountain slaveholders and nonslaveholders were bound together created an interclass consensus more pronounced than that which existed elsewhere in the South. As customers, consumers, clients, constituents, and perhaps most important, as fellow mountain residents, highland yeomen depended on, and rewarded with their loyalty, that very distinct and powerful class that ruled them.

Chapter 6

Mountaineers as Westerners:

"No white slaves in the western reserve"

In 1849 Thomas L. Clingman of Asheville, who represented North Carolina's mountain district in the United States Congress and was the most outspoken advocate of western rights within the state, told his constituents that they must dare to tell the eastern-controlled state government in Raleigh that "if they want white slaves they must look for them elsewhere than in the Western reserve." A year later, as one of the most fervent advocates of southern rights in Congress, Clingman told his fellow representatives from the North that "if you intend to degrade and utterly ruin the South, then we will resist. We do not love you, people of the North, well enough to become your slaves."[1]

In these statements, Clingman expressed the dual and often parallel themes that dominated the late antebellum politics of western North Carolina. There was probably no southern politician of the time who embraced more fully or expressed more effectively the republican ideology as it had evolved by the mid-nineteenth century. That concept of republicanism was basically an extension of the "country ideology" of eighteenth-century English political theorists that America's revolutionary generation had embraced, in turn, as the rationale for its quest for independence. Over the next several generations those ideas were refined into a concept of government as the central agent for the protection of individual liberty and equality. To see that it maintained that function, entrusted to it by the people it governed, the electorate and its representatives constantly must be on guard against inherent tendencies toward abuses of governmental power, whether from internal corruption, aristocratic privilege or self-interest, or [131]

other forms of oligarchical despotism. Minorities or even less-privi-
leged majorities were especially vulnerable to loss of liberty through
the potential tyranny such power engendered, and it was fear of their
"enslavement" that continued to permeate the republican rhetoric of
the mid-nineteenth century.[2]

Clingman was a master of that rhetoric and was quick to adapt it to
the particular sectional tensions of the Carolina mountains by articu-
lating what his constituents envisioned as two different threats to their
liberty.[3] As westerners within the state and as southerners within the
nation, North Carolina highlanders increasingly saw themselves as a
beleaguered and abused minority whose rights and interests were
threatened by governmental despotism on two fronts, federal and
state, controlled respectively by northerners and easterners whose values and goals conflicted with their own. Within the state, highlanders
saw themselves as victims of governmental neglect, as efforts to meet
their needs, promote their interests, and correct the inequities of the
power structure met with continued resistance or apathy. At the federal level, governmental power posed a very different problem, as
Congress's continued interference and its failure to leave them and the
institution of slavery alone became an ever greater source of worry. At
both levels, western North Carolinians saw themselves as underdogs
who had to resist further abuse through strong protest and more con-
certed efforts to claim and defend their rights. This chapter and those
that follow explore this dual sectionalism that shaped the course of
North Carolina's mountain region during the 1840s and 1850s and
helped to define the identities and allegiances of its residents as the crisis of secession and civil war approached.

As in national politics, the second party system in North Carolina
cut across sectional divisions and served to limit, or at least partially to
obscure, the extent to which western interests differed from those of
the rest of the state. The mountain electorate was always an integral
part of state politics, and several of its leaders gained prominent and
respected positions within their parties and throughout the state.
They exerted undue influence in both state and national elections, because the distribution and fluctuations of party strength elsewhere in
the state often gave the western section the balance of power in determining electoral results.

With the emergence of the second party system in 1830s, pockets of
Democratic strength developed throughout the mountains due to An-

drew Jackson's personal popularity. This strength was particularly widespread in the southwesternmost counties when Whigs, led by Gov. Edward B. Dudley, failed to support Cherokee Indian removal.[4] But once Jackson left office and Indian removal was carried out, highland Democrats lost much of the basis of their original support, and the Whigs quickly became the dominant party in most of the mountain counties. As both legislator and governor during those years, the region's most influential spokesman, Asheville native David L. Swain, led many of his fellow westerners into the Whig party by his strong opposition to Andrew Jackson and his policies.[5] As the Whigs emerged as the party of reform through their support of the state's new Constitution of 1835 and of federal and state aid for internal improvements and education, their popularity in the west grew.

By 1840, with the gubernatorial candidacy of Whig John Motley Morehead, who as an ardent supporter of state-funded transportation development was well known and liked in the mountains, the party's predominance in the region was firmly established. Throughout that decade, the Whigs were as solidly entrenched there as in any section of the state, so much so that the state's primary Whig newspaper, the *Raleigh Register*, in 1845 called the mountain district "the Gibraltar of Whig Principles." Governor Morehead himself had been among the first to recognize the significance of the mountains to the party's strength in the state. Just after the 1842 gubernatorial election, the *Raleigh Register* reported:

> The way the Western Whigs do their voting is a caution to Loco Focos. Until their thunder began to pour down upon us, we were quite chap-fallen even about the Governor's race. But Governor Morehead replied, in answer to some interrogatory implying doubt on the subject – 'Just wait until the Mountain boys launch their earthquake, and that will settle the question.' . . . And sure enough, the Governor was right. When Buncombe and Henderson came lumbering down with its 1000 majority, Rutherford with its 1300, old Iredell with her 1400, Burke with her 1200 &c, we felt truly proud of our glorious 'WESTERN RESERVE.' As long as the West thus does her duty, a little defection elsewhere, is but a 'flash in the pan.'[6]

In the three presidential elections of the 1840s, Whigs William Henry Harrison, Henry Clay, and Zachary Taylor each carried every mountain county but one. In five of the six gubernatorial races from 1840 through 1850, substantial majorities in all but two of the same counties supported the Whig candidates (see table 6.1).[7]

Figure 15. David L. Swain. North Carolina Division of Archives and History.

During the 1840s, Whigs enjoyed statewide dominance as well. Whig governors served throughout the period, Whig majorities controlled the state legislature through most of it, and the state's electoral votes all went to the Whig presidential candidates. But their majority was not a large one, and many of their victories were gained by only slim margins over their Democratic opponents. Thus the Whig strength in the mountain counties was vital to the party's statewide success, a fact that residents were quick to point out to North Carolina Whigs elsewhere. Tod R. Caldwell of Morganton urged Senator Willie P. Mangum to visit the area during the presidential election of 1844, reminding him that "the vote of No. Carolina for the last years has depended in a great measure upon us of the 'Western Reserve' " and that in an "emergency" the party always looked to the mountains to pull it through.[8] Clingman was even more straightforward in assessing the Whigs' dependence on his region's support. "East of this section the Whigs are beaten," he said in 1849, "and if this western region were equally divided, they could neither elect a governor nor a senator. . . . The West, by its heavy [Whig] majorities, neutralizes and overcomes the partial success of our opponents and gives us the control of the State."[9]

The mountain section was by no means a one-party stronghold, however; nor could its consistent delivery of Whig majorities be taken for granted. The Democrats were very much in evidence throughout the region, and, as in the state as a whole, their challenges to the Whigs were often formidable. Yancey County voted for Democratic gubernatorial candidates by substantial majorities in every election from 1836 through 1860 and regularly sent Democrats to the state legislature. Though the margins were slimmer, Ashe County voters cast a majority of their votes for Democratic candidates for governor in four of the six elections in 1840–50 and were represented by as many Democrats as Whigs in the General Assembly. In Buncombe and Burke counties, Democrats on several occasions during that decade beat their Whig opponents for legislative seats and ran close races in others.[10]

A number of the most prominent leaders of the western part of the state were Democrats. William Holland Thomas of Cherokee County, Robert Pearson of Burke, Samuel Fleming of Yancey, Robert Love of Haywood, and James B. Gordon of Wilkes were all Democrats who exerted considerable influence in state and local affairs. Equally influential in the party were the offspring of prominent Whigs. Despite the fact that they were the nephews of David L. Swain, both David and Newton Coleman of Buncombe County were active Democrats, as were William Waightstill and Clarke Moulton Avery, the sons of Burke County's wealthiest Whig, Isaac T. Avery.[11] Most of the men above managed to win election to the legislature from their counties or sen-

Table 6.1. *Gubernatorial Election Results in Western North Carolina,*
1840–1860

| Year | Democrats | | | Whigs* | | |
	Total Vote	Percentage	No. of Counties Carried	Total Vote	Percentage	No. of Counties Carried
1840	2,568	28.7	2	6,370	71.3	6
1842	2,496	28.0	2	6,410	72.0	6
1844	3,406	34.1	1	6,597	65.9	9
1846	3,186	30.4	1	7,287	69.6	9
1848	4,129	36.7	3	7,117	63.3	7
1850	4,124	34.5	2	7,818	65.5	8
1852	5,413	40.5	4	7,971	59.5	7
1854	5,863	44.7	3	7,249	55.3	11
1856	8,223	54.1	11	6,979	45.9	3
1858	7,841	54.1	9	6,643	45.9	5
1860	8,165	49.1	7	8,474	50.9	8

Source: Computed from Connor, *North Carolina Manual*, 993–1000.
*Includes American and Opposition parties where applicable.

atorial districts despite the fact that Whigs averaged from 60 to 70 percent of the vote in most antebellum elections.

The very popularity of the Whig party sometimes jeopardized its success. With no party primaries to narrow the field, several Whig candidates could split the votes of their party and allow a Democrat to win, a predicament of which the Whigs were well aware. Edmund Jones lamented in 1840, "It is strange the Whigs cannot act in concert. There never was a time when I thought there was more unanimity of feeling in our party and less selfishness—yet it seems we are composed of discordant material." He later concluded that the problem was the Democrats, who "want if possible to excite prejudices . . . divide the Whigs and slip in secretly and unknown to the Whigs one of their party."[12]

In the mountain district's first three congressional elections of the 1840s, for instance, two Whigs, James Graham and Thomas Clingman, competed against each other with no Democrat to challenge them. But in 1847, a third Whig, Gen. John Gray Bynum, also of Rutherford County, entered the race, and others seemed likely to follow suit. In response, Graham, the current incumbent, chose to give up his seat without a fight rather than risk the victory of a Democrat, most likely Samuel Fleming of Yancey County. As Graham explained, "There are about 10,000 votes in this District; of which 3,500 are Democratic. With three Whig Candidates, the success of a Democrat would be very good, with their drill and discipline." In at least two instances, Democrats actually won in heavily Whig counties because of multiple Whig candidates. William Waightstill Avery of Burke was sent to the state legislature as a result of "the field's being full of Whig candidates," as was James B. Gordon, who defeated seven Whig opponents in Wilkes, the region's solidest Whig stronghold.[13]

For a number of reasons, the two parties became even more evenly matched in the mountain counties during the 1850s. By the middle of that decade, the deterioration of the Whig party at the state level and its virtual demise at the national level left its western party members without a base.[14] Even earlier, the Whigs' failure to deliver much to the west in the way of internal improvements during the years in which they controlled the state had dampened the enthusiasm of the mountain electorate, particularly as Democrats in the state had increasingly embraced support for such development. Because of his considerable clout among fellow western North Carolinians, Clingman's own defection from the party was a serious blow to Whigs across the state, and his eventual move into the Democratic fold brought along many of his supporters as well.[15]

The Whig party never completely died in the mountains. As table 6.1 indicates, as late as 1854, over 55 percent of western North Carolina voters, and all but three of the fourteen westernmost counties, supported the state's last Whig candidate for governor. Many mountain Whigs reluctantly adopted the Know-Nothing, or American, party label during its brief life span in the mid-fifties and, by the end of the decade, after floundering as merely the "Opposition" in search of an affiliation, the Whig party itself enjoyed a brief revival.[16] The instability of the Whig party and its various transformations during the decade proved tremendous advantages to western Democrats, and, except for brief intervals, the 1850s were characterized by the most balanced, and thus the most competitive, two-party politics ever seen in North Carolina's mountains.

Between 1851 and 1859, Clingman's constituents sent him to Congress once as a Whig, once as an independent, and twice as a Demo-

Table 6.2. *Partisan Representation in the State Legislature*
by County, 1840–1860

	Whigs[1]	Democrats
House of Commons		
County (Senatorial District)		
Ashe (44th)[2]	6	5
Buncombe (49th)[3]	11	5
Burke (45th, 48th, 46th)	13	4
Caldwell (48th, 46th)	7	1
Cherokee (50th)	9	1
Haywood (50th)	3	8
Henderson (49th)	8	1
Jackson (50th)	—	4
Macon (50th)	10	1
Madison (49th)	2	2
McDowell (46th)	2	2
Watauga (44th)[3]	3	1
Wilkes (44th, 48th)	21	—
Yancey (45th, 49th)	—	11
Senate		
44th District (1844–1860)	3	6
45th District (1840–1842)	2	—
46th District (1854–1860)	2	2
48th District (1844–1852)	4	—
49th District (1840–1860)[4]	7	4
50th District (1844–1860)	2	8

Source: Computed from Connor, *North Carolina Manual*, 993–1000.
[1]Includes American and Opposition parties.
[2]Includes Alleghany County.
[3]For two legislators from Buncombe and Watauga counties, party affiliation cannot be determined; they are omitted from this table.
[4]Macon and Haywood counties were briefly a part of the 49th District, from 1840 to 1842.

crat. They then turned to a Whig, Zebulon Vance, whom they chose as their congressman twice at the decade's end. During the same period, almost every mountain county elected state legislators of both parties (see table 6.2). (Wilkes County never elected a Democrat, and Yancey County never elected anyone who was not a Democrat.) As table 6.3

indicates, mountain Democrats in the state legislature outnumbered Whigs or American party members by three to two during the 1850s, compared with Whig majorities of three to one in the 1840s.

The continued strength of two-party politics in western North Carolina paralleled the course of politics across the state, and the awareness by both parties that their success was dependent on statewide unity did much to contain sectional divisiveness. A less obvious but equally significant link between east and west was the fact that the political leaders of the mountains shared the same socioeconomic level with their counterparts elsewhere. As indicated in the last chapter (see table 5.2), the vast majority of elected officials from the westernmost counties were slaveowners with holdings fully equal to those of their peers in the legislature.

As both substantial slaveholders and party members, then, western legislators had bonds with their associates across the state that transcended sectional distinctions. Yet antebellum intrastate sectionalism was, as it long had been, a tradition deeply ingrained in North Carolina. Neither the unity of a statewide party organization nor class loyalties that bound mountain slaveholders to their eastern peers could obscure the economic, political, and social differences that divided mountain residents and the eastern half of the state.

Much of the division arose from geographical factors: the sheer distance between the two ends of the state; lack of an adequate transportation system connecting them; and differences in terrain and climate and their effects on agricultural production, economic conditions, and even the lifestyles of their inhabitants. As late as 1857, a North Carolina educator observed that mutual prejudices and lack of knowledge would prevent the gap between the state's two halves from closing any time in the near future:

> Our Western friends grow up too much with the notion that the East is a nation composed of "niggers," half-starved, half-clad and worked to death, of pale, pine-smoked whites born paupers, living off fish and "huckleberries," and of rich, proud, oppressive Nabobs, whose only god is money and whose only pleasure is the wine cup. While our Eastern friends are much of the notion that the West is a nation of semi-barbarians, destitute of good breeding, politeness and everything else like refinement, living in the woods and subsisting on roots and berries.[17]

Two years later, a Raleigh newspaperman returned from a trip to Asheville and revealed to his eastern readers what seems to have been

Table 6.3. *Western North Carolina Representation in the State Legislature,
by Party, 1840-1860*

	1840	1842	1844	1846	1848	1850
Whigs* (Senate/House)	3/12	3/11	4/12	4/10	2/9	2/6
Democrats (Senate/House)	0/1	1/4	0/2	0/2	2/4	2/4

Source: Computed from Connor, *North Carolina Manual*, 993–1000.
*Includes American and Opposition parties where applicable.

an unexpected discovery: "The people of the West are neither savages nor ignoramuses; but on the contrary, they are intelligent, high-minded, hospitable, and civilized."[18]

It was in the political sphere that the state's east-west rivalry became most pronounced and sectional battles proved most intense. The 1835 constitutional convention and the new constitution it produced under the leadership of Gov. David L. Swain (the first of several Asheville lawyers to achieve political prominence in the state during the antebellum period) did much to alleviate the major complaints of western Carolinians regarding the inequities of state government. But those reforms by no means eliminated all discriminatory features, and by the late 1840s and early 1850s, sectional divisiveness again had risen to the surface of state politics. As issues concerning western proportions of representation, taxation, and funding allocations within the state once more found their way to the center of the legislative stage, mountain residents again focused on their unjust treatment at the hands of what was still very much an eastern-dominated government in Raleigh. Partisan factors sometimes clouded the otherwise clear-cut sectional implications of these issues, but when sectional perspectives did prevail, the mountain counties often joined their piedmont neighbors to battle for measures beneficial to their entire half of the state. But those from the westernmost section, the most remote and thus most neglected area of North Carolina, were more sensitive about the discriminations they felt they suffered, and they often fought harder to correct those injustices.

The three major political issues that contributed to this resurgence of sectional feelings among mountain residents were equal suffrage, ad valorem taxation, and that to which they were most fervently com-

Table 6.3. Continued

	1852	1854	1856	1858	1860
Whigs* (Senate/House)	3/8	2/6	2/5	2/6	1/6
Democrats (Senate/House)	2/4	3/7	3/7	3/10	4/7

mitted, state aid for internal improvements. Both equal suffrage and the ad valorem tax were initiated as partisan proposals, but the appeal of both issues in western North Carolina indicated how difficult it was for mountain politicians to remain loyal to their party's prescribed platforms without violating an even more intense loyalty to their section of the state.

The only property qualification for suffrage that remained in North Carolina's new Constitution of 1835 was the stipulation that only owners of fifty acres of land or more were entitled to vote for state senators. That restriction had evoked very little discussion since then, and thus it took both parties by surprise when Democratic gubernatorial candidate David S. Reid, a former congressman from Rockingham County, as part of his 1848 campaign platform, proposed the elimination of that last vistage of pre-Jacksonian privilege. He introduced the idea of what he called "equal suffrage" (Whigs referred to it as "free suffrage") only after he had been nominated and apparently with no consultation with other party leaders. Though the Democrats quickly endorsed the cause, recognizing its popularity and political potential, most Whigs across the state were just as quick to denounce this "new innovation."[19] While Whigs elsewhere in the state floundered in their efforts to rationalize their opposition without confirming the "elitist" accusations of the Democrats,[20] those in the mountains recognized the proposal's obvious sectional appeal. A far larger proportion of landholders in their region (54.8 percent) than elsewhere in the state (38.8 percent in the piedmont and 39.3 percent in the coastal plain) owned less than fifty acres.[21]

The *Highland Messenger* in Asheville was one of only two Whig newspapers in the state to endorse the proposal, and Whig state senate candidates in two of the mountain's three senatorial districts openly supported it.[22] Congressman Clingman, still a Whig in name at least and dependent on the party's support, realized the issue's potency and dared not oppose it. He wrote Sen. Willie P. Mangum in September that, since arriving home from Washington, he had decided to support free suffrage. "I think from all I saw and heard as I came on that the west will generally unite in favor of such a change."[23] Mountain Whigs thus sought to neutralize the partisanship of the issue and for the most part succeeded in doing so. Reid, with 49.5 percent of the statewide vote, narrowly lost the election to Whig candidate Charles Manly. Reid had made a dramatic comeback for North Carolina's perpetual Democratic minority, but he carried only three highland counties, and the percentage of votes for Manly was just slightly less than that received by his Whig predecessor William A. Graham in 1846. Only in the westernmost senatorial district did the issue damage mountain Whigs. There, Democrat William Holland Thomas defeated Whig incumbent Michael Francis by a large majority and took the senate seat that he would continue to hold until the Civil War.[24]

The free suffrage issue, as it stood in 1848, could hardly be called a sectional one. Though it was decidedly more popular in the west than in the east, the fact that it affected only local races suggests that its passage would not have provided westerners with any political advantage at the state level. Though Whigs had withstood the most serious challenge yet to their mountain stronghold, they realized that merely assenting to a Democratic proposal could be no more than a stopgap measure. To maintain their support, they would have to turn free suffrage back into a partisan issue, though one on which their initiative would provide them with the offensive advantage. This they did by broadening the proposal so that its appeal would become sectional and its advantages to the west over the east more apparent.

The inequities in the composition of the senate were based not only on the qualifications of its electorate but also on the distribution of its representation across the state. Because North Carolina apportioned its senators according to the federal census formula, by which three-fifths of all slaves were included in population totals, the large slaveholding counties of the east enjoyed far more representation than did those in the mountains. As a western Whig pointed out in a letter to the *Raleigh Register*, Burke, Caldwell, McDowell, and Wilkes counties, with 3,873 voters, received the same representation in the state senate as did the single county of Hertford, with only 560 voters.[25] Thus, along with suffrage reform, the writer and others reasoned that state senate apportionment should be based on white population alone. By 1850, most western Whigs were committed to this and other more extensive reforms. Ashe County Whigs met in February 1850 and confirmed their support for free suffrage and the proposal to use the white population alone to determine apportionment, along with the popular election of judges and removal of property qualifications for all officeholders. Party leaders in Henderson, Watauga, and Buncombe counties did likewise.[26] The Buncombe County group issued a resolution declaring that "equal suffrage is the right of every white man in a Republican Government . . . property qualifications for members of the Legislature are unnecessary . . . [and] representation in both houses of the Legislature, should be founded on White population, and not on property exclusively, as it now is."[27]

The far-reaching extent of the measures proposed led their champions to call for a constitutional convention to consider them, since they knew that the legislature itself would never submit to such widespread reform.[28] Western legislators met in Raleigh late in 1850 and drew up a pamphlet, signed by almost all who were mountain Whigs, as well as several leading Democrats, which was circulated among their constituents. Commonly referred to as the "Western Address," the pamphlet declared that "a Free Convention, unrestricted by anything but the will of the People, was the only republican means for altering the fundamental law of the State." It pointed out that the "Senate represents property, not persons—money, not men—matter, not mind." The three-fifths slave count meant that "all the negros . . . are represented in the Senate; but your wives and children have no political rights."[29]

This strategy of redefining an issue thrust upon them and raising the stakes associated with it served the Whigs' purposes well, placing Democrats on the defensive for adhering to what westerners saw as a very limited and inadequate reform proposal. Reid, committed to no more than his original 1848 reform proposal, carried even less of the mountain vote in 1850 than he had previously.[30] By 1852, demands by mountain Whigs for a convention were stronger and more closely tied to western interests than ever before. Urging his party to nominate a pro-convention candidate for governor, Thomas George Walton of Morganton warned that the issue "will be paramount to all others in the extreme West in the next gubernatorial canvass—all who oppose a convention free and unrestricted will be politically annihilated so far as the extreme west has the power." Nicholas Woodfin, one of Asheville's most outspoken Whigs, reiterated Walton's prediction, declaring that "this Section of the State will not unite cordially (if at all) in the support of any one who is not for sustaining our rights."[31]

But conservative eastern Whigs feared the sweeping changes that could result from such a convention, and their control of the party led to the gubernatorial nomination of one of their own, John Kerr, who opposed both a convention and the proposed reforms, much to the disappointment of western Whigs. Despite their earlier defiant warnings, most of the Whig leadership reluctantly supported Kerr, since they had been urged by the *Asheville Messenger* to be patient, for "all will be gained after a while that is desirable."[32] Democrats were quick to accuse them of abandoning the interests of their section by their loyalty to a Whig platform that blatantly ignored them. Voters registered their disapproval of this slight of their region when an unprecedented five mountain counties delivered Democratic majorities, with Whig percentages lower in all twelve counties than they had been two years earlier.[33]

This setback to the party had even more damaging long-range effects. By their sectionalization of the equal suffrage issue, mountain Whigs had alienated party members in the east to the extent that party unity within the state was shattered. The process that would lead to the party's demise by the middle of the decade was well under way. After their 1852 failure, western North Carolinians' interest in further reform remained only intermittent through 1855, when the basic suffrage proposal—eliminating voter property qualifications—finally won legislative approval and was submitted to a popular vote during the 1857 congressional election.

By this time, the question of more equitable representation between sections had been eclipsed by the question of more equitable taxation. With the surge in state expenditures in the 1850s, resulting primarily from various improvement projects undertaken, the problem of how to secure additional revenue became of more practical and immediate concern. This was particularly true in the west, where the benefits of additional state spending were most eagerly anticipated. The means proposed for refilling state coffers was an ad valorem tax base, whereby slaves and other property would be taxed according to their value. This would be a far more equitable tax than the current poll tax, in which only those male slaves between the ages of twelve and fifty, regardless of their worth, were taxed at the same rate as white males. An ad valorem tax would shift far more of the increasing tax burden onto those wealthy citizens best able to bear it—the slaveholders.

The white basis for apportionment and other proposed reforms connected with the free suffrage issue all had entailed clearcut benefits to the western part of the state at the expense of the east. Thus the choice Whigs had had to make between party loyalty and regional interest had been a relatively easy one. In contrast, the ad valorem issue, with the obvious concrete financial burden it would impose on all slaveholders wherever they lived, added class loyalty to party and regional loyalties as factors to be considered by mountain political leaders, most of whom owned slaves themselves. It seems that neither individual nor class interest ever overrode mountain masters' commitment to their section. Almost all overlooked the expense the new tax base would impose on them personally (and for some, the cost would be substantial). Almost to a man, they approached the issue in terms of the far greater burden it would impose on the eastern part of the state and their far more numerous and wealthy counterparts there.

This time it was the Whigs (who, after the dissolution of the Know-Nothings, had become known merely as the Opposition) who initiated the proposal. They forced the Democrats to oppose it and boxed them into a defensive corner, much as the Democrats had done to them on the free suffrage issue. Western Whigs by now fully appreciated the strategic value of defining the issue in sectional terms and were quick to equate opposition to ad valorem taxation with regional disloyalty. In July 1856, two years before the issue fully emerged as a central one in state politics, the *Asheville Spectator*, then the predominant Whig-American voice in the region, criticized Buncombe County's Democratic state senator, David Coleman, for his rejection of an amendment to the free suffrage bill that would have removed "slaveholders' protection, by putting two great objects of taxation, (land and slaves) upon an equal footing." The paper made itself a guardian of republicanism, as its editorial continued:

> What could have been more just and proper? What could have been more desirable to the West? And yet, Mr. Coleman, representing a Western constituency, that has groaned, for lo! these many years under the weight of taxation for the benefit of the East votes against it on the ground that it would clog the Free Suffrage bill before the people! If the West desires ever to have any redress of her wrongs, it is time she should look closely to the

men who represent her, being well assured that if her own men are made to forsake her interests, by the power of party drill, she need not look to strangers for any better treatment.[34]

In February 1857, a letter published in the *Asheville News* from a "citizen of Buncombe" pointed out the direct link between taxation and internal improvements. "Are we," it asked,

to sit down and submit tamely and quietly to all the burdens of taxation and other inequalities that are being imposed on us and get nothing in return? Just think of it, in the Eastern part of our State they have their railroads and navigable rivers and we of the West are paying enormously high rates of taxes to aid them in building their roads and improving the navigation of their rivers – and now, I ask, what has been done for us in return, in our part of the State?[35]

By 1858, Democrats across the state had decided to oppose the ad valorem tax proposal. This forced mountain party members to make a choice between supporting the tax and thus rejecting their party's platform or finding the means to justify their opposition to it in terms of sectional interest. Initially, when the proposal was under discussion in the legislature from late 1858 through 1859, many western Democrats chose the first option. Marcus Erwin, editor of the *Asheville News*, supported the ad valorem bill introduced by Moses Bledsoe in the lower house, stating that "the principle is correct, and if the details of his bill are right, we hope it will go through."[36] William Holland Thomas, the long-time Democratic state senator for the southwestern section of the state, supported the measure on the grounds that it was unfair to tax land without taxing slaves as well. He supported equal suffrage, he said, but he also favored making men free and equal on tax-paying as well as on election days.[37]

The issue became central to the governor's race in 1860, and mountain residents had ample opportunity to hear the candidates debate it. In a series of joint appearances made around the state from April through July, Democratic incumbent John W. Ellis and his Opposition challenger John Pool spent over a third of their tour in the mountain counties.[38] The clarity of their opposing positions on the tax made party affiliation a higher priority than it had been, and many of those Democrats who had earlier gone along with the Whig's support of the tax now reversed their position to reenter their party's fold. An Asheville Whig observed that "the democratic Leaders have succeeded in pulling the wool over the eyes of many in regard to equal Taxation, and

accordingly things will be nearer on a party line than I anticipated."
Morganton Whig Burgess S. Gaither was glad to see this, believing
that their opposition would prove too unpopular to win them much
support in the region. "If the democracy will take issue upon ad va-
lorum," he wrote, "we will give them a Waterloo defeat in the West."[39]

But Gaither did not take into account the extent to which the Democrats would be able to diminish the popularity of the tax among
mountain voters by successfully reconciling opposition to the measure
with sectional concerns. Several sound arguments as to why the ad valorem tax would hurt, rather than help, western North Carolina soon
emerged. William Holland Thomas was among those who had moved
back into the Democratic fold on the issue, and he claimed that the
passage of the tax bill would threaten further support for the Western
North Carolina Railroad. He reasoned that, with easterners bearing
far more of the burden of financing state projects, they would be less
likely to allow those funds to be drained off from their own area to the
mountains. Thomas's opposition to the measure had become so
strong that he walked out of a rally in Jackson County where Burgess
Gaither was expounding the virtues of the proposal, and declared it
no place for a Democrat. Mountain Whigs worried that, in raising such
soundly commercial objections, Thomas might have discovered ad valorem's most basic liability within the region. Robert Vance of Buncombe County feared that "Bill Thomas will scare off hundreds out
west by making them believe it will Kill off the R.R."[40] The *Asheville
News* also reversed its position and pointed out that any increase in
taxation on slaves in the east would also increase their apportioned
representatives in the state senate. Others joined Democrats across
the state in questioning the timing of the debate. Any divisiveness
over slavery within the state, they warned, merely played into the
hands of slavery's critics in the North.[41]

An even more effective weapon against the proposed Whig reform
was one which played on what were by then long-nurtured republican
fears of creeping government encroachment. This so-called "tin cup"
argument Ellis fully exploited in canvassing the highlands in spring
1860. He pointed out, and local Democrats quickly agreed, that the
Whig's proposed system would tax not only slaves, but all property,
including farming implements, household furnishings, livestock, and
even one's tin cups. To do so would entail an invasion of privacy by tax
collectors and unwelcome interference, even oppression, by the gov-

Figure 16. John W. Ellis. North Carolina Division of Archives and History.

ernment. Just after Ellis and Pool had spoken in the area, an Ashe County Democrat wrote that "in this section ad valorem is not popular as advocated by the Opposition. Our people are afraid of a tax being imposed on their stock."[42]

In a lengthy editorial opposing the new tax, the *Asheville News* appealed to both slaveholding and nonslaveholding farmers by equating the injustice of taxing livestock with that of taxing slaves not in their prime. It argued that:

> A farmer who has no young negroes, has no right to complain that those belonging to his neighbor are not taxed so long as his own horses, cattle, sheep, hogs &c are not taxed . . . . Old Negroes and young, that are a burden upon the owner rather than a profit to him, are privileged from taxation because they can yield no profit. Horses, cattle, sheep, hogs, &c are privileged because they are necessary to the maintenance of one's family. But the great injustice of this ad valorem system lies in the fact that all property would be taxed according to value. Luxuries and vices, would be taxed as high, according to value, and no higher than necessities.

It concluded by accusing Whigs of seeking to ease the taxation burden from businessmen and bankers and predicting that it would instead "come down with a hand of iron on the farmers and laborers."[43]

Edward Jones Erwin, a Burke County banker and Democrat, explained to his son why he opposed the tax. "A Farmer," he wrote, "who is worth in land or Negroes $100,000 pays to the state a tax of $90 and the Bank who owns $100,000 in stock pays $320. Now if you take the worth of a man and then lay the tax, each of them will have to pay the same, while the Farmer is not getting one percent, the Banker is getting 8 percent on his capital." While Democrats pushed this line of reasoning among the predominantly rural mountain constituency, Erwin, as a slaveholder, was particularly concerned about the system's effect on slavery itself, which he predicted would be disastrous. If accomplished, he wrote, "this will carry out the very plan suggested by Hinton Rowan Helper, to usher every negro out of the state or render him worthless."[44]

Combined, these arguments dampened much of the earlier western enthusiasm for the ad valorem tax. The split on that issue, along with the ambiguities of the candidates' stands on internal improvements, made the 1860 gubernatorial race the most evenly divided ever held in the mountain counties. Pool won eight counties and 50.9 percent of the vote, while Ellis took seven counties and 49.1 percent of the vote (see table 6.1).

Significantly, the class conflict inherent in the tax issue was rarely, if ever, evident in the debate among western North Carolinians. Most spokesmen for both parties were slaveholders whose message was aimed at a predominantly nonslaveholding electorate. Thus the question of the effects of the proposed tax on individual slaveowners had no real place in public discussion in the mountain counties. Large slaveholding Whigs, in their strong public and private endorsement of the plan, clearly were sacrificing their own and their fellow slaveowners' interest to those of their party and region. Nicholas W. Woodfin of Asheville, for example, readily embraced the plan, despite the fact that in 1860 he owned 122 slaves and would have been among those taxed most heavily by it. Likewise, Thomas George Walton of Morganton, with 46 slaves; Montreville Patton of Asheville, with 30; and Samuel F. Patterson of Caldwell County, with 36, were all active advocates of the Whig party's platform.[45]

The initial support of slaveholding Democrats such as Marcus Erwin and William Holland Thomas indicates that their concern for the mountain region overrode both personal and party interests, while their later objections seemed to represent more a return to party loyalty than a retreat to self-interest. One of the few instances in which the direct effect of the tax on individual slaveowners was discussed was a letter from Edward J. Erwin to his son. Even in it, Erwin based his argument on the sectional discrimination suffered by westerners. "I look upon [the ad valorem bill] as one of the greatest humbugs of the day," he wrote. It would be most oppressive to mountain slaveholders "as our slaves are not worth as much to us as they are in the East yet the East can make from $400 to $500 per hand and pay the same tax we do here. Our negroes will not in the farm yield us more than $50 net."[46] The logic of his argument is somewhat questionable, since the same inequity he foresaw under ad valorem was applicable under the current poll tax system. Still, Erwin's letter suggests that western slaveholders' concern over tax reform was not whether it was disadvantageous to slaveholders compared to their non-slaveholding neighbors, but whether it was disadvantageous to them as western slaveholders compared to eastern ones. Even here, sectional loyalties took precedence over the bonds of class.

The issues of free suffrage and ad valorem taxation contributed much to the sense of regional distinctiveness among western North Carolinians. Compared to debates over internal improvements, the sectional implications of these controversies were not always so readily apparent nor the effects of their outcomes so obvious. But major themes of the republican ideology—particularly the vulnerability of minorities to government despotism—were inherent in both issues, and western leaders readily embraced and effectively employed them. Politicians of both parties, whether supporting or attacking the proposals themselves, in stressing these themes, framed the issues in sectional terms. As their leaders focused on specific advantages or disadvantages to their particular constituency, Carolina highlanders became all too aware that they had needs and interests not shared by those elsewhere in the state and that they would have to stand together as a section, despite partisan rivalries, to protect those interests. That realization was driven home even more fully in the third area of intrastate struggle. The campaign for state-funded internal improvements was fought simultaneously with the suffrage, representation, and taxation battles and, like them, helped to reinforce highlanders' identities as westerners. However, as the following chapter will demonstrate, the struggle over internal improvements was equally significant in raising other equally relevant questions regarding mountain residents' place within both the state and the South.

Chapter 7

Mountaineers as Westerners:

"Internal improvements . . . the main hinge
upon which western votes will turn"

For western North Carolinians, by far the most vital political issue was state aid for internal improvements. It was the struggle over that issue that most fanned the flames of North Carolina's intrastate rivalries and sectional tensions throughout the antebellum period. Because the economic effects of better roads, turnpikes, and railroads on the western region and its future were so direct and so obvious, any prospective officeholder from the mountain counties or from elsewhere in the state who sought backing in the region had to support, at least minimally, the cause of internal improvements. The comment of a Macon County resident on the governor's race of 1854 would have been equally applicable in most campaigns for state office during the 1840s and 1850s: "The main hinge upon which the votes of the western counties . . . will turn is the position the two candidates take respecting Internal Improvements."[1]

The degree to which this one issue dominated western Carolina politics and the overwhelming support it generated throughout the antebellum years attest to the strong entrepreneurial spirit that pervaded the region. Several recent local and regional studies of the nineteenth-century South's social economy suggest that such sentiments may have been atypical, since internal improvements, particularly railroads, met with decidedly mixed reactions elsewhere in the South; southern yeomen, above all others, were satisfied with the small-scale community economy and had grave doubts about the expansion of their markets.

Steven Hahn's Georgia upcountry farmers, for instance, worried about the impact of the railroad on their areas—its effects on present and future land ownership, the degree to which it might inhibit self-sufficiency and independence, or the threat it posed to local tranquility and safety. Even merchants and craftsmen opposed the railroad on the grounds that it would disrupt local business relations and make competing merchandise produced elsewhere more accessible to their customers.[2]

Lacy Ford noted that strong antimercantile biases among the agrarian interests in the South Carolina upcountry during the 1850s evolved into much more explicit tensions after the Civil War. Alabama yeomen, according to Mills Thornton, panicked at railroad and commercial development that contributed to greater prosperity for the merchant-planter elite but which they felt reduced their own chances of sharing in the expanding economic pie.[3] And in his intricate analysis of the social economy of two piedmont Virginia counties, John Schlotterbeck detected a retreat from extended trade networks in response to the economic stagnation that beset the state for much of the nineteenth century's first fifty years. That reversion to localized self-sufficiency apparently met with substantial compliance by most of those counties' residents, slaveholders and nonslaveholders alike.[4]

All of this was in marked contrast to the perpetual widespread popularity of internal improvement efforts in the Carolina highlands. Many others besides mountain merchants or even slaveholders embraced the campaign for state-granted corporate charters and subsidies for commercial and transportation development in their region. Substantial majorities of the electorate consistently backed those efforts. In a recent analysis of the effects of class on southern antebellum politics, Harry Watson acknowledged small farmers' cautionary stance toward the entrapments of the extended marketplace, as well as the appeal improved transportation networks held for them. He concluded, "Nothing so clearly indicates the superior power of the slaveholders as their ability to impose this course of accelerated commercial development on a reluctant class of white non-slaveholders."[5]

There is little evidence, however, to suggest that among Carolina mountain residents such sentiments were imposed from above. With the emergence of the second party system in North Carolina, regional representatives were quick to acknowledge and respond to an already obvious desire on the part of their constituents for such development. It was the Whigs' strong endorsement of government funding for various transportation projects that led the majority of mountain voters into the party in the late 1830s, and it was Whig promises of support that remained the basis of its strength throughout the 1840s. Likewise, the Whigs' failure to deliver results to that part of the state was a major factor in their declining popularity there during the 1850s.[6] David Swain, Thomas Clingman, and, to a lesser extent, Zebulon Vance all launched their careers by fighting vigorously for state-sponsored transportation facilities in the mountains.[7]

Even Democrats in the mountains embraced the cause, since to oppose it, or even to remain apathetic to it, would have amounted to political suicide. Three of the area's most successful Democrats, William Holland Thomas, W.W. Avery, and Samuel Fleming, were all instrumental in efforts to link their region with the rest of the state and the rest of the South.[8] Thomas Jeffrey has demonstrated through an analysis of votes on internal improvements in the General Assembly from 1836 through 1860 that support on that issue was based far more on sectional than on partisan loyalties. Such loyalty was particularly marked in the extreme west, "where legislators from both parties backed state-supported internal improvements with equal fervor throughout the antebellum period."[9]

The enthusiasm of mountain residents for internal improvements was not based on a desire to overcome present isolation and to enter the market economy. As has been demonstrated earlier, western North Carolinians had been actively engaged in interstate trade for many years. It was their very success in these ventures and the benefits they provided to both individual participants and the region as a whole that whetted their appetites for more.[10] The increased demand for mountain products by plantation markets, mountain residents' heightened awareness of the value of their region's natural and cultivated resources, and the simultaneous development of improved transportation facilities and more efficient trade networks elsewhere in the South combined to point up both the great commercial potential offered by greater accessibility to their markets and the serious limitations of their present situation.

The region's most important artery, the Buncombe Turnpike, completed in 1828, carried a phenomenal amount of traffic along the French Broad River from Tennessee almost due south into South Carolina through Madison, Buncombe, and Henderson counties. The commercial and tourist traffic that moved along it stood as the most

Figure 17. The Buncombe Turnpike in Madison County. North Carolina Division of Archives and History, Western Branch.

conspicuous example of the invigorating effects of such channels on those communities and individuals fortunate enough to be situated along its route.[11] With the rise of the Whigs and the new emphasis on an active state role in developing internal improvements, other parts of the mountain region clamored for state aid for similar thoroughfares that would at least link them to the Buncombe Turnpike.

At first, results were encouraging. The very first internal improvement measure considered by the General Assembly in its initial session under the new constitution in 1836 was a bill to construct a road across the Nantahala Mountains that would link Macon County's seat, Franklin, with Georgia.[12] With the help of Thomas Clingman, then a state senator, the bill passed. Soon afterward, a turnpike through the Oconaluftee Valley, crossing the Smoky Mountains into Tennessee, was well under way and promised to provide the southwestern corner of North Carolina with access both to Tennessee and South Carolina markets and to the benefits of contact with outside traffic moving through that area.[13] Fortuitous circumstances occasionally allowed other influential mountain Whigs in Raleigh to win concessions for their area. Samuel F. Patterson, for example, long active on the party's central committee in the state, found himself appointed chairman of both the Internal Improvements and Finance Committees during his first term in the General Assembly in 1846. The only internal improvement bill to win legislative approval that session was a turnpike for his own Caldwell County.[14]

In 1840, the most noted champion of statewide development, John M. Morehead, successfully campaigned for governor with a vow to push for internal improvements, the most pressing of which was an east-west highway linking the western mountains with North Carolina's coastal plain. Once in office, Morehead reiterated his commitment to the mountain counties, summing up the benefits that western Carolinians firmly believed would result from good roads in their region:

> It is believed the population will increase with rapidity, agriculture will improve, grazing will be extended, and manufactures and mechanic arts will flourish in a location combining so many advantages and inviting their growth. The improved highways will be additional inducements to citizens of other sections of our State to abandon their usual northern tours, or visits to the Virginia watering places for a tour more interesting among our own mountains, much cheaper, and much more beautiful – a tour in which

they will inspire health in every breath and drink in health in every draught.[15]

Among mountain residents, optimism soon gave way to cynicism and exasperation toward those in power in Raleigh, as appropriations for both the Cadlwell County and the east-west turnpikes were delayed for over a decade. Most other projects proposed to the legislature were either rejected outright or postponed indefinitely, due to either Democratic blockage or bipartisan opposition by the still dominant eastern half of the state.[16] In some cases in which schemes for matching state and local funds were formulated, it proved beyond the means of local citizens in some of the poorer, less densely populated counties to provide their share of either the cash or the labor necessary to qualify for state aid. In Yancey County, several such projects were attempted but failed. To cite but one example, the McDowell and Yancey Turnpike Company was formed in an effort to provide another road across the Blue Ridge Mountains. In order to qualify for a three-thousand-dollar subsidy from the state public improvement board, local residents of the two counties were required to raise seven thousand dollars. Even when the legislature approved reducing the amount to three thousand dollars, it proved too much for those who so desperately desired the road, and the project was not completed until after the Civil War.[17] Even more frustrating for local citizens were those projects which were approved during one legislative session, only to have funding revoked or even charters annulled during a later one. The Jonathan Creek and Tennessee Mountain Turnpike Company, for example, was incorporated by an act of the 1846–47 General Assembly but then dissolved by a more fiscally conservative legislature in 1849.[18]

Despite the increasing difficulties in obtaining state financing, roads continued to be built throughout the mountains during the 1840s and 1850s through the authorization of county courts with financing by local stock companies and construction by local labor forces. The Hickory Nut Gap Turnpike, for example, linking Asheville and Rutherfordton, became the state's first adequate thoroughfare across the Blue Ridge. Coordinated efforts by three counties resulted in its completion two years after legislators in Raleigh rejected attempts to extend the previously granted authorization for its construction.[19]

The success of such efforts led some regional entrepreneurs to take matters more and more into their own hands. Caldwell County residents, led by brothers Thomas and William A. Lenoir, formed their own company to finance and build the Caldwell and Ashe Turnpike. Thomas Lenoir wrote Gov. William A. Graham in 1848 that the road would "open an entirely new and much more direct channel of communication between our state, on one side, and E. Tennessee, West Va. & Kentucky on the other." He informed Graham that the Tennessee legislature would charter a road to join theirs and that he hoped North Carolina's legislature might also provide funds for the project.[20] His tone seemed to indicate that, while some state aid would certainly be welcome, the success of their venture by no means depended on it.

By the end of the 1840s, more and more western Carolinians had come to believe that the high hopes they had once held for the Whig government in Raleigh had been misplaced and that whatever they hoped to achieve would have to come from efforts made within their own section. This disillusionment with both the Whig party and the legislature turned to bitterness on the part of some who came to see the state's neglect as an affront to which they should no longer submit.

Thomas Clingman, in a printed address that he circulated among his constituents early in 1849, reflected the frustrations of a growing number in his district. He pointed out that the new constitution had been designed specifically "to put the West on an equal footing with the East as respects legislation." But, he asked mountain residents, "What has been the result, even under an ameliorated condition, after we have been advanced to a position of comparative equality, and are supposed to have had some share in the benefits of government? Since then, out of the State Treasury there has been appropriated for internal improvements one million and nine hundred thousand dollars, not one dollar of which has been expended west of Raleigh." For a long time, he continued, using the rhetoric of republicanism that served him so well, "we had acquiesced—too tamely perhaps—because we were 'willing that the elder branch of the family should be served first' . . . and since then, under our tame submission, the evil has been aggravated." The time had come, Clingman wrote, for westerners to assert their equality, and he concluded, in the defiant phrase cited earlier, that the "central managers" should be told "that if they want white slaves they must look for them elsewhere than in the Western reserve."[21]

As Thomas Lenoir perhaps inadvertently pointed up in his letter to the governor, private enterprise tended to augment rather than alleviate the problems of intrastate distance and access. Lenoir's emphasis on the way his project would link his area with Virginia, Kentucky, and Tennessee affirmed an emerging pattern: those roads being completed in the mountain region would do very little to link it with the eastern part of the state. Instead, they radiated north, south, or west, perpetuating the very problem that state aid for transportation had been meant to alleviate—the siphoning off of western trade to neighboring states.

As emphasized in chapter 2, western North Carolina's commercial ties with South Carolina and Georgia were well established, and tourists from those states far outnumbered eastern North Carolinians who enjoyed the scenic beauty and cool climate of their own state's mountains. Greenville and Spartanburg, South Carolina, were located much closer to most mountain residents than any of North Carolina's major cities. But proximity was not the only reason that mountaineers directed their attentions south rather than east. As Governor Morehead pointed out, the "vast productions of the fertile West" often sought markets even more distant than those in the state, because access to the former was easier. Thus, even "the towns of Cheraw, Camden, Columbia . . . and Augusta and Charleston are much more familiarly known in the far west than even Fayetteville or Raleigh, much less those towns farther Eastward."[22] The Buncombe Turnpike and the Hickory Nut Gap road greatly reinforced interstate contacts. As Tennessee and Kentucky farmers and traders moved in ever-increasing numbers along those and other routes toward their southern markets, their ties to western North Carolinians also were strengthened; projects ranging from the Caldwell and Ashe Turnpike in the state's northwest corner to the Oconaluftee and Cataloochee roads in the southwest corner, sought to exploit those out-of-state connections.

The implications of this trend disturbed North Carolinians both within the region and elsewhere. In a report to the legislature in 1846, Elisha Mitchell stressed the need for an east-west turnpike and warned of the growing division between the two ends of the state. He quoted "an intelligent gentleman" from the mountains who had told him "that as things now are he has less to do with people on the northern side of the Albermarle Sound than with those on some of the remotest regions of the globe."[23] Two years later, Samuel Patterson issued an even more urgent plea for action by the legislature. Unless the present session took action (presumably in sponsoring road construc-

Figure 18. Traffic to and from South Carolina through the Hickory Nut Gap
Turnpike. North Carolina Division of Archives and History, Western Branch.

tion across the state's east-west axis), he wrote, North Carolina "will be irretrievably ruined. We are being tapped on both sides by our Sister States, and before another session comes round, the process will be carried to such an extent by them that we can never recover from its effects."[24]

In 1849, the General Assembly finally responded to concern about increasing alienation between east and west by approving funds for a turnpike west from Salisbury. Arguments over what route the road would take within the region translated into electoral results in 1850 foreshadowing just what a "hinge" internal improvements would prove in turning western voters through much of the decade to come. Residents of both Burke and Rutherford counties had campaigned actively to bring the turnpike and its associated new trade through their county seats. Gov. Charles Manly named a commission to settle the matter, and it selected the more central route from Statesville on to Morganton rather than one slightly farther south from Shelby through Rutherfordton. Disappointed voters in the latter held Manly fully accountable for his appointees' decision and, in a dramatic reversal, gave him only 35 percent of their county's vote in 1850, compared to 74 percent of its support two years earlier. Neighboring Burke County, as the beneficiary of the commission's decision, rewarded Manly with almost 80 percent of its 1850 vote, the largest Whig majority it had yet bestowed on a gubernatorial candidate.[25]

By 1850, railroads rapidly were coming to be seen as a solution much more likely to unite the state than more turnpikes. Westerners again began to hope that state aid would bring economic transformation to their region, this time by linking them by rail with the rest of the state. Recent studies of southern social economies and market networks have reached contradictory conclusions as to the effects of railroad links on the local communities, and particularly the yeomen they served. While several scholars found evidence of positive economic benefits to the full range of white landholders and merchants, others revealed seriously restrictive, disruptive, or disorienting effects on those on the bottom rungs of the socioeconomic ladder.[26]

Again, however, there is no suggestion that any group of North Carolina's mountain residents opposed the advent of railroad lines that would strengthen their links with surrounding and even distant markets. To a striking degree, mountaineers enthusiastically predicted, often in romantically idealized terms, the vast opportunities

4 HORSE POST COACH,
FROM MORGANTON TO ASHEVILLE.

◆

J. H. & R. W. TATE,

HAVING become contractors of this Line of Mail Stages, inform the travelling public that they run once a week and back, from Morganton to Asheville, a distance of sixty miles, in two days, a line of four horse Post Coaches, which leave Morganton on every Saturday morning at 4 o'clock A. M. and arrive at Asheville at 6 o'clock. P. M., of the same day; and leave Asheville at 4 o'clock, the following morning, (Sunday) and arrive at Morganton at 8 o'clock. P. M.   This line immediately intersects with the line from Salem to Greenville at Morganton and also with the great Western line at Asheville.   The accommodation in this Line are excellent—having good coaches, able horses and experienced drivers.   This is the speediest and shortest route for those who are travelling either westwardly or eastwardly, as it harmonizes with the Salem, N. C. and Greenville line, which runs 50 or 60 miles per day.   ☞ FARE.—6¼ cents per mile.

N. B.   All possible care will be taken of baggage, bundles, &c.; yet the contractors will not be responsible for losses.

Morganton. May 12, 1831.   13tf

Figure 19. Stagecoach advertisement, *Raleigh Standard*, 1831. From copy in North Carolina Collection, UNC Library, Chapel Hill.

this mechanized bond would bestow on them and their region. A Macon County woman echoed the sentiments of citizens throughout the mountains in her expectations for the development of her community: "We hope ere long to hear the stately tread of the Iron-horse in our midst. Then indeed will open a new era among us."[27] The editor of the *Asheville News*, Marcus Erwin, was even more eloquent in his optimism: "Bore a tunnel through the ridge, let daylight shine under the mighty backbone and the iron horse break through to startle the peaceful vallies of the west into a new and more vigorous life, and the revolution that would follow would outstrip the wildest dreams of the most visionary among us."[28]

To some, increased contact with their fellow North Carolinians was itself a most welcome prospect. "Whose heart would not beat with quickened vibration at the idea of meeting his brethren from all parts of the State at Raleigh in 12, 24 hours, for either religious, political, or other purposes?" asked the *Highland Messenger* in 1852. "What poor man could not then visit his friends and relatives, and make life more social and endurable?"[29] At least one mountain resident was far more expansive concerning the links the coming railroad would establish for his area. Nimrod Jarrett of Macon County described the eventual route of the western extension as running "below Franklin and Murphy, thence to Ducktown's copper mines, thence to Cleaveland [*sic*], thence to Chatanuga [*sic*], thence to Memphis, and if congress should settle down on any plan to make the road to California . . . it will be the greatest road on our continent." Jarrett was so confident that this plan would be realized that he advised a friend that "now is a good time to purchase the Lands now along the expected line."[30]

Others stressed that if the mountains' vast untapped natural resources were made readily accessible, they could benefit the whole state. Typical of the many letters from western Carolinians to the state's agricultural journal, the *North Carolina Planter*, is one from Silas McDowell, in which he extolled the "superior grazing lands" of his region and predicted:

> The day will come when these rich mountains will be covered with herds of fine and well bred cattle and flocks of thorough bred sheep. Then will not Switzerland be superior to the "United States of Buncombe," and the old North will be proud of her west. Let the iron horse come whizzing through to the extreme west, and old Rip will shake off her mantle and stand out among her sisters in flame of light.[31]

The editors of a Franklin newspaper also bemoaned the inability of mountain farmers to participate in the annual state agricultural fair in Raleigh:

> Had we Railroad facilities as our middle and eastern people have, we would proudly exhibit at our State Fair specimens of our mineral, agricultural, and pomological resources and products. . . . But none of these products can we have present unless we could wagon them an hundred and forty or fifty miles to the head of North Carolina enterprise in the shape of a Railroad, or await the movement of a Van Winkle State policy. Our unsur-

passed water power and sites for manufacturing establishments, our inexhaustible forests of furniture timber . . . our rich mountains, pure water and mineral springs of Haywood, Jackson, Macon, and Cherokee, must all remain unappreciated and unvisited by the capital and enterprise of our own State unless the auspices of a brighter day should dawn upon us, and a more liberal and just sentiment possess North Carolina legislators.[32]

During the 1850s the discovery of valuable mineral deposits in the southwestern counties intensified the demand for a railroad link with the rest of the state, particularly as mining operations were proving so successful just across the border in Tennessee and Georgia.[33] In 1853, a Murphy resident wrote of the excitement at what was being found in his area. "This is a Mineral Kingdom," wrote S.R. Mount, "and it only wants energy upon the part of its inhabitants to unbed the precious Mettles, Gold, Silver, Led, [and] Copper." A Waynesville man reported on valuable veins of copper and marble found in Cherokee County. In addition, he wrote, "there may also be silver and gold enough . . . to depopulate California!"[34] State geologist Ebeneezer Emmons confirmed the presence of rich copper deposits in Jackson County and inexhaustible beds of iron ore in the Nantahala Valley, as well as marble, roofing slate, quartz, and, in Macon County, "the finest Porcelain clay." But, he wrote, all of these "under existing circumstances, are nearly useless; but [they] will become of immense value when a cheap and commodious way is opened to the markets of the world."[35]

It was by no means only mountain residents who were aware of and eager for the benefits of extending the railroad to the western counties. In 1855, a Fayetteville newspaper editorialized: "Let improvements be shoved inland, and the amount of produce carried on them to the seaboard will astonish every one who has never seen the noble mountains and beautiful and fruitful valleys of the West." For eastern slaveholders, the editorial continued, there were also benefits: "The Summer tourist also will have a chance to spend his money and his time visiting the beauties of his own beautiful State, instead of going among the abolitionists of Saratoga, Niagara, &c., where families cannot take their servants with them, without running a great risk of losing them."[36]

Certainly the most original argument for the westward extension of the railroad put forward by a nonwesterner was the effect it would have on the "morals of North Carolina." In an appeal to temperance advocates and to eastern prejudices against mountain residents, the same Fayetteville writer explained that "in almost every ravine and mountain gorge of Western North Carolina you will find a still house and an apple mill, placed there for the purpose of turning the healthy grains and fruits of the earth into a maddening and killing beverage." Despite his propensity for exaggeration, the writer gave an accurate explanation: that the only means western farmers had of making their fruits marketable commodities over long distances was to distill them as whiskey and brandy. The solution to such corruptions, according to this easterner, was simply to:

> Run improvements through those sections alluded to, so that the people can get remunerating prices for their fruits and grains in the natural and healthy state in which a kind providence gives those products to man, and . . . our temperance lecturers will soon quit holding up the mountain region of our State to their eastern brethren, as a land abounding in still houses and apple mills; while we of the east will get from the upcountry good fruit instead of fiery brandy, and good and sound grain and flour instead of mean corn whiskey.[37]

Despite the clamor by western Carolinians for a railroad through their section, and the recognition by others in the state of the benefits it could provide them, the bumpy course of state and local cooperation during the last antebellum decade proved fully as exasperating as had earlier efforts to secure funding from Raleigh. Once again, neglect by their own state led mountain residents to take up more promising opportunities elsewhere. Actually, these out-of-state prospects had been pursued long before the state-sponsored Western North Carolina Railroad was seriously considered. While North Carolina lines, public and private, were being constructed throughout the east and even into the piedmont during the 1830s and 1840s, it was South Carolinians who first proposed a railroad through North Carolina's mountains, with an 1835 plan for a line extending from Charleston to Knoxville, Tennessee, and eventually to Louisville and Cincinnati. As developed by Mitchell King and other Charlestonians, whose extensive property holdings at Flat Rock and Asheville gave them a vested interest in the region, a 107-mile section of the proposed route would cross western North Carolina from the Saluda Gap on the South Carolina line through Asheville and then on up along the French Broad River into Tennessee, paralleling the Buncombe Turnpike for much of its length.[38] Despite progress made in organizing the project over the next several years, in 1850, when both South Carolina and Tennessee refused to incorporate a company tied to an interstate organization, the plan collapsed.

By that time William Holland Thomas was involved in a similar project. The Blue Ridge Railroad, as it was called, would also link Charleston to Cincinnati, but would do so by passing through Rabun Gap in northeastern Georgia and crossing through North Carolina at its southwestern tip, following the Tennessee River through Macon County into Tennessee. Not until 1850, though, did Thomas feel ready to present his request to incorporate the Tennessee River Railroad Company (as the North Carolina section was called) to the legislature. The bill passed with little opposition, but there was a general feeling, both in Raleigh and among his own friends, that his effort was a futile one. Even he admitted that the measure had passed without serious discussion because of this lack of confidence.[39] Three years later, mountain residents still considered the the project's chances of succeeding slim. Fellow westerner Silas McDowell wrote, "Thomas is pushing his 'Humbug' ahead with a vengence, and should success crown his efforts he will be viewed by our kind friends of Asheville as Don Quixote when he charged and unhorsed the Knight of the Mirrors. My sympathies of course are all on the side of the Don with a slight touch of wrath against the knight."[40] Presumably the knight was the state government, which proved to be the major barrier with which Thomas had to contend. As the result of active lobbying and fundraising efforts in all of the states involved, as well as in Washington and New York, he had obtained the necessary charters, won private and county support by rallying enthusiastic crowds at barbecues, sold stock to northern and local investors, and gained substantial help from the South Carolina and Tennessee legislatures. But North Carolina's legislature repeatedly denied all requests for funding. Finally, in 1859, with fifteen miles of track laid and two-thirds of a major tunnel in South Carolina dug, Thomas and the Blue Ridge Railroad Company were forced to admit defeat and abandon the project.[41]

Even if that railroad had succeeded, it spanned only seventy-three miles in North Carolina and would have benefitted only the three or four westernmost counties. Far more significant for the region as a whole, both economically and politically, was the long-awaited Western North Carolina Railroad. Planned as an extension of the North Carolina Railroad, it was to run from Salisbury through or near

Asheville, then on to the Tennessee line, in order to "effect a communication between the North Carolina Railroad and the Valley of the Mississippi."[42] A bill introduced in the North Carolina legislature in 1850 to charter a company to build it met considerable opposition from eastern senators who preferred an extension aimed in their own direction and from Democrats reluctant to commit the state to such a costly venture. It was only when western Whigs introduced a substitute bill that reserved for the state the rights to two-thirds of the company's stock, appropriated funds only to survey proposed routes, and avoided any decision on the extent of funding for the project itself, that the Western North Carolina Railroad, along with its eastern counterpart, were approved in December 1852.[43] The project was strongly supported by western Democrats and Whigs alike, but Democratic opposition elsewhere in the state made its future uncertain.

The gubernatorial campaign of 1854 became a showdown on the issue. Asheville Democrat Marcus Erwin told his party that if its convention would "only lay down some acceptable ground on the subject of Internal Improvements . . . . the Democracy in the West are in fine spirits and confident of success." This question, he warned Gov. David Reid (who, like many Democrats, was only a recent convert on the issue) "overrides every other in the Counties West of Asheville & no candidate who stands upon a platform worse in this respect than that of the Whigs can in my opinion poll the full strength of the [Democratic] party vote."[44] The convention heeded his advice, as did the candidate they nominated, Thomas Bragg of Northampton County, who, in an effort to win votes away from the equally committed Whig candidate Alfred Dockery, also grew increasingly committed to a liberal policy of state aid. In the western region, the only question in voters' minds seemed to be which of the two men was more likely to give them a railroad. Robert Scott of Macon County observed: "The main hinge upon which the votes of the western counties . . . . will turn is the position the two candidates take respecting Internal Improvements, and especially the Central Road's extension west."[45] Apparently most voters felt that Dockery was the more reliable choice, for he carried eleven of the fourteen mountain counties, though Bragg won the election. The *Asheville News* claimed that misrepresentation of its candidate accounted for its failure to convince mountain readers of the Democrats' new commitment to what had traditionally been a Whig cause. Bragg lost the region as a result of "the unscrupulous and

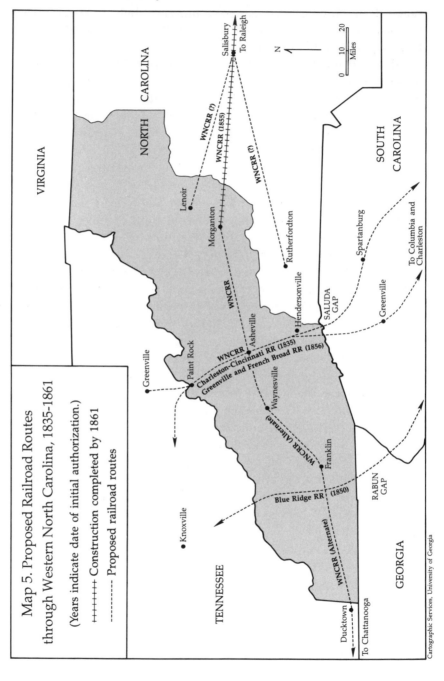

Map 5. Proposed Railroad Routes through Western North Carolina, 1835-1861

(Years indicate date of initial authorization.)
++++++ Construction completed by 1861
- - - - - - Proposed railroad routes

Cartographic Services, University of Georgia

unremitting efforts of our opponents to place him in an attitude of hostility to works of Internal Improvements," particularly the state railroad's westward extension.[46]

The campaign itself served to warn those easterners unenthusiastic about railroad extension that the prospect was increasingly popular across the state. A Democrat from the coastal plain assured a Caldwell County friend that easterners formerly opposed to increasing the state debt to build transportation facilities had indeed recognized that "a great change had taken place in public sentiment." He predicted that funding for the western railroad, among other internal improvement projects, easily would pass the next General Assembly.[47] Under Governor Bragg's leadership, strong support for these projects had become bipartisan, and within a month of their convening in 1855, legislators of both houses approved the charter of the Western North Carolina Railroad (WNCRR) by large majorities. But the four-million-dollar appropriation of public funds was among the higher price tags considered by the legislature, so its approval came only with the added stipulation that the road be built in sections, moving from east to west, with each section being fully completed before work on the next one could begin.[48]

The mountain counties rewarded Bragg for his support when he sought reelection in 1856. The *Asheville News* reminded its readers that "a Democratic Governor and a Democratic Legislature have brought our Rail Roads to the foot of the Blue Ridge, without oppressing the people and without any detriment to the credit of the State. Why turn a party out of power which is willing and able to prosecute these works successfully?"[49] In one of the most dramatic party reversals in the region's history, mountain voters responded by giving Bragg a majority in eleven of the fourteen westernmost counties, after opposing him in exactly the same number (eleven of fourteen supported Dockery) two years earlier.[50]

At this point, the route the railroad would take still had not been decided, and western North Carolina communities became fiercely competitive in their effort to bring the road—and the economic boom that would accompany it—through their area. East of the Blue Ridge, Rutherfordton, Lenoir, and Morganton each campaigned vigorously to become the terminus of the first section. Morganton won, because of both its more direct access to the Swannanoa Gap (which surveyors had determined to be the most feasible point at which to cross the Blue Ridge en route to Asheville) and the clout of leading citizens, who pledged $100,000 in subscriptions from Burke County and one of whom, Robert C. Pearson, was named president of the company.[51]

A far more heated debate concerned the route the railroad would take beyond Asheville. One alternative was to continue the line due west through Waynesville and Franklin, where it would intersect with Thomas's Blue Ridge Railroad, and on to Ducktown, Tennessee, the site of several very profitable copper mines. The other option was to turn north from Asheville and parallel the French Broad and the Buncombe Turnpike to the Tennessee border at Paint Rock. Because the section clause of the charter meant that no immediate decision was required for what would be the third and fourth legs of the project, the legislature delayed making any commitment to either route. It was only in February 1859 that it even authorized surveys of both, the results of which would not be considered until the next legislative session.[52] This uncertainty led to extended debates by local proponents of each proposal. Buncombe and Henderson county residents considered the Buncombe Turnpike their commercial lifeline, and they strongly favored reinforcing that well-traveled route with the railroad extension. Many in the area, including Zebulon Vance, preferred to see a revived South Carolina project, the Greenville and French Broad Company, provide the rails along that course.[53] But others sought to use their loyalty to their own state's project, along with the threat that a South Carolina company might further divert western goods out of state, as a means of persuading the legislature to choose the French Broad route. The management of the WNCRR Company also favored this route, on the more practical grounds that it was shorter and thus would cost far less.[54]

Even more impassioned arguments for the Ducktown route were made by residents of the southwestern counties. Chief among their spokesmen, of course, was William Holland Thomas. Claiming that many North Carolinians "regard Buncombe County as the western limit of the state," he launched an elaborate promotional campaign to stir awareness of the westernmost tip of the state.[55] It was, he claimed, the "New England of the South," and he compared its plentiful soil and mineral resources and salubrious climate most favorably to its northern counterpart. Most important to Thomas was his area's geographic advantage as "the centre of the Southern country." Located midway between the Atlantic Coast and the Mississippi River, and between Cincinnati and Louisville to the northwest and Charleston and Savannah to the southeast, the section would, within six years, he predicted, "be connected with every slaveholding State in the Union." Finally, he stressed the particular economic advantage of the southwestern route: it would provide the state with access to the extraordinary output of Ducktown's copper mines, which currently were not served by railroad connections.[56]

Eventually Thomas won his case (due in no small part to his position as chairman of the state Public Works Board), and the decision was made to continue the line due west from Asheville to Ducktown, with a secondary extension also granted along the French Broad route. But the General Assembly ratified this measure only in February 1861; two months later the war intervened and delayed the project's completion for over twenty years.[57]

Well before then, delays on the first section of the line and the restrictions imposed by the section clause had made westerners increasingly impatient with the project and disgusted with the state government. With only twenty miles of track laid after two and a half years of work, progress on the line from Salisbury proved so slow that residents of Asheville and those beyond worried that further delays might jeopardize the entire scheme. They realized that if their own allotted sections had to wait for the completion and operation not only of the first section to Morganton, but of the second to the Swannanoa tunnel as well, the chances of the railroad's ever crossing the Blue Ridge within their lifetimes were slim. Even if the line was ever completed, some feared that the completion would come too late for it to compete successfully with lines already finished or likely to be established soon. Yancey County citizens issued a formal protest which reflected the feelings of many others in the area:

> as citizens of the mountain section, we do most solomnly protest against the Legislation which has left us only deprived of the benefits, or the reasonable speedy prospect of the benefits, which all others have thus derived . . . and against the unwise, narrow and short sighted policy which by our delay, permitting ourselves to be forestalled by rival lines of other States, on the North and upon the South, have put at extreme hazard the eventual prosperity of our own works, when completed.[58]

As early as 1857 a strong resentment toward the state's cautious policy had developed. A "citizen of Buncombe" urged that the people of the west take drastic action regarding the railroad. He advocated secession from North Carolina and annexation to South Carolina. "If we can't get in there, try Georgia next, and then Tennessee. . . . It would be decidedly better," he explained, "for the counties west of the Blue Ridge to be attached to either of those states. If we belonged to any one of them we would have a railroad right off."[59] One of Asheville's leading citizens, Montreville Patton, voiced the same impatient defiance. "I despair of ever having any aid for our Rail Road," he wrote in 1859. "The section feature is too slow for men of my age. I do not like to pay taxes all my life and have no benefits from the Rail Road. I am for cutting loose from the Old North State and going to S. Carolina, and if we cannot get aid—I am for Rebellion—and let the balance of the State know, that we will not always submit to taxes without any equivalent."[60]

Less drastic, but with the same sense of urgency, an *Asheville News* editorial urged western North Carolinians not to despair of the state's delays in getting the railroad to their region, but rather to assert their independence through a boycott of the rest of the state:

> We have the means of independence. We have the elements of social pros-
> perity and individual wealth. Let us put a proper value upon our advan-
> tages, and give all the world to understand that we can live without their
> assistance.
>   To this end keep your money at home. Read home papers, patronize
> home schools—employ home mechanics, and as far as possible eat, drink
> and wear what is manufactured in the mountains of North Carolina, and
> the day is not distant when Mohamet will come to the mountain, seeing the
> mountain is disinclined to go to Mohamet. . . . Our people are waking up,
> and having grown tired of the condition of colonial vassalage, are deter-
> mined to take care of themselves. They can improve their farms without
> State Aid, thank God. They can adorn their homes, educate their children,
> fear God, hate the Devil, and loath two-faced demogogues, all without a
> charter from the Legislature! And we are glad of it.[61]

The obvious solution to the problem and the one means of abating this frustrated defiance was, of course, to repeal the section clause of the western railroad's charter. James C. Turner, the project's chief engineer, did proceed with the survey of the second section west of Morganton and claimed to have the manpower and resources to begin grading it if the restriction were lifted. The company's president, Robert Pearson, who favored the French Broad route, felt that work should begin at the far end of the line, at Paint Rock on the Tennessee border, and work backwards.[62] Despite the fact that only $1.2 million of the $4 million appropriated for the line had yet been spent, however, a majority of the legislators in Raleigh showed little inclination to alter the original charter, claiming that to allow work on more than one section at a time would place too great a strain on the state budget.

Once again, a gubernatorial race became, for the western section, a forum on this issue alone. Of the 1858 campaign, Augustus S. Merrimon, an Asheville judge, stated, "The election here will turn solely upon Internal Improvements."[63] Once again the Democrats were able to shape the issue to their advantage. Both candidates, Democrat John W. Ellis of Rowan County and Whig (or Opposition) Duncan K. McRae of New Bern, favored repealing the section clause. But sectional biases seem to have overridden what few traces of traditional party ideology remained, as McRae, the easterner, firmly refused to support additional appropriations, making western native Ellis's conditional approval of extra funding the clear preference of western Carolinians. Judge Merrimon, a confirmed Whig, bemoaned McRae's stand, which he called "ruinous in the extreme." "All our people," he wrote, "believe that Judge Ellis is devotedly in favor of extending the present system of Rail Roads West to the Tenn. line . . . the result will be that he will get almost the whole Western vote." He even confessed that "with the present lights before me, I would vote for Ellis if I had to vote for either of the Candidates." His prediction was a sound one, as Ellis carried Buncombe and eight more of the mountain counties.[64]

This time, a supportive governor alone was not enough to win the West's case. Because it was far more a sectional than a partisan issue, Ellis, unlike his predecessor, was unable to rally to the cause his fellow Democrats in the East. A bill to remove the section restrictions on the Western North Carolina Railroad, introduced in the legislature early in 1859, was quickly defeated by large majorities of fiscal conservatives in both house and senate. Mountain residents had been optimistic about its passage and were shocked at what they deemed a blatant display of sectional discrimination.[65] Many viewed the defeat as the final insult in a long tradition of neglect and insensitivity to their needs by the state government. The *Asheville News* reflected their bitterness in an openly defiant editorial which stated that the legislature had adjourned "followed by the curses of an oppressed, downtrodden, betrayed and plundered people. The people of the West have got nothing." The rhetoric of republicanism again blared forth as the paper warned:

> An act not more tyrannical led to the Revolutionary war, and this will lead to a peaceful revolution, quite as potent in remedying the evil. . . . We have no doubt the people of the West will readily embrace this tender of a dissolution of every tie that binds us together as one people, and will henceforth regard themselves as having neither part nor lot in the internal improvement system of North Carolina. . . . And we predict the people of the French Broad Valley will never again ask for a connection with any North Carolina Road.

The editor concluded by reminding readers of their out-of-state options: "We must be content to remain in our present condition, or revive and go to work under our Cross Charter. Surely the people of Spartanburg, Columbia and Charleston will lend a helping hand."[66]

That was something of an understatement, since South Carolinians had been eager to undertake their Greenville and French Broad Railroad, the so-called "Cross Charter," which would run through Henderson, Buncombe, and Madison counties, crossing at right angles the Western North Carolina Railroad's extension westward from Asheville, if the latter took that route. As long as the chances of their own state's railroad following that course had been good, local businessmen had been reluctant to encourage the South Carolina company. Now, however, citizens of all three counties quickly organized public meetings to formalize their rejection of the state project and to pursue the Greenville and French Broad option. Nicholas W. Woodfin told fellow Asheville residents that he hoped "no citizen of Buncombe would ever pay a single dollar toward the extension of the Western N.C.R.R."[67] Ashevillians obliged him by voting overwhelmingly to buy $125,000 of stock in the South Carolina company, and by the end of the summer, citizens in their neighboring counties had also purchased stock.[68]

The act of defiance disturbed eastern leaders, who saw this continued out-of-state preemption of highland commerce as defeating the purpose of the expensive western line they were providing to the region. To discourage the competing projects in the mountains, government leaders proposed that the mountain counties be allowed to buy stock only in the Western North Carolina Railroad. This prospect was particularly galling to westerners, for, as the *Asheville News* expressed it, "Our people have uncomplainingly assisted in paying for every railroad in the State, and now not only are we denied assistance, but positively forbidden to build a road with our own money!!"[69] Yancey County Democrats drew up a resolution in which they declared, "We hold it as to be a self evident truth, that every people have a right to construct their own improvements with their own means; the violation of such right is not only a fundamental error, unworthy of our enlightened age, but is gross usurpation and oppression towards those who are its victims." By preventing their participation in the Greenville and French Broad Rail Road Company through "restrictions calculated to destroy an enterprise of such vital importance to so many citizens," the state legislature was committing "a piece of capricious and short sighted oppression at which we are all ashamed and indignant."[70]

To some, John Pool, who became the Whig gubernatorial candidate in February 1860, was the main culprit. Soon after Pool's nomination, Woodfin predicted that his chances of support in the mountains would be slim, since "he of all others . . . sought to further oppress our people in relationship to the amendment of our cross charter, even after we had failed in the commons to repeal the most iniquitous and oppressive section restriction of our charter . . . he should be taught that even small sections have some influence if they have no rights." He expressed regret that his party had not nominated a more liberal advocate of internal improvements than Pool, particularly one who would "allow the poor the privilege of making their own roads to their own natural markets with their own money."[71] But as Ellis sought reelection against Pool, western resentment at the governor's failure to help the region on the railroad issue was still strong. That plus the predominance of the ad valorem issue combined to split mountain votes evenly between the two candidates. Although Ellis won reelection by a narrow margin statewide, he barely lost the mountain counties with 49.2 percent of the vote and seven counties, compared to Pool's 50.8 percent and eight counties.[72]

Thus an era that had begun with high hopes for linking North Carolina's mountains with the rest of the state and which had seen some very promising developments toward that goal ended with a resurgence of sectional antagonism as strong, at least among westerners, as it had ever been. Progress had been made on the railroad—it was within six miles of Morganton when the war broke out—and much more progress was expected soon, since no one yet foresaw the conflict that would disrupt and long delay further construction.[73]

On the other hand, many western Carolinians resented the fact that after a decade of struggle over this much anticipated railroad line in 1861, it was still east of the region's easternmost town. They continued to express a sense of having been both betrayed and oppressed by their state government. The apparent unanimity with which they had embraced the campaign for internal improvements demonstrated even more than did the ad valorem or free suffrage issues the degree to which regional concerns overrode partisan loyalties. Likewise, the emotionalism displayed in their anticipation of, and later their frustration over, governmental efforts regarding transportation development reflects more clearly than any other facet of antebellum politics the strong commercial orientation of mountain residents. This orientation was a central factor in their political conditioning as a regional minority; the setbacks to which they were so often subjected provided ample confirmation of the republican fears of the governmental abuses to which such a minority was vulnerable. By 1860, their confidence in the commitment of Raleigh to the western counties shaken, highlanders turned their sights both inward on themselves and outward on their out-of-state neighbors, as the keys to the continued economic development they sought so eagerly.

Chapter 8

Mountaineers as Southerners:

"Those transmontane fellows
cling to Clingman"

The intrastate struggles over suffrage, taxation, and internal improvements, fought simultaneously over the last antebellum decade, did much to make western Carolinians conscious of themselves as part of a distinctive section of North Carolina, with priorities, goals, and needs unlike those of other parts of the state. But such consciousness did not entail provincialism, insulation, or isolation from the world around them. As the preceding chapters have indicated, strong trade links with neighboring states, particularly South Carolina, Georgia, and Tennessee, compensated for and even contributed to Carolina highlanders' alienation from the eastern half of their own state. Thus, at the same time that their identities as westerners were coming into sharper focus, so too were their identities as southerners. Their sectional battles with fellow North Carolinians coincided with different sectional battles being played out on a much larger stage, and mountain residents became involved as fully in the latter as they were in the former. Their greater political sensitivity to southern interests resulted not only from their increasing commercial dependence on plantation markets to their south; it also reflected the effects of an extraordinary one-man campaign waged by their congressman, Thomas L. Clingman, to raise the consciousness of his constituents. He worked hard at, and to a large degree succeeded in, making them see themselves as victims, not only of more dominant eastern forces in Raleigh but also of more dominant northern forces in Washington.

A district's congressman was the most direct link between its citizens and the federal government. Choosing one among two or more [177] local people to participate in the national decision-making process in Washington gave voters their most clearcut forum on national issues affecting them and their region. Nowhere was this more true than in western North Carolina, where congressional races provided a thorough, constant gauge of the North-South sectional attitudes of its citizens. They did so in part because these races were neither tied as closely to party affiliation as were presidential contests in the area nor encumbered as heavily by local issues as were elections for state office. Moreover, throughout the late antebellum era, Clingman, the perpetual candidate, and his opponents kept the issues that divided North and South at the forefront of every congressional race, making them the primary subjects on which mountain voters had to base their ballot-box decisions.

Born in Huntersville in Surry County in 1812, Thomas Lanier Clingman was educated in the Iredell County public schools and at the University of North Carolina. He studied law under future governor William A. Graham in Hillsborough and returned home to open a law practice in 1834. He was elected to the state legislature the next year, but his defeat in the following election and his less than successful law practice led him to move west to Asheville, whose rapid growth and commercial potential he felt offered wider scope for his political aspirations. In 1841, after another term in the General Assembly, Clingman challenged Congressman James Graham of Rutherfordton (the brother of his former law teacher) for the seat from North Carolina's First (later Eighth) Congressional District, which then encompassed all but two of the mountain counties.[1] Both candidates were Whigs, and the strength of the party in the region was such that, although they opposed each other throughout the 1840s, they never faced a Democratic opponent. Losing in 1841, Clingman tried again and won by a narrow margin in 1843. Two years later, though, Graham defeated him. Reelected in 1847, Clingman was returned to Washington by his mountain constituents throughout the next decade, until in 1858 he was appointed to the United States Senate, where he served until the outbreak of the Civil War. Despite his gradual and controversial shift from the Whig to the Democratic party in the midst of his congressional career, no other North Carolina congressman during that period served as long as Clingman.[2]

Clingman's energies and interests seemed boundless. His commitment to the North Carolina mountains extended far beyond his political hold on the region. Although he never became more than an amateur in training or profession, his scientific interest in and studies of the region absorbed him as fully as politics. His research and writings embraced fields as diverse as astronomy, physics, botany, meteorology, and Darwinian evolution. His greatest interest was in geological and topographical studies of the Appalachian Mountains. As one of the most avid of the region's many commercial boosters, both before and long after the Civil War, Clingman was tireless in his promotion of the mineral resources, livestock productivity, and agricultural benefits of western North Carolina. Professor Elisha Mitchell once wrote that his illustrious former student "has long taken a deep interest in every thing connected with the mountain region" and "is well acquainted with the larger part of it." Mitchell even went so far as to describe Clingman as "my superior in all matters of science."[3]

As admirable as were his scientific enthusiasm and his commitment to the region, Clingman also exhibited a volatile belligerence that he vented as much in self-promotion as in sectional loyalty. His close friendship with Mitchell quickly deteriorated into a bitter battle of egos when each claimed to have been the first to recognize, climb, and measure the area's highest peak.[4] In politics such aggression ran rampant. As we shall see, Clingman was prone to interpret partisan challenges by both Whigs and Democrats or regional affronts, western and southern, as personal slights, to which he was quick to respond with angry diatribes and even, on occasion, violent conflict with his antagonists.[5]

Clingman's self-assertiveness, his impassioned and accomplished oratory, and his consistent popularity among his fellow highlanders made him a particularly visible and influential participant in the sectional battles of the 1850s. His role in those struggles tells us much not only about his own views on slavery and the South, but also about those of the constituents to whom and for whom he spoke, as they moved together toward the breaking point of 1861.

It is ironic that Clingman, who became one of the most ardent pro-slavery spokesmen in Congress throughout the 1850s, never owned a slave himself and represented a district with one of the smallest slave populations in the South. Most treatments of Clingman's career pass over the implications of this discrepancy without examining the values or attitudes of the voters on whom that career was so vitally dependent.[6] These accounts readily assume that because so few of those in his district owned slaves, they either opposed or were indifferent to

Figure 20. Thomas L. Clingman. North Carolina Division of Archives and History.

his outspoken defense of slavery and southern rights. Even those scholars who acknowledge this presumed discrepancy between the mountain congressman and those he represented reason that "the most ultra-Southern of the North Carolina delegation in Congress" continued to be reelected not because of that role but in spite of it. According to Thomas E. Jeffrey, it was "his personal popularity and his vocal support for 'western rights' and state reform" that kept mountain residents from holding his southern rights rhetoric against him.[7]

As for why Clingman adopted an increasingly impassioned proslavery stance, the most common explanation is his ambition to move from the House to the Senate. According to this reasoning, Clingman, in order to broaden his political appeal and win election by the state legislature to a senate seat, aimed his message at the influential planters of the eastern half of the state and sought to downplay it in his own section. This strategy finally paid off in 1858, when he was appointed to fill the unexpired term of Sen. Asa Biggs and was reelected on his own in 1860.[8]

While these arguments are factually based, since Clingman did aspire to become a senator, they overlook or at least vastly underestimate the all-important factor of the congressman's relationship with his constituents. Whatever his ultimate political goals, Clingman depended heavily on the support of his own mountain district, without which he could never expect to win statewide support. Nor is it reasonable to conclude that western North Carolinians would have made him the state's longest-serving member of the House of Representatives had they disapproved of the prosouthern, proslavery stand that became so central to his political platform. To say that his personality and support of western issues were enough to satisfy them, despite his primary identification with a cause that was unpopular in his district, or that he was able to, or even tried to, obscure the true nature of this cause that had gained him national prominence is to suggest that his constituents were practically blind and deaf.

An examination of Clingman's electoral fortunes within the state's First Congressional District not only reveals that the majority of mountain residents did support their congressman's increasingly "ultra-southern" stand, but also shows that he was well aware of their attitudes on these issues before he adopted them as his own. Indeed, his own first term in Congress and his subsequent defeat taught him just how strong the southern identity and sectional loyalty of mountain voters were.

During his first term in Congress, from 1843 through 1845, Clingman seemed determined to establish himself as a loyal nationalist Whig and to downplay sectional issues which threatened party unity. But his efforts failed to placate southern Whigs, including his own constituents. On 5 January 1844, in his first speech before the House, he drew widespread attention as the one southerner of either party to support the repeal of the "gag rule" that prevented abolitionist petitions from being introduced in Congress. As he explained from the House floor, his objection to the rule was that it violated the constitutional right of petition, and in any case such petitions posed no threat to slavery, since Congress would certainly reject or ignore them. He argued that the rule hurt rather than helped the southern cause because it provoked abolitionist agitation and exacerbated sectional tensions that otherwise would long since have been reduced. "Hence ill-feeling grows out of it both at the South and in the North . . . and all arising from this foolish struggle about petitions."[9]

Despite the logic of his argument and his obvious concern for the rule's detrimental effect on southern interests, southerners of both parties immediately subjected Clingman to a barrage of attacks and accused him of befriending the North and betraying the South. Southern Whigs were particularly offended. According to Clingman, they were "especially vehement in their denunciation of me," and in Congress "set speeches have been made against me daily for two months." But in defending himself, he attempted to proclaim his party loyalty by lashing out recklessly at the Democrats. He accused their most extreme spokesman of southern rights, John C. Calhoun, of using such issues as an attempt "coolly and deliberately to break up the Union and substitute a Southern confederacy." When the gag rule was overturned, Clingman was as ready to blame his Democratic critics as they were to blame him. Although southern Democrats had supported the rule and made dire predictions that its repeal "would be a virtual dissolution of the Union," Clingman claimed that they had tried harder to cast blame for its defeat than to save it:

> There all of these gentlemen sat, quiet and mute . . . and saw, with much seeming unconcern their favorite rule killed off by a large majority. There was no burst of indignation; no exclamation to the South, 'Samson, the Philistine be upon thee!' . . . Were they asleep? No, no, sire; they were

awake, but they were false watchmen of the South—traitor sentinels! I have a right so to call them; for, in denouncing me at the last session, some of them declared that any man who did not sustain the rule by all proper means was a renegade and a traitor to the Southern States.[10]

This speech actually offended more southerners than had the original speech Clingman was attempting to explain. William L. Yancey of Alabama, one of Congress's most prominent "fire-eaters," called these comments "an insult to us in our defeat . . . which could only have found prompting in the heart of one who had given a stab to the institutions of his own land, and wears the garb of the enemy." This accusation eventually resulted in a duel between the two men, one which Yancey provoked under pressure from other southern Democrats, who wanted him, according to Clingman, to "assail me violently."[11]

Such verbal and physical attacks on some of the South's most prominent defenders did little to convince Clingman's constituents that he did indeed have the best interests of his section at heart. Their suspicions were confirmed when he again supported a nationalist Whig position over a more popular southern stand. Unlike most of his fellow southerners, he opposed all of the various proposals for the annexation of Texas in 1844 because of its divisive sectional effects and because Henry Clay, whom Clingman greatly admired, opposed it.[12] When warned that his positions might prove unpopular among those who had sent him to Congress, Clingman expressed unabashed confidence that his consistent party loyalty on these issues would prove no impediment to his reelection in 1845 in a district as solidly Whig as his was. "My district is unapproachable," he said. "She stands alone in her strength, and dreads no contact with the Democracy . . . She would gladly embrace in either arm the two strongest Democratic districts in the state; and they would fall under that grasp as did the columns of the Philistine edifice before the strength of Sampson [sic]." Clingman predicted that Henry Clay too could count on that strength in the upcoming 1844 presidential contest: "He will find that the Whiggism of that district has lost none of its spirit since 1840, but that it exists in increased strength and energy, and when November comes, the western reserve will send down from her mountains such a majority for Harry of the West as will sweep unresisted over the old North State."[13] Clingman's confidence in Clay's popularity in the North Carolina mountains was justified. Although he lost the election to Polk,

Clay carried every western North Carolina county, with two of the most populous counties delivering well over 80 percent of their votes to him.[14]

This demonstration of party loyalty by his constituents must have been reassuring to Clingman, who fully expected to be its beneficiary the following August, when the same voters would duly reward him for his staunch adherence to party doctrine. But while party affiliations at that point may still have overshadowed southern sectional interests in his district, his stands proved too dissonant with his constituents' southern identities to withstand the challenge of another Whig who was more clearly aligned with the South.

Until less than a month before the congressional election of 1845, it looked as if Clingman would be unopposed. Then his regular rival for the seat, James Graham, entered the race, sensing that Clingman's seemingly antislavery positions in Congress and his duel with one of the most prominent prosouthern spokesman in Congress made him particularly vulnerable among First District voters. There was, Graham reported to his brother the governor, "a deep and abiding dissatisfaction among the people with regard to Clingman's course." He was urged to run by his "old Whig friends," who had never voted for Clingman before and "since his voting with the North against the South [said] they never would."[15] Emphasizing in his campaign Clingman's opposition to the annexation of Texas and to the ban on abolition petitions, Graham stressed his own support for both. In portraying his opponent as an abolitionist and a traitor to southern interests, Graham defined the issues so that the choice before mountain voters became, for the first time, one in which North-South sectionalism preempted East-West sectionalism; they had to decide which candidate would best represent the South as a whole rather than merely western North Carolina. Graham was able to raise enough doubts about Clingman's loyalties to defeat him in what most observers considered a major upset, though he won with only 54 percent of the vote. Reporting the defeat of one of their party's most outspoken critics, the Democratic *Raleigh Standard* happily proclaimed that it was "an important triumph for the friends of the South" and that North Carolina, as always, had defeated "the aider and abettor of the Abolitionists and spurned him from her service."[16]

His defeat was a rude awakening for Clingman. It taught him an important lesson about his mountain constituency, one that would instigate one of the most complete political transformations ever witnessed in North Carolina politics. The results of that 1845 campaign showed that, despite the strength of its Whig support, Clingman's district shared with the rest of the state and the rest of the South loyalties that were even stronger than party ties. The subsequent course of his own career would demonstrate that the sectional identities of western Carolinians as southerners ran far deeper than their partisan identities as Whigs.

Clingman's constituents gave him a second chance to prove himself in 1847, when he once again challenged Graham for the congressional seat they had alternately occupied. Graham, however, withdrew from the race when the entry of other Whigs threatened to allow a Democrat to defeat them all.[17] In the end, Clingman's only opposition was fellow Whig John G. Bynum of Rutherford County. By emphasizing his precongressional record as a champion of western interests, rather than his nationalist record in Congress, Clingman easily defeated Bynum with 57 percent of the vote, carrying every county except Bynum's own and its adjacent piedmont county, Cleveland.[18]

Once back in office, Clingman soon seized the opportunity to demonstrate what he had learned from his defeat two years earlier. Though still eager to avoid sectional divisiveness and still on the defensive concerning his opposition to the gag rule, he also began to adopt a more traditional, more acceptable southern Whig stance. All of these themes were embodied in his long first speech in the new Congress on 22 December 1847. In it he spoke out against the Wilmot Proviso, which would have banned slavery from any territory acquired from Mexico. While attacking the Democratic party, Clingman continued to focus on John C. Calhoun, depicting him as the major source of North-South tensions. "Being ambitious of popularity and influence," Clingman said of the South Carolina senator, "he sought to restore himself to the confidence of the South in the first place, and seized upon the slave question as the means to effect that end."[19] Ironically, that statement aptly delineates Clingman's own strategy as he took the first step in a transformation that would allow him to rival both Yancey and Calhoun as the most proslavery and prosouthern of antebellum congressmen.

Much of Clingman's speech was merely a defense of the "peculiar institution" and an attack on northern abolitionists. He reasoned that while the South would have been better off with an all-white populace than with a "mixed race," because of the presence of blacks who could not be eliminated, slavery was the only means to ensure white security and care for blacks. "The physical wants of the slaves are sure to be provided for," he said, "because he can never be owned by a pauper." Phrases that he had often used specifically to describe the favorable conditions of slavery in the mountains he now applied more broadly, noting that "the negro race in the Southern States, when considered with reference to their physical comforts, industry and moral qualities, are in advance of the same race either in Africa or in the Northern States." He increased his attacks on abolitionists by calling their schemes "absurd and visionary" and "reckless of their consequences to the well-being of society."[20]

Southerners of both parties opposed the Wilmot Proviso, and split only on whether it was unconstitutional and beyond congressional authority, as the Democrats maintained, or merely an unjust and unwise precedent, as Whigs suggested. In addressing this issue, Clingman embarked on a long and complex argument in which he attempted to find a middle ground between the two. Like most Whigs, he affirmed Congress's right to exert "general legislative powers over the territories." But he reasoned that any use of that authority which would give "greater advantages to the people of one section than to those of the other would be unjust and unconstitutional."[22] Here Clingman even veered from his own party's stand to embrace the Democrats' argument about constitutionality. He flatly stated that "Congress has no authority to object to the admission of any State because she tolerates slavery."[23]

This speech gave the first hint of the more open defiance Clingman would soon adopt regarding the South's future role in the Union. Though much of his message had been conciliatory, he ended his speech by saying that he would support the Constitution "as long as any amount of human exertion can uphold it," but that the passage of the Wilmot Proviso would be a violation of its principles and might force the South to more drastic action: "When an organic change is made in that Constitution—a change which is to degrade those who have sent me to represent them here—then, sir, at whatever cost of feeling or of personal hazard, I will stand by the white race, the freemen of the South. Should we be forced away, we will control as we best can the inferior race which Providence has placed under our charge." Clingman stressed the disastrous consequences of a separation of

South and North, but he warned that such a calamity might be a heavier burden for the latter: "Though the slave States are not equal to the free in population and wealth, yet the strength they have is amply sufficient for purposes of defence, either as against the North or against foreign nations." Citing the weakness of Mexico in comparison with Canada's strong British backing, he went on to point out that the South's chances of "extending its dominions" were better than those of the North. Likewise, the South could develop the commercial and manufacturing resources it presently lacked by excluding northern competition through tariffs, navigation laws, and control of the Mississippi and even the Ohio rivers.[24]

The belligerence of such a statement in 1847 was extraordinary, particularly coming from a man who represented far fewer slaveholders than did most of his southern colleagues and whose nationalistic and conciliatory sentiments had led to accusations of northern and even abolitionist sympathies just two years before. Still, Clingman's transformation, though well under way, was by no means complete. His attacks on Democrats such as President Polk and Senator Calhoun indicated that his anti-Democratic partisanship was as firmly entrenched as ever.[25] His ardent support of the proposed Clayton Compromise in 1848 (which would have kept New Mexico and California from passing any laws regarding slavery until the Supreme Court had ruled on its legality in the territories) and of the Walker Amendment later that year, even though their advantages to the South were questionable, indicates that Clingman was still genuinely interested in avoiding sectional strife and was willing to make some regional concessions in order to do so.[26]

On the basis of this speech of 22 December 1847, it seems safe to conclude that Clingman had spent his two years out of office rethinking his role in relation to the South and to his mountain constituents. Moreover, he had decided that his full support of the former was necessary to assure him of the full support of the latter. Although he himself admitted in retrospect that his efforts on behalf of the South and in defense of slavery resulted from "information I obtained during my first term in Congress," it was his failure to win a second consecutive term that had proved even more significant in redirecting his course.[27]

During the next year Clingman's alienation from his fellow Whigs began in earnest. A tour through the North made him painfully aware of the strength of antislavery sentiment there, and it became apparent to him that the northern wing of the party was firmly committed to the Wilmot Proviso and the abolition of slavery in the District of Columbia. At the end of 1848, he repeated his conviction, this time with no qualification, that the proviso or any other effort to exclude slavery from the territories was "as gross a violation of the constitution as the government could commit, a violation of such a character as would justify the Southern States in resisting its execution by all means in their power." His realization that loyalty to the Whig party would be increasingly difficult to reconcile with a strong defense of slavery led Clingman to cast his fate with the latter. He correctly guessed that, despite Whiggery's solidity in his district, his support among mountain voters would remain just as strong if he took a pro-South, proslavery stand, regardless of his party affiliation. This realization inevitably led Clingman to make peace with Calhoun, whom Clingman admitted he had attacked unfairly. When he called Calhoun a "friend of the Union" for his support of the Clayton Compromise, Clingman moved one step closer to the Democratic party himself.[28]

Clingman may well have been courting state Democratic support in his bid for the senate seat to be filled by the state legislature late in 1848, but his statements then were not at all inconsistent with the course he had steered since his reelection to Congress a year earlier. He enjoyed the almost unanimous support of the legislature's Democrats, but sectional divisiveness among its Whigs led him finally to concede the election to incumbent George E. Badger of Raleigh, generally acknowledged to be the head of the state's Whig organization. That members of his own party, rather than the Democrats, denied him his goal of moving over to the upper house of Congress came as a bitter blow to Clingman, and caused a mutual disaffection between him and the state's Whig leadership that never healed. Both parties were fully aware of the congressman's hold over the mountain district, and Democrat William W. Holden predicted that the Whigs would downplay their increasing differences with Clingman rather than risk offending his constituents, whose support was so vital to the party's strength in the state. They would not attack Clingman publicly, Holden wrote, "for they know their assaults upon him would bring 'thunder from the mountains' and recoil upon their heads."[29] Clingman, however, was fully ready to exploit his defeat among his fellow western Carolinians. He equated the legislature's rejection of him with a rejection of the section for which he spoke. The so-called "central managers" of the party were dependent on the support of the "Western reserve" but rarely rewarded it for that support. He called on his constituents to recognize the offense just committed against them by the General Assembly in reelecting Badger. At the same time, Clingman warned the state government, and particularly the Whig caucus controlling it, that slighting him was an offense not to be taken lightly by his section:

> If men of worth and talent over the State generally are to be proscribed because of their location . . . and the most inefficient and unpopular men are to be pushed up from time to time into high places merely because they are their favorites, then they must expect to meet with resistance. They will find arrayed against them some whose aid they have needed in times gone by, men who are not to be put down without much effort, men who are willing long to struggle against tyranny.[30]

Although statements such as these and those he was making in Congress made him many enemies among Whigs across the state, Clingman's support within his own district was stronger than ever. His position seemed so impregnable in the summer of 1849 that no one challenged him in his August reelection campaign. Thus he returned to Congress confident that the vast majority of mountain voters approved of his role as a states' rights advocate, even though it was, by then, widely recognized that he was "with the Democrats on the slavery question."[31]

Bolstered by this support, Clingman moved steadily toward a more aggressive stance built on fears of northern encroachment on southern rights. In November, he wrote to one of the Senate's extremist Democrats, Henry S. Foote of Mississippi, and sent the letter to the *National Intelligencer* for publication, in order to warn southerners of "the danger that was impending" from the increased likelihood that the Wilmot Proviso would be passed. In his letter, he stated that any attempt by Congress to exclude slavery from the territories would invalidate the authority of the United States government and that the southern states should resist "this utter disregard of plain constitutional guarantees." Although he did not yet openly advocate secession, he implied none too subtly that their degree of resistance "should be commensurate with the violence of the attack." He expressed his confidence that, with the possible exception of Kentucky, the entire South would stand with even more unanimity "in the struggle for the preservation of the rights and liberties of the white race" than did "the old thirteen slave States, when they decided to resist British aggression."[32]

This correspondence was a clear indication that Clingman was fast approaching the extremist prosouthern position. As tensions in the new Congress mounted over the question of the status of California and New Mexico, states' rights sentiment became more vocal in North Carolina, and Clingman was encouraged to carry the implications of his recent sentiments on to their logical conclusion.[33] On 22 January 1850, he gave a speech in Congress, entitled "In Defense of the South Against the Aggressive Movement of the North," that placed him firmly and irrevocably in the "ultra" camp. He recounted his earlier support for conciliatory measures to ease tensions between North and South, and even reminded Congress of his support for the gag rule's repeal six years earlier. The failure of these efforts, due largely to the North's inflexibility, had convinced him that the South must no longer follow a policy of mere appeasement. Still insisting that his region would "acquiesce in any reasonable settlement," he complained that its efforts to obtain justice or to be left alone were "met by the senseless and insane cry of 'Union, union!' " "I am disgusted with it," he declared. If, under the constitution, "gross injustice is done, insurrections incited, and the citizens of part of the States politically enslaved, then the Union ought not to stand, as an instrument of wrong and oppression." He warned that recent events were rapidly weakening southerners' once-strong attachments to the Union, and that "many of our people, regarding a dissolution of the Union as the inevitable result of this aggression, have looked forward to the consequence of such a state of things." In a rousing conclusion, Clingman declared defiantly:

> Gentlemen may call this treason—high treason—the highest treason ever known. But their words are idle. We shall defeat their movement against us. . . . If we repel the wave of aggression now, we shall have peace. The Abolitionists defeated before the country on the main issue, will not have the power to molest us. . . . Gentlemen of the North, . . . should circumstances divide us, I wish that you may prosper. From all my knowledge of the elements of your society, I have doubts. That we shall . . . take care of ourselves, I have no fears. In conclusion, I have to say, do us justice and we continue to stand with you; attempt to trample on us, and we separate.[34]

With this speech, one of the most blatantly secessionist yet made in

Congress, Clingman established himself as North Carolina's most ultrasouthern representative in Washington.[35] His popularity among
Democrats throughout North Carolina and the South soared, just as
many Whigs became increasingly alarmed by his reckless threats and
skeptical of his continued identification with their party. While on a
trip to Baltimore, a Whig planter from the far eastern part of the state
met Clingman and reported that "the celebrated Mr. Clingman . . .
seemed to be full to overflowing of himself, talking as if he were Sampson [sic] who would pull down by his individual strength the pillars
that support the Union."[36]

Though his secessionist tendencies and his weakening Whig ties
alienated some within his own district, Clingman was sensitive to the
attitudes of his constituents and had laid out his defense of a southern
nation in terms with which they could identify. As the various
speeches just cited clearly indicate, his attacks on both antisouthern or
antiwestern factions were unrelenting in evoking republican images of
government tyranny wreaking havoc with minority interests.

But equally significant were his appeals to his constituents' economic sensibilities. In arguing that the South would prosper outside
the Union, Clingman made no mention of the plantation system, slavery, or the cotton economy. Rather he stressed those factors particularly beneficial to the financial state of western Carolinians. As
examples of the burdens that protective tariffs had imposed on the
South, he cited the high prices his constituents had to pay for iron,
whether it was manufactured in Pennsylvania or Great Britain. Becom-
ing a separate nation would not only eliminate such inequities but also
provide the South with a much-needed inducement to develop its
commercial interests and to improve the links between southern markets. As an example of the benefits of the internalization of southern
commerce, Clingman noted that Kentucky and Tennessee livestock,
much of which moved through North Carolina's mountains, would no
longer have to compete with that of Ohio and other northwestern
states for the plantation markets.[37]

Clingman's theme, then, differed from the more reactionary and
purely defensive rhetoric of other secessionists. He stressed the idea of
creating a "new" South while protecting the "old," by developing both
untapped natural resources and commercial prospects, unhindered
by northern domination and restrictions.[38] These were goals which,
regardless of their feelings on disunion, entrepreneurially-oriented

mountain residents would recognize as desirable. In a speech before Congress, Clingman even pointedly linked his constituents with the mainstream of southern thought. "I thank God," he said, "that there is no one in my district that I think so meanly of, as to believe that he would not readily come into whatever movement might be necessary for the protection of our rights and liberty." He warned those northerners who hoped that areas like his own would be divided on this matter "that we shall not have half as many traitors to hang as we did Tories in the Revolution."[39]

On the racial issue too, Clingman aimed much of his message at the highlanders he represented, the majority of whom were small, nonslaveholding farmers. Though he never shied away from an explicit defense of slavery, he put more emphasis on the threat to the South as a whole if slavery were not allowed to expand into new territory. If the South did not resist northern legislative efforts to restrict such expansion, he warned of demographic consequences that were as alarming to western North Carolinians as to other southerners:

> Slavery is to be kept, they say, where it is now; and we are to be surrounded with free States. These States not only prohibit the introduction of slaves, but also of free negroes, into their borders. Of course the whole negro population is to be hereafter confined to the territory of the present fifteen slave States. That population in twenty-five years will amount to seven or eight millions, and in fifty years to fifteen millions. However dense the population might become, the negroes will not be gotten away, but the wealthier portion of the white population (I mean such as were able to emigrate) would leave the territory. The condition of the South would, for a time, be that of Ireland; and soon, by the destruction of the remnants of the white population, become that of St. Domingo.[40]

A week after Clingman's speech, on 29 January 1850, Henry Clay introduced his compromise proposals in the Senate. Clingman opposed the compromise formula as requiring too many concessions from the South. His region would receive little except stricter enforcement of the Fugitive Slave Act, which, he reasoned, the North was already legally obligated to provide. He urged his fellow southern congressman to hold out for a more equitable plan and argued that their approval of Clay's proposal would be yet another act of "slavish submission" to the North.[41]

The issue that carried most weight at home was California's status as a free or slave state. The gold rush of 1849 had enticed a number of slaveholders from western North Carolina to cross the continent with their slaves, but the risk of forfeiting their legal ownership there probably deterred many others from taking advantage of the opportunities available. Clingman blamed these uncertainities on northern abolitionists. "But for the anti-slavery agitation," he claimed, "our Southern slaveholders would have carried their negroes into the mines of California in such numbers, that I have no doubt but that the majority there would have made it a slaveholding State. We have been deprived of all chance of this by the Northern movements . . ." This failure to insure the security of their property amounted to a "farce," he said, in that it, in effect, "excluded a whole class of our citizens from the territory."[42] Although he was willing to let California remain free, provided that slavery be allowed east of it below the Fortieth Parallel, Clingman was also receptive to the proposal of splitting the state by extending the Missouri Compromise line through it.[43] His major objection to that part of the proposal was that it merely evaded a final settlement on California's status and thus prolonged the uncertainties for slaveholders interested in moving there.

Clingman's efforts to rally southern Whigs behind a revised version of the compromise more beneficial to the South seems to have been his last effort to work with his own party to promote sectional unity. Its failure convinced him that it was futile to make any strong southern defense within the framework of the Whig party. By the time the eight compromise measures were put to a vote, Clingman was the only southern Whig who still opposed the plan and who voted against all of the resolutions except more rigid enforcement of the Fugitive Slave Law.[44]

His opposition to the compromise and the secessionist tone he took in doing so became the central issues confronting Clingman's constituents as he faced reelection in 1851. Mountain voters once again faced a choice in which the key issues revolved more around their sectional feelings as southerners than as westerners. Although his break with the Whig party was virtually complete, Clingman was not yet ready to label himself a Democrat in what was still a staunchly Whig district. He even flirted briefly with the idea of forming a third party. Both the Whigs and the Democrats, he said in a speech before Congress in February 1851, "have now become mere factions." No longer were they "separated by well-defined principles, but only by political animosity."

He called on his fellow mountain residents to display the independence in which they took such pride and join him in creating a state
reform party based on "the Old Republicanism of Jefferson and Madison," which was always "regardful of the rights of the States, strictly
defining the powers of the Federal government."[45] He wished to
combine this principle with a strong defense of western rights within
the state; thus the party would embody both of the sectional interests he represented, western North Carolina and the southern United
States—a combination he believed would draw strong support from
mountain Whigs as well as Democrats. Despite the fact that his loyal
spokesman Thomas W. Atkins, editor of the *Asheville News*, circulated
the proposal widely throughout the district, traditional party labels
were too firmly entrenched for it ever to win much support.[46]

Clingman thus called himself a States' Rights Whig in his bid for reelection to Congress, while his challenger, Burgess S. Gaither of Burke
County, entered the race as a Consolidationist Whig. He attacked
Clingman's secessionist sentiments and, with South Carolina actually
threatening to secede, Gaither joined most of the state's Whig leadership in advocating the use of federal force, if necessary, to prevent
such a step.[47] Clingman's confusing political status, strong support for
the 1850 Compromise among many western Carolinians, and their
alarm over the radical actions of their southern neighbor all seemed to
indicate that Gaither would prove Clingman's most formidable opponent since 1845.

Conservative Whig Robert Love of Waynesville probably reflected
the consensus of opinion, among mountain residents at least, on the
actions of their southern neighbors, when he wrote, "The course
which the state of South Carolina pursued in her late convention has
produced much excitement against her in this section of our state." He
urged South Carolinians to "pause and reflect . . . recede from her
mad and fanatical course" which would "bring ruin and devastation
upon herself and perhaps the whole South, whose course is a common one and whose destiny is the same." His prediction that "the firing of the first gun at Charleston will be the means of arousing the
South" was uncanny in its foreshadowing of events a decade later. But
his short-term prediction of the upcoming congressional contest was
far less accurate. "Secession and disunion," he stated, "receive no
countenance here—and the people appear to be pleased that they have
an opportunity, in the coming elections, to signalize their attachment

to the Union of the States. Secession will be killed as dead as nullification was in the year '32."[48]

A so-called "Union meeting" of Buncombe County residents earlier in the year also had expressed disapproval of South Carolina's threats to secede. It passed a resolution that stated, "We see secession as the exploded doctrine of Nullification, re-christened, and we ask friends of Union of either party to join us in meeting this political heresy as we did in 1832–33, and prove ourselves American patriots, not sectional ultraists." But the conviction behind this document was far weaker than this opening statement implied. For the resolution went on to defend the right of secession. As long as the 1850 Compromise was carried out in good faith, those meeting vowed to remain in the Union. But any violation of it, such as repeal of the Fugitive Slave Act, refusal to admit new slave states, or any attempt to abolish slavery in the District of Columbia, "will meet most determined resistance by freemen of North Carolina and justify them in joining with other slave states to uphold and maintain their rights." Any further interference with slavery would lead them to "recommend all southern merchants to cease all further intercourse with the North and if the Southern states are compelled by the aggressions of the North to dissolve the Union, we pledge ourselves and our honor to sustain the South." The resolution's bottom line, not surprisingly, was an endorsement of the "enlightened and fearless zeal of our distinguished Representative T.L. Clingman."[49]

This bipartisan meeting, with even Gaither in attendance, apparently reflected mountain sentiment more accurately than Love's statement, in that it distinguished between disapproval of South Carolina's proposed secession in response to existing conditions and the right to take such a step should further encroachment of southern rights warrant it. A month after the Buncombe meeting, William Holland Thomas echoed this conviction before the state senate in a debate over the right of secession. He stressed the mountain region's commitment to the defense of the southern cause, although his attempt to portray its major motive as loyalty to the state was somewhat less than convincing. "I have the honor to represent a portion of the state," he told his fellow legislators, "which is a grazing country, where slave labor yields but small profits; yet my constituents will unite in sustaining and defending an interest in which any portion of the State is interested." He, like Clingman, fell back on the rhetoric of republican ideology in declaring that, if North Carolina were ever

forced to the alternative of deciding between dishonor and political degra-
dation and maintaining her political rights as secured by the Constitution of
the United States, I am in favor of our doing as our ancestors did— pledge
our *lives, fortunes,* and *sacred honor* to preserve the rights and liberties of the
Old North State and defend her to the last, and fight the last battles in the
Mountain passes of my native portion of the State; and that none of her
sons, if she is crushed by superior power, survive her downfall.[50]

Such a statement from Thomas, one of the mountain's most ardent
Democratic leaders, reflected an adherence to his party's policy. More
important for Clingman's political future, however, was the response
of Whigs to his position. The issues at hand convinced many of them
that they and their interests were southern in character and thus won
them over to Clingman's pro-South policies, even if it meant desert-
ing their party. An account of how one mountain Whig made the
transition, probably typical of many similar transitions, indicates the
extent to which republican theory, more than any tangible concern for
slavery's future, was of most immediate concern. J.R.N. Bennet of
Waynesville wrote to a friend in June 1851:

I am very sorry that I shall have to go counter to some of my warmest
friends. . . . It is true that I have heretofore gone with the Whigs. . . . But
you must know that the old issues between the two great parties are nearly
extinct, and of course I go for what I conceive to be the honor of the South,
the home of my kindred, and the land of my love, and in doing so I consider
myself bound to vote for Mr. Clingman.

Clingman's warnings concerning continued southern appeasement
had struck a responsive chord within the district. As Bennet observed,
"It is evident that whenever a compromise have [sic] been made the
South has been the looser [sic]—the South has got nothing by this last
compromise, as it is called—the fugitive slave law she had before, and
my great astonishment is that *our* representatives in Congress should
be so cheated by our *bastard brethren* of the North."[51]

In light of such sentiments, Clingman himself felt confident of a
strong mandate from mountain voters. "Not withstanding the stren-
uous efforts of my opponent," he wrote, "I believe myself stronger by
far in the district than I ever was." The election results in August
proved him right, as a solid Democratic backing combined with a large
proportion of his Whig following to send him back to Congress with
more than a 70 percent majority over Gaither, who was defeated in
every county in his district, including his own.[52]

The western Whig leadership found Clingman's continued strength disconcerting, and they were reluctant to accept it as a mandate for his ultrasouthern positions. Nicholas Woodfin accused Clingman of "deceiving a large portion of the voters by pretending to be for the Union and Whig policy." "He insists," Woodfin claimed, "that he is a stronger Union man than Gaither." Others seized upon this idea as consolation for the Whig party's first major setback in the mountain region. One disappointed Whig claimed to be incredulous "that Clingman could so far blind the eyes of our citizens, as to make them think that he was in favor of the Union." Even if he did soften his secessionist threats somewhat during the campaign, claims that voters were unaware of Clingman's views and that his election actually was based on Union sentiment in the region remain unconvincing. Gaither's accusations alone must have kept voters well aware of Clingman's "extremist" tendencies, and even Whig leaders acknowledged that he had the full support of "the Locos and the Disunionists."[53]

On the other hand, Clingman's broad-based support in 1851 was not necessarily an endorsement of secession. As the statements quoted above indicate, most western Carolinians clearly disapproved of South Carolina's move in that direction. But they were troubled by fears of northern (or majority) tyranny and took comfort in Clingman's strong defense of southern (or minority) rights. His supporters seem to have had no problem distinguishing between the right to secede as a last resort and South Carolina's present threats, which as yet seemed unjustified, a vast overreaction to the current situation.

The 1853 congressional race was a virtual repeat of the 1851 campaign, as Gaither again challenged Clingman. Clingman by then had dissolved his affiliation with the Whig party but had not yet completed his shift to the Democratic party, and he ran as an "independent in favor of Southern Rights." Redistricting had removed the heavily Democratic Cleveland County from the mountain district and added to it "two very decided Whig counties," Wilkes and Watauga; and this, plus Clingman's open break with the Whigs, gave Gaither hopes for a stronger showing against the formidable incumbent.[54] He and the Whig establishment had even matched Clingman's most formidable weapon within the district, the *Asheville News*, with a newspaper of their own, the *Asheville Spectator*, which began circulation throughout the western counties in March 1853.[55]

Though the distribution of proceeds from federally-owned lands dominated most congressional races in the state that year,[56] the same sectional issues, with some modifications, continued to be the main theme of the contest in the state's westernmost district. Gaither seemed to have learned that the strong prosouthern sentiments of the district called for a different battle plan than the unionist versus disunionist lines he had defined in the preceding contest. Still believing the region to be the Whig party's solidest stronghold, despite evidence of its rapid erosion, Gaither and his supporters saw Clingman's defection from the Whigs as the issue on which he was most vulnerable. Thus they centered their attack on his betrayal of the party. "The Old Whig Spirit is aroused," the *Spectator* proclaimed. "Judas-like, Clingman has betrayed the Whig party into the hands of the Gentiles (democrats), and every true Whig in the District, sensible of his treachery, in the true spirit that animates every friend of the Union and the Compromise is determined to vote for Col. Gaither."[57]

Recognizing that his ultrasouthern stance was the greatest source of Clingman's appeal, the Whigs refrained from any direct criticism of Clingman's southern rights policies other than occasional references, like that above, to the Compromise of 1850. Gaither himself even tried to capitalize on the sectional loyalties of mountain voters by questioning Clingman's claim to being a greater friend of the South than Gaither was. He claimed that, as a Whig, he denied Congress's right to deal with slavery in the territories, which in itself reflected a definite shift toward a stronger proslavery stand. Gaither also cited a statement made many years earlier by Clingman, in which he admitted Congress's power to pass the Wilmot Proviso, "and yet Mr. Clingman claims to be, par excellence, the friend of Southern Rights."[58]

The effort was a feeble one, as was a second strategy aimed at questioning Clingman's commitment to his section. Whigs tried to raise suspicions about his dedication to defending slavery, since he owned no slaves himself. This charge led Clingman's supporters to turn the tables and make their congressman's "honest poverty" an asset by ridiculing the "scrub Aristocracy of this District" as snobs. This led to a ludicrous debate by both parties as to which candidate was poorer and thus had the greater claim to their fellow westerners' support.[59]

Clingman stood firmly on his record, and called on voters to "let the [decision] be so overwhelmingly in favor of Southern Rights, against Consolidation and Federalism that it may silence forever" the petty efforts of his opposition. Still, he too resorted to petty "side issues" at least once in the campaign, when he accused *Spectator* editor John Hyman of being a Free-Soiler, on the grounds that, as a former editor of a Wisconsin newspaper, Hyman had supported a free-soil candidate for governor there.[60] But none of these distractions did much to alter the outcome of this race, and Clingman once again won an easy victory over Gaither. His share of the vote, however, was reduced to 59 percent, largely because of the addition to the district of Wilkes County, the region's most heavily Whig county and the only one Clingman lost.[61]

Stephen Douglas's Kansas and Nebraska bills in 1854, which introduced the idea of "popular sovereignty" as the determinant of a territory's status regarding slavery, were enthusiastically embraced by Clingman as "the best species of nonintervention" and "for the South the best measures yet presented," in that they would "allow every portion of the country to regulate its own affairs, whether States or Territories." Clingman was ecstatic over its passage, and in a letter written soon afterwards, he declared:

> The importance of the Kansas and Nebraska act cannot be overrated. It removed from the statute book an odious and unjust discrimination [the Missouri Compromise] which had existed there for nearly half a century. That restriction, a mark of inferiority, was degrading to the South, and as such, ought never to have been originally submitted to by her. . . . We now stand as equals in the Union with our brethren of the North.[62]

The benefits to the South were so obvious that southern Whigs had little grounds to oppose this Democratic measure. The *Asheville News* said of it that "if nothing else, it presents a gratifying spectacle of a united South."[63] But the act's passage brought about the collapse of the Whig party, already seriously weakened by sectional divisiveness at the national level and by the defection of Clingman and many of his mountain followers, among other reasons, at the state level.[64] The need for a national party affiliation led many North Carolina Whigs to embrace the only real alternative, the American or Know-Nothing party. This essentially one-issue party was based on prejudices triggered by the influx of Irish and German immigrants into northern cities, and thus had little relevance to western North Carolinians. Yet most Whig leaders in the mountains, however reluctantly, joined its ranks. The *Asheville Spectator* dutifully made itself the new party's organ, printing on its front page "Our Principles," which consisted of the repeal of naturalization laws and various other restrictions against immigrants.[65]

Many mountain Whigs hoped to maintain the party's former strength in the district by openly identifying with Whig principles and even calling themselves Whigs. Several saw the Unionist cause as the issue most likely to appeal to highland voters and to serve as an effective challenge to Clingman. Know-Nothing lawyer Nicholas Woodfin of Asheville wrote that, in making his circuit through the courts of the western counties, he had been "talking for the Union where I could find time. We have a hope of saving the Union by the native Americans."[66]

Clingman was the real beneficiary of his former party's demise. He gained considerable new support from those whose loyalty to the Whig party, as long as it still existed, had made them reluctant to stray from it. In the 1855 congressional campaign, he openly declared himself a Democratic candidate for the first time, though most voters realized that the new label merely acknowledged a transition that had been virtually completed several years earlier. He stressed the northern origins of the new Know-Nothing party, attacked it as nothing more than "a mask for the great abolition crusade of the North," and called its secrecy "demoralizing and mischievous in the extreme." By capitalizing on the sectional loyalties of his constituents and on the very limited appeal of the nativist issue in the mountains, Clingman, as a Democrat, by a wide margin easily defeated his American opponent, Leander B. Carmichael of Wilkes County.[67]

By 1856, Clingman believed that the Know-Nothing party was destined to fail and that it was the more blatantly sectional Republican party, also emerging from the ruins of the Whig party in 1854, that posed a far greater threat to the South. In a letter meant for general circulation within the district prior to the presidential campaign of 1856, he warned his constituents that "the danger which now menaces the Federal Union arises from the feeling of hostility entertained in the North toward the Southern section, and especially the institution of negro slavery as it exists among us." He characterized the Republicans as a sectional party of abolitionists and free-soil Democrats "held together mainly by its hostility to the South." He called its designation as the Black Republican party appropriate because "it is devoted to the elevation of the negroes" and "ignores, disregards, and condemns the rights of white men." Arguing that such intentions could only be thwarted by a Democratic victory in the upcoming election, Clingman warned that support for Know-Nothing candidate Millard Fillmore might allow the Republicans to seize victory. Such a result would require more drastic action, and prompted his most direct call yet for secession: "We are called upon, fellow citizens to make a manly stand for the Constitution and the rights of our section. If beaten, we may be forced to declare independence, to maintain equality and honor."[68]

In a letter published in the *Asheville News*, Clingman reiterated his conviction that "should the black republicans prevail . . . it would not only justify the action of any single State, but even authorize individual resistance; for any free white American might well refuse to be so degraded as to become the slave of negro-worshipping abolitionists."[69] Significantly, this statement again pulled the race issue to center stage in the debate. Even more important, Clingman introduced his constituents to the idea that the election of a Republican president was sufficient cause for southern withdrawal from the Union—an idea that would, of course, assume much greater immediacy in the next presidential election.

Despite such declarations, the only defense Clingman's opposition seemed able to muster was the old accusation that because he did not own slaves himself, his commitment to slavery's preservation was less than wholehearted. In an editorial entitled "Niggers and Patriotism," the *Asheville News* challenged that argument:

> Know-Nothings try to attack Mr. Clingman and weaken the estimation of him by Southern people by the oft-repeated story that he is not a slaveholder. Wonderful logic! Tried by this rule, ninety-nine hundredths of the soldiers of the Revolution were not patriots, nor were those who fought in the Mexican War. In the company that went from Buncombe County, not one in twenty owned slaves.
>
> Mr. Clingman, although a Southern man by birth, education, interest, feeling, and every tie which can bind a man to his section, and thoroughly identified with the South by past efforts in her behalf, and by all his hopes for the future, is not a slaveholder, and cannot therefore, according to these "new lights," be an honest man and a patriot!! How long will these Know-Nothing editors continue to insult the good sense of the community with such twaddle—the natural offspring of an effete aristocracy, as disgusting to the intelligent slaveholder as to everyone else.[70]

This editorial and others like it led to another strange debate in the

North Carolina press over whether Democratic or Know-Nothing editors owned more slaves and thus were more loyal to the South.[71]

In 1856, Clingman became chairman of the House Committee on Foreign Affairs, and he managed to use even that role to expand on his pro-South rhetoric. Much of his attention centered on the foreign threat, particularly that of the British government, to southern interests. In several speeches, he accused the British of conspiring with American abolitionists to renew the antislave agitation in hopes of splitting the Union, and thus separating northern shipping from southern production and giving Great Britain "dominion of the ocean."[72]

In what was to be Clingman's final congressional race, in 1857, the debate returned to the more basic issue of unionism versus disunionism, as fellow Asheville resident Zebulon B. Vance, an ardent unionist and assistant editor of the *Asheville Spectator*, challenged the seemingly invincible incumbent for his seat. Through the *Spectator*, Vance called the congressman "a liar and a scoundrel" and wrote that, "unlike the mean and contemptible demagogue who has received the suffrage of the people of this district, I desire to maintain some vistage [sic] of private character and truth." He attacked Clingman as a secessionist and a radical whose reckless pronouncements seriously threatened the Union. Like others before him, Vance also resorted to more desperate efforts to show inconsistencies in Clingman's prosouthern stand. He tried to demonstrate that by voting to grant Minnesota statehood, Clingman had "sided with the Black Republicans," even though Clingman argued that opposing the entrance of that state would have left southerners without "ground to complain if Southern territories are rejected."[73]

In light of Clingman's strength in the district, efforts to discredit him seemed futile. In response to the resigned observations of an American party paper in Wilmington that "those 'transmontane' fellows . . . will cling to Clingman with a pertinacity only equalled by the love a Loco has for the spoils of office," the *Asheville News* quickly affirmed that "the people of this district . . . have always found Mr. Clingman as true to their interests as the needle to the pole, and they will cling to him with a pertinacity inspired by his long and faithful public services in their behalf." Nor did the paper attempt to downplay the reason for Clingman's success. The continued support of his constituents, it explained, was based simply on the fact that "his efforts have placed the South upon safer and better ground than she has occupied for thirty years. . . . His sentiments are the sentiments of the overwhelming majority not only of the people of this district, but of the entire South."[74]

But Clingman's supporters did not merely rest on his laurels. They boldly took the offensive against those like Vance, who insisted that the Union should be preserved at all costs. "This is precisely the doctrine of the Black Republicans of the North," wrote the editor of the *Asheville News*, and it merely encouraged northerners to believe that slavery could be abolished without risking loss of the South: "True Southern men are those who stand up for the Union as it is founded upon the Constitution. They are not a set of whimpering dough faces and overgrown children who blubber about the sacredness of the Union, while the abolitionists steal their property and sap the very foundations of their social and political existence."[75]

The election results once more proved the *News* right in its estimation of Clingman's invincibility within his district. Despite his personal popularity among mountain residents and his reputation for "militant Whiggery," Vance was burdened with the rapidly declining Know-Nothing party affiliation. Their convention in Morganton to choose a candidate to challenge Clingman had been so poorly attended (only two of the district's fifteen counties were represented) that Democrats urged them to admit defeat and disband. Vance lost to Clingman by almost 5,500 votes, a wider margin than in any of Clingman's previous races. Vance failed to carry a single county.[76]

On 6 May 1858, Clingman finally achieved the political goal he had sought for over a decade. Gov. Thomas Bragg appointed him to fill the Senate seat of Asa Biggs, who had been appointed a federal judge. A special election to fill Clingman's House seat soon followed, providing Vance with a second chance to represent his district in Congress. But the strength of his Democratic opponent once again made the prospect a slim one for him. William Waightstill Avery was a member of a prominent Burke County family with a distinguished record in North Carolina's legal and political affairs, a family which had long been among the largest slaveholders in the western part of the state. Having served as the speaker of the state senate and as head of the North Carolina delegation to the Democratic convention in 1856, Avery was second only to Clingman as an active states-rights Democrat.[77] The only blemish on Avery's record was an 1851 incident in which he had shot and killed, in the Burke County Courthouse, another prominent Democrat, Samuel Fleming of Yancey County, who had attacked him with a horsewhip three weeks earlier.[78] Although he was acquitted within the week and public opinion at the time accepted Fleming's death as "righteous retribution" for his humiliating attack on Avery, the long-term effects of the incident seems to have dampened much of the enthusiasm Avery otherwise might have rallied.[79]

The emphases in this campaign were somewhat different from those in which Clingman had kept sectional divisiveness at the forefront. The final two years of the 1850s saw what was to be only a brief lull in national tensions over slavery and states' rights. Southerners' paranoia, at least, had cooled, if only because they were still basking in their only clear-cut sectional victory of the decade—the Supreme Court's 1857 decision that neither Dred Scott nor any other slave could claim freedom on free soil. Perhaps remembering his stinging defeat to Clingman the year before, Zebulon Vance took a different approach toward his Democratic opponent. In the wake of the Panic of 1857, his primary foci became the continued extravagant and irresponsible spending by congressional Democrats and the hints of corruption behind it, charges that Avery made little effort to refute.[80]

The issue of national unity was by no means dead, and both candidates echoed the earlier campaign rhetoric of Clingman and his opponents. Vance denounced Avery's secessionist tendencies, and risked offending the district's Democrats, not in a majority, with his outspoken expressions of contempt for the party. He called the Democrats in Congress "half-brained fire-eaters" and opposed everything they stood for. In particular he spoke out against "the sectionalism which it has engendered & fostered with paternal care, the wild, reckless, lawless, violent and loathsome corruption which has made it smell to high heaven," though such charges seem more apt descriptions of financial abuses than of disunity.[81]

Avery, like Clingman, sought to equate southern loyalty with the Democratic party. He urged voters to elect him, because "those of this district need someone who will support the interests of the South and defend Southern rights," unlike Vance, "who can see nothing higher than party, nor dearer than factions' opposition to everything."[82] Without any specific concern—such as Clingman had in the Compromise of 1850 and Kansas and Nebraska—on which to hang the partisan diatribes, such accusations seemed somewhat hollow.

Figure 21. Zebulon B. Vance. North Carolina Division of
Archives and History.

Vance proved to be a vigorous and increasingly skillful campaigner, even managing to upstage Avery in several of their debates with his quick wit and sheer bravado. Stories of his performances spread widely throughout the district, so that even before the election in August, it was said of Vance that "a new star of the first magnitude had risen in the mountains." He defeated Avery by a comfortable margin of two thousand votes, in what was considered a major upset by most observers in the state. The next year Vance won reelection to a full term, the last prior to secession, in an even closer race, defeating Asheville Democrat David Coleman. The 1859 campaign itself was more lackluster than that in 1858, centering mainly on Vance's unimpressive record during his few months in Congress and on his former association with the Know-Nothing party.[83]

Zebulon Vance's electoral success as a conservative Unionist during the latter part of the 1850s might suggest that western North Carolina's consistent support of Clingman over the previous decade was based less on strong secessionist tendencies within the district than on the remarkable personal allegiance voters felt toward Clingman. One cannot separate the popularity of the man from support for the issues he stood for, however—particularly when he was identified as closely and as single-mindedly with a cause as Clingman was with his defense of slavery and southern rights. Nevertheless, feeling less threatened by northern aggressions than they had earlier in the decade, mountain voters in 1858 and 1859 responded to the other issues—more partisan than sectional—that Vance most effectively laid before them. Whereas Clingman had received increasingly large proportions of the vote in the congressional races from 1847 through 1857, Vance obtained much narrower winning margins in both 1858 and 1859. The shift indicates that mountain voters were by no means averse to a strong defense of southern rights or even to secession as a last resort.

Perhaps the most important effect of Clingman's congressional career on the citizens of the state's westernmost district was to keep sectional issues constantly before them. His ultimate goal well may have been statewide office and his intention to broaden his appeal within the state by embracing a proslavery stand as fully as he could. Even so, he was a skillful politician who always aimed his message as much at his mountain constitutents as at Congress or eastern North Carolina. Confident that his fellow western North Carolinians were just as receptive to that message as others in the state or in the South, he never softened its intensity for home consumption.

Clingman and his message shaped the politics of western North Carolina far beyond the bounds of his own congressonal races. In each of the presidential elections of 1848, 1852, and 1856, he played a central role in casting voters' judgments of the candidates in sectional terms, so that the principal criteria for many voters was the candidates' commitment to southern interests. Clingman helped to infuse campaigns for state-level offices—from gubernatorial to state legislative races— with North-South sectionalism, along with the more dominant East-West state issues. In 1852, for example, several legislative candidates from the mountain counties ran on Clingman's coattails as "Southern Rights Whigs."[84] During the governor's race that year, a letter from Clingman to one of Asheville's leading Democrats, Dr. J.F.E. Hardy, claimed that a victory for Whig candidate John Kerr would be a victory for the North, since he was "a Southern man with Northern feelings . . . going in all issues for the North and against his own section."[85] Though the pro-Clingman legislative candidates were less than successful in their use of his name, Clingman's influence did contribute to Kerr's diminished support in the west, which in turn contributed to his loss statewide.[86]

Even in 1854, when state issues dominated the gubernatorial campaign and Whig candidate Alfred Dockery's stands on free suffrage and internal improvements won strong support in the mountain counties, the Democrats believed that his extreme Unionist views could be used to make an effective case against him among western Carolinians. *Asheville News* editor Marcus Erwin wrote that "neither Mr. Clingman nor any other States-Rights man could be complacent about the triumph of such an out and out, full-blooded Consolidationist as General Alfred Dockery, who declared he'd vote men and money to whip North Carolina into the Union, in the event the Federal Government should force her to set up for herself."[87] In his first bid for political office in 1854, Zebulon Vance ran for and won a seat in the state House of Commons over another Asheville Whig, Daniel Reynolds, in a race that echoed Clingman's own by contrasting the merits of the Compromise of 1850 and those of the Kansas-Nebraska Act.[88]

Throughout his career, one of Clingman's predominant themes and a major reason for his success in his district was his recognition that westerners did and should think of themselves as southerners. In assessing Clingman's popularity among his constituents, the *Asheville News*'s observation that "his sentiments are the sentiments of an overwhelming majority, not only of the people of the district, but of the entire South" seems fully substantiated by both his rhetoric and his electoral success. In eulogizing South Carolina Congressman Preston S. Brooks, who had achieved notoriety by his 1856 caning of Republican Senator Charles Sumner on the floor of the Senate, Clingman told his fellow congressman that "coming as I do from the same section of the country . . . such was the intercourse between our constituents, that he was well known and highly honored among those whom I represent."[89]

A Buffalo, New York, newspaper stated in 1857 that Clingman came from "one of the most sterile, impoverished and poverty-stricken Congressional districts in the United States–where the people drink yapon tea and pay for all the luxuries they enjoy in turpentine, lightwood, top fodder, and corn-shucks." The response by the editor of the *Asheville News* was a spirited defense of western North Carolina that, in contrasting the republican virtues of agrarianism with the evils of urban and industrial life, was indistinguishable from a defense of the entire South. The description of this district, he wrote, "was about as truthful as most pictures of the South drawn by Northern writers." The editor's attack on northern society and its accompanying moral endorsement of slavery could hardly have been more forceful had it come from any other part of the South:

> The people of the District, it is true, are generally of moderate means—independent farmers, who cultivate their own land, and honestly earn their bread by the sweat of the brow. We have not many overgrown capitalists among us—men who have acquired great wealth by monster frauds, speculations and forgeries, a la Huntington, of New York celebrity! Nor have we many among us who have acquired wealth by extracting the lifeblood from the veins of the poor and destitute, requiring them to work from twelve to sixteen hours a day for a pittance barely sufficient to protract their miserable existence. . . . The squalid wretchedness, hopeless misery, and degrading vices, which render the streets of all Northern cities, and particularly those of New York, more dangerous after nightfall than the mountain fastnesses of Mexico or South America, do not find their counterpart in Western North Carolina. The people of Mr. Clingman's district, in all the elements that constitute a truly happy, independent, virtuous and Christian community, are far ahead of any District in the State of New York.

Indeed we hazard but little in saying that our slave population are more comfortably provided for, more honest and moral, than the mass of fanatical, ignorant and stupid human machines who pay the fiddler that a few leading Abolition scoundrels may have an opportunity to do the dancing.[90]

Why did Clingman's strong pro-South message strike such a responsive chord among North Carolina's mountain electorate? Few of them would ever be going west into the disputed territories, and of those who might, few would have had slaves to take with them. (The experiences of those slaveholders who joined the California gold rush, of course, may well have instilled in them and their families back home an awareness of the restrictions and risks involved in such situations.) Few mountain residents saw any tangible threat to their own freedom or to that of slavery in their area. Unlike Charlestonians, for instance, whose daily commercial enterprises were affected by federal tariff and trade policies and for whom the blockade of their port or its occupation by troops was a very real threat, western Carolinians were far removed from any such arm of federal power. Yet those in the mountains were, over the last antebellum decade, sensitized to the threat of northern interference and aggression as much as were southerners in far more vulnerable areas. Certainly their vital economic and commercial ties with South Carolina and Georgia markets played a significant role in shaping their identities as southerners and in assuring them a vested interest in the security and prosperity of the South. So, to a lesser extent, did the influence of those planters and their families who swarmed into the highland region every summer.

As important as these tangible contacts, it seems, was the fact that North Carolina mountain residents, through their sectional struggles within the state, were already accustomed to the role of regional underdog. Clingman was among the first to recognize the striking parallels between the abuses, or perceived abuses, inflicted on his constituents by the governments in both Raleigh and Washington. While he first won the support of his fellow mountaineers through an outspoken defense of western interests within North Carolina, it was through his even more fervent defense of southern rights in Congress that he maintained it. As his republican rhetoric indicates, he saw the threat that his region's residents might be "enslaved" as resulting from their status as both westerners and southerners. He made the most of the emotional and political potential of that threat throughout his congressional career, constantly nourishing the mountaineers' dual identities, so that each served to reinforce and complement the other.

By the end of the decade, this larger struggle dominated the thoughts and worries of mountain residents. With Clingman at the forefront of the nation's growing political crisis and with commercial ties between North Carolina and the Lower South stronger than ever, Carolina highlanders were fully aware of the extent to which their interests were the same as those of the larger South. The mountaineers' attitudes toward secession from the Union—and Vance's success at the end of the decade suggests that they remained flexible—were based as much on how secession would affect the South as a whole as on its effect on their small corner of it. By the time the crisis reached the point at which the possibility of a separate South approached reality, western North Carolinians long had been familiar with the assets and liabilities of participation in a southern nation. Having listened for over a decade to one of secession's foremost proponents and his critics, they were probably caught off guard by its impending actuality far less than those in some other parts of the South.

Chapter 9

Secession:

Feeling "awful Southern"

A desperate scheme and its reckless enactment by a fanatical abolitionist named John Brown did in a matter of weeks what Thomas
Clingman had tried for over a decade to do. The raid on Harpers Ferry
and, even more, its apparent approval by many northerners, made
western North Carolinians believe that a serious threat to their rights,
particularly to their "peculiar institution," existed, if only because so
much of the nation seemed so apathetic toward the violation of those
rights. Just as Clingman himself had become aware of the true scope
of northern hostility to slavery only after an extended trip through the
Northeast in 1848, so his constituents were rudely awakened by the
heroic stature which Brown seemed to achieve above the Mason-Dixon
Line. His attempt to incite a slave insurrection and his subsequent
martyrdom turned what they had previously known only as abstract
rhetoric or legislative debate into a shocking reality. As the climax of a
decade of tensions between North and South, Harper's Ferry and its
aftermath led to a sectional fervor unprecedented in the mountains—
one which nevertheless would be overshadowed within the year by
feelings of even greater proportions and significance.

As the reaction to Nat Turner's rebellion thirty years earlier had
demonstrated, a slave uprising was among the prospects most feared
by southerners; the mountain residents of North Carolina responded
just as passionately to that dreaded possibility as did their counterparts elsewhere throughout the slaveholding states. Zebulon Vance
conveyed the emotional intensity of his constituents' fears as he worried what would result now that "good and true men of the North" [211]

were converted "into aliens, acknowledging no longer any constitutional obligations or brotherly regard for us." Thus he wondered in a message to citizens of the Eighth District: "What restraint is there upon the furious and bloodthirsty fanaticism which led John Brown, bristling with arms, into a sleeping southern city? What mother within a hundred miles of that long and defenceless border could kiss her infant to sleep without the horrid thought that before the morning's sun her home might become the funeral pile [*sic*] of herself and child!"[1]

Senator Clingman directed his indignation toward his northern colleagues in the Senate. Nothing, he told them, had made a "stronger impression on the minds of the Southern people . . . than the manner in which the acts of John Brown were received in the North. Instead of the indignation and abhorence which his crimes ought naturally have excited, there were manifestations of admiration and sympathy." He later observed that "this fact alone, showing as it did that the feeling in the North was so strong against the South that any crime committed against our section was applauded there . . . ought to have united the whole South for its common defense."[2]

It did indeed unite mountain communities in their resolve to defend themselves against what they saw as "a studied and determined intention on the part of some of the insane elements at the North to make war directly on the South." To many, it merely confirmed what had all along been the self-proclaimed purpose of "Black Republicanism." Even before public reaction in the North had become apparent, the *Asheville News* wrote, "Now, when we see what the irrepressible conflict of Seward means—when we see the feast of blood to which [the Republicans] will invite the South—we have but to be ready with measures firm, quiet and decided, when the popular majority of the North shall evince their approbation of it."[3]

Public meetings were held in several mountain counties and vigilante committees were formed.[4] In Buncombe and Henderson counties, particularly, with their constant influx of visitors, many of them accompanied by slaves, strong measures were deemed necessary. Asheville citizens met at the courthouse on 20 December 1859, and drew up a resolution stating:

> Whereas, having reason to believe that this portion of the country, like many other portions of the slaveholding states, is infested with itinerant Abolitionists, who, under various disguises are endeavoring to sow the seeds of dissatisfaction among our slave population. Therefore . . . be it re-

solved that all strangers, particularly those from non-slaveholding States, who come in our midst *under suspicious circumstances*, although claiming to be in pursuit of peaceful occupation, shall be subjected to the most rigid scrutiny, and if there is probable cause to believe they are abolition emissaries they shall be taken up and made to undergo a searching examination and be dealt with accordingly.[5]

"Abolition emissaries, either native or foreign," wrote one Asheville resident, "will meet with as little favor in this region as they would in the household of Governor Wise [of Virginia] himself."[6]

More general reactions across the South took two forms: the formation of local military units based on "a rekindling of the martial spirit" and efforts at economic and social boycotts of the North. Here too, the participation of North Carolina's mountain residents was well within the mainstream of southern activity. At least five of the twenty-three counties in the state that formed volunteer militia companies in late 1859 or early 1860 were in the mountains.[7] Their stated purpose was not only the defense of their own communities but that of other parts of the South as well. The public safety required such measures in order "to put down insurrection, quell rebellion, or resist invasion at home; to tender their services to the Governor of any sister southern State, or to render any service patriotism and the exigencies of the times might require at their hands."[8]

Marcus Erwin reported to Governor Ellis on the formation of such a company, the "Buncombe Rifles" in Asheville. While inquiring as to the procedure for procuring arms and equipment from the state, he declared that "the military spirit is fully aroused here & I am satisfied that upon any collision or any immediate prospect of one in or out of Congress I could raise a thousand men in this country." Through notices headed "Arm! Arm!" the *Asheville News* urged outlying areas of the county to follow such examples in order to "prepare against the evil day."[9]

Equal enthusiasm met proposals to declare economic independence from the North in preparation for a possible political separation, thus underscoring once again the strong entrepreneurial spirit that motivated so much of the mountain region's response to the crisis. This movement had been evident in the mountains even before the shock waves of Brown's raid. In 1857 an Asheville resident, who had attended the Southern Commercial Convention in Savannah, returned home urging his fellow citizens, as southerners, to buy southern prod-

ucts to "contribute to the industrial welfare of the section." Soon afterward, the *Asheville News* took up the cause and scolded Buncombe
residents for their tendencies "to cry down every article of ornament
or utility that is not manufactured by a hatchet-faced yankee, or
vended by a sixpence-adoring Jew . . . Our houses are filled with articles of Yankee production—the niggers being, in many cases, the
only Southern production on the place."[10]

Harpers Ferry, however, inspired much more intense and specific
efforts by western Carolinians to demonstrate to themselves and to the
North that they could stand very well on their own. The *Asheville News*
set forth the purpose of suspending trade with the North in no uncertain terms:

> The only way to stop the infernal whining of Northern Abolitionists is to
> cut of[f] the supplies on which they grow fat. Let us trade at home and
> drink at home, travel for business and pleasure in the South; learn to sup-
> ply each other's wants and to rely on ourselves, and soon the voice of Ab-
> olition will cease, not only along the busy mart, but in the pulpit, for the
> philanthropy, freedom and religion of a Yankee-slave-stealing fanatic all
> dwindles into contemptible insignificance when you touch the breeches
> pocket.[11]

In January 1860, a meeting of Asheville women was held in which
they were urged "to take active part in the movement now so general,
the encouragement of Southern enterprise." Marcus Erwin and Nicholas Woodfin addressed the group, calling for a return to the self-sufficiency of home manufactures. The latter pointed out, "Twenty years
ago, there were looms to be found in every farm house—now it is hard
to get a good piece of homemade jeans."[12] Proposed resolutions declared that during the next three years, no local residents should buy
men's clothing or farm implements made outside the area, and merchants should limit their merchandise to products either made in the
South or imported directly through southern ports.[13]

In Jackson County two months later, "an ardent friend of the South
and southern independence" urged the "farmers, merchants, me-
chanics and all who are interested in the county's prosperity" to follow the lead of neighboring Macon County in forming an agricultural
society "for the encouragement of home manufactures [which by] increasing our resources and wealth, will contribute to the independence and prosperity of the South." Even as ardent a unionist as
Zebulon Vance conceded that if abolitionist efforts continued una-

bated, the South would soon have to develop its own "manufactures and mechanic arts," rather than continuing to rely on the North to provide them.[14] Local residents also questioned the practice of hiring northern teachers for their schools. When a public meeting in Asheville on this issue was postponed, a local merchant wrote to protest the lack of action. "This sort of measure," he said, "forms the very ground work of what we are pleased to denominate 'Southern Independence' and I look upon all the 'fuss and feathers' about emancipating the people of the South from their subserviency to the North, as of little value, while a large majority of our public schools are in the hand of Yankee teachers."[15]

For some, such efforts at military preparedness and economic or educational self-sufficiency were aimed at increasing southern bargaining power within the Union, but others urged that such steps be followed to their logical conclusion and that all ties with the Union be broken. Marcus Erwin observed that "disunion is a thing freely talked of & openly advocated by many." He seemed so enthusiastic about the military unit he headed that he declared his own willingness "to break up the Government" on such a minor pretext as Ohio Congressman John Sherman's selection as speaker of the House of Representatives.[16] In an editorial in the *Asheville News*, Erwin surveyed the collective efforts under way and wondered how they could be reconciled with any desire to maintain the Union:

> As far as we know the sentiments of the people in this section of the State, a large majority of them are in favor of a perpetual non-intercourse with the North. If they had their choice they would never again buy a dollar's worth of goods in any Northern State. Well, what does all this amount to—coupled with the formation and action of Vigilante Committees in this State and throughout the South—the mustering and arming of the militia and volunteer forces? Who are we resolving not to trade with? Our *brethren* of the North. Whom do we find it necessary to establish committees of safety to watch, and hustle out of our midst when they come in on business? Our *brethren* of the North . . . If this be so, and it is, is not the Union already virtually dissolved? Why continue it longer, if we can only remain in it with arms in our hands?[17]

Such blatantly disunionist sentiment does not seem to have been widespread in the region during this period. By late spring of 1860, the sectional excitement itself had died down, as the gubernatorial election and the issue of ad valorem taxation moved back to the center of the political stage. But 1860 was a presidential election year as well, and the results of the parties' nominating conventions that spring and summer portended renewed sectional tensions ahead.

The Democrats met in Charleston in April 1860, and W.W. Avery of Burke County played a prominent role in its proceedings. Far less conservative than most of the North Carolina delegation, Avery headed the committee on resolutions and presented the party's proposed platform to the convention. He stood firm on making congressional protection of slavery in the territories a part of that platform, despite the reluctance of his fellow North Carolinians to commit the party to such a blatantly sectional, potentially divisive position. Defending his stand, Avery said: "We regard this principle as more important in its ultimate effects than any principle ever discussed before in the South." He urged northern Democrats to accept it, too, since it would have no adverse effects on either their constitutional rights or their material interests.[18] When this majority report was ultimately voted down, most of the Lower South delegates walked out. Those who remained, including the North Carolina and border state delegations, failed to agree on a candidate and adjourned to meet again in Baltimore in June. There they nominated Stephen A. Douglas as the party's presidential candidate. That group's failure to readmit those delegates who had walked out in Charleston led the North Carolina and Virginia delegations to withdraw and join the "Seceders Convention" there a week later. The later convention nominated John C. Breckinridge of Kentucky and Gen. Joseph Lane of Oregon (a native of Asheville) as presidential and vice-presidential running mates. Remnants of the old Whig party reunited as the Constitutional Union party and chose John Bell of Tennessee as their presidential nominee and Edward Everett of Massachusetts as his running mate.

In the campaign that followed, the major consideration of North Carolina's political leaders was to determine which of these three candidates stood the best chance of winning enough votes from North and South to prevent that most dreaded of possibilities, a victory by the Republican candidate, Abraham Lincoln. Even before the nomination of two sets of Democrats, western North Carolinians of both parties saw ominous implications in the Democratic division at Charleston. Just a week after the nomination of Bell and Everett, Whig Nicholas Woodfin expressed his approval of the Constitutional Union convention's choice. Then, following the common assumption that William Seward would be the Republican nominee, he declared: "Un-

Figure 22. William Waightstill Avery. North Carolina Division of Archives and History.

der existing circumstances I suppose a Black Republican must be elected if any one by the people . . . The failure to unite on Douglas at Charleston put an end to my hopes of seeing Seaward [*sic*] beaten before the people & I am now satisfied that the Secession democracy will not unite with supporters & I fear not with any party to save but rather to destroy the Union."[19]

Despite his strong secessionist tendencies over the previous decade, Thomas Clingman sincerely hoped for a united Democratic front to prevent the Republican victory, which he too saw as inevitable. He was even more upset by the course of events at the Charleston convention, claiming that the "harmonious nomination" of Douglas would have prevented the Whigs from making any nomination and thus would have provided a single candidate to whom the South could give its entire vote. But the split among the Democrats had ruined any chance of such a scenario. Clingman, still quick to hurl accusations, blamed President Buchanan, Jefferson Davis, and others for conspiring to divide and destroy the party, calling their so-called conspiracy "unsurpassed in its insanity and wickedness." He compared the irrationality of their action to that of "a man about to do battle for his life, who should, as a preparatory step, cut off one arm and one leg, in order that he might march and strike with more efficiency."[20]

Clingman stood by Douglas and urged North Carolinians to do so on the grounds that Douglas alone could draw the intersectional support necessary to defeat Lincoln. Douglas was, Clingman assured his constituents, "a very thorough Democrat, who has fought the Abolitionists for the last twelve or fifteen years with as much zeal and effect as any man in America."[21] One of only three meetings in the state endorsing Douglas was held in Buncombe County in July, at which it was resolved "that we will never give support or countenance to any party that is sectional in its character, or the success of which would in the slightest degree tend to the dissolution of the Union." The meeting also echoed Clingman's argument that Douglas was the only electable alternative to "the Abolition candidate."[22]

Senator Clingman's support of Douglas implied a somewhat more temperate approach to the crisis than had his previous outspoken pronouncements. In 1856, when the party's first candidate, John C. Fremont, had offered a real possibility of a chief executive elected because of his hostility to slavery, Clingman had viewed the election of a Republican president as sufficient cause for the South's withdrawal from the Union.[23] Again in 1860, he warned of the consequences of a Republican in the White House. He sounded just as determined in January 1860, when he told the Senate that "hundreds of disunionists . . . would willingly today see the Union dissolved" and that the majority of southerners would readily join them "upon the happening of some further causes. In my judgement, the election of a presidential candidate of the Black Republican party will furnish that cause." In response to those who felt that the South should wait for some overt action before resorting to secession, he argued that a Republican's very inauguration would make him the commander of the army and navy. This, along with the political appointments in the South at his disposal, would allow him to station troops advantageously, remove all public arms from the South, and divide southern whites while "forming connections with the negroes." Thus, he reasoned: "No other 'overt act' can so imperatively demand resistance on our part, as the simple election of their candidate. Their organization is one of avowed hostility, and they come against us as *enemies*; and should we submit we shall be in the condition of an army which surrenders at discretion, and can only expect such terms as the humanity of the conqueror may grant."[24]

Yet Clingman's most pressing concern after the conventions in spring 1860 was that such a scenario be prevented, and he saw Douglas as the only means of doing so. Even though Clingman was far less the "ultra" during this period than he had been or soon would be again, his mountain constituents had retreated to an even more cautious stand, and he failed to win much support for his candidate either among them or elsewhere in the state. That, along with a meeting between Clingman and the Illinois senator, in which the latter indicated some reluctance to defend southern interests, caused Clingman's own enthusiasm for Douglas to wane.

Thus, the campaign soon shaped itself as a usual two-way contest between Whigs and Democrats, with Bell and Breckinridge filling those party roles despite the fact that both actually represented variations of those traditional parties. Both candidates received strong support in western North Carolina, in a contest based almost solely on their electability and their stand on southern rights. Democrats stressed the fact that theirs was the only platform that "fairly and squarely recognizes the rights of the South and the equality of the States." They also emphasized vice-presidential candidate Lane's early years in their own region.[25] In response to Whig attempts to label Breckinridge a "disunionist," they maintained somewhat vaguely that a strong defense of the South was the best means of preserving the Union.[26]

Mountain Democrats took the offensive against the Constitutional Unionists by questioning their commitment to southern interests. At an Asheville rally for Bell in late October 1860, Burgess Gaither of Morganton made a speech in which he took an "unconditional unionist" stand that proved too extreme even for his Unionist party. He declared not only that he opposed North Carolina's seceding, but also that he would refuse to come to the aid of any other seceded state "that Lincoln might attempt to whip into submission." Gaither's intention to remain neutral came under sharp attack from opponents, who leaped at the chance to exploit the unpopularity among moutain voters of such aloofness, which Gaither's opponents maintained implied a disloyalty to both the state and the South. The *Asheville News* warned Gaither that a lack of allegiance to either was unacceptable. "If the struggle should come, and it is not improbable, the South will say in the language of the holy writ: 'He that is not for me is against me'; and your 'neutral' ground might prove unhealthy."[27]

By this time, most realized that such divisions within the South had made Lincoln's election inevitable. The comments of a Caldwell County woman a week before the election typified the apprehension with which western Carolinians, like most southerners, approached the fateful decision. "Great excitement now about the coming election," Sallie Lenoir wrote to her husband Rufus from Fort Defiance: "Dick says that Lincoln will be elected and there seems to be a gloom over nearly every heart. How dark the future!"[28]

This sense of impending doom was combined with frustration at the fact that none of the three names appearing on their ballots had much chance of defeating the one name that did not. This resulted in a western voter turnout (see table 9.1) considerably lower than that in the gubernatorial election in August, when voters had believed that they were contributing to the selection. Breckinridge carried North Carolina by only about 800 of more than 96,000 votes cast, a bare majority of 50.4 percent of the vote. Bell carried two-thirds of the mountain counties, with 55 percent of the vote there. Only in the five northwestern counties (and one southwest county), did Bell's total support exceed 60 percent. In the rest of the region, the race was a close one—so close, in fact, that, excluding the five northernmost counties, only 25 votes separated Breckinridge and Bell in the rest of the mountain region.[29]

The western election results indicated a relatively strong commitment to the Union, one slightly stronger than that evinced by the state as a whole. The southern passions so aroused by John Brown's raid had abated by the time of the presidential campaign, and the preceding winter's reckless talk of secession was notably absent during the summer and fall. But the mood among political leaders and voters was

Table 9.1. Presidential Election Results in Mountain Counties,
          November 1860

County	Bell Votes	(Const. Union) Majority Percent	Breckinridge Votes	(Ind. Dem.) Majority Percent	Douglas (Dem.) Votes
Ashe/Alleghany*	717	76.0	229		1
Buncombe	705	49.5	662		49
Burke	447		470	51	4
Caldwell	449	65.0	229		9
Cherokee	667	59.0	459		15
Haywood	248		367	58	13
Henderson	496	54.0	435		4
Jackson	142		403	74	—
Macon	469	67.0	221		13
Madison**					
McDowell	349	56.0	276		1
Watauga	322	69.0	147		—
Wilkes	1,323	78.0	363		—
Yancey	275		500	64	4
WNC Total	6,008	55.3	4,761		93
NC Total	44,990		48,539	50.4	2,701

Source: Computed from Burnham, *Presidential Ballots*, 648–68; and Connor, *North Carolina Manual*, 985–86.
   *Alleghany County voted with Ashe County through 1860.
   **Madison County election results were so confused and so questionable that they were thrown out. Paludan, *Victims*, 58.

by no means so conciliatory that southern interests were submerged merely for the sake of unity. Slavery and the question of who would best defend it remained at the forefront of the debate. Only because Whigs argued convincingly that southern rights, including slavery, could best be protected within rather than without the Union did they win the confidence, or at least the resigned acceptance, of a small majority of mountain voters.

On the other hand, Breckinridge's support in the area, which was considerable in at least half of the western counties, did not result from the disunionist label he wore. Rather, his stand for a strong defense of southern rights appealed enough to voters that they were

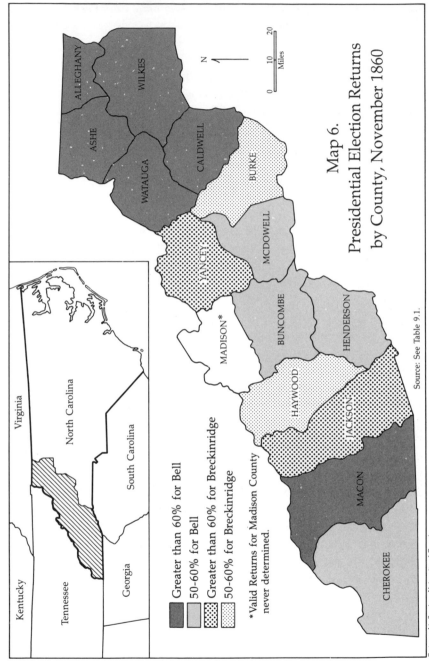

Map 6.
Presidential Election Returns
by County, November 1860

Greater than 60% for Bell

50–60% for Bell

Greater than 60% for Breckinridge

50–60% for Breckinridge

*Valid Returns for Madison County
never determined.

Source: See Table 9.1.

Cartographic Services, University of Georgia

willing to risk, or more likely to overlook, the more radical implications of his position. Thus, after Lincoln's election, with the possibility of secession suddenly very real and the future of the state and the South suddenly in doubt, western North Carolinians continued to argue for or against withdrawal from the Union, in terms of how the South's interests could best be served.

As was true throughout the Upper South, the vast majority of mountain residents did not find Lincoln's election alone sufficient cause for seceding and adopted a "watch and wait" policy. Yet from November 1860 through February 1861, when the vote for a state secession convention was held, the issue was hotly debated by advocates of all sides of the issue. The Republican victory, along with South Carolina's secession in December, inspired forceful arguments for North Carolina to follow South Carolina's lead.

Immediate secessionism would have been assured a hearing in the region, if only because Clingman advocated it. But he never was alone; other equally respected western political leaders joined him in pushing for immediate, decisive action. Among these were Democrats W.W. Avery, William Holland Thomas, and Marcus Erwin, all of whom, during the secession crisis, happened to be the state senators from the mountain's three senatorial districts. Avery, of course, had achieved prominence in his role at the Charleston convention; indeed, because of the controversial platform proposals he presented, he bore important responsibility for the Democratic party breakup and subsequent Republican victory. Erwin was the longtime editor of the area's Democratic voice, the *Asheville News*, and an avid supporter of Clingman. Thomas, though maintaining an apparently cautionary stance, in some ways was the most enthusiastic of the three about the idea of a southern confederacy. They, and others in the mountains, supplemented the arguments of Clingman and provided their fellow citizens with the full range of reasons why their state should cast its fate with its southern neighbors, and opinions as to when it should do so.

Once the election results confirmed Clingman's worst fears, he quickly reverted to his role as an ardent secessionist, strengthening his resolve that his state could not remain subject to a government headed by Abraham Lincoln or part of the nation that had elected him. "It is not," Clingman said, "that a dangerous man has been elected to the Presidency of the United States . . . But I assert that the President-elect has been elected *because he was known to be a dangerous man* . . . he declares that it is the purpose of the North to make war upon my section until its social system is destroyed, and for that he was taken up and elected. It is that great, remarkable and dangerous fact that has filled my section with alarm and dread for the future." Before South Carolina seceded in December 1860, both Clingman and Avery pushed for a state convention which would issue an ultimatum to Lincoln that unless he promised not to interfere with southern rights or make war on any states that might secede, North Carolina too would leave the Union.[32] As the intentions of South Carolina and the Gulf states became apparent, other mountain secessionists became as vocal and as determined as Clingman in urging that North Carolina follow these states' example. When the first southern states left the Union, it became obvious to some that a separate South was inevitable and that the sooner they themselves joined in, the better.

In mid-November 1860, W.W. Avery's father noted that "conservative men of all political opinions . . . seem to consider the Election of Lincoln as a declaration of war, and talk of a second declaration of independence." He concluded that, "if the conflict must come, perhaps it is as well now, as any time."[33] The conversion of Edward Jones Erwin of Burke County provides an example of how such realizations made disunionists out of former unionists. His initial reaction to Lincoln's election had been, "I am with the South; yet the time has not yet arrived for any one to take action." But on the last day of the year, he declared, "I am now for immediate secession as I have lost hope of the Union. The time is fast approaching to the situation that those who now advocate submission & renounce the South will be looked upon as Tories [were] in 1776." He berated those who still clung to the Union "when any man of common sense not warped by prejudice can't but see the Union is gone forever."[34]

For others, it was less the inevitability of eventual secession than the belief that an ensuing war was not inevitable that served as the best argument for North Carolina to secede. Their rationale was that Lincoln would be tempted to resort to military force against a fragmented South but would not dare to confront a united one. As Edward Erwin put it simply, "If the border states go out, there will be no war. If they do not, there will be war." He hoped that North Carolinians would declare immediate secession, so that "we would not seem to be kicked out."[35] James W. Patton of Asheville believed that only the

South as a whole could bargain effectively for terms by which reunion could be possible and war averted. "A Southern united separation is inevitable," he said, "before any favorable reconstruction of the government can be had."[36]

Clingman felt that evidence of delay and hesitation on the part of the Upper South encouraged "our enemies" to believe that they would have no resistance outside the cotton states, where they felt they could easily crush resistance with military force. They thus felt no need to make any substantive concessions to the South. He explained to William Holland Thomas:

> The obvious policy and purpose of the Black Republicans is to keep the South unprepared and divided until they can get into power, and then their intention is unmistakable – to use all the power of the government to compel the South to submit to their domination, to the extent even of abolishing slavery, should civil war afford them a tolerable pretext. If, however, North Carolina, Virginia and the border States will act at once, they may, by preserving a united South, avert the evils of civil war.[37]

Most of these opinions were expressed in private correspondence, though the essence of these arguments certainly would have been familiar to most politically aware citizens of the region. The most effective arguments issued by mountain secessionists specifically for public consumption—the arguments they felt their fellow westerners would most readily respond to—stressed the effect of "submission" on the institution of slavery. Once again, those who knew it best considered their area—in which almost 90 percent of the residents owned no slaves—to be as repelled as any other part of the South by that most unthinkable of consequences, the abolition of slavery. A circular issued by David W. Siler for distribution among Macon County citizens bluntly stated: "There are persons at the North who profess to believe that they commit a sin against the Almighty in supporting a Constitution that guarantees to the people of the South the right to hold slaves; whenever . . . the Government must be controlled by those who entertain this opinion, we must separate."[38]

Early in February 1861, Clingman made a speech before the U.S. Senate, which was issued two or three days later as a pamphlet and widely distributed throughout the mountain district and across the state. In it, he said that the North, in considering the most effective means of subjugating the South, recognized that "the greatest possible injury would be to liberate the slaves, and leave them as free negroes in those communities." In appealing to the nonslaveholding populace, he stressed not so much the obvious property losses to slaveholders, but rather the economic ruin such a financial disaster would bring on the region as a whole. Even that, however, was not the "greatest evil." Clingman once again appealed to deep-seated concerns over race control, by warning of the "social destruction of society by infusing into it a large free negro population that is most dreaded." Such would be the result if North Carolina remained in the Union under Lincoln. The state not only would be expected to "join him in the war against the Southern seceding States," but also must "expect to have slavery abolished by force of arms, and to see the South reduced to the condition of Jamaica or St. Domingo; or in other words, to a condition of free negro equality."[39]

W.W. Avery and Marcus Erwin also addressed this theme in circulars of their own distributed among their constituents and/or readers. After pointing out, as Clingman had, that separation could be achieved without war, and indeed could prevent it, they moved quickly to the racial theme. Emphasizing the effect of an emancipated slave populace which Republican coercion would bring with it, they noted:

> In addition to the terrible calamity of having three hundred thousand idle, vagabond free negroes turned loose upon you with all the privileges of white men—voting with you; sitting on juries with you; going to school with our children; and intermarrying with the white race . . . wages of all kinds of labor will be diminished; the price of agricultural productions of all kinds will fall so low that our farmers will be ruined.[40]

Another argument never used overtly by western North Carolina secessionists, but which had proved most effective in gaining the support of Georgia mountaineers, had been voiced by their governor, Joseph E. Brown. A native of the north Georgia mountains himself, Brown called attention to the effect of abolition on the mobility of freed slaves. "So soon as the slaves were at liberty," he wrote, "thousands of them would leave the cotton and rice fields in the lower part of our State, and make their way to the healthier climate in the mountain region. We should have them plundering and stealing, robbing, and killing; in all the lovely vallies [sic] of the mountains."[41] Western North Carolinians were equally susceptible to such fears. Indeed the seasonal influx of slaves from the low country to the resort communities had often increased racial tensions in the area, as had the presence of almost any strangers in the aftermath of the insurrections of both John Brown earlier that year and Nat Turner almost thirty years earlier. The sensitivity of western North Carolinians to these outsiders meant that Governor Brown's scenario, even if envisioned in less dramatic terms, at least must have crossed the minds of some.

As usual, economic arguments found a ready audience among commercially minded highlanders. Advocates of secession sought to localize the issue by predicting both the handicaps to the mountain counties if they were not a part of the Confederacy and the benefits to their region if they were. North Carolinians all over the state worried that the secession of Virginia and Tennessee would leave them no choice but to join the southern nation, since remaining in the Union while surrounded by Confederate territory was inconceivable. For the southwestern counties, which were closer to Georgia, South Carolina, and Tennessee than even to Asheville, the prospect of being hemmed in by Confederate states was even more alarming. That area's chief spokesman, William Holland Thomas, pointed out that the highlands would face economic ruin if North Carolina did not also secede, for that region in particular "would be surrounded by foreign territory into which her citizens could not go without passports and with which she could not trade except through customhouses."[42]

Clingman, too, recognized that tariffs and possibly nonimportation restrictions would be imposed on North-South trade at whatever northern boundary was fixed for the Confederacy. For western North Carolinians, such barriers would be far less harmful along the Mason-Dixon line, or even between North Carolina and Virginia, than they would between the two Carolinas. In response to tariff threats by northern senators, Clingman replied that "if you establish a line of custom houses and make us in North Carolina pay as high duties as you please . . . the merchants from my region will go down to Charleston, as they often do." He also pointed out that the lower tariff on imported goods already established by the Confederate government would be an improvement to mountain consumers over the federal rates to which they were presently subject.[43]

On a more positive note, some claimed that, with independence from the North, voluntary efforts at developing local manufacturing, so widely discussed a year earlier, would blossom under the added impetus of necessity. The long-term result would be diversity and prosperity for the mountain economy. Likewise, the inaccessibility of popular northern "watering holes" would drive more planters from across the South to the Carolina highland resorts, already well known to Charlestonians. Its geographical location and the fact that Flat Rock and Hendersonville were already the summer homes of several prominent southern officials, most notably Confederate Treasury Secretary Christopher G. Memminger, led some to speculate that the government itself might establish headquarters in the area. In this "mountain kingdom," wrote a Henderson County visitor, "it is contemplated to place the capital city of the Southern Confederacy, having its seat of government within 100 miles of the capitals of six other states."[44]

Clingman, having envisioned most of these possibilities for his section of the state long before the current crisis, was enthusiastic about them. But it was William Holland Thomas who best summed up these aspirations. "The mountains of Western North Carolina would be the centre of the Confederacy," he pointed out; as a result, "we shall then have one of the most prosperous countries in the world. It will become connected with every part of the South by railroad. It will then become the centre of manufacturing for the Southern market. The place where the southern people will spend their money, educate their children and very probably make laws for the nation."[45] Curiously, these speculations on the glorious benefits of joining the Confederacy were made largely in private correspondence and were never widely circulated among mountain residents.

Despite the undeniable appeal of the various secessionist arguments set forth by highly respected leaders, the vast majority of mountain residents seems to have been much more cautious toward these developments from Lincoln's election in November 1860 through the state's convention vote late in February 1861. Maintaining peace, defending slavery, and advancing regional well-being were the priorities of mountain unionists as much as of their secessionist opponents. So only the question of what course would best ensure those goals caused disagreement between the two sides and led most Western Carolinians to resist any action before it was absolutely necessary.

The outcome of the presidential election alone was not cause enough, they felt, for breaking up the Union. Their "watch and wait" stance was based as much on assurance that their options for later action remained open as it was on a fear of disunion. David W. Siler of Macon County summed up the majority of mountain opinion during November and December 1860 when he wrote, "My policy is to hold

Figure 23. William Holland Thomas. North Carolina Division of Archives and History.

on to the Union, until every remedy has been and if that fails it will be time enough then to get out." Congressman Vance, the region's most prominent unionist, pointed out, "We have everything to gain and nothing on earth to lose by delay, but by too hasty action we may take a fatal step we can never retrace—may lose a heritage that we can never recover."[46]

Many of those who agreed with Siler and Vance still saw the election result as an omnious signal that sooner or later they would have to act. Sallie Lenoir, her preelection fears confirmed, reiterated her sense of foreboding the day after hearing that Lincoln had been elected: "I dread the dark future. If the South would only keep cool and try him first I think we need not fear much but I cannot hope that."[47] Her brother-in-law in Haywood County, too, harbored few illusions that the crisis could be resolved without separation. "I do not yet think we have had sufficient cause to secede," Thomas Isaac Lenoir wrote late in December, "but this aggressive policy of the Black Republicans will sometime, if they do not now, drive us from a Union once so dear but now so little respected." He labeled himself a "co-operationist" rather than a secessionist, "not a minute man, yet not old fogey enough to be a member of the 'cob-pipe association' " (a group presumably made up of diehard unconditional unionists).[48]

To many mountain residents, South Carolina's secession on 20 December 1860 merely confirmed the inevitability of North Carolina's course. Just after hearing of it, James Gwyn wrote: "I dare say most of the Southern States, if not all, will soon follow. No hope for the Union I fear . . . No chance to make any amicable settlement of the difficulties between the North & South."[49] Despite their close association with and economic dependence on South Carolina, western North Carolinians had little sympathy for the situation into which that state had put itself. As in the crises of 1832 and 1850, most mountaineers expressed disapproval at the recklessness of their southern neighbor in declaring independence. A much-quoted story probably reflects the attitude of many. At a local secession meeting, a North Carolina mountaineer grew so impatient at the seemingly endless discussion of South Carolina's bold action that he jumped up and shouted, "For God's sake! Let South Carolina nullify, revolute, secede, and BE DAMNED!"[50]

Indeed, some condemned the Palmetto State's rashness as strongly as they did the fanaticism of northerners and blamed both for bringing about the crisis at hand. A Buncombe County father, in explaining the crisis to his son in Australia, said that it was "all brot about by the corruption of scheming, designing, demagogue politicians & office seekers, that deserve to be shot & hung for treason, both North and South."[51] Zebulon Vance actually accused the two groups of collusion in bringing on the crisis. "The rabid abolition element of the North," he informed his constituents, "has been working side by side with southern disunionists for the destruction of the Union, though for different reasons: the one because it protected slavery at all, the other because it did not protect it enough. Both alike rejoice in the prospect of disunion."[52]

As the Deep South states followed South Carolina's lead, mountain unionists expressed keen resentment at the rash behavior of those states and doubts about their own participation in a confederacy dominated by the "cotton oligarchy." Vance, in the House of Representatives, believed that the seceded states had, in effect, deserted the rest of the South and the southern cause by the resignation of their congressmen. They are "leaving us completely in the power of the Republicans of both branches!" he wrote with disgust from Washington. "A more ruinous and suicidal policy . . . could not have been pursued." Moreover, the disunion leaders of South Carolina and Georgia "are scorning every suggestion of compromise and rushing everything with ruinous and indecent haste that would seem to imply that they were absolute fools." But, he warned, "they are acting wisely for their ends—they are precipitating the people into a revolution without giving them time to think—*They fear lest the people shall think*; hence [their] hasty action."[53]

In the face of pressure from those who had already seceded, mere pride led some mountain residents to oppose secession. "It is deeply humiliating (or ought to be)," said Calvin C. Jones of Lenoir, "to any citizen of a border state if they allow these arrogant Cotton Oligarchies south of them to dragoon them into their service."[54] A Haywood County farmer based his resentment on earlier economic grievances toward the naughty South Carolinians with whom he had traded. In an anonymous letter to the *Raleigh Register*, he stated:

> We should never leave the Union on account of South Carolina. We should not follow the example of such a domineering State. If we have to leave the Union, we should not be dragged out by a State whose citizens consider themselves our superiors in every respect. They would want to lead us continually, and we could not get along in peace with them five years. For ex-

ample think how they have shaved North Carolina money, when it was really as good as their own: and yet we are her sister State, and called by the same name.[55]

C.D. Smith of Macon County was among those who resented the attempts of South Carolina and Georgia "to seduce and coerce" the border states to join the Confederacy. He even implied that their policies favored the North more than the South. Offended by the recommendation of Gov. William H. Gist of South Carolina that slaves from Virginia and other border states not be allowed to be sold in his state, Smith asserted that such a betrayal of fellow slave states would "disturb our intercommercial relations amongst ourselves." Moreover, it was, he said, "a most remarkable discrimination in favor of the North [since] he says nothing against the people of South Carolina buying goods, merchandise, hay, fruit, powder, lead, arms, bacon, corn, flour, clocks, clothes, and almost every thing else from Abolitionists and Yankees."[56] Mountain residents also found offensive the more subtle means by which individual South Carolinians sought to pressure their business acquaintances in the mountain counties. Businessmen sometimes called in the debts of their North Carolina customers and implied that such credit was risky as long as the two states remained in different countries. A Spartanburg merchant, for example, asked Edmund Jones to pay a four-hundred-dollar note not due for almost a year, because of "great pressure in the money market due to the crisis." The merchant then launched into a rousing tribute to the Confederacy and its virtues and expressed his hopes that North Carolinians soon would be a part of it.[57]

Others who opposed immediate secession were more concerned about the differences in the mountains and the Deep South if they were united in the Confederacy. A unionist broadside circulated in Buncombe County stressed the fact that the "cotton monopoly is at the bottom of the revolution," but claimed that secessionists had "concealed the fact from the people from Western North Carolina, because cotton is not raised here." The circular also pointed out that policies beneficial to "the rich cotton, sugar, and rice planters of the Cotton States," such as free trade and direct taxation, would not be in the best interest of western Carolinians, and might in fact prove "oppressive and ruinous to the poor farmer and mechanic." The writer predicted that the Lower South states "are to reap golden rewards, while the middle States . . . are to be 'hewers of wood and drawers of water' for

King Cotton."[58] W.W. Lenoir stated that he too opposed "joining our state with the schemes and politics of the cotton states," because "I am utterly opposed to reopening the slave trade [with Africa], have no faith in the new political dogmas which I believe they will engraft in their constitution, and have no desire to engage in the silly project of trying in vain to carry slavery into Mexico and Central America."[59]

Significantly, however, western North Carolina unionists did not criticize the Lower South's large slaveholdings. In mountaineers' expressions of disapproval at the seceded states' actions or of reluctance to cast their own fate with those states, they referred to "cotton states" and never used the term "slaveocracy," which was in such common use elsewhere. No one in the mountains ever implied that discrepancies between the interests of the Deep South and those of their own area were based on the number of slaves held in each. The one slave-related policy they opposed, the reopening of the African slave trade, posed a threat to the value of their own slave property—a fear widely felt throughout the Upper South. Thus they objected to the Confederacy's actions because the latter threatened the system's survival, rather than because they insured it. The emphasis was on avoiding any change in the racial status quo, whether instigated by the North or by the Lower South.

As the Confederacy took shape, mountain unionists found additional arguments against North Carolina's entry. The Buncombe County broadside pointed out that the effect of southern secession on North Carolina thus far had been to depreciate property values, disturb industrial pursuits, destroy confidence in business transactions, and "bring much distress to our people." "If such has been the effect upon North Carolina while she remains in the Union," the broadside reasoned, "we may reasonably conclude that these evils would be greatly multiplied if she should go out of the Union."[60]

An argument particularly effective with the poorer mountain populace pointed out the heavy tax burden that had already been imposed on South Carolina citizens and that most likely would become even more oppressive with the added cost of financing a war. Opponents of secession warned that if North Carolina followed a similar course, it "will be foolishly involved in debt for arms and ammunition." One particularly ardent Buncombe County unionist predicted that "the Southern States will be ruined by the taxes to keep up a government & standing army," a fate he felt was well deserved. "It is hoped they will be made to suffer," he went on, "for their hot-headed arrogance & foolhardiness & premeditated wickedness in doing as they have done, bringing ruin on themselves & the bal[ance] of the States."[61] Vance reminded his constituents that a war against the North was not the only one they might be required to finance. "As soon as we join the confederacy," he pointed out to them, "suppose we are called on to furnish men and money for the conquest of some Mexican provinces on the Gulf, or perhaps merely money to purchase them . . . So of Cuba, Nicaragua, or any other country we might annex."[62]

For some western Carolinians, the sheer instability of the Confederate government and its component parts was the biggest source of worry. Calvin Cowles called the seceded states "little republics" and wondered "if they will not quarrel and fight as do states in S[outh] America—do you think the interest of the negro requires so great a sacrifice?" Late in February 1861, a Morganton man expressed dismay over the changes wrought over the last two months. Already, he wrote, "we behold the remains of a shattered and dismembered confederacy—a people overwhelmed with commercial and financial distress and a government thoroughly revolutionized."[63] Some perceptive mountain residents recognized that because it had to incorporate the doctrine of secession into its constitution, the Confederacy carried within itself the seeds of its own destruction and might remain a nation short-lived and of little consequence. An Asheville unionist pointed out that it was "held together by ropes of sand." Allen T. Davidson, a Cherokee County banker, wrote home from a business trip in Georgia and Florida in early April 1861, describing the chaotic conditions he found. "If ever the liberty of speech and the press was under the direct control of a despotism," he reported from Atlanta, "it is here. God save our glorious old state from the damnation of such a lawless and desperate *Mob*—for mob rules here in all its peculiar force."[64]

These reservations about the Confederacy and worries about incompatibility with the Deep South led some western Carolinians to consider seriously, if only briefly, the idea of a "Central Confederacy." As chances of preserving the Union seemed to wane, the proposal of a third unit composed of border free and slave states provided one last desperate means to effect a reconstruction of the Union. Though it was considered throughout the Upper South, the idea seems to have carried special appeal in North Carolina's mountain counties, perhaps because their residents felt they had less in common with the Lower South, though they were equally threatened by Republican ascendency in the North. The plan was never widely publicized in the region, but a number of western unionists, most notably Zebulon Vance and W.W. Lenoir, enthusiastically discussed it among themselves. Based on the theory that the real enemy of slavery and southern rights was New England, rather than the northern states as a whole, moderates in several of the middle states, slave and free, felt that a union free of both extremist elements would form a solid core which the seceded states one by one would be willing to rejoin.[65]

Vance saw this plan as a stop-gap alternative to the bleak choices then available to North Carolinians. Their options at that point, he explained, were either to join the Confederacy after its policies had been established, and have to accede to its "own peculiar dogmas"; or to "stay out and be their border Guard against abolitionism." At this point, he declared, the Confederacy did not care which course they took. A central confederacy offered distinct advantages over either course. For Vance, still in Washington, it meant that "we preserve this Capitol, the public lands, the form and prestige of the old government [and] secure greater homogeneousness."[66] Lenoir added that joining a central confederacy was far preferable to secession, which would be "to abandon to wrong-doers our vast and increasing national wealth, our magnificient capitol and public buildings, our archives, our soul-stirring national traditions, our army, our navy, and our proud flag." It would be better to destroy the latter than to "desert it to be waived [*sic*] in defiance and insult over the hosts of a mad fanaticism."[67]

Of course, this proposal's greatest advantage was that it offered a means not only of restoring the Union, but also of making reforms that would assure a more stable balance of power within the federal government. According to the scenario foreseen by Vance, Georgia would be the first of the seceded states to return to the fold, and its withdrawal from the Confederacy "would break the backbone of the whole seceding Kingdom." New England, on the other hand, would not be allowed back (in fact, Vance said, "we would *kick* it out if it refused to secede") except as a single state "with only two Sumners in the Senate to play the blackguard."[68]

Vance never openly advocated this plan, since he was still publicly trying to convey confidence in compromise measures to avert further secession. But Lenoir told him that the idea not only was widespread in his mountain district but was the only one viewed with favor. "Any means which may be prudent and necessary to inaugurate it," he assured Vance, "will be sustained with enthusiasm."[69] Given the obvious impracticalities of the plan and the sheer speed with which developments were unfolding, however, such enthusiasm for the plan proved short-lived and had faded completely by mid-January.

Only in East Tennessee, the South's most firmly entrenched unionist stronghold, did the scheme remain alive beyond that point. Just prior to Tennessee's convention referendum on 9 February 1861, "Parson" William G. Brownlow, East Tennessee's most outspoken antisecessionist, set forth an interesting variation on the plan. In his *Knoxville Whig*, he proposed the formation of an "independent Mountain State of Frankland," composed of the highland regions of Tennessee, Virginia, and North Carolina, each of which would separate from its own state "if they shall be so reckless as to consent to go out of the Union." Even after the April 1861 attack on Fort Sumter and Lincoln's subsequent call for troops, A.W. Howard of Greeneville, Tennessee, raised the cry for a separate central confederacy. He suggested that "if the border States secede that does not necessarily connect them with the South. . . . I am for the Border States declaring themselves to be the United States—and that the North and South have both gone off."[70]

There is no indication that anyone across the state line to the east acknowledged, or much less embraced, Brownlow's idea of a mountain republic. Only W.W. Lenoir seemed to hold out any hope for such a scenario. In early February 1861, well after most others had given it up as futile, he proposed that in the event of war, North Carolina declare itself "an armed neutrality." Other border states would follow suit, and "the fight would thus whittle down to a broil between New England and South Carolina and such of their excited neighbors as were mad enough to join in with them."[71] Lenior stood alone on the issue even in February. By mid-April, of course, when Howard still clung to the possibility, western North Carolinians had moved well beyond such implausibilities.

More traditional unionist arguments within the mountains resembled secessionist views, in that they were based firmly on the anticipated effects of disunion on slavery's survival. The most basic point was simply that, in the Union, the Constitution protected slave property. Thus, to secede from the Union would mean casting aside that most basic of securities. Alexander H. Jones, Henderson County's most vocal unionist, declared that "by throwing off those guarantees—the Constitution and the Union—southern states have done the cause of slavery more injury than anything else could have done."[72]

Others emphasized a more specific protective device that North Carolinians would sacrifice if they left the Union—the Fugitive Slave Law. A Nantahala man stated that he would be satisfied to remain in the Union under a Republican administration "if Lincoln will pledge himself to execute the fugitive slave law."[73] Vance reminded mountain residents that, with the border states as part of the Confederacy, everything north of the Mason-Dixon Line would be what Canada was throughout the antebellum period, a foreign nation beyond any legal jurisdiction of slaveholders. Thus, "the moment a negro stepped across that line he would be forever gone, for there is not a civilized nation on earth, so far as my knowledge extends, that returns fugitive slaves to their foreign masters." He went on to trace the effects of this situation: the risks of slave ownership in Virginia and other border states would become so great that the value of black property would depreciate until masters, either by sale or emigration, would move them farther South. Those states would thus gradually become free, North Carolina and Tennessee would then form slavery's northernmost border, and the process would repeat itself. "So destruction marches southward," he warned.[74] An Ashe County unionist also warned of depreciation of slave values, but for another reason. The Lower South's real motive in seceding, he claimed, was to reopen the African slave trade as a cheaper source of black labor, thus undercutting the market for North Carolina slaves.[75]

Like their opponents, unionists were also quick to equate war with an unleashing of black power across the South. An Asheville resident pointed out that the very ownership of slaves gave southerners a decided disadvantage "if the two sections . . . become engaged in deadly conflict," for the North "can do awful damage & destruction by & through our slaves. Once arouse them to insurrection & they will carry murder, Rape & arson into the midst of our firesides." He reported that "all the principal cities S[outh] are in commotion & fear both from bad Negroes & from Abolitionists lest they come down in an army and incite the Negroes to insurrection." If they could only convert their slave property into funds, he concluded, southerners might survive the struggle intact. But, with the presence of slaves, they should do all they could to preserve the Union and avoid war.[76]

In Raleigh, late in November 1860, Zebulon Vance challenged the arguments of two South Carolina congressmen who were passing through the city on their way home from Washington. These men argued that British support and protection would prevent any problem of race control in a seceded South. Vance retorted that it was that very protection for which "our forefathers had waged a seven years war to escape." As evidence that British allies would not necessarily safeguard slavery, he reminded his listeners of the *London Times'*s indignant reaction to the Prince of Wales' recent visit to Richmond slave pens, an appearance it called a blot on the English character. To those who believed slave property would be more secure under British protection than under the United States Constitution, Vance asked how many runaway slaves had ever been returned by Canadian authorities.[77] Such arguments by mountain unionists once more point up the fallacy of equating unionism with antislavery sentiment.

Despite the passion with which unionism was advocated throughout the mountain counties, it was, to an overwhelming degree, what can be termed cautionary, or conditional, unionism. Few if any of the spokesmen opposing immediate secession ever saw that position as an irrevocable one. They were usually quick to affirm that their first loyalty was to the South and that their commitment to the Union was based entirely on the assumption that southern interests, particularly slavery, would be protected under the incoming administration. A statement by East Tennessee's "Parson" Brownlow aptly summed up the sentiments of most western North Carolina unionists as well, in what also proved to be an accurate prediction. "The Union men of the border slave states," he wrote,

> are loyal to their Government and do not regard the election of Lincoln as any just cause for dissolving this Union . . . But, if we were once convinced in the border states that the Administration at Washington, and the people of the North who are backing up the Administration with men and money, contemplated the subjugation of the South or the abolishing of slavery, there would not be a Union man among us in twenty-four hours. Come what might, sink or swim, survive or perish, we would fight you to the death. And we would unite our fortunes and destinies with even those demoralized seceded states, for whose leaders and laws we have no sort of respect.[78]

For the vast majority of North Carolina's mountain residents, a commitment to the Union was a means toward an end, rather than an end in itself. Only when they saw allegiance to the Union, rather than withdrawal from it, as the option most likely to protect their interests as individuals, as North Carolinians, and as southerners, did they advocate continued association. From November 1860 on, most highlanders indicated that there were limits beyond which that commitment could not endure. Secessionists found that the term "submissionist," implying a willingness to submit to any federal policy for the sake of preserving the Union, was an epithet which made unionists flinch, and most of the latter were quick to deny accusations that their commitment to the Union was so intense as to merit that label.

Far more often than not, the various expressions of unionist sentiment cited thus far were qualified by statements either of loyalty to the South and slavery or of limits within which such sentiments applied. A Baptist minister in Madison County, for example, wrote a letter to Vance condemning the actions of secessionists and affirming his area's support for the Union. But he ended his message by saying, "This people is As true to the south As Any people that every trod the soil But Let it [secession] be The Last Resort."[79] W.W. Lenoir expressed his "abhorrence of those who have been and are busy destroying the constitution and the Union" and called their actions "the greatest crime that has been done in the world since the temptation of Eve." Nevertheless, he continued, "while I religiously believe that to be true, it does not follow that I would think the more formal act, when necessary, of arresting its machinery and declaring its nonexistence would be criminal. . . . I stand out as stout as any Southern man ought for full justice from the north as an indispensible condition to union with the north, or any part of it."[80] Even Allen Davidson, whose trip through the Deep South filled him with contempt for the mob rule and chaotic conditions of the Confederacy, concluded his description by saying, "If however, 'Old Abe' does make war on the south, our destiny must be with the south as a state. I would not encourage disloyalty to our section."[81]

Vance himself was fully aware that conditions might lead to his state's withdrawal from the Union. He assured his constituents that, should that be the case, "then your fate is mine . . . You shall have, if necessary, even my blood upon the battle field. Having resisted the tide of destruction as long as possible, it will nevertheless be the duty, as, I doubt not, it will be the pleasure, of Union men to show the foes of our State and section, should the dreadful necessity arise, that if slow to take the field, we are none the less resolute to maintain it."[82]

Communities all over the state held public meetings in December 1860 and January 1861 and drew up resolutions declaring their allegiance to the Union. Of those held in western North Carolina, all but one qualified their present course of action with strong conditional statements.[83] Caldwell County residents, for example, reaffirmed the constitutional right of secession and declared that if the nonslaveholding states failed to guarantee "the preservation of the constitutional rights of the Slaveholding States," the latter had not only a right, but a duty to form a "separate political existence." Even the citizens of Wilkes, considered the most solidly unionist county in western North Carolina, declared that "if after exhausting such means as are consistent with our rights and common safety, we are unable to secure safety in the Union, we are as ready as any people to sacrifice our blood and treasure to maintain and preserve our institutions out of the Union."[84]

What it would take to convert these men into secessionists varied somewhat. Certainly, as Brownlow made clear, any attempt to interfere with slavery where it presently existed would have dissolved any unionist sentiment immediately. That reaction was so obvious and so predictable to both North and South that it rarely had to be verbalized. Far more often discussed, was the less obvious and far more likely possibility that Lincoln might apply military force to hold the nation together. Despite strong disapproval of South Carolina's secession, nearly all mountain unionists were adamant in their conviction that South Carolina had had the right to secede and that any attempt to force it or any other state back into the Union would justify North Carolina's joining forces with the states so threatened.

On 22 December 1860, two days after South Carolina withdrew from the Union, Caldwell County citizens met and declared that, because free governments are maintained by the consent of the governed, "we believe that if any one or more of the States shall secede from the Union in its present condition, it is the wisest policy of the federal government to recognize immediately their separate national existence."[85] "Coercion" quickly became the key word signifying the limit beyond which tolerance for the new administration would not extend. Only one day after South Carolina initiated the separation process, a Macon County man reported an increase in southern feeling there, along with a general attitude that "if our Sister States should secede that coercion or an attempt to coerce on the part of the north will be a signal for 'to strike.' "[86]

Western Carolinians opposed coercion so strongly that Vance's supporters feared that rumors that he approved such a move could be a major political liability. A resolution approving Maj. Robert Anderson's bold stand to hold federal property in Charleston's harbor and President Buchanan's support of him was introduced in the U.S. House of Representatives early in January 1861 and passed by a vote of almost two to one. Though Vance voted against the bill, secessionists within his district tried to interpret his stand as approval of military force in South Carolina. His brother in Asheville told him that he "would be astonished at the activity of one horse politicians here in circulating that you voted to coerce So. Ca. I don't regard it of course, I only hate to see people lie so."[87] Late in January, James Gudger also informed Vance of circulating reports that "Zeb Vance is a dead dog, he's gone in for coercion." He added contemptuously that "one half of the cussed devils don't know what coercion means."[88] Whether or not Vance actually was able to correct these deliberate distortions, they damaged him little, as new events and changing issues quickly diverted public attention. But the very facts that Vance's opponents had viewed such charges as an effective weapon and that his supporters had seen them as a source of concern indicate just how conditional the unionist feelings of his constituents were, and how sensitive they were to any use of federal force against their southern neighbors.

After much delay and with considerable pressure on the part of secessionist leaders in the state, the General Assembly, on 29 January 1861, approved a measure calling for North Carolinians to vote on 28 February whether or not to hold a convention to consider secession. At the same time, delegates to that convention were to be selected. During the month of February 1861, both unionists and disunionists campaigned intensely throughout the mountain counties, and western leaders closely scrutinized popular opinion. Calvin Cowles' observation that "public sentiment here amongst the rank & file is decidedly averse to extreme measures" applied to most of the mountain district. As a Lenoir resident warned, however, "the nature of the Southern people is impulsive and sectional feeling contagious."[89] Unionists in most counties remained confident that voters were not yet ready for a

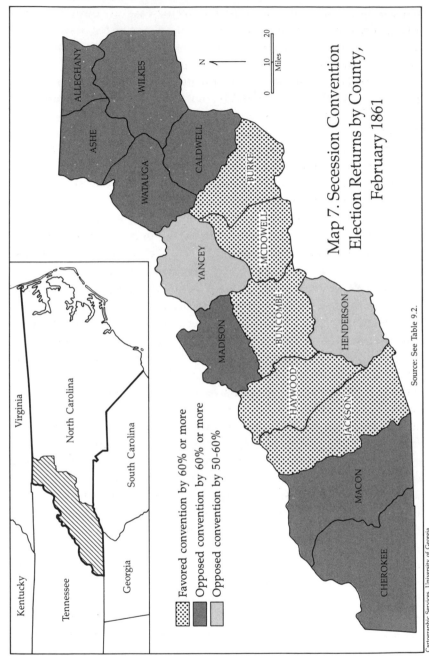

Map 7. Secession Convention
Election Returns by County,
February 1861

Source: See Table 9.2.

Favored convention by 60% or more

Opposed convention by 60% or more

Opposed convention by 50-60%

Cartographic Services, University of Georgia

convention which many saw to be the last step toward secession.[90] Yet others, whatever their own sympathies, predicted strong showings by secessionists in many parts of the region and felt that the momentum of the crisis would work to the latter's advantage.[91]

The correlation between party affiliation and secessionist attitudes was also hotly debated. Though somewhat exaggerated, a Madison County man's observation that "it has split Whig & Democracy all into h—l" suggested the confusion. Party leaders Clingman and Vance did keep many of their supporters in their respective disunion and Union camps. Tod R. Caldwell described Burke County Democrats as "all secessionists, while our Whig friends [are] generally firm for the Union and conservatism."[92] But several prominent mountain Democrats, particularly in Buncombe and Polk counties, strongly supported the Union. Likewise, Vance learned that many of his former Whig supporters had become secessionists.[93]

The campaign was hard fought, and violence almost erupted in some areas. David Coleman, one of Buncombe County's leading secessionists, was almost tarred and feathered when he carried his message over into Madison County. Yancey County secessionists burned Vance in effigy in Burnsville and attempted to equate his unionism with abolitionism.[94] Hostility toward a unionist minister at Cane Creek and fear of his influence from the pulpit made three local secessionists agree that they should make him either "pray for Jeff Davis and the Confederacy, or ride him on a rail." Only another minister's taking over that pulpit prevented a possibly violent confrontation there.[95]

Unionist tactics in delaying approval of a convention referendum in the legislature paid off. The momentum for secession created by the rapid succession of Lower South state withdrawals had somewhat abated by the latter part of February 1861. During the month, hopes for a peaceful resolution to the crisis were revived. As Congress reconsidered the Crittendon Compromise proposal, a peace conference met in Washington, and the states of Virginia and Tennessee rejected secession. All of these developments gave unionist sentiment in the region "a chance to jell."[96]

By a slim majority (50.3 percent of the vote), North Carolinians rejected the call for a convention on 28 February. The turnout in the western counties was almost one-and-a-half times greater than it had been in the presidential election three months earlier. This increase seems to have indicated not so much greater interest in the stakes, as a greater sense that each vote could make a difference. This shift was particularly true of Democrats, who had been so discouraged by their divided party's poor prospects that many had chosen not to vote at all for a presidential candidate.[97]

In the mountains, results of voting on the convention issue were mixed. Five of the fifteen counties (Buncombe, Burke, Haywood, Jackson, and McDowell) voted for a convention by margins of over 60 percent. In three others (Henderson, Macon, and Yancey), the electorate was almost evenly divided, with opposition to a convention carrying by less than 60 percent in each (see table 9.2). The other seven counties—the five northernmost counties and Cherokee and Madison counties —opposed a convention by heavy majorities.

These figures alone do not indicate the extent of unionist sentiment in the region. Voters did not, in the end, equate a vote for a convention with a vote for secession. Rather, many seem to have followed the lead of unionist leaders like Vance, who advocated a convention. He had said that he did not regard the call for a convention as a disunion movement. He believed that the convention could serve purposes other than North Carolina's secession, such as making collective demands on the North and "if they are refused, then for making our voice heard with the Southern States." Above all, Vance believed a convention to be the only democratic means by which a people should commit themselves to war. He wrote: "Though some of our Southern sisters have contemptuously refused to consult the wishes of 180,000 fighting men, over whose dead bodies an invading host, treading through the ashes, must reach them, yet there are others who anxiously seek general and fraternal counsel, and their desire we should regard."[98] Though Vance was one of the first both to oppose secession and to favor a convention, other conservatives later came to see such a gathering as a means of slowing the pace of secessionist fervor and calming the public mind. For others, the mere lack of any action implied weakness, and a convention would at least confirm the state's position in a more forceful way. In explaining why he had voted for a convention, unionist Samuel F. Patterson said, "I could not see how North Carolina could stand still with either honor or safety."[99]

Apparently such was the feeling of much of the mountain electorate, for the votes for a convention far exceeded those for secessionist candidates. Of fifteen delegates elected from the westernmost counties, all but three were unionists.[100] Voters had clearly indicated that

Table 9.2. *Secession Convention Election Results in Mountain Counties, February 1861*

County	Favor[1] Convention	Majority Percent	Oppose[1] Convention	Majority Percent	% Slaves[2] in Population 1860	Party[3] Affiliation 1850–1860
Alleghany	115		255	69	5.7	D
Ashe	144		758	84	4.9	D
Buncombe	1,219	76	389		15.3	D/W
Burke	718	78	273		31.6	W
Caldwell	186		615	78	14.5	W
Cherokee	149		901	86	5.6	D/W
Haywood	504	62	307		5.4	D
Henderson	573		647	53	13.2	W
Jackson	435	84	83		4.8	D
Macon	250		359	59	8.6	W
Madison	345		532	61	3.6	D
McDowell	638	75	217		18.3	D/W
Watauga	72		536	88	2.0	W
Wilkes	51		1,895	97	8.2	W
Yancey	556		598	51	4.8	D
WNC Total	5,955		8,401	59		
NC Total	46,671		47,333	50		

[1]Computed from Connor, *North Carolina Manual*, 1013–15; and Kruman, *Parties and Politics*, table 31, 276–78.

[2]Computed from *Population of the U.S. in 1860*, 358–59. See also table 2.2 in this book.

[3]Party labels are based on election results in the 6 gubernatorial and state legislative races from 1850 through 1860. These were determined by the number of times a county voted for a Democrat or Whig candidate for governor, and by the party affiliation of a majority of its state legislators. D/W indicates a fairly even split between Whig and Democratic majorities in both types of race over the decade. American and Opposition party members were counted as Whigs.

they were not yet ready to abandon the Union, but many (almost half) did not oppose the idea of a convention through which the state could make a firm defense of their rights either within or outside of the Union. For this, they were willing to risk what convention opponents had stressed was simply a disunion scheme. By the same token, the majority of those delegates to the convention, had it been approved, were clearly so-called "conditional unionists." Their commitment was to oppose immediate secession, but most of them had publicly indicated their opposition to coercion and their willingness to cast their lots with the Confederacy when and if further developments warranted it.[101]

The mountains' electoral results reflected geographical factors more than party affiliation, slave population, or other variables. Just as the largest slaveholders in the region were divided in their attitudes toward secession, so there was little correlation between the proportion of slaves in a county and February 1861 voting patterns (see table 9.2). Though the largest slaveholding county, Burke, was also the most pro-convention county and the only one to elect a secessionist delegate, the connection was a tenuous one elsewhere in the region. Of the four counties with the next greatest number of slaves in 1860, only two, Buncombe and McDowell, voted heavily for a convention. Caldwell County voted just as heavily against one, and Henderson voted against by a much closer margin. Likewise, of the six counties where slaves made up 5 percent or less of the population, two favored a convention, three opposed it, and one was fairly evenly split on the issue. Just over 8 percent of the populations of both Wilkes and Macon counties were slaves, yet in the former, over 97 percent of its voters opposed a convention, while in the latter, less than 59 percent did so.

There was some correlation between party affiliation and secessionist sentiment, particularly in relation to the recent presidential election. As tables 9.1 and 9.2 indicate, the residents of six of the eight counties that opposed a convention in February 1861 had cast a majority of their votes in November 1860 for the Constitutional Unionist (Whig) candidate John Bell. Likewise, four of the five counties in which a majority supported a convention had supported Democrat John Breckinridge three months earlier.[102] Beyond that, partisan correlations remain tenuous. The heavier voter turnout in February made parallels difficult to draw, particularly considering the November election's significant absence of Democrats. Nor did the mountain counties' long-term party affiliation ensure as consistent a relation to secessionist sentiments as it did elsewhere in the state.[103] In the two mountain counties with the most consistent Democratic voting records, based on gubernatorial and legislative elections from 1850 through 1860, Ashe County strongly opposed a convention, while Yancey was almost evenly divided, with 51.8 percent opposing it. The discrepancies in votes on the convention in the two most predominantly Whig counties, Wilkes and Macon, have been noted above.[104]

Probably the most consistent variable correlating with unionist support within a county was its geographical position within the region. The largest majorities opposing a convention and the most unconditional unionist delegates were those from the block of counties which made up the northwestern corner of the state. Commercial ties with northern markets were certainly stronger in that area than in any other part of North Carolina's mountains. It is no coincidence that Calvin Cowles, whose business activity was oriented more northward than southward, was one of the most outspoken unionists in the state. Rather than trading primarily with firms or individuals in Charleston, Spartanburg, Athens, and Augusta, he and other merchants from Wilkes, Caldwell, and Ashe counties in particular carried on regular transactions with the larger cities to the North. Cowles' annual trips to Washington, Philadelphia, New York, and Boston, like those of James Harper of Lenoir, partners Lytle and Hickerson of Wilkesboro, and others, reinforced an intersectional perspective on the crisis and raised fears about how separation from those markets would harm business. The fact that all of these men were among the largest slaveholders in their counties indicates that a vested interest in slavery was by no means the primary determinant shaping their attitudes toward secession.[105]

These men and their commercial ties were influential in shaping the attitudes of their communities. An even more important factor in the northwestern counties' cautious stance, however, was the more immediate prospect that North Carolina's secession would make them, as the Confederacy's northern border, particularly vulnerable to federal attack. These counties realized early, and the realization soon spread through the rest of the mountain region, that North Carolina's course would be determined almost entirely by that of Virginia, if the latter chose to secede.[106] When Virginians, earlier in February, elected to their convention an overwhelmingly unionist slate of delegates, it all but settled the way in which those mountain counties along its southern border would vote later that month.[107]

Similar concerns probably contributed to opposition to a convention in Watauga, Madison, and Yancey counties, each of which bordered Tennessee. Either seepage of East Tennessee's almost rabid unionism across the state line or, more likely, the concern of those westernmost North Carolinians for their own security if their state joined the Confederacy and Tennessee (or merely East Tennessee) did not, may account for the stronger unionist sentiment the three counties, and particularly Yancey County—which, unlike the other two, had long been a Democratic stronghold—displayed in the convention referendum.[108]

Historians have taken too seriously and relied too exclusively on the February election results as a definitive demonstration of North Carolinians' stand on secession prior to Fort Sumter. While it is indeed the best indicator we have of popular opinion on the issue, it is important to remember that those results reflect public sentiment at a very specific moment in a fluid, evolving process during which such views were constantly reshaped. The same election, held a month earlier or a month later, might have yielded very different results, particularly since the outcomes in so many counties hung on such narrow margins. Only when events as clear-cut in their implications as the attack on Fort Sumter and Lincoln's subsequent call for troops occurred did the attitudes of western North Carolinians solidify and a decisive, unified consensus of public reaction emerge.

The mood in the region changed quickly after the convention vote in February 1861. News of the failure of the Washington Peace Conference, in which so many had placed so much hope, reached the area early in March and led some to resign themselves to inevitable separation from the Union and to war. James Gwyn seemed disgusted by the fact that "it has adjourned & done nothing or that which amounts to nothing . . . its not worth the paper its written on." As a result, he wrote, "There seems to be very little hope now of any settlement of the national difficulties."[109]

The biggest question in the minds of western Carolinians, indeed of all southerners, was what stand Lincoln would take toward the seceded states in his inaugural address on 4 March 1861. Mountain opposition to "coercion" remained so strong that any indication that the new president had such intentions suddenly could have reversed the sentiments expressed at the ballot box less than a week earlier. His message, when received by mountain residents a few days after it was delivered in Washington, was ambiguous enough to allow unionists to label it conciliatory and secessionists to call it belligerent. The former, however, remained wary and seemed disappointed that Lincoln did not state his peaceful intentions more clearly. A Wilkes County man said, "I understand Lincolns inaugural is conciliatory, [but] I suppose it was prepared by Seward & may mean anything they choose to adopt." J.R. Siler of Macon County felt that "if it had been from any other than Lincoln I would say it was very good," but, based on the Republican president's former statements, as well as those of Seward (who many seemed to think would be the real power in the White House), Siler was not encouraged.[110]

Secessionists in the area were quick to stress Lincoln's implied willingness to use force to retain federal property in the seceded states. In a Senate debate two days after Lincoln took office, Thomas Clingman insisted that the president's pledge to use his authority to take control of those forts taken over by Confederates and to collect taxes from those in seceded states meant that "collision is inevitable." "If Mr. Lincoln intends to use the power in his hands, as he states in his inaugural," Clingman said, "we must have war. If he does not, I think he is unfortunate in his declarations."[111]

The combined effect of these less than encouraging developments was that from mid-March to mid-April 1861, the conviction grew among western Carolinians, both secessionists and waning unionists, that decisive southern action sooner would have resolved the crisis at hand. On 11 March, James Gwyn wrote, "I think if all the Southern States had acted promptly & together that we might have had a peaceable separation, which would have been greatly preferable in my opinion to the Condition we shall be in for a year or two perhaps."[112] William Holland Thomas agreed that "no attempt would have been made to coerce the South if our people had been united." If the North had realized that the southern people could not be divided, he felt sure they would have proposed peace rather than declare war.[113]

The necessity of united action became a major theme of Clingman's during that period, as he continued to call for decisive action by North Carolina. He claimed that Lincoln had planned to call a special session of Congress to attempt another compromise settlement, until he heard that Virginia had rejected secession in mid-February. Then, confident that federal forces would have only the cotton states to contend with, he was willing to risk war. As the senator explained in retrospect:

> These facts tend to show how near we were of escaping war at that time. Had either North Carolina, or Tennessee, or Virginia, shown a purpose to act with the confederacy before the fight at Sumter, instead of war there would have been an appeal to Congress, to ascertain if an accommodation

could not be made; and in the event of failure, it is not unlikely that the "erring sisters" would have been allowed to "go in peace," and Lincoln would have "run the machine as he found it," to use his homely but striking phrase.[114]

Former unionists were put on the defensive. The ones who agreed that the time had now come for taking a stand did not necessarily regret the Upper South's earlier united front. In response to charges that their indecisiveness had allowed Lincoln time to take control of and prepare "the military arm of the Government," David Siler argued that, by waiting for a more justified provocation, a solider South had been assured. He told Macon County citizens that "the unanimity at the South, that an unquestioned, righteous cause must have produced, would abundantly compensate for any loss in the munitions of war."[115]

Even before the decisive events of mid-April, then, western North Carolinians, like other North Carolinians, were, if not accepting, at least resigning themselves to the inevitability of their own state's secession and of war. Despite February election results that should have encouraged unionists in the region, their efforts over the next month seemed relatively subdued and defensive, while secessionists became more and more outspoken and confident that their cause ultimately would prevail.

The attack on Fort Sumter by Confederate forces on 12 April did not come as a great surprise to mountain residents, since the possibility of a clash there had been openly discussed for several weeks.[116] It was Lincoln's response three days later that ended any complacency or reluctance about leaving the Union. On 15 April the president called for seventy-five-thousand troops, including two regiments from North Carolina, to supress the rebellion. With their almost unanimous opposition to "coercion," North Carolinians now had what David Siler had called "an unquestioned, righteous cause" to unite them.[117]

If any still had lingering doubts as to the state's course, Virginia's secession on 17 April ended them. In Charles Manly's words "All are unanimous. Even those who were loudest in denouncing secession are now hottest & loudest the other way." The statement applied to mountain residents as much as to those in any other part of the state.[118] The most ardent western unionists described their conversion experiences as sudden and dramatic. Zebulon Vance's often quoted recollection reflects the impact of these events on union sentiment in the area:

I was canvassing for the Union with all my strength; I was addressing a large and excited crowd . . . and literally had my arm upward in pleading for peace and the Union of our Fathers, when the telegraphic news was announced of the firing on Sumter and the President's call for seventy-five thousand volunteers. When my hand came down from the impassioned gesticulation, it fell slowly and sadly by the side of a Secessionist. I immediately, with altered voice and manner, called upon the assembled multitude to volunteer, not to fight against but for South Carolina.[119]

Likewise, Josiah Cowles, the father of Calvin Cowles, Wilkes County's most committed unionist, explained his own reversal to his son. "I was as strong a union man as any in the state up to the time [of] Lincoln's proclamation calling for 75,000 volunteers. I then saw that the South had either to submit to abject vassallage or assert her rights at the point of a sword." Though with somewhat less conviction than his father, Calvin Cowles resigned himself to the inevitability of his state's withdrawal from the Union. Early in May he wrote to a friend in New York: "Congress should be assembled as quickly as possible and should recognize the Confederate States as an independent nation. I think the good sense of the North will quickly see the folly of the effort to coerce 15 states (for it amounts to that and nothing less) and give it up."[120]

The remarkable haste with which this new surge of secession sentiment was translated into action suggests that, to the majority of western North Carolinians, the events of mid-April did not so much lead to many dramatic conversions as confirm expectations and trigger a conditioned reflex action for which they already had actively, even eagerly, prepared. In Hendersonville, a banner proclaiming "Old Rip's Awake," was stretched across the main street in anticipation of the inevitability of North Carolina's secession; impatient secessionists felt that their state had re-earned its "Rip Van Winkle" nickname because of its long delay in making that move. By 18 April, just three days after Lincoln's proclamation and less than a week after Fort Sumter, volunteer companies were organized in both Burke and Buncombe counties. In Asheville, men and boys made up the "Buncombe Riflemen." After a speech by one of the county's leading secessionists, Nicholas Woodfin, and a rousing send-off by local residents, they began their march to Raleigh.[121] This "large and enthusiastic meeting" of Buncombe County citizens drew up a resolution to send a committee to Governor Ellis "to procure arms for such volunteer companies as may be now in this section, or which may hereafter be raised." It concluded by resolving that "we are rejoiced at the entire unanimity which pervades our community in this trying emergency, and that as one man, we are determined to defend the honor and dignity of our State to the last extremity."[122]

One day earlier, a group toured Yancey County with a brass band in order to raise troops. Both there and in Madison County it was reported that "all turned out for the South."[123] In the southwestern corner of the state, William Holland Thomas met with Cherokee Indians late in April and soon after organized two hundred of them into a guard unit known as the "Junaluska Zouaves."[124] Even in the northwestern counties where unionism had been most widespread, the response was as enthusiastic as elsewhere in the region. Before the end of April, Caldwell County had raised a hundred-member company known as the "Caldwell Rough and Ready Boys." Lenoir that day was in "a state of feverish excitement," as its citizens declared themselves "in readiness at any and all times . . . to march in defense of the rights and honors of the South against the aggressions of the North."[125]

In the west's real bastion of unionism, Wilkes County, the situation on the surface seemed very much like that in the other mountain counties. James Gwyn recorded in his diary that the "general convention" he attended in Wilkesboro consisted of "a large collection of people & a great deal of excitement—most everybody now for the South." But in a letter to a friend, he reported that "not many volunteered, only 40 or so & only 6 or 700$ raised to pay them." He confided that "the people seemed pretty nearly united in the Cause of the South— but I think if an influential man had got up and espoused the other side, he would have had a good many to join him."

In Watauga County, almost equally committed to the Union in February, enthusiasm for the Confederacy seemed more unequivocal. Harvey Davis, an eager twenty-year-old resident, recorded in his diary on 11 May, "After a some-what firey speech by G.N. Folk a brilliant lawyer in the Town of Boone, in which the speaker dwelt at large on the attempt of the North to dominate the South and abrogate her rights under the Constitution, A call was made for volunteers. . . It seemed as if the whole assembly of citizens soon were in line."[126]

Two days later, on 13 May, voters elected delegates to a convention on 20 May. (This time, whether or not to hold a convention was not an issue.) The brief campaigns for those positions reflected, for the most part, the unanimity of spirit on which at this point most counties prided themselves. Party alignments proved inconsequential, since most candidates ran unopposed within their counties. In the few two-man races, the debate centered primarily on which of the two candidates was, and had been, the most committed to secession throughout the crisis. In Buncombe County, for example, Nicholas Woodfin, running against Montreville Patton as he had in February, reminded voters that he had warned all along that Lincoln could not be trusted and that a united South had offered the safest recourse to northern aggression. Patton, like Vance and others, spoke of his dramatic conversion from union to disunion and claimed that he was now as staunch a supporter of a united southern confederacy as his competitor. But Woodfin harped unmercifully on Patton's former opposition to the very actions he now endorsed and on how poor his judgment had been. "I need not remind you," he told voters, "how fearfully my worse fears have been realized, and how entirely all of his predictions have been falsified."[127] Woodfin easily won the election, as did other long-term secessionists wherever they ran. Former conditional unionists now committed to secession won when unopposed.[128] Only two unionists who still opposed secession, Tod R. Caldwell of Burke County and Alexander H. Jones of Henderson County, made any effort to run, though support for them seemed virtually nonexistent.[129]

The fact that every mountain county elected prosecession delegates and had already raised Confederate military companies did not mean that harmony prevailed everywhere. Divisive tensions still ran high in certain sections of several counties. In Marshall, Madison County's seat, the election was the scene of a widely-publicized shoot-out over the issues at hand. The sheriff's enthusiasm for secession and his probable intoxication led him to stand in the center of town shouting, "Hurra[h] for Jeff Davis and the Southern Confederacy." When a Unionist shouted back for George Washington and the Union, the sheriff drew his pistol, fired into the crowd and accused them of being "a set of Damd Black republicans & lincolnites." In the ensuing gun-fire, he wounded a young boy and in turn was shot and killed by the boy's father.[130]

In Henderson County, voters in the precinct of Edneyville witnessed a "free-for-all combat" between unionists and secessionists just before the polls opened. In a nearby community, skirmishes and pillaging were already under way, and the captain of the local Confederate company complained to Governor Ellis that not one man in that

Figure 24. Nicholas W. Woodfin. Pack Memorial Library, Asheville, North Carolina.

area had yet volunteered to join his unit. "They are," he explained, "as deadly hostile to our raising volunteers & the whole defence of the south as any portion of Pennsylvania."[131] Even in Hendersonville, the county seat, secession forces threatened violence. According to the unionist candidate on the ballot, he was "invited from the stump and threatened with a ride on one of Lincoln's rails" on the day before the election. He claimed that guards at the polls the next day announced that they would hang or shoot anyone who voted for him, and that several who did were mobbed. On 20 May when its convention approved North Carolina's break with the Union, one enthusiastic young secessionist exchanged shots with a local unionist and then proceeded to chop down the pole bearing the American flag, in front of a tense but generally approving crowd.[132]

These incidents were exceptions to the generally enthusiastic secessionist spirit that pervaded western North Carolina; and even they seem to have reflected more an unrestrained exuberance and cockiness on the part of local secessionists who finally saw their cause triumphant than any formidable unionist opposition. As North Carolina finally severed its ties with the Union on 20 May, the vast majority of its western citizens approved the action. With this reaction, as throughout every phase of the crisis, mountain residents were in step with the state and with much of the rest of the Upper South. Like all of that region, western North Carolina included spokesmen advocating both extremes—immediate secession after Lincoln's election and preservation of the Union at all costs. But the views of the vast majority of western Carolinians fell on a continuum between those two positions, with most embracing a "watch and wait" attitude that opposed rash action until events fully warranted it, but without precluding the possibility of seceding from the Union if northern provocation made it necessary.

In their responses to the developments of late 1860 and early 1861, highlanders thought of themselves as both North Carolinians and southerners and saw their region as an integral part of both their state and the larger South. In identifying themselves with the South as a whole, what little consciousness of class distinctions mountain residents might have had was further eroded. Both slaveholders and non-slaveholders in the region seem to have been divided almost equally on both sides of the secession question. The leadership of the area and most of those quoted in this chapter were slaveholders who were well aware that their arguments were directed at a vast nonslaveholding electorate. Yet, whether unionists or disunionists, they kept the defense of slavery central to their reasoning about why they should remain a part of, or separate from, the Union. The fact that the most outspoken unionists were among the area's largest slaveholders discredits the widespread assumption that the strength of unionism in the mountains was a function either of the relative scarcity of slaves there or of opposition to the slave system.

A further indication that any such correlation is a fallacy is that those Union spokesmen openly appealed to a basically nonslaveholding electorate on the grounds that secession posed a serious threat to the system's survival. Though most western Carolinians owned no slaves, the institution's presence in their midst was enough to make its fate the most tangible aspect of the secession debate. The possibility of slavery's abolition, in fact, was probably even more frightening to most mountain residents than the prospect of armed conflict, and unionists played on that fear of slavery's demise just as effectively as secessionists did.

Within North Carolina, any distinctiveness that the mountaineers had felt as westerners within an eastern-oriented state was almost totally submerged under the more immediate threat posed by perceived northern aggression. They had focused their attention on the state fight over ad valorem taxes up until three months before the November 1860 election. Nevertheless, any intrastate divisiveness that issue had engendered was all but eclipsed by far more omnious preoccupations. Residents of the mountain counties now expressed their concern for the fate of the state as a whole and saw their own interests as synonymous with those of all fellow North Carolinians. Throughout the crisis, profuse declarations of loyalty to the state were paired with similar ones toward the South. Such declarations especially marked the rhetoric of mountain unionists, who were quick to avoid any hint that their devotion to the nation compromised their devotion to state or region. Some even went so far as to argue that remaining in the Union would heal intrastate sectional wounds. With the possibility that the markets of South Carolina and Georgia were, or would soon become, unavailable, unionists suggested that the commercial interdependency of eastern and western North Carolina would be greatly enhanced, binding the two sections more closely together.[133] Since the range of opinion among western Carolinians paralleled that across the state, no section ever became identified with a particular stand on secession. Thus mountain unionists and secessionists joined forces with their respective counterparts all over North Carolina, and in doing so, they strengthened statewide political, as well as economic, bonds.

On the eve of their entry into the Civil War, western North Carolinians transcended local and regional identities to an extent unparalleled either before or afterward. An old man in Yancey County spoke for the vast majority of his fellow western Carolinians when he said, "When the war come, I felt awful southern."[134]

Epilogue

During November and December 1861, with the war still in its opening throes, James W. Taylor, a Minnesota journalist, laid out a set of
proposals for Union military and political strategists that he believed
could bring the South to its knees and the war to an end. Published
first as a series of articles in the *St. Paul Daily Press* and then as a pamphlet widely distributed in the North in 1862, it was titled *Alleghania:
A Geographical and Statistical Memoir Exhibiting the Strength of the Union
and the Weakness of Slavery in the Mountain Districts of the South*. On the
basis of 1850 and 1860 census figures and published geographical descriptions of the Southern Appalachians, Taylor maintained that
"within the immense district to which the designation of Alleghania is
here applied, the slaves are so few and scattered" that its residents
have "a complete dedication . . . to Free Labor" and thus no sympathy
for the Confederacy or its cause. Slavery in the mountains "sits like an
incubus—not desired by the people and alien to the climate and agriculture. It is a tyranny imposed, not an institution adopted by the majority of the People." Because of this, Taylor argued, the mountain
populace, with some protection and encouragement from federal authorities, might well instigate a counterrevolution against the Confederacy to which they had unwillingly been bound, be reinstated into
the Union, emancipate what few slaves they held, and then serve as a
military base of operations from which the northern army, along with
the southern mountaineers, could launch "a powerful diversion of a
hostile character" against the insurrectionists.[1]

North Carolina's mountain region was vital to Taylor's plan, and he applauded President Lincoln's assurance "that a military highway will be opened between 'the loyal regions of East Tennessee and Western North Carolina, and other faithful parts of the Union.' "[2] "Why might we not expect," he asked, a sweep of force from Watauga, from the Catawba, and from the French Broad, that would break "the spinal column of the rebel confederacy" and lead to "now in 1861, as on Oct. 7, 1780, a victorious counterpart of the struggle and victory of King's Mountain?" (As has been noted, that battle's legacy could be claimed for any number of situations or ideologies.) In conclusion, Taylor urged, "Within this Switzerland of the South, Nature is at war with Slavery, and the People are ready to strike for Liberty and Union. If so, will not the Government recognize Relief to the Loyal South as the first great emergency, and as the most urgent expediency in the suppression of the insurrection?"[3]

As Taylor's report indicates, the myths of Appalachia were already firmly entrenched. Much later in the war, disaffection not only in the Carolina highlands but throughout the state and much of the South would have lent considerably more credibility to Taylor's ideas.[4] But in 1861, they made no sense, and merely indicated how out of touch this Minnesotan was with the political and military realities of at least this one section of the southern mountains. The euphoric reaction with which most western Carolinians greeted their own and their state's official commitment to the southern nation in May in fact continued unabated throughout the rest of the year. James Whitaker, a more detached observer than most, wrote of his fellow Cherokee County residents in June, "The war excitement has engaged the minds of every man in the County. The Preachers have quit preaching, the Churches are lingering under a fatal disease . . . it seems that they are all gone astray mixing and mingling with the world."[5]

This fervor was not so chaotic, however, that organizational priorities were neglected. Certainly the most tangible evidence of mountain residents' firm commitment to their new nation was their enthusiastic response to the call for Confederate troops. The western counties were among the first to fill the volunteer quotas requested by Gov. John Ellis, their enlistees following quickly in the wake of those Carolina mountain volunteers already actively engaged in Virginia before North Carolina's secession became official. Mountaineers also enlisted in greater numbers than did North Carolinians elsewhere; one in fifteen of all people in the thirteen westernmost counties had enlisted by October 1861, as compared with an average of only one in nineteen for the rest of the state.[6]

In Rutherford County, two communities—Rutherfordton and Burnt Chimney (now Forest City)—competed to see which could have a volunteer company in service first. The "Burnt Chimney Vols" won the contest by departing for Raleigh on 3 June, though the Rutherfordton "Riflemen" were only a day behind and became a part of the same regiment upon reaching the state capital.[7] By July, almost half of the voting population of Burke County was armed, and Caldwell County soon after boasted an even higher percentage of enlistments.[8] Before the end of June, Jackson County officials proudly informed Governor Ellis that they had already met their quota and that the two companies formed in doing so had taken so many of the county's young single men that the next company formed was made up almost entirely of family men.[9]

All of these men gathered and departed from their county seats amid overwhelming community support. The words of a Rutherford County woman, Ellen Mitchell, echoed both the conviction and the spirit of the rhetoric heaped upon such warriors-to-be not only throughout western North Carolina, but in almost any part of the South where the die had been cast. As spokeswoman for the "ladies of Rutherfordton," Mitchell addressed the eager young "Riflemen" as they set out for Raleigh:

> The ladies feel proud of the Sunny South, proud of the Old North State, but prouder still of this glorious mountain county whose sons, at the first sound of the tocsin of war, have rushed to the standard of our insulted country; and who being among the first in the field, will bear a part of the glorious work of driving out of Virginia the vandal hordes, who have dared to desecrate the soil where rests the ashes of Washington.[10]

Mitchell's family owned no slaves, nor did the vast majority of those citizens—both soldiers and civilians—who heard her words and "cheered riotously" at their conclusion. Many other nonslaveholding mountaineers expressed similar resolve and equal pride as they watched their sons march off to war. Was such emotion not the ultimate manifestation of the success of the so-called "slaveholders' revolution"? These were not merely yeomen induced by southern slaveholders to fight what was to become a long and bloody war in order to defend those slaveholders' black property. These were, in addition, yeomen who, although they lived in a part of the South only peripherally bound to slave labor and far removed from the plantation South, pledged themselves enthusiastically to fight for its survival.

In 1905, before an Asheville literary club, Theodore Davidson of Cherokee County reflected on the distinctive character of Carolina highlanders. Regarding their role in the Civil War, he said:

> One of the most significant proofs of the fact that the status of the negro was not at the South regarded as the issue in the War between the States, was the ardor with which the mountain and non-slaveholding portions of the population flew to arms at the call of their respective states, and the fidelity they exhibited for the cause throughout four years of struggle, self-denial, suffering death and social destruction. This fact has been often commented upon with surprise by intelligent persons in the North. How utterly they fail to comprehend the real issue, or the lofty and patriotic sense of duty which animated the Southern people of all classes.
>
> Especially was this true of the North Carolina Mountaineer. In . . . that section of the State . . . the slave owners of 1861 were so rare that the institution of slavery may be said practically to have had no existence, and yet that region sent more than fifteen thousand fighting men—volunteers—into the field. . . . They had inherited from their ancestors the political idea that the people of every government had the inalienable right to ordain and regulate that form of government which they believed their conditions demanded; and this fundamental and vital principle they were convinced was assailed—hence their ardor and determination.[11]

Davidson's reasoning as to why slavery was not the central issue in driving the South from the Union is, of course, based on counterfactual logic, and he neglects to mention what, if not slavery, led his ancestors to feel that the government was assailing their rights. Yet there are elements of truth and insight in his statement. It is not surprising that this is among the very few turn-of-the-century accounts to acknowledge highlanders' commitment to the Confederacy, since Davidson's father, Col. Allen T. Davidson, represented his county in North Carolina's secession convention and his district in the Confederate Congress. Indeed, as one of Cherokee County's most prominent lawyers, bankers, legislators, and slaveholders before the war, Allen Davidson was the very embodiment of the type of leadership that shaped western North Carolina's response to the sectional crisis.[12] He and his counterparts never shied away from the issue of slavery in addressing their constituents. He remained consistent in his outspoken defense of the institution throughout those decisive months prior to Fort Sumter. In doing so, he and others like him played to the same racial fears and bigotry of the yeomanry manipulated so effectively for so long by slaveholders across the South.

It was as not as slaveholders, but rather as commercial lynchpins in the economic well-being of their region, that these mountain masters gained the hegemonic control that served them so well. It was they who established and maintained the lucrative markets for mountain produce and livestock in the Lower South and they who, as often as not, served as conduits that allowed their fellow mountaineers, regardless of how small or how remote their holdings, access to that extended trade network. It was these masters who primed the region's economic pump even further by promoting its scenic and agricultural bounty, attracting both tourists and outside investors eager to take advantage of its resources. It was these masters who fought members of their own class and even, on occasion, sacrificed their own individual interests in legislative battles over taxation, representation, and budgetary allotments, both to gain justice and to enhance prosperity for their corner of the state. In the marketplace and in the legislative halls, this mountain elite had so effectively demonstrated its loyalty and usefulness to the region and its people that, when these slaveholders rallied the yeomen to fight for slavery's defense, none of them could entertain suspicions that class-based interests at odds with their own motivated the call.

Despite his son's claims to the contrary, Allen Davidson's contemporaries were never shielded from, nor did they lose sight of, the fact that slavery's fate was at the heart of the debates in those tension-filled weeks of late 1860 and early 1861. Slavery was by no means the only factor that shaped their identities as southerners or their loyalties to the South, however. Equally important, even central, to their decision-making process was the more immediate, practical consideration of those vital commercial links with the rest of the South. Which course, remaining in or withdrawing from the Union, would more likely ensure (or could even enhance) their thriving economy? Here, too, the fact that their leaders' self-interest and regional interest coincided inspired confidence that the concerns of the nonslaveholding majority would be served as well.

Finally, the long, hard-fought intrastate sectional battles against an entrenched eastern oligarchy made the task of proslavery, secessionist spokesmen much easier. Their western constitutents had been made fully aware of the dangers that could beset a minority subject to governmental purposes and policies at odds with its members' interests. Thus the republican ideology that shaped so much of the South's consciousness, and an almost paranoid fear of the threats posed by a federal government ruled by a hostile majority, struck among mountain residents more resonant chords of recognition than was the case elsewhere in the Upper South. Firmly identifying themselves as victims, whose "inalienable right to ordain and regulate that form of government which they believed their conditions demanded . . . had been assailed" (to repeat Theodore Davidson's words), western Carolinians promptly recognized the parallels to their plight in the larger sectional tensions between North and the South. Their political, economic, and ideological character as westerners was smoothly and naturally transformed into an equally defensive stance as southerners.

In many respects—from its class structure and racial demography to its agrarian brand of commercial enterprise and the variety of its agricultural output—Southern Appalachian society had more in common with the preindustrial North than did any other part of the South. In other ways, though, western North Carolina shared a great deal with the South around it. It was the combination and interaction of those various features that stamped this mountain region as unique. While its responses to secession—both pro and con—were very much within the mainstream of Upper South reaction, the reasons behind those very southern reactions were quite distinctly its own.

Appendix

Western North Carolina's Fifty Largest Slaveholders and Their Wealth, 1860

Name	County	No. of Slaves	Value of Estate	
			Real	Personal
William F. McKesson	Burke	174	$80,000	$185,000
N. W. Woodfin	Buncombe	122	60,000	100,000
Jacob Harshaw	Burke	121	31,000	116,150
Issac T. Avery	Burke	103	45,300	73,450
William C. Erwin	Burke	80	17,950	55,000
James W. Patton	Buncombe	78	67,000	193,390
Abraham Suddereth	Cherokee	72	25,000	28,400
Dillard Love	Macon	71	60,000	102,000
Mary G. Erwin[1]	McDowell	69	20,000	50,000
John E. Patton	Buncombe	68	16,500	180,783
John Suddereth	Burke	65[2]	58,500	64,640
Thomas Lenoir	Caldwell	65[3]	27,500	59,000
David E. Horton	Caldwell	62	15,000	60,450
John Witherspoon	Caldwell	59	8,000	37,000
Daniel Blake	Henderson	59	30,000	50,000
Hannah Caldwell[4]	Burke	59	20,000	35,000
James R. Love	Haywood	58	100,000	86,200
Robert C. Pearson	Burke	57	26,000	76,500
Edmund W. Jones	Caldwell	55	106,800	65,000
William Johnson	Buncombe	55	40,000	135,665
John W. Woodfin	Buncombe	54	44,000	73,200

Appendix, Continued.

Name	County	No. of Slaves	Value of Estate	
			Real	Personal
Charles Fisher	Burke	52	28,000	72,000
John Rutherford, Jr.	Burke	52	40,000	128,000
V. Ripley	Henderson	51	30,000	95,000
John B. Love	Jackson	49	18,000	50,000
Thomas G. Walton	Burke	46	30,900	63,500
T. Y. Greenlee	McDowell	43	18,000	40,000
A. Hamilton Erwin	Burke	42	8,800	28,450
J. F. E. Hardy	Buncombe	40	8,000	55,000
W. W. McDowell	Buncombe	40	23,000	47,100
G. M. Carson	McDowell	40	20,000	43,000
J. H. Greenlee	McDowell	39	18,300	40,000
F. W. Johnstone	Henderson	39	30,000	40,000
C. M. Avery	Burke	38	15,000	29,000
R. V. Michaux	Burke	37	15,300	30,000
Walter Blake	Henderson	36	10,000	50,000
Samuel F. Patterson	Caldwell	36	30,000	45,000
Joseph Corpening	Caldwell	36	10,080	27,000
Alney Burgin	McDowell	34	20,000	25,500
George Bower	Ashe	34	22,590	100,375
Mitchell King	Henderson	34	30,000	30,000
J. I. Erwin	Burke	34	14,560	29,000
Joshua Harshaw	Cherokee	33	40,000	42,000
J. W. Patton	McDowell	33	16,500	32,000
E. Molyneax	Henderson	33	21,500	34,000
William C. Kilgore	Henderson	33	13,000	23,000
William H. Thomas	Jackson	32	22,725	27,000
Milton Penland	Yancey	31	20,000	36,000
Lytle Hickerson	Wilkes	31	15,000	24,000
Montraville Patton	Buncombe	31	40,000	68,130

[1]Slaves shared with six heirs.

[2]Figures represent combined Burke and Cherokee County holdings of John Suddereth.

[3]Figures represent combined Haywood and Caldwell County holdings of both slaves and property of Thomas Lenoir.

[4]Widow of John Caldwell.

Notes

Abbreviations

Duke Duke Manuscript Department, Duke University, Durham, North Carolina

NCC North Carolina Collection, University of North Carolina, Chapel Hill, North Carolina

NCDAH North Carolina Department of Archives and History, Raleigh, North Carolina

Pack Pack Memorial Library, Asheville, North Carolina

SHC Southern Historical Collection, University of North Carolina, Chapel Hill, North Carolina

WCU Hunter Library Special Collections, Western Carolina University, Cullowhee, North Carolina

Preface

1. Bernard C. Steiner, ed., "The South Atlantic States in 1833, As Seen By a New Englander [Henry Barnard]," *Maryland Historical Magazine* 13 (Sept. 1918): 344–45.

2. Carl N. Degler, *The Other South: Southern Dissenters in the Nineteenth Century* (Boston: Northeastern Univ. Press, 1982).

Introduction

1. William Faulkner, *Absalom, Absalom!* (New York: Vintage, 1936, rptd. 1951), 221–22. For further discussion of Faulkner's interpretation of Appalachia, see Lynn Dickerson, "Thomas Sutpen: Mountain Stereotypes in *Absalom,*

Absalom!," *Appalachian Heritage* 12 (Spring 1984):73–78; and John C. Inscoe, "Faulkner, Race, and Appalachia," *South Atlantic Quarterly* 86 (Summer 1987):244–53.

2. Faulkner, *Absalom, Absalom!*, 227.

3. This term was coined by Will W. Harvey in the title of an article he published in 1873, after a trip through the Cumberland Mountains of Kentucky. Will Wallace Harvey, "A Strange Land and Peculiar People," *Lippincott's Magazine* 12 (Oct. 1873), 429–38. See Henry D. Shapiro, *Appalachia on Our Mind: The Southern Mountains and Mountaineers in the American Consciousness* (Chapel Hill: Univ. of North Carolina Press, 1978), 3. Many of the ideas discussed in the early part of this introduction are based on Shapiro and on Cratis D. Williams, "The Southern Mountaineer in Fact and Fiction," (pt 1), *Appalachian Journal* 3 (Autumn 1975): 8–61.

4. William G. Frost, "Our Contemporary Ancestors in the Southern Mountains, *Atlantic Monthly* 83 (Mar. 1899):311–19; Julian Ralph, "Our Appalachian Americans," *Harper's Monthly Magazine* 107 (June 1903): 36.

5. Frost, "Our Contemporary Ancestors," 311; Julian Ralph, *Dixie; or Southern Scenes and Sketches* (New York, 1896), cited in James C. Klotter, "The Black South and White Appalachia," *Journal of American History* 66 (Mar. 1980):834.

6. John Fox, Jr., *Blue–Grass and Rhododendron: Out–doors in Old Kentucky* (London: Archibald Constable & Co., 1905), 3–4; James W. Raine,*The Land of Saddle–bags: A Study of the Mountain People of Appalachia* (New York: Council of Women for Home Missions, 1924), x. See also Margaret W. Morley, *The Carolina Mountains* (Boston: Houghton Mifflin, 1913), 144–45.

7. Ulrich B. Phillips, *Life and Labor in the Old South* (Boston: Little, Brown, rpt. ed., 1969), 342. "Narrative of Col. John Stuart of Greenbriar," *William and Mary Quarterly* 22 (Apr. 1914):234.

8. Klotter, "Black South and White Appalachia," 882–49.

9. Ralph, "Our Appalachian Americans," 37; James W. Taylor, *Alleghania, A Geographical and Statistical Memoir* (St. Paul, Minn.: James Davenport, 1862), 1.

10. Frost, "Our Contemporary Ancestors," 313; Samuel T. Wilson, *The Southern Mountaineers* (New York: J.J. Little and Ives, 1914), 57.

11. Samuel Wilson, *Southern Mountaineers*, 57. For similiar views, see also Ralph, "Our Appalachian Americans," 36; John C. Campbell, *The Southern Highlander and His Homeland* (New York: Russell Sage, 1921), 94–95; Walter C. Whitaker, *The Southern Highlands and Highlanders* (Hartford, Conn.: Church Missions Publications, 1916), 17–18; James M. Dabbs, "Beyond the Appalachians," *Appalachian Journal* 2 (Winter 1975): 88–90; and Shapiro, *Appalachia on Our Mind*, 97.

12. Frost, "Our Contemporary Ancestors," 314.

13. Raine, *Land of Saddle–bags*, 138. See also Carter G. Woodson, "Freedom and Slavery in Appalachian America," *Journal of Negro History* 1 (Apr. 1916):142; Campbell, *Southern Highlander*, 95.

14. Theodore F. Davidson, "The Carolina Mountaineer: The Highest Type of American Character," in *First Annual Transactions of the Pen and Plate Club of Asheville, N.C.* (Asheville: Hackney and Mole, 1905), 84. For similar references

to the Battle of King's Mountain, see Frost, "Our Contemporary Ancestors,"
313; Ralph, "Our Appalachian Americans," 37; Wilbur G. Zeigler and Ben S.
Grosscup, *The Heart of the Alleghanies of Western North Carolina* (Raleigh, N.C.:
Alfred Williams & Co., 1883), 217–20; Taylor, *Alleghania*, 12–13, 22–23.

15. Campbell, *Southern Highlander*, 91. In a recent study of contemporary
community structure in western North Carolina, Patricia Beaver discusses
these and other traditions as a "mythic past" that even now provides ideological sustenance and definition of local identities and bonds. See Patricia D.
Beaver, *Rural Community in the Appalachian South* (Lexington: Univ. Press of
Kentucky, 1986), 140–44.

16. Horace Kephart, *Our Southern Highlanders* (New York: Macmillan, 1913,
rev. ed., 1941), 382–83. See also Phillips, *Life and Labor in the Old South*, 342–44.
Phillips drew heavily on Kephart's book in his brief discussion of mountain
life.

17. Jack E. Weller, *Yesterday's People: Life in Contemporary Appalachia* (Lexington: Univ. of Kentucky Press, 1965), 88–89, cited in Ronald D Eller, "The
Search for Community in Appalachia" (Keynote Address, Ninth Annual Appalachian Studies Conference, Boone, N.C., 21 Mar. 1986). Eller's address in
itself constitutes an important discussion of the themes of individuality and
community as inherent aspects of the highland heritage. See also John B.
Stephenson, *Shiloh: A Mountain Community* (Lexington: Univ. Press of Kentucky, 1968), 102–106.

18. For residents' perpetuation of these ideas, see various statements in
Laurel Shackelford and Bill Weinberg, eds., *Our Appalachia: An Oral History*
(New York: Hill and Wang, 1977), 67, 172, 261–62; Davidson, "The Carolina
Mountaineer," 84–86; and Beaver, *Rural Community*, Ch. 6.

A recent scholarly treatment of these themes is Ronald Eller's discussion of
preindustrial Appalachia, in which he emphasizes its basic values of land and
family and its atmosphere of "self–sufficiency, traditionalism, and a certain independence from the larger society." Ronald D Eller, *Miners, Millhands, and
Mountaineers: Industrialization of the Appalachian South, 1880–1930* (Knoxville:
Univ. of Tennessee Press, 1982), 37–38. Phillip S. Paludan, in *Victims: A True
Story of the Civil War* (Knoxville: Univ. of Tennessee Press, 1981), 37–38, implies
that the isolation and alienation of the Shelton Laurel community was typical
of Appalachia on the eve of the Civil War. See also Robert B. Phillips, *One of
God's Children in Toe River Valley* (Bakersville, N.C.: Privately published, 1983),
5–6.

19. Edward Pessen, "How Different from Each Other Were the Antebellum
North and South?", *American Historical Review* 85 (Dec. 1980):1146–47.

20. F.N. Boney, *Southerners All* (Macon, Ga.: Mercer Univ. Press, 1984):3,
106–107.

21. Robert H. Wiebe, *The Opening of American Society From the Adoption of the
Constitution to the Eve of Disunion* (New York: Vintage, 1984), xii–xv, 256, 353–
75.

22. Two major works embracing both these themes—the ideological and
economic links between North and South and between Old South and New

South—are Carl N. Degler, *Place Over Time: The Continuity of Southern Distinctiveness* (Baton Rouge: Louisiana State Univ. Press, 1977; and Laurence Shore, *Southern Capitalists: The Ideological Leadership of an Elite, 1832–1885* (Chapel Hill: Univ. of North Carolina Press, 1986.)

23. Dwight B. Billings, Jr., *Planters and the Making of a "New South": Class, Politics, and Development in North Carolina, 1865–1900* (Chapel Hill: Univ. of North Carolina Press, 1979), 70–95; Jonathan M. Wiener, *Social Origins of the New South: Alabama, 1860–1885* (Baton Rouge: Louisiana State Univ. Press, 1978), 137–48. It is important to distinguish here between such historians as Kenneth Stampp, Lewis Gray, Robert Fogel, Stanley Engerman, and Laurence Shore, who have interpreted the planters' activities and attitudes *as* planters as capitalistic in nature, and the historians dealt with in the present context— those who focus on planters, or mere farmers, with mercantile or other commercial interests apart from, and in addition to, agricultural concerns.

24. Paul D. Escott, *Many Excellent People: Power and Privilege in North Carolina, 1850–1900* (Chapel Hill: Univ. of North Carolina Press, 1985), 5. It is noteworthy that both Billings and Escott single out a western Carolinian, Samuel F. Patterson of Caldwell County, as an example of the state's entrepreneurial leadership.

Chapter 1

1. Mrs. John C. Campbell, "Flame of New Future for the Highlands," *Mountain Life and Work* 1 (Apr. 1925): 9.

2. Among the most perceptive works on this theme are Gene Wilhelm, Jr., "Appalachian Isolation: Fact or Fiction?", and Wilma Dykeman, "Appalachia in Context," both in J.W. Williamson, ed., *An Appalachian Symposium* (Boone, N.C.: Appalachian Consortium Press, 1977); Gene Wilhelm, Jr., "Folk Settlements in the Blue Ridge Mountains," *Appalachian Journal* 5 (Winter 1978); Ralph Mann, "Isolation and the Social Economy of an Appalachian Community: Burkes Garden, Virginia, in the 1840s and 1850s," (Paper delivered at the Fifth Citadel Conference on the South, Charleston, S.C., Apr. 1987); and Dwight Billings, Kathleen Blee, and Louis Swanson, "Culture, Family and Community in Preindustrial Appalachia," *Appalachian Journal* 13 (Winter 1986): 154–70.

3. J.G. de Roulhac Hamilton, ed., *The Papers of Randolph Abbott Shotwell*, vol. 2 (Raleigh: North Carolina Department of Archives and History, 1931), 280–281.

4. "Letter from James Patton to his Children, 1837" (Privately printed, 1841, 1970), in possession of the Patton family, quoted in H. Tyler Blethen and Curtis Wood, "A Trader on the Western Carolina Frontier: James Patton, 1783–1845," unpublished manuscript.

5. Francois André Michaux, *Travels to the Westward of the Alleghany Mountains* (London: Richard Phillips, 1805), rptd. in Reuben G. Thwaite, ed., *Early Western Travels, 1748–1846* (Cleveland, Ohio: Arthur H. Clark Co., 1904).

6. Wilhelm, "Folk Settlements," 207; Beaver, *Rural Community*, 11. Edward W. Phifer, Jr., has demonstrated the tendency of Burke County residents to settle at junctures of rivers and streams, where the richest soil was deposited. Such a tendency was probably operative throughout the mountain region, the topography of which created an abundance of such converging waterways. See Edward W. Phifer, "Slavery in Microcosm: Burke County, North Carolina," *Journal of Southern History* 28 (May 1962): 140.

7. Wilhelm, "Folk Settlements," 207–208.

8. In 1850, the population of the twelve westernmost counties was 10 percent of the state total. In 1860, 12 percent of those in the state lived in the same area (by then redivided into 15 counties). Thus table 1.2 includes those agricultural products of which more than 10 percent in 1850 and more than 12 percent in 1860 were raised in those counties.

9. William Wyndam Malet, *An Errand to the South in the Summer of 1862* (London: R. Bentley, 1863), 250–51.

10. Watauga, Yancey, and Cherokee counties were ranked first, second, and third in the state in 1860, but this category was not included in either table because the census figures for it, for both 1850 and 1860, are so incomplete.

11. Corn and other crops are not included in the tables because their per capita production in the mountains was only equal to or less than that of the state as a whole.

12. Burke County was by far the leading tobacco–producing county in the region, with over 160,000 pounds raised in 1860. It was followed by Wilkes County, with 93,000 pounds, and McDowell, Caldwell, and Buncombe, with between 50 and 20,000 pounds each. Yet these counties, along with the others in the mountains, produced only 1 percent of the tobacco raised in North Carolina that year. *Agriculture of the United States in 1860*, 106–10.

13. Elisha Mitchell to Thomas L. Clingman, n.d., in Charles Lanman, *Letters from the Allegheny Mountains* (New York: Putnam, 1849), 195.

14. For a thorough discussion of the problems of livestock production in the Lower South, see Julius Rubin, "The Limits of Agricultural Progress in the Nineteenth Century South," *Agricultural History* 49 (Apr. 1975): 362–73. See also John Solomon Otto, "Southern 'Plain Folk' Agriculture: A Reconsideration," *Plantation Society in the Americas* 2 (Apr. 1983): 29–36; and Robert E. Gallman, "Self–Sufficiency in the Cotton Economy of the Antebellum South," *Agricultural History* 44 (Jan. 1970), 5–23.

15. *Agriculture in 1860*, 106–10.

16. The twelve farmers were Joseph Shepherd (Yancey), Daniel T. Ramseur (Cherokee), Joseph Hayes (Wilkes), A.B. Chunn (Buncombe), James Patton (Haywood), Sidney Thompson (Caldwell), Absalom Bower (Ashe), Hugh Johnson (Henderson), Martin Hurst (Macon), John Wittington (Watauga), Joseph Conley (McDowell), and Joseph Scott (Burke). See appropriate counties in Seventh U. S. Census, 1850, Agriculture Schedule. (The one common link among these men is that each owned 10–12 slaves in 1850. The implications of this fact will be discussed in ch. 3.)

17. George Swain to David L. Swain, 6 Dec. 1822, David L. Swain Papers, Epistulary Correspondence, vol. 2 (typescript), SHC.

18. T. McGimsey to Thomas Henderson, 3 May 1811, in A.R. Newsome, ed., "Twelve North Carolina Counties in 1810–1811," *North Carolina Historical Review* 5 (Oct. 1928), 419.

19. See Elisha Mitchell to his wife Maria, 20 July 1828, Elisha Mitchell Papers, SHC; Robert S. Lambert, "The Oconaluftee Valley, 1800–1860: A Study of the Sources for Mountain History," *North Carolina Historical Review* 35 (Oct. 1958): 418; Julian Margaret Connor Diary (typescript), p. 26, SHC; and Lanman, *Letters from the Allegheny Mountains*, 85–86, for descriptions of each of the valleys. For more objective observations about those and other areas of western North Carolina, see Myron H. Avery and Kenneth S. Boardman, eds., "Arnold Guyot's Notes on the Geography of the Mountain District of Western North Carolina," *North Carolina Historical Review* 15 (July 1938): 251–318.

20. H.E. Colton, "Picturesque America: On the French Broad River, North Carolina," *Appleton's Journal* (17 Dec. 1870): 737.

21. Malet, *Errand to the South*, 236. Of Watauga County, William Lenoir wrote, "Here . . . apples, peaches and the more delicate fruits, especially grapes of several varieties, grow in greatest perfection." William Lenoir to the Editors, 8 Jan. 1859, *North Carolina Planter* 2 (Feb. 1859).

22. See "Our Trip to Buncombe," *North Carolina Planter* 3 (Oct. 1860): 330; and Thomas L. Clingman, *Selections from the Speeches and Writings of Hon. Thomas L. Clingman* (Raleigh, N.C.: John Nichols, 1877), 125–26, for descriptions of the Woodfin farms.

23. Malet, *Errand to the South*, 255–56.

24. Elisha Mitchell to his wife Maria, 20 July 1828, Elisha Mitchell Papers, SHC.

25. Lanman, *Letters from the Allegheny Mountains*, 197.

26. Clingman, *Speeches and Writings*, 113–15.

27. J.S. Goe, "Sheep and the Mountains of North Carolina," *North Carolina Planter* 3 (Mar. 1860): 90.

28. Gary S. Dunbar, "Silas McDowell and the Early Botanical Exploration of Western North Carolina," *North Carolina Historical Review* 41 (Autumn 1964): 125–26.

29. Silas McDowell to the Editors, *North Carolina Planter* 1 (Apr. 1858): 125–26. Dunbar, "Silas McDowell," 435.

30. *Agriculture, in 1860*, 104, 108. See also J. Carlyle Sitterson, *The Secession Movement in North Carolina*, James Sprunt Studies in History and Political Science, vol. 23, no. 2 (Chapel Hill: Univ. of North Carolina Press, 1939), 19–20.

31. Sitterson, *Secession Movement*, 19–20; *Agriculture in 1860*, 104, 108.

32. For discussions of highland farming patterns, see Beaver, *Rural Community*, 16; Blethen and Wood, *From Ulster to Carolina: The Migration of the Scotch–Irish to Southwestern North Carolina* (Cullowhee, N.C.: Mountain Heritage Center, 1983); and Blethen and Wood, "Land and Family in the Tuckaseigee Valley, 1800–1850" (Paper presented at Ninth Annual Appalachian Studies Conference, Boone, N.C., Mar. 1986).

Chapter 2

1. Thomas Wolfe, *The Hills Beyond* (New York: New American Library, 1935; rptd. 1982), 187. Wolfe used the name Libya Hill for Asheville in this book.

2. Edward W. Phifer, Jr., *Burke: The History of a North Carolina County* (Morganton, N.C.: Privately published by the author, 1977), 66–67.

3. Mildred B. Fossett, *History of McDowell County* (Marion, N.C.: McDowell County American Revolution Bicentennial Commission, 1976), 85; Ora Blackmun, *Western North Carolina: Its Mountains and Its People to 1880* (Boone, N.C.: Appalachian Consortium Press, 1977), 266; Jody Higgins, ed., *Common Times* (Burnsville, N.C.: Yancey Graphics, 1981), 57; John P. Arthur, *Western North Carolina: A History from 1730 to 1913* (Raleigh: Edwards & Broughton, 1914), 169–74.

4. Nancy Alexander, *Here Will I Dwell: The Story of Caldwell County* (Salisbury, N.C.: Rowan Printing, 1956), 93–95.

5. Betty McFarland, *Sketches of Early Watauga* (Boone, N.C.: The Branch, 1973).

6. Blackmun, *Western North Carolina*, 274.

7. Arthur, *Western North Carolina*, 174. See also Blethen and Wood, "Land and Family in the Tuckaseigee Valley."

8. Foster A. Sondley, *Asheville and Buncombe County*, vol. 1 (Asheville, N.C.: Citizen Co., 1922), 72–73.

9. George W. McCoy, "Madison County Marks Its Centennial," *Asheville Citizen-Times*, 14 Jan. 1951; Manly Wade Wellman, *The Kingdom of Madison: A Southern Mountain Fastness and Its People* (Chapel Hill: Univ. of North Carolina Press, 1973), 66. See also Frontis W. Johnston, "The Courtship of Zeb Vance," *North Carolina Historical Review* 31 (April 1954):222–39.

10. Wellman, *The Kingdom of Madison*, 63, 66.

11. James T. Fain, Jr., *A Partial History of Henderson County* (New York: Arno 1980), 15–18.

12. Blackmun, *Western North Carolina*, 289–95.

13. Wilhelm, "Appalachian Isolation," 78, 85.

14. Zeigler and Grossup, *Heart of the Alleghanies*, 342.

15. Wolfe, *The Hills Beyond*, 186.

16. Lanman, *Letters from the Allegheny Mountains*, 427. See also Milton Ready, *Asheville, Land of the Sky: An Illustrated History* (Northridge, Cal.: Windsor Publications, Inc., 1986), 19–21.

17. Sondley, *Asheville and Buncombe County*, 84.

18. Advertisement, *North Carolina Standard*, Raleigh, 16 July 1859.

19. H.E. Colton, *Guidebook to the Scenery of Western North Carolina* (Asheville: Western Advocate Office, 1860), 14–15.

20. Ibid., 17–18.

21. Mollie Carrie to Leander Gash, 3 Aug. 1855, Gash Family Papers, NCDAH.

22. Laura Siler to "Leon," 29 Sept. 1847, Lyle and Siler Family Papers, SHC, quoted in Laurel Horton, "Nineteenth Century Quilts in Macon County,

North Carolina," in *The Many Faces of Appalachia: Exploring a Region's Diversity*, ed. Sam Gray (Boone, N.C.: Appalachian Consortium Press, 1985), 15.

23. Malet, *Errand to the South*, 215. See also Blanche Marsh, *Historic Flat Rock* (Asheville: Biltmore Press, 1961).

24. Colton, "Picturesque America"; James S. Buckingham, *The Slave States of America*, vol. 2 (London and Paris: Fisher, Son & Co., 1842), 197.

25. Malet, *Errand to the South*, 235–37; Marsh, *Historic Flat Rock*, 3.

26. Marsh, *Historic Flat Rock*, 3.

27. Lanman, *Letters from the Allegheny Mountains*, 125. For brief descriptions of Warm Springs and other western North Carolina resorts, see John Disturnell, *Springs, Waterfalls, Sea-bathing Resorts and Mountain Scenery: Of the United States and Canada* (New York: J. Disturnell, 1855), 137–38.

28. A.R. Newsome, ed., "A.S. Merrimon Journal, 1853–54," *North Carolina Historical Review* 8 (July 1931):315.

29. Ibid., 319.

30. Ibid., 311.

31. George W. Featherstonhaugh, *A Canoe Voyage Up the Minnay Sotor*, vol. 2, (London: R. Bentley, 1847), 281.

32. Avery and Boardman, "Arnold Guyot's Notes," 272; Walter Lenoir to his wife, 19 Aug. 1856, Lenoir Family Papers, SHC; John P. Arthur, *A History of Watauga County, North Carolina* (Richmond: Everett Waddey Co., 1915), 147–53. For a similar description of Bakersville, Yancey County's seat, see Porte Crayon, *The Old South Illustrated*, ed. Cecil D. Eby, Jr., (Chapel Hill: Univ. of North Carolina Press, 1959), 230–31.

33. Art Gallaher, Jr., "The Community as a Setting for Change in Southern Appalachia," in *The Public University in its Second Century*, ed. Lloyd David, (Morgantown: West Virginia Center for Appalachian Studies and Development, 1967), 26.

34. Darrett B. Rutman, "The Social Web: A Prospectus for the Study of the Early American Community," in *Insights and Parallels: Problems and Issues of American Social History* ed. William L. O'Neill (Minneapolis: Burgess, 1973), 61–87.

35. Col. Allen T. Davidson, "Reminiscences of Western North Carolina," *Lyceum* 1 (Jan. 1891):4. The most comprehensive account of antebellum merchants and mercantile operations remains Lewis E. Atherton, *The Southern Country Store, 1800–1860* (Baton Rouge: Louisiana State Univ. Press, 1949).

36. *Asheville Spectator*, 19 July 1853, 19 July 1856. For other references to the barter system in mountain stores, see Susan F. Cooper, ed., *William West Skiles: A Sketch of Missionary Life at Valle Crucis, 1840–1862* (New York: Pott, 1890), 27–28.

37. Wilma Dykeman, *The French Broad* (New York: Rinehart, 1955), 59.

38. Otto H. Olsen and Ellen Z. McGrew, eds., "Prelude to Reconstruction: The Correspondence of State Senator Leander Sams Gash, 1866–67," pt. 1, *North Carolina Historical Review* 60 (Jan. 1983): 40.

39. See survey and various entries in Calvin J. Cowles Papers, NCDAH,

and Calvin Josiah Cowles Papers, SHC; "The Late Bacchus J. Smith," *Asheville Citizen*, 6 August 1886, in Gudger-Love Papers, SHC.

40. For a description of these "sang" gatherers, see entry for 15 Aug. 1859, William C. Daily Journal, Duke.

41. These conclusions are based on a sample of 52 customers recorded by name in the account books of Joseph Cathey, Leander Gash, William Holland Thomas, James W. Terrell, William C. Erwin, and Calvin Cowles. The customers also appear in the Agricultural Schedule of the 1850 or 1860 U.S. Censuses for Haywood, Henderson, Cherokee, Jackson, Burke, and Wilkes counties, respectively. Forty of the 52 had 20–100 improved acres. Of the remaining 12, 5 owned less than 20 acres, and 7 owned more than 100. The inclusion of so few large landholding customers in these records suggests that more of them dealt with South Carolina and Georgia markets, either directly or through their own agents.

42. For a more thorough discussion of this limited market economy, see John T. Schlotterbeck, "The 'Social Economy' of an Upper South Community: Orange and Green Counties, Virginia, 1815–1860," and Steven Hahn, "The Yeomanry of the Nonplantation South: Upper Piedmont Georgia, 1850–1860," both in *Class, Conflict, and Consensus: Antebellum Southern Community Studies*, ed. Orville V. Burton and Robert C. McMath, Jr. (Westport, Conn.: Greenwood, 1982), 3–28, 32–36; Mann, "Isolation and the Social Economy of an Appalachian Community"; and Billings, Blee, and Swanson, "Culture, Family, and Community in Preindustrial Appalachia."

43. Robert D. Mitchell, *Commercialism and Frontier: Perspectives on the Early Shenandoah Valley* (Charlottesville: Univ. Press of Virginia, 1977), 140–46, 234–35; Paul Salstrom to Editor, *Appalachian Journal* 13 (Summer 1986):345. Salstrom's letter is in response to Billings, Blee, and Swanson, "Culture, Family, and Community in Preindustrial Appalachia."

44. Michaux, *Travels to the West of the Alleghanies*, 290.

45. This account of Patton's career is taken from Bethen and Wood, "A Trader on the Western Carolina Frontier." Their primary source was an autobiographical letter by Patton to his children in 1837.

46. Mitchell, *Commercialism and Frontier*, 147–49. On Cowles, see esp. vols. 54, 59, 65, 67, 72, Cowles Papers, SHC; Cowles Papers, NCDAH; and Alexander, *Here Will I Dwell*, 93–95.

47. Lewis C. Gray, *History of Agriculture in the Southern States to 1860*, vol. 1 (Washington, D.C.: Carnegie Institution, 1933), 454–58.

48. See various bills, receipts, and correspondence, 1850–54, in Joseph Cathey Papers, NCDAH. For accounts of such trips by other mountain merchants, see Thomas D. Johnston to his father, 7 May 1857, in Thomas D. Johnston Papers, SHC; Joseph Livingston to nephew, 7 Dec. 1856, and others, Gash Family Papers, NCDAH; Nathaniel C. Browder, *The Cherokee Indians and Those Who Came After* (Hayesville, N.C.: Privately published, 1973), 174–75; Arthur, *Watauga County*, 114–15; Doris Cline Ward, ed., *The Heritage of Old Buncombe County*, vol. 1 (Winston-Salem, N.C.: Hunter Publishing, 1981), 142.

49. Nimrod S. Jarrett to John McKee Sharpe, 4 Jan. 1852, in John McKee Sharpe Papers, SHC. For more on Jarrett's activity in Macon County, see Weimer Cochran, *Nantahala People and Events* (Berea, Ky.: Berea College Appalachian Center, 1987), 5–6, 13–16, 22.

50. 1844–45 entries, Johnson W. King Diary, Duke; Eli Sharpe to John McKee Sharpe, 15 May 1854, Sharpe Papers, SHC. See Browder, *Cherokee Indians*, 175, for a discussion of professional wagoners in the western part of the state.

51. George L. Hicks, *Appalachian Valley* (New York: Holt, Rinehart & Winston, 1976), 19. Kent County is a fictional name for Yancey County.

52. I.T. Avery to Thomas Lenoir, 29 Nov. and 29 Dec. 1829, 8 Dec. 1830, Lenoir Family Papers, SHC.

53. *Asheville News*, 24 June 1858.

54. Ibid.

55. Forrest McDonald and Grady McWhiney, "The Antebellum Southern Herdsman: A Reinterpretation," *Journal of Southern History* 41 (May 1975):160.

56. George Swain to Zebulon Baird, 15 Nov. 1822, David L. Swain Papers, Epistulary Correspondence, NCC (typescript in SHC).

57. Eli Sharpe to John McKee Sharpe, 1 Feb. 1845, Sharpe Papers, SHC.

58. Dykeman, *French Broad*, 139.

59. Lanman, *Letters from the Allegheny Mounains*, 123.

60. Clingman, *Speeches and Writings*, 116.

61. Lanman, *Letters from the Allegheny Mountains*, 386.

62. James M. Ray, "Reminiscences of Forty Years Ago." *Lyceum* 1 (Dec. 1890), quoted in Arthur, *Western North Carolina*, 286.

63. William A. Lenoir to Thomas Lenoir, 13 Nov. 1849, Lenoir Family Papers, SHC.

64. Jane Lenoir to her mother, 7 Nov. 1849, Lenoir Family Papers, SHC.

65. Wellman, *Kingdom of Madison*, 45.

66. Kephart, *Our Southern Highlanders*, 123.

67. Phifer, *Burke*, 208.

68. Blackmun, *Western North Carolina*, 224.

69. Jason Basil Deyton, "The Toe River Valley to 1865," *North Carolina Historical Review* 24 (Oct. 1947):457–58.

70. See Sherrill's Inn Registers (microfilm), SHC; originals in possession of James Clarke, Hickory Nut Gap, N.C.

71. Ray, "Reminiscences," 16.

72. James Sharpe to John McKee Sharpe, 8 Jan. 1846, Sharpe Papers, SHC; and Arthur, *Western North Carolina*, 287.

73. James S. Sharpe to John McKee Sharpe, 17 May 1854, Sharpe Papers, SHC.

74. Clingman, *Speeches and Writings*, 166.

75. Dykeman, *French Broad*, 146.

76. Eli Sharpe to John McKee Sharpe, 30 Sept. 1851, Sharpe Papers, SHC.

77. N.W. Woodfin to D.L. Swain, 28 Nov. 1857, Walter Clark Papers, NCDAH.

78. Hamilton, *Shotwell Papers*, vol. 2, p. 280.

79. The best example of this was the Toe River Valley. See Deyton, "Toe River Valley," 446.

80. See John Opie, "Where American History Began: Appalachia and the Small Independent Family Farm," in *Appalachia/America: Proceedings of the 1980 Appalachian Studies Conference*, ed. Wilson Somerville (Boone, N.C.: Appalachian Consortium Press, 1981), 61; and Marion Pearsall, *Little Smoky Ridge: The Natural History of a Southern Appalachian Neighborhood* (University, Ala.: Univ. of Alabama Press, 1959), 28.

81. Paludan, *Victims*, 8–9. See also Deyton, "Toe River Valley," 434.

82. Beaver, *Rural Community*, 12. See also Wilhelm, "Folk Settlements," 208. Lambert, "Oconaluftee Valley," 419–20; and Elizabeth D. Powers and Mark E. Hannah, *Cataloochee: Lost Settlement of the Smokies* (Charleston, S.C.: Powers-Hannah Publishers, 1982), 30–35.

83. Lanman, *Letters from the Allegheny Mountains*, 446–47, 449–50; Higgins, *Common Times*, 9, 13–25.

84. Frederick Law Olmsted, *A Journey in the Back Country in the Winter of 1854–55* (New York: Mason Bros., 1860; rptd. Putnam, 1907), 258–59.

85. Arthur, *Western North Carolina*, 145; Arthur, *Watauga County*, 114.

86. Margaret Walker Freel, *Unto the Hills* (Andrews, N.C.: Published by the author, 1976), 44; Mattie Russell, "William Holland Thomas, White Chief of the North Carolina Cherokees" (Ph.D. diss., Duke Univ., 1956), 230–231.

87. Elisha Mitchell to his wife Maria, 20 July 1828, Elisha Mitchell Papers, SHC.

88. Olmsted, *Back Country*, 258–59.

89. Lanman, *Letters from the Allegheny Mountains*, 384.

90. Ibid., 386.

91. Beaver, *Rural Communities*, 12.

92. Vladimir E. Hartman, "A Cultural Study of a Mountain Community in Western North Carolina" (Ph.D. diss., Univ. of North Carolina, Chapel Hill, 1957), 58.

93. Hewitt, John, "My People of the Mountains," John Hewitt Memoir (typescript), SHC, p. 7–8.

94. Olmsted, *Back Country*, 231, 246. See also Cratis D. Williams, "The Southern Mountaineer in Fact and Fiction" (Ph.D. diss., New York Univ., 1961), 73; Lanman, *Letters from the Allegheny Mountains*, 396, 456–58; Buckingham, *Slave States of America*, vol. 2, 155–60; Muriel E. Sheppard, *Cabins in the Laurel* (Chapel Hill: Univ. of North Carolina Press, 1935), 45.

Chapter 3

1. Campbell, *Southern Highlander*, 94; Blackmun, *Western North Carolina*, 132.

2. Wolfe, *The Hills Beyond*, 250, 263; David Donald, *Looking Homeward: A Life of Thomas Wolfe* (Boston: Little, Brown, 1987), 79.

3. Other works which have implied that slavery or blacks had little influ-

ence in the mountains include Morley, *Carolina Mountains*, 149; Arthur, *Western North Carolina*, 636; W.J. Cash, *The Mind of the South* (New York: Knopf, 1941), 219; and Dykeman, "Appalachia in Context," 29. Carter G. Woodson, in his landmark article, "Freedom and Slavery in Appalachian America," 132–50, emphasized antislavery sentiment but applied the term "Appalachian" so loosely that he dealt with an area encompassing most of the Upper South. He addressed neither the demographics nor the economics of slavery in the mountains. Among the few works which have recognized the demographic significance of slavery in the mountains are Robert P. Stuckert, "Black Populations of the Southern Appalachian Mountains," *Phylon* 48 (June 1987):141–51; James M. Gifford, "Our Pioneer Heritage," in Clifford R. Lovin, ed., *Our Mountain Heritage* (Cullowhee, N.C.: Mountain Heritage Center, Western Carolina University, 1979), 106–107; Martin Crawford, "Slaveholding and Power in the New River Valley: Ashe County, North Carolina, in 1860," in *Proceedings of the New River Symposium, May 1982* (Wheeling: National Park Service and the West Virginia Dept. of Archives and History, 1983):30–35; Richard B. Drake, "Slavery and Antislavery in Appalachia," *Appalachian Heritage* 14 (Winter 1986), 25–33; Ralph Mann, "Master and Slave in the Other South" (Paper delivered at Conference for Carl Degler, Stanford Univ., Palo Alto, Calif., May 1987); and Phifer, "Slavery in Microcosm: Burke County, North Carolina." Phifer's article, it should be noted, deals with the one western county whose slave demography more resembled that of piedmont counties than that of neighboring mountain ones.

4. Out of Burke County's total population of 9,237 in 1860, 2,371 (25.7%) were slaves. In 1850, slaves made up 20.2% of the population in McDowell County, and 19% in Caldwell County. In ten piedmont counties (Montgomery, Moore, Union, Randolph, Davidson, Guilford, Forsyth, Alexander, Yadkin, and Stanley), slaves made up less than one–fourth of the population in both 1850 and 1860, and in all but the first three counties listed, slaves made up less than one–fifth. Eighth U.S. Census, 1860, Population Schedule, Burke County; Seventh U.S. Census, 1850; Population Schedule, Caldwell and McDowell counties; *Agriculture in 1860*, 235–236.

5. Eighth U.S. Census, 1860, Population Schedules for Buncombe, Henderson, Madison, and Watauga counties. The upper Toe River Valley of Madison County and the Rock Creek section of Watauga County had virtually no slaves. See Sheppard, *Cabins in the Laurel*, 60; and Deyton, "The Toe River Valley to 1865," 459.

6. For comparison with the demographics of slavery in Kentucky's mountains, see James B. Murphy, "Slavery and Freedom in Appalachia: Kentucky as a Demographic Case Study," *Register of the Kentucky Historical Society* 80 (Spring 1982): 151–69.

7. Olmsted, *Back Country*, 253. For further discussion of Olmsted and his trip through this area, see ch. 4.

8. The sample counties are Buncombe, Burke, Ashe, Cherokee, and Yancey. Because these data are derived from a wide variety of sources, these figures are only approximate. Information derived from U.S. Census occupation list-

ings alone is incomplete and misleading, because many slaveholders identified themselves as farmers despite their involvement in one or more nonagricultural activities. The term "agriculture alone" is applied to those slaveholders who either were known to have had no other business pursuits or for whom no supplementary information is available. The percentages listed exceed 100% because, as is explained in the next few paragraphs, many large slaveholders were involved in several of the categories listed. The best general discussion of slaveholders engaged in nonagricultural careers is James Oakes, *The Ruling Race: A History of American Slaveholders* (New York: Knopf, 1982), 58–65.

9. Ibid., 61. In 1860, Woodfin owned 122 slaves. (Only William F. McKesson, discussed later in the chapter, owned more.) Eighth U.S. Census, 1860, Slave Schedules, Buncombe and Burke counties; Phifer, *Burke*, 51–52. In 1850, Caldwell owned 17 slaves. In 1860 Vance owned 6 and his brother, R.B. Vance, also a young lawyer, owned 7. Seventh U.S. Census, 1850, Slave Schedule, Burke County; Eighth U.S. Census, 1860, Slave Schedule, Buncombe County.

10. Gaillard S. Tennent, "Medicine in Buncombe County Down to 1885: Historical and Biographical Sketches," pamphlet rptd. from *The Charlotte Medical* (1906). Other doctors in the region with substantial slaveholdings included J.F.E. Hardy, who owned 42 slaves in 1850; and J.D. Boyd, with 18 in 1860.

11. Phifer, *Burke*, 260–61, 462; Eighth U.S. Census, 1860, Slave Schedules, Cherokee and Henderson counties.

12. Arthur L. Fletcher, *Ashe County: A History* (Jefferson, N.C.: Ashe County Research Association, Inc., 1963), 87–88; Seventh U.S. Census, 1850, Slave Schedules, Ashe and Macon counties; Eight U.S. Census, 1860, Slave Schedules, Ashe and Macon counties; Arthur, *History of Watauga County*, 114–15; Jesse R. Siler Book, SHC.

13. James Gwyn Books, vols. 4 and 5, SHC; Seventh U.S. Census, 1850, Slave Schedule, Wilkes County. Other successful merchant slaveholders include James Harper, who owned several stores in and around Lenoir and had 20 slaves in 1860, and Bacchus J. Smith and John W. McElroy, merchants and one-time partners in ginseng production in Yancey County, where each owned 15 slaves in 1850. See Alexander, *Here Will I Dwell*, 78, 93–95; Ward, *Old Buncombe County*, 142–43; Olsen and McGrew, "Prelude to Reconstruction," 40; "The Late Bacchus J. Smith," *Asheville Citizen*, 6 Aug. 1886; Fourth U.S. Census, 1820, and Fifth U.S. Census, 1830; Slave Schedules, Buncombe and Caldwell counties; Eighth U.S. Census, 1860: Slave Schedule, Yancey County.

14. Phifer, *Burke*, 185–86, 214, 258, 465; Eighth U.S. Census, 1860; Slave Schedule, Burke County.

15. James W. Terrell, "Manuscript Sketch of William Holland Thomas's Life," 29 Jan. 1906, in James W. Terrell Papers, WCU; Mattie Russell, "William Holland Thomas," 223–34.

16. Blackmun, *Western North Carolina*, 291–92. See also Sondley, *Asheville and Buncombe County*, vol. 1, 771–72; Eighth U.S. Census, 1860, Slave Schedule, Buncombe County. Both Love's White Sulphur Springs and Robert Henry's

Sulphur Springs just west of Asheville were discovered by slaves they owned. See Sadie Patton, "Fame of WNC as Major Health Resort Dates from 18th Century," *Asheville Citizen*, 26 Mar. 1950. Other successful hotel owner–slaveholders included George Bower and John Happoldt, already mentioned; Calvin S. Brown (Burke County); Henry Farmer (Henderson County); David Vance; and Robert Henry (Buncombe County).

17. Margaret W. Freel, *Unto the Hills* 22; Seventh U.S. Census, 1850; Slave Schedule, Wilkes County.

18. Vols. 54, 59, 65, 67, and 72 and other account books and ledgers, Calvin J. Cowles Papers, SHC and NCDAH. See also Susan Sokol Blosser, "Calvin J. Cowles's Gap Creek Mine: A Case Study of Mine Speculation in the Gilded Age," *North Carolina Historical Review* 51 (Autumn 1974):379–400.

19. Richard A. Shrader, "William Lenoir, 1751–1839" (Ph.D. diss. Univ. of North Carolina, Chapel Hill, 1978), 189–90; Margaret E. Harper, *Fort Defiance and the General* (Hickory, N.C.: Clay Printing Co., 1976), 86–87.

20. Edward W. Phifer, Jr., "Saga of A Burke County Family," *North Carolina Historical Review* 39 (1962): 140.

21. Contract, 3 Oct. 1854, Thomas George Walton Papers, SHC.

22. Olmsted, *Back Country*, 254.

23. Seventh U.S. Census, 1850, Slave and Agriculture Schedules, Burke, Caldwell and McDowell counties.

24. Works dealing with the movement of hogs through the North Carolina mountains include Edmund C. Burnett, "Hog Raising and Hog Driving in the Region of the French Broad River," *Agricultural History* 20 (Apr. 1946):86–103; "The Age of the Drovers," *The State* 27 (25 July 1959):11–12; McDonald and McWhiney, "The Antebellum Southern Herdsmen," 147–66; Wilma Dykeman, *French Broad*, 137–51; and Sam B. Hilliard, *Hog Meat and Hoecake: Food Supply in the Old South, 1840–1860* (Carbondale: Southern Illinois Univ. Press, 1972), 193–96.

25. See Ch. 1, n. 13.

26. These four were James Gudger of Buncombe County, and Thomas Gardner, Joseph Shepherd, and Samuel Fleming (sometimes spelled Flemming) of Yancey County. Seventh U.S. Census, 1850; Slave and Agriculture Schedules, Buncombe and Yancey counties.

27. Seventh U.S. Census, 1850, Slave and Agriculture Schedules, Cherokee County; Eighth U.S. Census, 1860, Slave and Agriculture Schedules, Madison County. Nonslaveholders with up to 200 or so improved acres were not uncommon in these counties—another variable in the region's land–slave ratio.

28. The number of slaves too young or too old to work made up roughly the same proportion of all of these holdings, as did the proportions of male and female slaves, so that age and sex do not account for the variables in number. Temporary hired white labor may have been used to supplement slave labor, although there is little evidence that slave owners in the region made much use of this option, or even that such an option was readily available in most areas of the mountains.

29. William A. Lenoir to William Lenoir, 16 Oct. 1835, Lenoir Family Papers, SHC.

30. James S. Buckingham, *Slave States*, 193; Lanman, *Letters from the Alleghany Mountains*, 433; George W. Featherstonaugh, *Canoe Voyage*, vol. 2, 314–17.

31. Johnson W. King Diary, various entries, 1844–45, Duke (King was an earlier business partner of Thomas's); James W. Terrell to William H. Thomas, 5 Jan. 1860, William Holland Thomas Papers, Duke.

32. Fletcher, *Ashe County*, 233.

33. Ruth W. Shepherd, ed., *The Heritage of Ashe County, North Carolina* (Winston–Salem, N.C.: Hunter Publishing, 1984), 47; Phifer, *Burke*, 183–84, 215; Eighth U.S. Census, 1860, Slave and Manufactures Schedules, Burke County.

34. George Swain to David L. Swain, 23 May 1822, David Lowry Swain Epistolary Correspondence, NCC (typescripts in SHC).

35. William Coleman to David L. Swain, 3 Dec. 1839, 18 Dec. 1841, 25 Feb. 1842, David L. Swain Papers, NCDAH; Sondley, *Asheville and Buncombe County*, Vol. 2, 768.

36. Fletcher M. Green, "Gold Mining: A Forgotten Industry in Antebellum North Carolina," *North Carolina Historical Review* 14 (Jan. 1937): 12, 15. See also Edward W. Phifer, Jr., "Champagne at Brindletown: The Story of the Burke County Gold Rush, 1829–1833," *North Carolina Historical Review* 40 (Oct. 1963), 489–500. For a discussion of slaves employed as miners elsewhere, see Robert S. Starobin, *Industrial Slavery in the Old South* (New York: Oxford Univ. Press, 1970), 23–24, 214–19; Brent D. Glass, "Midas and Old Rip: The Gold Hill Mining District of North Carolina" (Ph.D. diss., Univ. of North Carolina, Chapel Hill, 1980), 133–43; Ronald L. Lewis, *Coal, Iron, and Slaves: Industrial Slavery in Maryland and Virginia, 1715–1865* (Westport, Conn.: Greenwood, 1979); John Edmund Stealey III, "Slavery and the Western Virginia Salt Industry," *Journal of Negro History* 59 (Apr. 1974): 105–31; and Mann, "Master and Slave in the Other South," which also deals with slave labor in Virginia saltworks.

37. Featherstonhaugh, *Canoe Voyage*, 333.

38. For a discussion of the risks encountered by slave miners, see Starobin, *Industrial Slavery*, 45–48; and Lewis, *Coal, Iron and Slaves*, 90–94.

39. James G. Scott to John Scott, 12 Nov. 1833, Dr. John Scott Papers, SHC.

40. Phifer, *Burke*, 213, 463.

41. Record of W.W. Avery and Co., 4 Nov. 1844, George Phifer Erwin Papers, SHC; Phifer, *Burke*, 214; "Report on Baker Mine," Oct. 1857, Calvin J. Cowles Papers, SHC. Curiously, there is no evidence of the use of slave labor at the area's largest mining operation, the Cranberry Iron Mines, then in Yancey County.

42. *Asheville News*, 2 Mar. 1854.

43. Phifer, "Burke County Family," 337; J. Lenoir Chambers, *The Breed and the Pasture* (Charlotte, N.C.: Stone and Barringer 1910), 72; Isaac T. Avery to his son, 26 Nov. 1852, George Phifer Erwin Papers, SHC. For treatments of the legal uncertainties of slaves' status on free soil prior to the Dred Scott decision,

see Paul Finkelman, *Slavery in the Courtroom: An Annotated Bibliography of American Cases* (Washington, D.C.: Library of Congress, 1985), 19–57; and Don E. Fehrenbacher, *The Dred Scott Case: Its Significance in American Law and Politics* (New York: Oxford Univ. Press, 1978),152–208.

44. Thomas G. Walton, "Sketches of Pioneers in Burke County History," typescript, p. 10–11, Thomas George Walton Papers, SHC.

45. *Asheville News*, 2 Mar. 1854.

46. Isaac T. Avery to James Avery, 20 Feb. 1853, Avery Family Letters, in possession of Mrs. Cliff Avery of Morganton, N.C. For further reports on the loss of slaves due to illness and death, see I.T. Avery to W.W. Avery, 14 Oct. 1852, George Phifer Erwin Papers, SHC.

47. Malet, *Errand to the South*, 242.

48. Shrader, "William Lenoir," 82; "Memorandum of Cloth made at F.D. [Fort Defiance]," 1849, Thomas Lenoir Papers, Duke; Lenoir Family Papers, various entries, vols. 196 and 203, SHC.

49. James Hervey Greenlee Diary, various entries, 1847 and 1852, SHC. For another look at the versatility of a mixed–farm slave labor force, see Schlotterbeck, "Social Economy of an Upper South Community," 10–11.

50. E.J. Erwin to George P. Erwin, 9 Dec. 1858, George Phifer Erwin Papers, SHC.

51. Eugene D. Genovese, *Roll, Jordan, Roll: The World the Slaves Made* (New York: Vintage, 1974, 1976), 390.

52. James Hervey Greenlee Diary, various entries, 1847–49, 1852–54, SHC; Eighth U.S. Census, 1860, Slave Schedule, Burke County.

53. James G. Scott to John Scott, 12 Nov. 1833, Dr. John Scott Papers, SHC; Calvin J. Cowles to "Andrew," 11 Feb. 1862, Cowles Papers, NCDAH.

54. Shrader, "William Lenoir," 82; Silas McDowell to David L. Swain, 1 Jan. 1831, David L. Swain Papers, SHC; various entries, 1861 (e.g., 20 Jan., 11 Feb., 14 Apr.), Cowles Papers, NCDAH.

55. Contract between Thomas and Love, 13 July 1835, William Holland Thomas Papers, WCU; Russell, "William Holland Thomas," 237.

56. L. Williams to W.H. Thomas, 24 Oct. 1859, William Holland Thomas Papers, Duke.

57. Charles White to Hamilton Brown, 20 Dec. 1832, Hamilton Brown Papers, SHC.

58. Entries for 1 July 1855 and 1 July 1861, Account Book, David L. Swain Papers, SHC.

59. Various entries, James Hervey Greenlee Diary, SHC. Some county courts required owners to provide slave labor for a certain number of days annually for road work. See Alexander, *Here Will I Dwell*, 119; and Court Summons, 3 Aug. 1845, George W. Hendrix Papers, Duke; Johnson W. King Diary, Duke.

60. It is probable that Jordan Councill, Jr.'s slaves helped build the Watauga County Courthouse, just as David Coleman's did for Macon County, and Judge Mitchell King's did for Henderson County. The slaves of George Bower

and Jesse Siler built the Methodist churches in Jefferson and Franklin respectively, and those of Ned Wilson erected Yancey County's first church, Cane Creek Baptist. There is no record, though, of whether or by whom these owners were paid for the labor provided. See Arthur, *Watauga County*, 115, 126; Fain, *Partial History of Henderson County*, 19; Fletcher, *Ashe County*, 167; Jesse R. Siler Book, SHC; Higgins, *Common Times*, 57.

61. Phifer, "Champagne at Brindletown," 492.

62. Contract, 6 Jan. 1838, Wilkes County Slave Records, NCDAH; Record of W.W. Avery and Co., 4 Nov. 1844, George Phifer Erwin Papers, SHC.

63. Greenlee Diary, vol. 1, typescript, pp. 79, 100, 103, et passim, SHC; "Report on Baker Mine," Oct. 1857, Cowles Papers, SHC; L. Williams to W.H. Thomas, (24 Oct. 1859), William Holland Thomas Papers, Duke.

64. James Patton to David L. Smith, 5 Feb. 1861, David L. Swain Papers, NCDAH.

65. Phifer, *Burke*, 185, 187; Eighth U.S. Census, 1860, Slave Schedule, Burke County. Slaves were hired on a yearly basis at varying rates for skilled and unskilled labor. See also Fossett, *History of McDowell County*, 85.

66. B.H. Nelson, "Some Aspects of Negro Life in North Carolina During the Civil War," *North Carolina Historical Review* 25 (Apr. 1948):161.

67. William H. Abrams, Jr., "The Western North Carolina Railroad, 1855–1894" (M.A. thesis, Western Carolina Univ., 1976), 13.

68. Good examples are found in James Gwyn Books, vols. 4 and 5, SHC; Lenoir Family Papers, vols. 196 and 203, SHC; and Diary, 1848–49, Thomas Lenoir Papers, Duke.

69. Olmsted, *Back Country*, 253; John Hall to David L. Swain, 3 Jan. 1842, David L. Swain Papers, NCDAH; Thomas Lenoir to Rufus Lenoir, 5 Sept. 1844, Lenoir Family Papers, SHC.

70. Figures for the South are taken from Richard Sutch, "The Profitability of Antebellum Slavery—Revisited," *Southern Economic Journal* 31 (Apr. 1965), 367–68. Calculations for slave prices in western North Carolina are based on recorded prices of 182 slaves sold in various combinations ranging from 1 to 23 slaves per sale in 1850–59.

71. Examples of estate settlements which included slave sales are found in James Gwyn Papers, various entries, 1859, SHC; Notice, 22 May 1846, *Highland Messenger* (Asheville); George Swain to David L. Swain, 8 Nov. 1822, David L. Swain Epistolary Correspondence, NCC; Account, 20 Mar. 1848 and 15 July 1851, Thomas George Walton Papers, SHC; Robert Penland Will, n.d., Penland Family Papers, WCU.

72. Examples include L.G. Jones to Thomas Lenoir, 23 Dec. 1839, Lenoir Family Papers, SHC; Statement by Terrell, 26 Mar. 1842, William Holland Thomas Papers, Duke.

73. John A. McLeod, *From These Stones: Mars Hill College, 1856–1968* (Mars Hill, N.C.: Mars Hill College, 1968), 22–23. Other examples of slaves sold to pay debts include Court Order, 9 Nov. 1853, McDowell County Slave and Free Black Records, NCDAH; William Coleman to David L. Swain, 3 Dec. 1839,

D.R. Lowry to Swain, 29 Nov. 1840, and numerous other examples in Swain Papers, NCDAH; promissory note, 5 May 1842, William Holland Thomas Papers, Duke; and Notice, 3 July 1846, *Highland Messenger*.

74. Eli McKee to John McKee, 8 Aug. 1847, and other correspondence in John McKee Sharpe Papers, SHC.

75. Mary Barbour interview in George P. Rawick, ed., *The American Slave: A Composite Autobiography*, vol. 14, *North Carolina Narratives, Part I* (Westport, Conn.: Greenwood, 1972), 79. The only reason she and the others were not sold was the disruption brought on by the war.

76. Shrader, "William Lenoir," 223–33.

77. See, e.g., Phifer, "Slavery in Microcosm," 155; James Gwyn to Rufus T. Lenoir, 15 May 1861, Lenoir Family Papers, SHC; Wilkes County Deposition, 18 Aug. 1859, James Gwyn Papers, SHC; Waightstill Avery's and Nathaniel Gordon's Wills, in Thomas Felix Hickerson, ed., *Echoes of Happy Valley: Letters and Diaries, Family Life in the South, Civil War History* (Chapel Hill, N.C.: Published by the author, 1962), 12, 33.

78. These figures are based on the Eighth U.S. Census, 1860, Slave Schedules for all fifteen of the state's westernmost counties.

79. For purchases of slaves by western Carolinians from Richmond, Norfolk, Charleston, Georgia, and eastern North Carolina, see Calvin J. Cowles to J.A. Bitting, 5 July 1851, Cowles Papers, NCDAH; Walton, "Sketches of Burke County Pioneers," in Thomas George Walton Papers, SHC; Isaac T. Avery to Thomas Lenoir, 17 Dec. 1821, Lenoir Family Papers, SHC; J.R. Siler to David L. Swain, 30 Nov. 1843, Swain Papers, SHC; James Avery to Isaac T. Avery, 1 Sept. 1852, in Avery Letters, in possession of Priscilla Schoenen, Morganton, N.C.

80. Sarah Gudger interview in Rawick, *American Slave*, vol. 14, 354–55.

81. Phifer, "Slavery in Microcosm," 154.

82. Willa Cather, *Sapphira and the Slave Girl* (New York: Knopf, 1940), 7.

83. This figure is based on the number of slave children under age 10 listed in the Eighth U.S. Census, 1860. For the state as a whole, 109,627—out of the total slave population of 331,059—were under ten years old. For the 15 westernmost counties, the comparable figures are 4,250 out of 12,812 slaves. *Population of the United States in 1860* (Washington, D.C.: Government Printing Office, 1864), 352–57.

84. There were 7,519 slaves in the state's 10 westernmost counties in 1840. In 1860, there were 12,182 in the same area (by then divided into 15 counties). The comparable figures for the state as a whole were 245,817 in 1840 and 331,059 in 1860. Sixth U.S. Census, 1840, and Eighth U.S. Census, 1860, Population Schedules. In a sample made of 10 counties across the state, the only mountain county included (Cherokee) was one of just two in which slave population increased rather than decreased between 1850 and 1860. See Yasuko I. Shinoda, "Land and Slaves in North Carolina in 1860" (Ph.D. diss., Univ. of North Carolina, Chapel Hill, 1971), 82.

85. In 1850, there were 1,648 slaveholding families in western North Caro-

lina. In 1860, there were 1,877 in the same area. Seventh U.S. Census, 1850, Slave Schedule for appropriate counties; *Agriculture in 1860*, 236–37.

Chapter 4

1. Phifer, *Burke*, 151, 256.

2. Walton's nephew's account of this incident is found in Walton, "Sketches of Burke County Pioneers," 10–11. Tamishan's descendant is John Fleming, a historian who heads the National Afro-American Museum and Cultural Center, Wilberforce, Ohio. His version, which he first heard from his grandfather and verified through interviews with other relatives still living in Burke County, varies only slightly from Walton's. See "Descendant Traces Family Roots to Burke," *Morganton (N.C.) News-Herald*, 16 June 1986.

3. Featherstonhaugh, *Canoe Voyage*, 314.

4. Olmsted, *Back Country*, 226–27.

5. Lanman, *Letters from the Alleghany Mountains*, 314.

6. Malet, *Errand to the South*, 215.

7. Lanman, *Letters from the Alleghany Mountains*, 434–35, 439–44. See also Featherstonhaugh, *Canoe Voyage*, 317.

8. See, e.g., Albert D. Richardson, *The Secret Service, the Field, the Dungeon, and the Escape* (Hartford, Conn.: American Publishing Co., 1865), 440, 462–63; J. Madison Drake, *Fast and Loose in Dixie* (New York: Authors' Publishing Co., 1880), 173; William Burson, *A Race for Liberty; or My Capture, Imprisonment and Escape* (Wellsville, Ohio: W.G. Forester, 1867), 79.

9. See ch. 3 for more on the Brown and Walker situations; Russell, "William Holland Thomas," 232–33, 235; James W. Terrell to W.H. Thomas, 5 Jan. 1860, William Holland Thomas Papers, Duke.

10. Various entries, Greenlee Diary, SHC.

11. See Contract, 3 Oct. 1854, Thomas George Walton Papers, SHC; Powers and Hannah, *Cataloochee*, 21–22.

12. Lanman, *Letters from the Alleghany Mountains*, 154.

13. Shrader, "William Lenoir," 208.

14. Harper, *Fort Defiance and the General*, 75; Thomas Lenoir to William Lenoir, 28 Mar. 1827, Lenoir Family Papers, SHC; Phifer, "Slavery in Microcosm," 154.

15. Will of Henry Hardin, 16 June 1846, in Will Book D, Ashe County Court Records, reproduced in Shepherd, *Heritage of Ashe County*, 48.

16. Russell, "William Holland Thomas," 237.

17. J.H. Coleman to David L. Swain, 17 Apr. 1853, Walter Clark Papers, NCDAH.

18. N.W. Woodfin to David L. Swain, 21 Aug. 1843, David L. Swain Papers, NCDAH. There were, of course, exceptions to this general respect for slave family ties. See, for example, Phifer, "Slavery in Microcosm," 155. The number of single-slave owners in the region, discussed in ch. 3, would seem to un-

dermine the case for mountain masters' respect for black family ties. But Phifer presents several explanations to resolve this seeming contradiction. Most notably, legal necessities—estate settlements, auctions, and other actions against indebtedness—overrode local moral guidelines regarding the dispersal of slavery property and forced owners to sell. Also evident were inheritance patterns in which black family members were dispersed among an owner's offspring, so that a number of single-slave owners who appeared on census records lived with or in close proximity to other members of their own families and those of their slaves. See ch. 3 of this book, including n. 71, 72, 74, 76–79, 81.

19. Douglas Swaim, ed., *Cabins and Castles: The History and Architecture of Buncombe County, North Carolina* (Raleigh, N.C.: NCDAH, 1981), 17.

20. Contract, 20 June 1859; James Gwyn to Philip Dowell, 4 July 1859; and Bills of Sale, 4 July 1859, all in James Gwyn Papers, SHC.

21. Lou Rogers, *Tar Heel Women* (Raleigh, N.C.: Edward and Broughton, 1949), 87. For other examples of efforts made to respect family ties at slave auctions, see L.G. Jones to Thomas Lenoir, 23 Dec. 1839, and Lenoir to Jones, 10 Jan. 1840, Lenoir Family Papers, SHC.

22. Swaim, *Cabins and Castles*, 17; L.G. Jones to Thomas Lenoir, 23 Dec. 1839, and Lenoir to Jones, 10 Jan. 1840, Lenoir Family Papers, SHC.

23. William L. Gwyn to Hamilton Brown, 1 Mar. 1836 in Hickerson, *Echoes of Happy Valley*, 27; Greenlee Diary, vol. 1 (typescript), p. 103, SHC.

24. James S. McKee to John McKee, 4 Feb. 1850, John McKee Sharpe Papers, SHC.

25. Ibid., 5 Dec. 1850.

26. Ibid., 30 Sept. 1851.

27. Ibid., 2 Jan. 1853.

28. Ibid., 30 Sept. 1851. See also 4 Jan. 1852, 16 Feb. 1852, and 23 Jan. 1854.

29. In his recent study of southern planters' lifestyles, Steven Stowe observes that slaveholders rarely if ever mentioned their slaves in letters to family or acquaintances. The regularity with which slaves are discussed by the McKee family, as well as by the Lenoirs, the Averys, the Swains, and others cited in this chapter indicates yet another distinctive characteristic of the relationship between owned and owner in western North Carolina. Steven M. Stowe, *Intimacy and Power in the Old South: Ritual in the Lives of the Planters* (Baltimore: Johns Hopkins Univ. Press, 1987), xvi. See also Jane T. Censer, *North Carolina Planters and Their Children, 1800–1860* (Baton Rouge: Louisiana State Univ. Press, 1984), 143.

30. Phifer, "Saga of a Burke County Family," 142.

31. 31 Dec. 1848 entry, Greenlee Diary, SHC.

32. W.W. Lenoir to Thomas I. Lenoir, 19 Apr. 1858, in Hickerson, *Echoes of Happy Valley*, 53.

33. Nimrod S. Jarrett to John McKee, 4 Jan. and 20 Feb. 1854; Eli McKee to John McKee, 18 Oct. 1853, all in John McKee Sharpe Papers, SHC.

34. Helen T. Catterall, ed., *Judicial Cases Concerning American Slavery and the Negro*, vol. 2 (Washington, D.C.: Carnegie Institution, 1929), 200.

35. William Coleman to David L. Swain, 16 Aug. 1852, David L. Swain Papers, SHC.

36. Ibid.

37. James Avery to Isaac T. Avery, 1 Sept. 1852, Avery Letters, in possession of Priscilla Schoenen, Morganton, N.C. See also reply from Isaac to his father, 20 Feb. 1853, in possession of Mrs. Cliff Avery, Morganton, N.C.

38. George Swain to David L. Swain, 2 Aug. 1822, in David L. Swain Epistolary Correspondence, NCC (typescript in SHC). See also Thomas Lenoir Papers, Greenlee Diary, etc., SHC.

39. Gudger-Love Family History (typescript), p. 2, Gudger-Love Family Papers, SHC.

40. Chambers, *Breed and Pasture*, 48–50.

41. Russell, "William Holland Thomas," 232–33.

42. James Gwyn to Thomas Lenoir, 28 Mar. 1856, James Gwyn Papers, SHC.

43. Walton, "Sketches of Burke County Pioneers," 11. Full accounts of these two incidents are found at the beginning of this chapter and in ch. 3, respectively.

44. Phifer, "Slavery in Mirocosm," 151; *Raleigh Register*, 3 Sept. 1851. The author is grateful to Martin Crawford for supplying the information on the Ashe County cases. See Crawford, "Slaveholding and Power in the New River Valley," 30–31, for other instances of slave disciplinary problems.

45. Phifer, "Slavery in Microcosm," 150; Henderson County Slave Records, 1856–57, NCDAH; Sondley, *Asheville and Buncombe County*, vol. 2, 481–82. For other evidence of the mistreatment of mountain slaves (though none from western North Carolina), based largely on the slaves' own testimony, see Drake, "Slavery and Antislavery in Appalachia," 26–29.

46. The description of this episode is found in George Swain to David L. Swain, 17 May 1822, David L. Swain Epistolary Correspondence, NCC.

47. John Hewitt, "My People of the Mountains," 9–10, John Hewitt Memoir, SHC. The *Asheville News* and *Asheville Spectator* often carried runaway notices from owners in South Carolina, Georgia, and eastern North Carolina who suspected that their slaves had headed for the North Carolina mountains.

48. For comments on the problem of slave intoxication in his area, see George Swain to David L. Swain, 26 Apr. 1823, David L. Swain Epistolary Correspondence, NCC. For other offenses, see the county court slave records for Buncombe, Burke, Caldwell, McDowell, Henderson, and Wilkes counties, NCDAH.

49. George Swain to David L. Swain, 17 May 1822, David L. Swain Epistolary Correspondence, NCC.

50. Buckingham, *Slave States*, 209–10.

51. Freel, *Unto the Hills*, 103–106.

52. Russell, "William Holland Thomas," 238.

53. Mrs. E.C. Alexander to W.L. Alexander, 2 Apr. 1850, Hoke Papers, SHC, cited in Guion G. Johnson, *Ante-Bellum North Carolina: A Social History* (Chapel Hill, Univ. of North Carolina Press, 1937), 469.

54. Rawick, *American Slave*, vol. 14, 352–55.

55. See Phifer, "Slavery in Microcosm," 151; Johnson J. Hayes, *The Land of Wilkes* (Wilkesboro, N.C.: Wilkes County Historical Society, 1962), 142–45; McDowell County Slave Records, Oct. 1844, NCDAH. For a brief reference to a mistress who beat a female slave to death in anger, see Cochran, *Nantahala People and Events*, 22.

56. Ira Berlin, *Slaves Without Masters: The Free Negro in the Antebellum South* (New York: Random House, 1974), 367.

57. James Oakes, *The Ruling Race: A History of American Slaveholders* (New York: Knopf, 1982), 167; Genovese, *Roll, Jordan, Roll*, 63–67; Kenneth Stampp, *The Peculiar Institution: Slavery in the Ante-Bellum South* (New York: Random House, 1956), 174.

58. Austin Steward, *Twenty-two Years a Slave and Forty Years a Freeman* (Rochester, N.Y.: Allings & Cory, 1857), 28, cited in Oakes, *Ruling Race*, 168. Eugene Genovese contends that the qualitative difference in slave treatment in the Upper and Lower South, so apparent during the colonial period, had all but disappeared by the nineteenth century. Genovese, *Roll, Jordan, Roll*, 54.

59. Censer, *North Carolina Planters*, 136, 144.

60. Ibid.

61. The fifteen estates in which family units were respected in the dispersement of slave property were those of William McEntire (Thomas George Walton Papers, SHC); James Lowry and Silas McDowell (Walter Clark Papers, NCDAH); Waightstill Avery (Waightstill Avery Papers, SHC); John Lenoir (Lenoir Family Papers, SHC); W. White (David L. Swain Papers, SHC); Priscilla Dowell and James Gwyn (James Gwyn Books, SHC); James R. Love (W.W. Stringfield Papers, WCU); John Scott (Freel, *Unto the Hills*, 91); W.W. Erwin (Chambers, *The Breed and the Pasture*, 72); and Maria L. Gordon (Catterall, *Judicial Cases*, vol. 2, p. 200).

The three cases in which family members were separated or in which no mention was made of keeping family units intact were the estates of Joseph S. West (Thomas George Walton Papers, SHC) John Penland, and Robert Penland (both, Penland Family Papers, WCU).

62. Censer's sample is made up of those North Carolina planters with 70 or more slaves in 1830. The only western Carolinians in that group are Isaac T. Avery, W.W. Erwin, and James Murphy, all of Burke County. See Censer, *North Carolina Planters*, Appendix, 155–60.

63. Ibid., 136.

64. These incidents are discussed earlier in this chapter. In Rodman's case, it well could have been the security of belonging to such a large slaveholder, after the uncertain future he faced under an owner less financially stable, that made ownership by Avery so appealing.

65. Carter G. Woodson, "Freedom and Slavery in Appalachian America," 140, 149.

66. Campbell, *Southern Highlanders*, 95.

67. Loyal Jones, "Appalachian Values," in *Voices from the Hills: Selected Readings on Southern Appalachia*, Robert J. Higgs, ed. (New York: Unger, 1975), 512.

68. Cash, *Mind of the South*, 219.

69. Sheppard, *Cabins in the Laurel*, 60.

70. Johnson, *Ante-Bellum North Carolina*, 584.

71. See H.M. Wagstaff, ed., *Minutes of the North Carolina Manumission Society 1816–1834*, James Sprunt Historical Studies, vol. 22, no. 1–2 (Chapel Hill: Univ. of North Carolina Press), 122–24; Gordon E. Finnie, "The Anti-Slavery Movement in the Upper South Prior to 1840," *Journal of Southern History* 25 (Aug. 1969), 329–30; John Michael Shay, "The Anti-Slavery Movement in North Carolina," (Ph.D. diss., Princeton Univ., 1970), 355–56; and Drake, "Slavery and Antislavery in Appalachia," 30–32.

72. Hewitt, "My People of the Mountains" (typescript), pp. 9–10, John Hewitt Memoir, SHC.

73. The fullest treatments of Olmsted's careers are Laura Wood Roper, *FLO: A Biography of Frederick Law Olmsted* (Baltimore: Johns Hopkins Univ. Press, 1973); John Emerson Todd, *Frederick Law Olmsted* (Boston: Twayne, 1982); and Broadus Mitchell, *Frederick Law Olmsted: A Critic of the Old South*, Johns Hopkins Univ. Studies in History and Political Science, vol. 42 (Baltimore: Johns Hopkins Univ. Press, 1924). Mitchell provides the best treatment of Olmsted's antebellum southern travels and writings, along with Charles E. Beveridge, "Introduction," *Papers of Frederick Law Olmsted*, vol. 2: *Slavery and the South, 1852–1857* (Baltimore: Johns Hopkins Univ. Press, 1981), 1–39.

74. Frederick Law Olmsted, *A Journey in the Seaboard Slave States* (New York: Dix & Edwards, 1856), 176.

75. Olmsted, *Back Country*, 103–104. See also Mitchell, *Frederick Law Olmsted*, 88–89.

76. Todd, *Frederick Law Olmsted*, 57.

77. Olmsted, *Seaboard Slave States*, 146–48. Olmsted, "The South," nos. 7 and 47, *New York Daily News*, 17 Mar. 1853, and *New York Daily Times*, 26, Jan. 1854, rptd. in Beveridge, *Papers of Olmsted*, vol. 2, 103–10 (no. 7), 247–54 (no. 47); see also "Introduction," 13–15.

78. *Papers of Olmsted*, vol 2, 252.

79. Todd, *Frederick Law Olmsted*, 57–58; Mitchell, *Frederick Law Olmsted*, ch. 2, 68–113.

80. For Olmsted's schedule and route, see *Papers of Olmsted*, vol. 2, pp. 309 (map), and 481–82 (itinerary).

81. See introduction to this book.

82. Olmsted, *Back Country*, 293.

83. Ibid., 268–70. This was a point Olmsted seemed to push too far. His comparison of the homes and lifestyles of a mountain slaveholder and his non-slaveholding neighbor, with the latter a big improvement over the former, is less than convincing.

84. Ibid., 239, 259–60.

85. Ibid., 263–64.

86. Ibid., 237.

87. Harry M. Caudill, *Night Comes to the Cumberlands: A Biography of a Depressed Region* (Boston: Little, Brown, 1962), 38.

88. Olmsted, *Back Country*, 163, 240.

89. See Wilson, *Southern Mountaineers*, 57–58; Campbell, *Southern Highlanders*, 94; and Phifer, "Saga of a Burke County Family," 145.

90. Ralph, "Our Appalachian Americans," 36.

91. Cratis D. Williams, "The Southern Mountaineer in Fact and Fiction," (Ph.D. diss., New York Univ., 1961), 379.

92. Though the correlation between total population and the percentage of slaves in the mountain counties is not a direct one, the four most populous counties (Buncombe, Burke, Henderson, and Wilkes) also ranked among the top five counties in slave population in 1860. Likewise, the five least populous counties, those in which Olmsted traveled (Alleghany, Watauga, Jackson, and Haywood), had among the fewest slaves. *Population of the United States in 1860*, 358–59.

93. Frank L. Owsley, *Plain Folk of the Old South* (Baton Rouge: Louisiana State Univ. Press, 1949), 133–34; Shay, "Antislavery Movement in North Carolina," 490; Genovese, "Yeomen Farmers in a Slaveholders' Democracy," *Agricultural History* 49 (Apr. 1975): 339–40; and Oakes, *Ruling Race*, 38–42.

94. See ch 3.

95. Starobin, *Industrial Slavery*, 128–30.

96. See ch. 3.

97. Alden B. Pearson, Jr., "The Tragic Dilemma of a Border-State Moderate: The Rev. George E. Eagleton's Views on Slavery and Secession," *Tennessee Historical Quarterly* 32 (Winter 1973):373.

98. Harry Caudill has suggested (*Night Comes to the Cumberlands*, 37) that the resentment and envy of Kentucky mountaineers toward their slaveholding neighbors' economic superiority led them to use moral objections to justify their antagonism toward the system. There is little evidence of such resentment among western North Carolinians toward local slaveholders, at least. Therefore was no need for the yeomen to concern themselves with the moral implications of the system.

99. E. Merton Coulter, *William G. Brownlow: Fighting Parson of the Southern Highlands* (Chapel Hill: Univ. of North Carolina Press, 1937), 89, 109. Though a historian at the University of Georgia, Coulter himself was a western North Carolinian, a native of Burke County.

Chapter 5

1. Alexis de Tocqueville, *Journey to America*, ed. J.P. Mayer (New York: Anchor, 1971), 102; Olmsted, *The Cotton Kingdom* (New York: Mason Bros., 1861), 558.

2. The most thorough treatment of the class structure of antebellum North Carolina is Escott, *Many Excellent People*, xv–xviii, 3–31.

3. Phifer, "Slavery in Microcosm," 140–41, 161 (map); Phifer, *Burke*, 37–39; Walton, "Sketches of Burke County Pioneers."

4. Crawford, "Slaveholding and Power in New River Valley," 3–4.

5. For fuller treatments of the Bairds, Pattons, and Jordan Councill, see ch. 2. For the Loves, see Allen, *Annals of Haywood County*, (Spartanburg, S.C.: Reprint Co., 1935, rptd. 1977) 31, 38–39; Eighth U.S. Census, 1860, Slave Schedules, Haywood, Jackson, and Macon counties.

6. Seventh and Eighth U.S. Censuses, 1850 and 1860, Slave Schedules, Cherokee and Burke counties; and Cochran, *Nantahala People*. See Browder, *Cherokee Indians*, 77, for a list of the 1838 auction purchases.

7. Arthur, *Western North Carolina*, 359–63; Sondley, *Asheville and Buncombe County*, vol. 2, 760–61.

8. Censer, *North Carolina Planters*, and Escott, *Many Excellent People*, are surveys of the state as a whole. Crawford, "Slaveholding and Power in New River Valley," and Robert C. Kenzer, *Kinship and Neighborhood in a Southern Community: Orange County, North Carolina, 1849–1881* (Knoxville: Univ. of Tennessee Press, 1988), are in-depth analyses of the same themes within single counties in the state. Recent similar studies of other parts of the South include Stowe, *Intimacy and Power in the Old South*; Orville Vernon Burton, *In My Father's House Are Many Mansions: Family and Community in Edgefield, South Carolina* (Chapel Hill: Univ. of North Carolina Press, 1985); Bruce Collins, *White Society in the Antebellum South* (London: Longman, 1985), ch. 8; J. William Harris, *Plain Folk and Gentry in a Slave Society: White Liberty and Black Slavery in Augusta's Hinterlands* (Middletown, Conn.: Wesleyan Univ. Press, 1985); and Mann, "Isolation and the Social Economy of an Appalachian Community."

9. Kephart, *Our Southern Highlanders*, 197.

10. Kenzer, "Portrait of a Southern Community, 1849–1881: Family, Kinship, and Neighborhood in Orange County, North Carolina" (Ph.D. diss., Harvard Univ., 1982), 22–24; Censer, *North Carolina Planters*, 88–89.

11. Crawford, "Slaveholding and Power in New River Valley," 7; Sondley, vol. 2, *Asheville and Buncombe County*, 742, 747–48; *Heritage of Burke County*, 173–74, 196.

12. See genealogical tables in Hickerson, *Echoes of Happy Valley*, 176–77.

13. Olsen and McGrew, "Prelude to Reconstruction," 37–38.

14. Sondley, *Asheville and Buncombe County*, vol. 2, 764.

15. Censer, *North Carolina Planters*, 84; Escott, *Many Excellent People*, 7; and Thomas E. Jeffrey, "The Second Party System in North Carolina, 1836–1860" (Ph.D. diss., Catholic Univ. of America, 1976), 164–66.

16. See correspondence in Calvin J. Cowles Papers, NCDAH and SHC.

17. See correspondence in James Harper Diaries, James Gwyn Books, Jones and Patterson Family Papers, Edmund Walter Jones Papers, all SHC; Thomas Lenoir Papers, Samuel Finley Patterson Papers, both Duke. For a convenient compilation of material from most of these collections, see Hickerson, *Echoes of Happy Valley*.

18. Diary of Augustus W. Finley, Sept. 1834–Feb. 1835, reproduced in Hickerson, *Echoes of Happy Valley*, 23–26.

19. Walter W. Lenoir to Thomas I. Lenoir, 12 Nov. 1860, Thomas Lenoir Papers, Duke.

20. Olmsted, *Cotton Kingdom*, 558.

21. See table 5.5 in Lee Soltow, *Men and Wealth in the United States, 1850–1870* (New Haven: Yale Univ. Press, 1975), 142.

22. Gavin Wright, *The Political Economy of the Cotton South: Households, Markets, and Wealth in the Nineteenth Century* (New York: Norton, 1978), 36.

23. See table 5.1 and appendix.

24. Otto Olsen, "Historians and the Extent of Slave Ownership in the Southern United States," *Civil War History* 18 (June 1972):101–116. Though published earlier than some of the most significant work on the topic by Lee Soltow and Gavin Wright, Olsen's article is the best overview of these variations in calculations and interpretation.

25. William A. Lenoir Diary, 15 and 21 Feb. 1851, Thomas A. Lenoir Papers, Duke. See Marc W. Kruman, *Parties and Politics in North Carolina, 1836–1865* (Baton Rouge: Louisiana State Univ. Press, 1983), 9–10, for a fuller and somewhat different interpretation of this incident.

26. Edmund W. Jones to Samuel F. Patterson, 12 May 1840, Jones–Patterson Papers, SHC.

27. A total of 108 men were elected to the legislature from the mountain counties during those two decades, but 16 are not included in their county's census records for either 1840, 1850, or 1860.

28. Statewide figures and those from the Upper South are from Ralph A. Wooster, *Politicians, Planters, and Plain Folk: Courthouse and Statehouse in the Upper South, 1850–1860* (Knoxville: Univ. of Tennessee Press, 1975), 40. Figures for western North Carolina legislators were computed from U.S. Census 1840, 1850, and 1860, Slave Schedules.

29. Wooster, *Politicians, Planters, and Plain Folk*, 39–40.

30. The eleven House members listed in the 1850 census owned a total of 120 slaves, but this figure is most likely well below the real slaveholding capacity of this group, since two of them, Robert G. Love and David W. Siler, were not listed in the slave schedule, but were members of the largest slaveholding families in Haywood and Macon counties, respectively. Likewise, W.W. Avery is cited as having only eight slaves, though his father was western North Carolina's fourth largest slaveholder, with 103 slaves in 1860. The area's four senators in 1850—George Bower, N.W. Woodfin, Tod R. Caldwell, and William H. Thomas—owned a total of 123 slaves (these four men owned a combined total of 195 slaves in 1860). Comparable figures for the area's four senators in 1860 cannot be cited accurately, since one of the senators that year was W.W. Avery, who is not included in the slave schedule, though his slaveholdings had probably increased substantially since 1850. The other three senators alone—Joseph H. Dobson, Marcus Erwin, and W.H. Thomas—whose holdings averaged 21 slaves each, exceeded the 1860 statewide average of 20 slaves per legislator.

31. For comparable figures for South Carolina and the Lower South, see table 6 in Wooster, *The People in Power: Courthouse and Statehouse in the Lower South, 1850–1860* (Knoxville: Univ. of Tennessee Press, 1969), 41.

32. Oakes, *Ruling Race*, 7.

33. The best sources on political campaign practices in ante-bellum North

Carolina are Jeffrey, "Second Party System," ch. 6; Kruman, *Parties and Politics*, ch. 2; and Johnson, *Antebellum North Carolina*, 104–105. See also William J. Cooper, Jr., *The South and the Politics of Slavery, 1828–1856* (Baton Rouge: Louisiana State Univ. Press, 1978), 38–43; Collins, *White Society in the Antebellum South*, 142–43. For a more specific description of political rallies in Asheville, see Ready, *Asheville, Land of the Sky*, 24–25.

34. James Graham to William A. Graham, 8 Apr. 1836, and 20 May 1840, in Joseph G. de Roulhac Hamilton and Max R. Williams, eds., *The Papers of William Alexander Graham*, 5 vols. (Raleigh: NCDAH, 1957–73), 1:424 and 2:91–92. For biographical sketches of both brothers, see William S. Powell, ed., *Dictionary of North Carolina Biography* (Chapel Hill: Univ. of North Carolina Press, 1979), vol. 2.

35. Kruman, *Parties and Politics*, 41.

36. For a complete schedule of their tour of the state, see William F. Burton, Jr., "The Issue of *Ad Valorem* Taxation in Ante-Bellum North Carolina" (Master's thesis, Univ. of North Carolina, Chapel Hill, 1940), 29–30.

37. See next three chapters for several examples.

38. Blackmun, *Western North Carolina*, 309–11; Guion Johnson, *Ante-Bellum North Carolina*, 774–80.

39. James Graham to William A. Graham, 12 July 1842, 21 Apr. 1850, in Hamilton and Williams, *Papers of William A. Graham*, 2:352, 3:320.

40. Jeffrey, "Second Party System," 186–88.

41. Fred A. Bailey, *Class and Tennessee's Confederate Generation* (Chapel Hill: Univ. of North Carolina Press, 1987), 60, 64–65.

42. Among the most influential proponents of white solidarity in antebellum southern society are George Frederickson, *The Black Image in the White Mind: The Debate on Afro-American Character and Destiny, 1817–1914* (New York: Harper & Row, 1971); Genovese, "Yeomen Farmers," 331–42; Fletcher M. Green, "Democracy in the Old South," *Journal of Southern History* 12 (1946):117–92; Owsley, *Plain Folk of the Old South*; Cash, *Mind of the South*; Kenzer, *Kinship and Neighborhood in a Southern Community*; Collins, *White Society in the Antebellum South*; and Harris, *Plain Folk and Gentry*. Harris provides a valuable overview of the historiographic debate in his introduction, pp. 1–7.

Chapter 6

1. Thomas L. Clingman, "Address to the Freemen of the First Congressional District of North Carolina on the Recent Senatorial Election, December 18, 1848 with additions January 6, 1849" (Washington, D.C.: J. and G.S. Gideon, 1849), 15; and "In Defense of the South Against the Aggressive Movement of the North, Delivered in the House of Representatives, January 22, 1850," in Clingman, *Speeches and Writings*, 252.

2. The most basic treatments of revolutionary republicanism are Bernard Bailyn, *The Ideological Origins of the American Revolution* (Cambridge, Mass.: Harvard Univ. Press, 1967); and Gordon S. Wood, *The Creation of the American*

Republic, 1776–1787 (Chapel Hill: Univ. of North Carolina Press, 1969). Recent treatments on its evolution in the nineteenth century include Michael F. Holt, *The Political Crisis of the 1850s* (New York: Norton, 1978); J. Mills Thornton III, *Politics and Power in a Slave Society: Alabama, 1800–1860* (Baton Rouge: Louisiana State Univ. Press, 1978); Kenneth S. Greenberg, *Masters and Statesmen: The Political Culture of American Slavery* (Baltimore: Johns Hopkins Univ. Press, 1985); Harris, *Plain Folk and Gentry*; Eric Foner, *Free Soil, Free Labor, Free Men: The Ideology of the Republican Party before the Civil War* (New York: Oxford Univ. Press, 1970); Robert Shalhope, "Toward a Republican Synthesis: The Emergence of an Understanding of Republicanism in American Historiography," *William and Mary Quarterly* 34 (1982); and Carl J. Vipperman, "Civic Virtue, Country Ideology, and the Machiavellian Moment in Southern History," in *Citta e Campagna Nell'Eta Dorata: Gli stati Uniti Tra Utopia e Reforma*, ed. Valeria G. Lerda (Rome: Bulzoni Editore, 1986).

3. For the fullest discussion of Clingman's use of republicanist rhetoric, see Marc W. Kruman, "Thomas L. Clingman and the Whig Party: A Reconsideration," *North Carolina Historical Review* 64 (Jan. 1987):1–18.

4. Max R. Williams, "The Foundations of the Whig Party in North Carolina," *North Carolina Historical Review* 47 (Spring 1970):124–25. See also Jeffrey, "Second Party System," 247–48, 277–78.

5. William K. Boyd, *The History of North Carolina: The Federal Period* (Chicago: Lewis Publishing, 1919); Jeffrey, "Second Party System," 71; Blackmun, *Western North Carolina*, 306–307.

6. *Raleigh Register*, 12 Aug. 1842. Only Yancey County cast a majority of its votes for Democratic presidential candidates in each of those elections.

7. W. Dean Burnham, *Presidential Ballots, 1836–1891* (Baltimore: Johns Hopkins Univ. Press, 1955), 648–66. Democratic gubernatorial candidates carried Yancey County in all six races and Ashe County in four of them. R.D.W. Connor, ed., *A Manual of North Carolina* (Raleigh: E.M. Uzzell, 1913), 993–96.

8. Tod. R. Caldwell to Willie P. Mangum, 21 Aug. 1844, in Henry T. Shanks, ed., *The Papers of Willie Person Mangum*, vol. 4, *1844–1846* (Raleigh: NCDAH, 1956), 179.

9. Clingman, "Address on Recent Senatorial Election," 1849, pamphlet in Rare Book Collection, Duke, p. 1.

10. Democrats Newton Coleman, Thomas Atkins, and Marcus Erwin of Buncombe County, and W.W. Avery of Burke County all served in the legislature between 1840 and 1850. Connor, *North Carolina Manual*, 517, 522–23, 933; see also Jeffrey, "Second Party System," Appendix B, p. 434.

11. Jeffrey, "Second Party System," 171; Phifer, *Burke*, 77.

12. Edmund W. Jones to Samuel F. Patterson, 12 May 1840, in Jones-Patterson Papers, SHC.

13. James Graham to William A. Graham, 10 May 1847, in Hamilton and Williams, *Papers of William A. Graham*, 3:193–94; *Raleigh Register*, 12 Aug. 1842; Jeffrey, "Second Party System," 206.

14. For discussions of the Whig party's decline, see James R. Morrill, "The Presidential Election of 1852: Death Knell of the Whig Party in North Caro-

lina," *North Carolina Historical Review* 44 (Oct. 1967):342–59; Herbert D. Pegg, *The Whig Party in North Carolina* (Chapel Hill: Colonial Press, 1968), 156–210; and Jeffrey, "Second Party System," 268–366.

15. Thomas E. Jeffrey, "Internal Improvements and Political Parties in Antebellum North Carolina, 1836–1860," *North Carolina Historical Review* 55 (Apr. 1978):143; Morrill, "Presidential Election of 1852," 359; Jeffrey, " 'Thunder from the Mountains:' Thomas Lanier Clingman and the End of Whig Supremacy in North Carolina," *North Carolina Historical Review* 56 (Oct. 1979):366–95; and Kruman, "Clingman and the Whig Party." Clingman's role in western North Carolina politics is discussed more fully in ch. 8.

16. See Kruman, *Parties and Politics*, and Jeffrey, "Second Party System," for the most comprehensive accounts of two-party politics in the state throughout the 1850s.

17. "The East and the West," *North Carolina Journal of Education* 1 (1857):13, quoted in Johnson, *Ante-Bellum North Carolina*, 36.

18. *North Carolina Standard*, 7 Sept. 1859.

19. Clarence C. Norton, *The Democratic Party in Ante-Bellum North Carolina, 1835–1861* (Chapel Hill: Univ. of North Carolina Press, 1930), 132.

20. For discussions of how Whigs argued against free suffrage, see Pegg, *Whig Party*, 114–17; and Kruman, *Parties and Politics*, 88–90.

21. Sitterson, *Secession Movement*, 7, 13, 19.

22. Nicholas W. Woodfin of the 49th District (Buncombe, Henderson, and Madison counties) and Michael Francis of the 50th District (Haywood, Macon, and Cherokee counties) were both Whig incumbents who came out in support of free suffrage. Francis lost to Democrat William Holland Thomas. See below.

23. Thomas L. Clingman to William A. Graham, 1 Sept. 1848, in Hamilton and Williams, *Papers of William A. Graham*, 3:109–10.

24. Graham received 67.6% of the vote and carried all but one of the 10 mountain counties in 1846. Manly received 62.7% in the same area, but only carried 7 counties. Reid won a majority of the votes in Ashe, Haywood, and Yancey counties, the last of which had always been Democratic. Thomas's influence was enough to give Reid a slim majority in his home county of Haywood. Connor, *North Carolina Manual*, 995–96. See also Jeffrey, "Second Party System," Appendix B, p. 434; Russell, "William Holland Thomas," 284, 286.

25. *Raleigh Register*, 3 June 1848, cited in Pegg, *Whig Party*, 116.

26. *Raleigh Register*, 13 Mar. 1850; Kruman, *Parties and Politics*, 95.

27. *Highland Messenger*, 30 Apr. 1850.

28. The most thorough treatment of the convention itself as an issue in the equal suffrage debate is Thomas E. Jeffrey, "Beyond 'Free Suffrage': North Carolina Parties and the Convention Movement of the 1850s," *North Carolina Historical Review* 62 (Oct. 1985):387–419.

29. Thomas L. Clingman, "An Address to the People of North Carolina on the Subject of Constitutional Reform," 1 Jan. 1851, pamphlet in Clingman-Puryear Papers, SHC.

30. In 1850, Reid received only 35% of the vote in the ten mountain counties in which he had received 37.3% two years earlier. He regained his 1848 per-

centage (37.3%) in his reelection bid in 1852. Connor, *North Carolina Manual*, 995–98.

31. T. George Walton to Calvin H. Wiley, 26 May 1851 and N.W. Woodfin to Calvin H. Wiley, 13 Jan. 1852, both in Calvin H. Wiley Papers, NCDAH.

32. *Asheville Messenger*, 30 June 1852.

33. Connor, *North Carolina Manual*, 995–98; see also Jeffrey, "Second Party System," Appendix B, p. 434.

34. *Asheville Spectator*, 16 July 1856.

35. *Asheville News*, 12 Feb. 1857.

36. *Asheville News*, 20 Jan. 1859; Donald C. Butts, "A Challenge to Planter Rule: The Controversy Over the Ad Valorem Taxation of Slaves in North Carolina, 1858–1862," (Ph.D. diss., Duke Univ., 1978), 65.

37. Russell, "William Holland Thomas," 298; Burton, "Issue of *Ad Valorem* Taxation," 9.

38. For a complete schedule of their tour of the state, see Burton, "Issue of *Ad Valorem* Taxation," 29–30.

39. Robert B. Vance to Zebulon B. Vance, 16 Apr. 1860, in Frontis W. Johnston, ed., *The Papers of Zebulon Baird Vance*, vol. 1, *1843–1861* (Raleigh: NCDAH, 1963), 67; Burgess S. Gaither to William A. Graham, 9 Mar. 1860, in Hamilton and Williams, *Papers of William A. Graham*, 5:147.

40. *Raleigh Register*, 18 Apr. 1860; Robert B. Vance to Zebulon B. Vance, 18 Apr. 1860, in Johnston, *Papers of Vance*, vol. 1, p. 67.

41. *Asheville News*, 11 July 1860, 17 Nov. 1859; Kruman, *Parties and Politics*, 193; Donald C. Butts, "The 'Irrepressible Conflict': Slave Taxation and North Carolina's Gubernatorial Election of 1860," *North Carolina Historical Review* 58 (Jan. 1981):51.

42. *North Carolina Standard*, 13 June 1860, quoted in Burton, "Issue of *Ad Valorem* Taxation," 42. See Kruman, *Parties and Politics*, 193–95, and Jeffrey, "Second Party System," 395–96, for discussions of Democratic opposition and the reasons behind it.

43. *Asheville News*, 11 July 1860.

44. E.J. Erwin to George Phifer Erwin, 19 Mar. 1860, George Phifer Erwin Papers, SHC; Phifer, *Burke*, 52, 153.

45. N.W. Woodfin to David L. Swain, 1 Mar. 1860, M. Patton to David L. Swain, 18 Feb. 1859, both in Walter Clark Papers, NCDAH; Jeffrey, "Second Party System," 390; Eighth U.S. Census, 1860, Schedule 2, Buncombe County.

46. E.J. Erwin to George Phifer Erwin, 19 Mar. 1860, George Phifer Erwin Papers, SHC.

Chapter 7

1. R.B. Scott to William L. Scott, 4 July 1854, William L. Scott Papers, Duke, quoted in Kruman, *Parties and Politics*, 78.

2. Steven Hahn, *The Roots of Southern Populism: Yeomen Farmers and the Trans-*

formation of the Georgia Backcountry, 1850–1890 (New York: Oxford Univ. Press, 1983), 36–40.

3. Lacy K. Ford, "Rednecks and Merchants: Economic Development and Social Tensions in the South Carolina Upcountry, 1865–1990," *Journal of American History* 71 (Sept. 1984):298–99; Thornton, *Politics and Power in a Slave Society*, 305–11.

4. Schlotterbeck is never very explicit about either individual or class attitudes toward these developments. See Schlotterbeck, "Plantation and Farm," 211–14. For similar conclusions on a North Carolina piedmont county (Union County), see Wayne K. Durrill, "Producing Poverty: Local Government and Economic Development in a New South Country, 1874-1884," *Journal of American History* 71 (Mar. 1985):765–66.

5. Harry L. Watson, "Conflict and Collaboration: Yeomen, Slaveholders, and Politics in the Antebellum South," *Social History* 10 (Oct. 1985):282–83, quote on 294.

6. Pegg, *Whig Party*, 50. For the best analysis of the issue as a reason for Whig decline, see Jeffrey, "Internal Improvements," 135–38.

7. Carolyn A. Wallace, "David Lowry Swain, The First Whig Governor of North Carolina," in *Studies in Southern History*, ed. J. Carlyle Sitterson, James Sprunt Studies in History and Political Science, vol. 39 (Chapel Hill: Univ. of North Carolina Press, 1957), 67–70; Clarence N. Gilbert, "The Public Career of Thomas L. Clingman" (M.A. thesis, Univ. of North Carolina, Chapel Hill, 1946), 15–22; Johnston, *Papers of Vance*, xxx.

8. Russell, "William Holland Thomas," 282, 287; Phifer, "Saga of a Burke County Family," 214–313; Jeffrey, "Internal Improvements," 133.

9. Jeffrey, "Internal Improvements," 150, and tables 2, 3, and 4, 152–56.

10. Kruman recognized this distinction in the motives of mountain residents in *Parties and Politics*, 9–10.

11. See ch. 2 for an extended discussion of the Buncombe Turnpike.

12. Jeffrey, "Internal Improvements," 121.

13. Robert S. Lambert, "Oconaluftee Valley," 423; see also Russell, "William Holland Thomas," 287–88.

14. Kruman, *Parties and Politics*, 52.

15. Burton A. Konkle, *John Motley Morehead and the Development of North Carolina, 1796–1866* (Philadelphia: William J. Campbell, 1922), 248–49.

16. For explanations of the anti–internal-improvement stances of the state's eastern elite, see Harry L. Watson, "Squire Oldway and His Friends: Opposition to Internal Improvements in Antebellum North Carolina," *North Carolina Historical Review* 54 (Apr. 1977):105–19; Harry L. Watson, *Jacksonian Politics and Community Conflict: The Emergence of the Second American Party System in Cumberland County, North Carolina* (Baton Rouge: Louisiana State Univ. Press, 1981), 50–57, 154–71; and Kruman, *Parties and Politics*, 7–8, 25–26, 55–58.

17. Deyton, "Toe River Valley," 443–44. See also William A. Lenoir to John M. Rose, 7 Jan. 1850, Lenoir Family Papers, SHC, for comments on the futility of the project.

18. Powers and Hannah, *Cataloochee*, 45.

19. Clarence W. Griffin, *The History of Old Tryon and Rutherford Counties, 1730–1930* (Asheville: Miller Printing, 1937), 214; Jeffrey, "Internal Improvements," table 2, p. 153.

20. Thomas Lenoir to William A. Graham, 27 June 1848, Lenoir Family Papers, SHC.

21. Clingman, "Address on Recent Senatorial Election," 1–2, 15.

22. Konkle, *John Motley Morehead*, 244–45.

23. Johnson, *Ante-Bellum North Carolina*, 28.

24. Samuel F. Patterson to Walter W. Lenoir, 27 Dec. 1848, Lenoir Family Papers, SHC.

25. Manly took only 500 votes of 1,437 cast in Rutherford County in 1850, compared with 1,341 out of 1,685 total votes cast in Burke County. Kruman, *Parties and Politics*, 74–75; *North Carolina Manual*, 995–96.

26. For examples of the positive roles played by railroads, esp. in stimulating commercialization, see Schlotterbeck, "Plantation and Farm," ch. 8; and Harris, *Plain Folk and Gentry*, 14, 26. Those stressing less desirable effects, economic and social, include Thornton, *Politics and Power in a Slavery Society*; Hahn, *Roots of Southern Populism*, 40–49; William L. Barney, "Toward the Civil War: The Dynamics of Change in a Black Belt County," in *Class, Conflict, and Consensus*, ed. Burton and McMath, 146–71; Ford, "Rednecks and Merchants"; Durrill, "Producing Poverty"; and John J. Beck, "Building the New South: A Revolution from Above in a Piedmont County" [Rowan County, N.C.], *Journal of Southern History* 53 (Aug. 1987):441–70; and again, Harris, *Plain Folk and Gentry*, 26, 71.

27. Cousin Mollie to Leander Gash, Mar. 1855, Gash Family Papers, NCDAH.

28. *Asheville News*, 8 Jan. 1858.

29. *Highland Messenger*, 1 Nov. 1852.

30. N.F. Jarrett to Col. John McKee, 20 Feb. 1854, John McKee Sharpe Papers, SHC.

31. Silas McDowell, "Our Trip to Buncombe," *North Carolina Planter* 3 (Oct. 1860):331.

32. "Western North Carolina," *North Carolina Planter* 2 (1859):323, quoted from the *Franklin Observer*.

33. See Eli McKee to John McKee, 18 Oct. 1853; N.F. Jarrett to John McKee, 20 Feb. 1854, John McKee Sharpe Papers, SHC; and various letters from Thomas D. Johnston to William Johnston, 1853–57, Thomas D. Johnston Papers, SHC.

34. S.G.R. Mount to William H. Thomas, 5 Apr. 1853, and H. Johnson to William H. Thomas, 13 May 1853, both in William Holland Thomas Papers, Duke.

35. E. Emmons to the Editors, *Franklin Observer*, 29 Aug. 1859, in *North Carolina Planter* 2 (1859):326.

36. *North Carolina Argus* (Fayetteville), 20 Jan. 1855, quoted in Russell, "William Holland Thomas," 300–302.

37. Ibid. On the need to liquify mountain fruit crops for market, see Hicks, *Appalachian Valley*, 19.

38. Blackmun, *Western North Carolina*, 319.

39. Russell, "William Holland Thomas," 302.

40. Silas McDowell to David L. Swain, 8 Aug. 1853, Walter Clark Papers, NCDAH.

41. The best discussion of the Blue Ridge Railroad project is found in Russell, "William Holland Thomas," 305–14. See also extensive correspondence among Thomas and Henry Gourdin, Anson Bangs, and H.W. Conner, 1852–58, in William Holland Thomas Papers, Duke.

42. Arthur, *Western North Carolina*, 470.

43. Cecil K. Brown, *A State Movement in Railroad Development: The Story of North Carolina's First Effort to Establish an East and West Trunk Line Railroad* (Chapel Hill: Univ. of North Carolina Press, 1928), 98–99.

44. Marcus Erwin to David S. Reid, 31 Mar. 1854, Reid Papers, NCDAH.

45. R.B. to William L. Scott, 4 July 1854, William L. Scott Papers, Duke.

46. *Asheville News*, 6 Sept. 1854.

47. Thomas D. McDowell to Walter W. Lenoir, 8 July 1854, Lenoir Family Papers, SHC.

48. "An Act Incorporating the Western North Carolina Rail Road," 15 Feb. 1855, in North Carolina General Assembly, *Acts Relating to the Western North Carolina Railroad* (Raleigh, n.d.) 1–17. See also Brown, *State Movement in Railroad Development*, 103.

49. *Asheville News*, 8 May 1856.

50. Connor, *North Carolina Manual*, 997–98; J.G. de Roulhac Hamilton, *Party Politics in North Carolina, 1835–1860*, James Sprunt Historical Publications, vol. 15, nos. 1 and 2 (Chapel Hill: Univ. of North Carolina, 1916), 176–78.

51. William J. Abrams, "Western North Carolina Railroad," 11.

52. "An Act to Amend an Act Entitled 'An Act to Incorporate the Western North Carolina Rail Road Company,' Passed at the Session of 1854–55" 15 Feb. 1859, in North Carolina General Assembly, *Acts Relating to the Western North Carolina Railroad*, 22–23; Brown, *State Movement in Railroad Development*, 144–45.

53. Z.B. Vance to the Editors, *Raleigh Register*, 7 Feb. 1855.

54. Brown, *State Movement in Railroad Development*, 138–39.

55. William Holland Thomas to Editors, *Asheville News*, 13 Apr. 1854.

56. W.H. Thomas, "Report on the Extension of the North Carolina Rail Roads West to Cowone or Ducktown, by the Committee on Internal Improvements," 1 Jan. 1857, pamphlet, William Holland Thomas Papers, Duke. For more on the copper mines at Ducktown, see no. 30 above.

57. The line to Paint Rock was completed in 1882, while that to Murphy was not finished until 1891. Abrams, "Western North Carolina Railroad," 11; Russell, "William Holland Thomas," 316–17; Arthur, *Western North Carolina*, 479.

58. *Asheville News*, 4 Feb. 1858.

59. *Asheville News*, 12 Feb. 1857.

60. Montreville Patton to David L. Swain, 18 Feb. 1859, Walter Clark Papers, NCDAH.

61. *Asheville News*, 2 Apr. 1857.

62. Brown, *State Movement in Railroad Development*, 136.

63. A.S. Merrimon to David F. Caldwell, 11 May 1858, David F. Caldwell Papers, SHC.

64. Ibid. Connor, *North Carolina Manual*, 997–98. See table 6.1 of this book.

65. The House voted 34 to 55 against it on 14 Feb. 1859. The Senate voted 15 to 24 against it the next day. Brown, *State Movement in Railroad Development*, 141. See Tod R. Caldwell to Thomas George Walton, 19 Jan. and 6 Feb. 1859, Thomas George Walton Papers, SHC, for examples of western expectations of bill's passage.

66. *Asheville News*, 24 Feb. 1859.

67. *Asheville News*, 9 June 1859; Blackmun, *Western North Carolina*, 323.

68. Brown, *State Movement in Railroad Development*, 142.

69. *Asheville News*, 25 Feb. 1859.

70. *Asheville News*, 4 Feb. 1859.

71. N.W. Woodfin to David L. Swain, 1 Mar. 1860, Walter Clark Papers, NCDAH. Woodfin later wrote Swain that it had been a mistake to label Pool the instigator of that "odious restriction," but said that Pool had voted for it and that he still regarded Pool's nomination "as harmful to our railroad prospects." See 19 Mar. 1860 letter.

72. Connor, *North Carolina Manual*, 999–1000. See last chapter of this book for a more extended discussion of this election.

73. Phifer, *Burke*, 186.

Chapter 8

1. Until 1852, the First Congressional District consisted of all the mountain counties except Ashe and Wilkes, and one piedmont county, Cleveland. In 1852, the First District became the Eighth District, with Cleveland County dropped and Wilkes and Watauga counties added, so that all mountain counties, with the exception of Ashe, fell into the same district.

2. Clingman was elected to the House of Representatives seven times. John R. Daniel of Halifax County served six terms. No other North Carolina congressman between 1840 and 1860 served more than five terms. Connor, *North Carolina Manual*, 929–36.

3. No full-length biography of Thomas L. Clingman exists. Among the works examining his antebellum political career are John S. Bassett, *The Congressional Career of Thomas L. Clingman*, Trinity College Historical Papers, ser. 4 (Durham, N.C.: Trinity College Historical Society, 1900); Gilbert, "Public Career of Clingman"; Marlene D. Siegmann, "Thomas Lanier Clingman, Political Pilgrim, 1843–1852," (M.A. thesis, Wake Forest Univ., 1964); Thomas E. Jeffrey, "Thunder from the Mountains,"366–95 (taken from Jeffrey, "Second Party System," ch. 9, 313–36); H. Thomas Kearney, Jr., "Thomas Lanier Clingman," in William S. Powell, *Dictionary of North Carolina Biography*, vol. I, 387–

88; Kruman, "Clingman and the Whig Party," 1–18; and Inscoe, "Thomas Clingman, Mountain Whiggery, and the Southern Cause," *Civil War History* 33 (Mar. 1987), 42–62.

4. S. Kent Schwarzkopf, *A History of Mt. Mitchell and the Black Mountains: Exploration, Development, and Preservation* (Raleigh: NCDAH, 1985), 51. See also Joanna Nicol Shields, *The Line of Duty: Maverick Congressmen and the Development of American Political Culture, 1836–1860* (Westport, Conn.: Greenwood, 1985), 89–90. On Clingman's postwar scientific endeavors, see Thomas E. Jeffrey, "Thomas Lanier Clingman and the Invention of the Electric Light: A Forgotten Episode," *Carolina Comments* 32 (May 1984):71–82.

5. Schwarzkopf, *History of Mt. Mitchell*, ch. 5, is the most thorough account of the Mitchell-Clingman feud.

6. Shields, *Line of Duty*, 53.

7. Siegman, "Thomas Lanier Clingman," 80–81, 94, 113–14; Jeffrey, "Thunder from the Mountains," 369–70. See also Clarence C. Norton, *Democratic Party in Ante-Bellum North Carolina*, 239. Quote is from Sitterson, *Secession Movement*, 157.

8. Jeffrey, "Thunder from the Mountains," 387, 395.

9. "Speech of Mr. Clingman of N.C. in the House of Representatives, January 5th [1844] on the Twenty-First Rule," rptd. in *Raleigh Register*, 1 Feb. 1844.

10. Clingman, "On the Principles of the Whig and Democratic Parties, Delivered in the House of Representatives, March 7, 1844," in Clingman, *Speeches and Writings*, 157; Clingman, "On the Causes of Mr. Clay's Defeat, Delivered in the House of Representatives, January 6, 1845," in *Speeches and Writings*, 193–194, 174.

11. Gilbert, "Public Career of Clingman," 37, 39–40.

12. Kruman, *Parties and Politics*, 110–11. Clingman also chose party over section by supporting a protective tariff, though here he seems to have risked little opposition from his district, whose commercial ties would benefit from it. See Siegmann, "Thomas Lanier Clingman," 22–23, and Clingman, *Speeches and Writings*, 152–55.

13. Clingman, "Principles of Whigs and Democrats," in *Speeches and Writings*, 159.

14. Clay's majority of 67.8% in the mountain counties was larger than in any other area of the state, which he carried by 52.7%. Burke County gave Clay 84% of its vote, and Wilkes County 87%. Burnham, *Presidential Ballots*, 648–67.

15. The sheer act of dueling proved unpopular with some mountain voters. Senator Willie P. Mangum wrote to Tod R. Caldwell asking about how the incident would be viewed by "religionists and churchmen" in western North Carolina, and Burgess S. Gaither worried about "what Whig Churchmen would do about voting for Mr. Clingman." Willie P. Mangum to Tod R. Caldwell, 19 Feb. 1845, in Shanks, *Papers of Mangum*, vol. 4, p. 267; sister Harriet to Thomas George Walton, 10 Feb. 1845, Thomas George Walton Papers, SHC; James Graham to William A. Graham, 19 Aug. 1845, in Hamilton, *Papers of William A. Graham*, 3:63.

16. Siegmann, "Thomas Lanier Clingman," 38–39; Jeffrey, "Thunder from the Mountains," 375; *Raleigh Standard*, 20 Aug. 1845.

17. James Graham to William A. Graham, 10 May 1847, in Hamilton and Williams, *Papers of William A. Graham*, 3:193–94.

18. *North Carolina Standard*, 25 Aug. 1847.

19. Clingman, "On the Political Aspect of the Slave Question, Delivered in the House of Representatives, December 22, 1847," in *Speeches and Writings*, 225.

20. Ibid., 211, 214.

21. Kruman, *Parties and Politics*, 116–17; Pegg, *Whig Party*, 138.

22. Clingman, "Political Aspect of Slave Question," in *Speeches and Writings*, 202–204, 210. Pegg and Jeffrey take single statements from this speech out of context to show that Clingman fully supported the Whig viewpoint and opposed Calhoun's conclusion himself, which he called "most shallow and superficial" (p. 200). Pegg, *Whig Party*, 138n; Jeffrey, "Thunder from the Mountains," 379.

23. Clingman, "Political Aspect of Slave Question," in *Speeches and Writings*, 210. Jeffrey and Pegg also overlook this statement and conclude that it was a year later before Clingman took this view, thus implying a more gradual pace of transformation than Clingman actually seems to have experienced. Pegg, *Whig Party*, 138n; Jeffrey, "Thunder from the Mountains," 376.

24. Clingman, "Political Aspect of Slave Question," in *Speeches and Writings*, 223, 225.

25. See Gilbert, "Public Career of Clingman," 52–54, for the best account of Clingman's opposition to Polk.

26. Ibid., 60.

27. Clingman, "Conclusion of the Slavery Discussion," in *Speeches and Writings*, 568.

28. Clingman to Calvin Graves et al., 18 Dec. 1848, rptd. in *North Carolina Standard*, 24 Jan. 1849; Clingman, *Speeches and Writings*, 229–30.

29. Jeffrey, "Thunder from the Mountains," 377, 381; Kruman, "Clingman and the Whig Party," 11–14; and Brian G. Walton, "Elections to the United States Senate in North Carolina, 1835–1861," *North Carolina Historical Review* 53 (Apr. 1976):184.

30. Clingman, "Address on Recent Senatorial Election," 1, 15.

31. *North Carolina Standard*, 8 Aug. 1949. Clingman won 6,085 votes, with 1,146 "scattered" votes, *Hillsborough Recorder*, 22 Aug. 1849.

32. Clingman to Henry S. Foote, 13 Nov. 1849, rptd. in Clingman, *Speeches and Writings*, 231–32.

33. For a discussion of states' rights sentiment in North Carolina in 1849–50, see Sitterson, *Secession Movement*, 55–60.

34. Clingman, "In Defence of the South Against the Aggressive Movement of the North, Delivered in the House of Representatives, January 22, 1850," in *Speeches and Writings*, 245, 251, 253–54.

35. Robert Toombs had made an earlier "discord speech" before Congress in Dec. 1849, which Clingman had applauded. Ibid., 255.

36. Ibid.; James C. Johnston to William S. Pettigrew, 6 Mar. 1850, Pettigrew Papers, SHC.

37. Clingman, "In Defence of the South," in *Speeches and Writings*, 250.

38. Clingman, "Political Aspect of Slave Question, in *Speeches and Writings*, 223.

39. Clingman, "In Defence of the South," in *Speeches and Writings*, 245.

40. Ibid., 244. For a Deep South version of this scenario a year later, see the *Montgomery Advertiser*, 12 Feb. 1851, cited in Thornton, *Politics and Power in a Slave Society*, 206.

41. Clingman to Editors of *The Republic*, 22 Mar. 1850, rptd. in *Speeches and Writings*, 267.

42. Clingman, "In Defence of the South," in *Speeches and Writings*, 239. See ch. 4 and 5 of this book for references to western North Carolina slaveholders who took slaves to California.

43. Clingman, "In Defence of the South," in *Speeches and Writings*, 251; Clingman to Editor of the *Herald*, 13 Aug. 1876, in *Speeches and Writings*, 271.

44. Gilbert, "Public Career," 83. For a breakdown of the compromise votes by North Carolina congressmen, see Pegg, *Whig Party*, 193.

45. Clingman, "On the Future Policy of the Government, Delivered in Committee of the Whole of the House of Representatives, February 15, 1851," in *Speeches and Writings*, 285–86; Siegmann, "Thomas Lanier Clingman," 98.

46. Jeffrey, "Thunder from the Mountains," 387–88.

47. J.G. deRoulhac Hamilton, *Party Politics in North Carolina*, 146; Kruman, *Parties and Politics*, 131.

48. Robert G.A. Love to James Love, 1 June 1851, William W. Stringfield Papers, WCU.

49. *Asheville News*, 9 Jan. 1851.

50. *North Carolina Standard*, 5 Feb. 1851.

51. J.R.N. Bennet to Jacob Siler, 30 June 1851, Lyle-Siler Family Papers, SHC.

52. Clingman to William H. Thomas, 22 June 1851, William Holland Thomas Papers, Duke. Clingman had 6,660 votes to Gaither's 2,819. *North Carolina Standard*, 27 Aug. 1851; Siegmann, "Thomas Lanier Clingman," 100.

53. N.W. Woodfin to David L. Swain, 28 July 1851, Walter Clark Papers, NCDAH; A.R. Bryan to Thomas I. Lenoir, 4 Sept. 1851, Lenoir Family Papers, SHC.

54. Jeffrey, "Thunder from the Mountains," 392. *Asheville Spectator*, 27 Apr. 1853. See n. 69 (Jeffrey) for a discussion of the uncertainties as to when Clingman actually adopted the Democratic label.

55. The *Highland Messenger* had been an earlier Whig organ in Asheville, but had had only limited success. Blackmun, *Western North Carolina*, 309–10.

56. Kruman, *Parties and Politics*, 136; Sitterson, *Secession Movement*, 127.

57. *Asheville Spectator*, 13 July 1853; see also editorial, 11 May 1853.

58. *Asheville Spectator*, 27 Apr. 1853.

59. *Asheville News*, 28 July 1853; *Asheville Spectator*, 13 July 1853.

60. *Asheville News*, 28 July 1853, *Asheville Spectator*, 13 July 1853.

61. *Asheville News*, 23 Feb. 1854; Jeffrey, "Thunder from the Mountains," 392n.

62. Clingman, "On Nebraska and Kansas, Delivered in the House of Representatives, April 4, 1854," in *Speeches and Writings*, 337, 354.

63. *Asheville News*, 13 Apr. 1854.

64. Jeffrey, "Thunder from the Mountains," makes a strong case for Clingman's defection as a major factor in the decline of the Whig party in North Carolina. See also Morrill, "Presidential Election of 1852."

65. *Asheville Spectator*, 21 Apr. 1855. The best accounts of the American party in North Carolina are Thomas H. Leath, "The Know-Nothing Party in North Carolina" (M.A. thesis, Univ. of North Carolina, Chapel Hill, 1929); Kruman, *Parties and Politics*, ch. 7, 159–79; and Jeffrey, "Second Party System," ch. 10, 267–80.

66. Kruman, *Parties and Politics*, 172; N.W. Woodfin to David L. Swain, 1 July 1855, Walter Clark Papers, NCDAH.

67. Sitterson, *Secession Movement*, 131–32; Clingman, "To the Freemen of the Eighth District [of N.C. on the Political Condition and Prospects of the Country, March 16, 1856]" [sic], in *Speeches and Writings*, 388; Jeffrey, "Thunder from the Mountains," 394.

68. Clingman, "To the Freemen," in *Speeches and Writings*, 377, 385, 388.

69. *Asheville News*, 30 Oct. 1856.

70. *Asheville News*, 20 Nov. 1856.

71. *Asheville News*, 4 Dec. 1856.

72. Clingman, "To the Freemen," in *Speeches and Writings*, 381–84.

73. *Raleigh Register*, 6 Oct. 1855, quoted in Pegg, *Whig Party*, 31.

74. *Asheville News*, 12 Mar. 1857, 2 Apr. 1857.

75. *Asheville News*, 16 July 1857.

76. Ibid. The election results gave Clingman 8,673 votes to Vance's 3,211, while a third candidate, William J. Wilson, received 446 votes. *Asheville News*, 20 Aug. 1857.

77. Phifer, "Saga of a Burke County Family," 306–307.

78. The most thorough account of the incident is found in W. Conrad Gass, "'The Misfortunes of a High-Minded and Honorable Gentleman': W.W. Avery and the Southern Code of Honor," *North Carolina Historical Review* 56 (July 1979): 278–97. See also *Raleigh Standard*, 1851; Kemp P. Battle, *Memories of an Old-Time Tar Heel*, ed. William J. Battle (Chapel Hill: Univ. North Carolina Press, 1945), 92; and Phifer, "Saga of a Burke County Family," 307–12.

79. Battle, whose father was both a witness to the crime and the presiding judge at Avery's trial, felt that it had increased his popularity, but Vance himself felt that it was a factor in his defeat. Battle, *Memories*, 102; Z.B. Vance to John E. Brown, 22 Aug. 1859, in Johnston, *Papers of Vance*, 56.

80. Kruman, *Parties and Politics*, 184–86; *Raleigh Standard*, 18 and 24 July, 25 Aug. 1858.

81. Z.B. Vance to David F. Caldwell, 19 Feb. 1858, in Johnston, *Papers of Vance*, 33. For a similar anti-Democratic tirade, see speech by Vance quoted in the *Asheville News*, 4 May 1858.

82. *Asheville News*, 28 June 1858.

83. Johnston, *Papers of Vance*, xxxiv–xxxv. The best account of the Vance-Avery contest is found in Glenn Tucker, *Zeb Vance: Champion of Personal Freedom* (Indianapolis: Bobbs-Merrill, 1965), 67–71, 77–78.

84. Samuel F. Patterson to William A. Graham, 2 Sept. 1852, Hamilton and Williams, *Papers of William A. Graham*, 4:386; Jeffrey, "Thunder from the Mountains," 388 and Appendix B. Though Jeffrey stresses the failure of these candidates, at least one "States Rights Whig" was elected in 1852, and four were elected in 1854.

85. Clingman to J.F.E. Hardy, 18 July 1852, Clingman–Puryear Family Papers, SHC. Clingman asked Hardy to publish it, while denying that he intended it for publication.

86. Patterson to William A. Graham, 2 Sept. 1852, Hamilton and Williams, *Papers of William A. Graham*, vol. 4, 386; Kruman, *Parties and Politics*, 153.

87. *Asheville News*, 20 Apr. 1854; see also Kruman, *Parties and Politics*, 77–78, 101.

88. Johnston, *Papers of Vance*, xxix–xxx.

89. *Asheville News*, 12 Feb., 2 Apr. 1857.

90. *Buffalo Advertiser*, quoted in *Asheville News*, 12 Mar. 1857.

Chapter 9

1. Zebulon B. Vance, "To the Citizens of the Eighth Congressional District of North Carolina," 13 Feb. 1861 (Washington, D.C.: H. Polkinhorn, 1861), 3.

2. Clingman, "Against the Revolutionary Movement of the Anti-Slavery Party, Delivered in the Senate of the United States, January 16, 1860," in *Speeches and Writing*, 475, 451.

3. *Asheville News*, 27 Oct. 1859.

4. At least five counties (Buncombe, Caldwell, Henderson, Madison, and Yancey) held such meetings before the end of the year. *Asheville News*, 19 Nov. and 29 Dec. 1859; Alexander, *Here Will I Dwell*, 126; Henderson County Slave Records, NCDAH.

5. *Asheville News*, 29 Dec. 1859.

6. Marcus Erwin to John W. Ellis, 22 Dec. 1859, in *The Papers of John Willis Ellis*, vol. 1, *1841–1859*, ed. Noble J. Tolbert (Raleigh: NCDAH, 1964), 335.

7. Ashe, Buncombe, Burke, Wilkes, and Watauga all formed military companies during this period. Raymond A. Heath, Jr., "North Carolina Militia on the Eve of the Civil War" (M.A. thesis, Univ. of North Carolina, 1974), 46; John B. Todd to John W. Ellis, 15 Dec. 1859, and Marcus Erwin to Ellis, 22 and 23 Dec. 1859, in Tolbert, *Ellis Papers*, 333–36.

8. *Asheville News*, 29 Dec. 1859.

9. Erwin to Ellis, 22 Dec. 1859, in Tolbert, *Ellis Papers*, 335; *Asheville News*, 29 Dec. 1859.

10. *Asheville News*, 15 and 29 Jan. 1857.

11. Ibid., 29 Jan. 1857.

12. James H. Boykin, *North Carolina in 1861* (New York: Bookman Associates, 1961), 185–86; Johnson, *Ante-Bellum North Carolina*, 89.

13. *Asheville News*, 19 Jan. 1860.

14. *Franklin Observer*, 16 Mar. 1860; Vance speech, 16 Mar. 1860, cited in Shore, *Southern Capitalists*, 71.

15. Edward J. Alston to the Editors, *Asheville News*, 19 Jan. 1860.

16. Ollinger Crenshaw, *The Slave States in the Presidential Election of 1860* (Baltimore: Johns Hopkins Univ. Press, 1945), 187; Marcus Erwin to John W. Ellis, Dec. 22, 1859, in Tolbert, *Ellis Papers*, 335.

17. *Asheville News*, Dec. 29, 1859.

18. Avery's role within the Democratic Party in 1860 is discussed in detail in Owen M. Peterson, "W.W. Avery in the Democratic National Convention of 1860," *North Carolina Historical Review* 21 (Oct. 1944):463–78. Dwight L. Dumond, *The Secession Movement, 1860–1861* (New York: Macmillan, 1931), 45. See also Sitterson, *Secession Movement*, 162; and William B. Hesseltine, ed., *Three Against Lincoln: Murat Halstead Reports the Caucuses of 1860* (Baton Rouge: Louisiana State Univ. Press, 1960).

19. N.W. Woodfin, to D.L. Swain, 17 May 1860, Swain Papers, SHC.

20. Clingman, *Speeches and Writings*, 484–85.

21. Clingman, "Speech on the Subject of Congressional Legislation as to the Rights of Property in the Territories, Delivered in the Senate of the United States, May 7 and 8, 1860," in *Speeches and Writings*, 450–51.

22. *Asheville News*, 9 Aug. 1860; Sitterson, *Secession Movement*, 170; Clingman, *Speeches and Writings*, 449–51.

23. See ch. 8 of this book; Sitterson, *Secession Movement*, 135–36.

24. Clingman, "Speech Against the Revolutionary Movement of the Anti-Slavery Party, Delivered in the Senate of the United States, January 16, 1860," in *Speeches and Writings*, 479–81.

25. *Asheville News*, 1 Nov. 1860; William D. Cotton, "Appalachian North Carolina: A Political Study, 1860–1899" (Ph.D. diss., Univ. of North Carolina, Chapel Hill, 1954), 76. See *Asheville News*, 4 July 1860, for the most thorough argument in support of Breckinridge and Lane.

26. Sitterson, *Secession Movement*, 170–71; Kruman, *Parties and Politics*, 199.

27. *Asheville News*, 1 Nov. 1860.

28. Sallie L. Lenoir to Rufus T. Lenoir, 29 Oct. 1860, Lenoir Family Papers, SHC.

29. Statewide, only 70% of the electorate voted in November, as compared with 82% in August. Kruman, *Parties and Politics*, 199; Burnham, *Presidential Ballots*, 648–666.

32. Clingman, *Speeches and Writings*, 514n, 515; W. W. Avery and Samuel P. Hill to Thomas Ruffin, 4 Dec. 1860, in J.G. de Roulhac Hamilton, ed., *The Papers of Thomas Ruffin*, vol. 2 (Raleigh: Edwards and Broughton, 1920), 106–107.

33. Isaac T. Avery to David L. Swain, 16 Nov. 1860, Swain Papers, SHC.

34. E.J. Erwin to George P. Erwin, 9 Nov. and 9 Dec. 1860, 10 Jan. 1861, George Phifer Erwin Papers, SHC.

35. Ibid., 6 Feb. 1861.

36. James W. Patton to D.L. Swain, 5 Feb. 1861, Swain Papers, NCDAH.

37. Thomas Clingman to William H. Thomas, 9 Jan. 1861, in Clingman, *Speeches and Writings*, 553.

38. Circular, "David W. Siler to Fellow Citizens of Macon County," 4 Mar. 1861, Mary Gash and Family Papers, NCDAH.

39. Clingman, "On the State of the Union, Delivered in the Senate of the United States, February 4, 1861," in *Speeches and Writings*, 531, 554–55. See also Clingman to Editor, *Asheville News* Extra, 21 Feb. 1861, broadside in NCC.

40. Sitterson, *Secession Movement*, 220–21.

41. Michael P. Johnson, *Toward a Patriarchal Republic: The Secession of Georgia* (Baton Rouge: Louisian State Univ. Press, 1977), 49–50. Another argument that Brown aimed at north Georgia nonslaveholders was that freeing the slaves would mean reimbursement to slaveholders of up to $2 billion. Not only would these funds come from higher taxes for all citizens, but slaveholders would likely use that compensation to buy up land, forcing small landholders and tenants out. See Derrill C. Roberts, *Joseph E. Brown and the Politics of Reconstruction* (University, Ala.: Univ. of Alabama Press, 1973), 13.

42. William Holland Thomas to his wife, 14 Jan. 1861, William Holland Thomas Papers, Duke.

43. Clingman, "On the War Policy of the Administration, Delivered in the United States Senate, March 19, 1861," in *Speeches and Writings*, 562.

44. Malet, *Errand to the South*, 248.

45. Thomas to his wife, 1 Jan. and 17 June 1861, William Holland Thomas Papers, Duke.

46. David W. Siler to Rufus S. Siler, 7 Dec. 1860, Jacob Siler Papers, SHC; Zebulon B. Vance to William Dickson, 11 Dec. 1860, in Johnston, *Papers of Vance*, 72.

47. Sallie L. Lenoir to Rufus L. Lenoir, 12 Nov. 1860, Lenoir Family Papers, SHC.

48. Thomas Isaac Lenoir to Rufus L. Lenoir, 26 Dec. 1860, Thomas Lenoir Papers, Duke.

49. James Gwyn Diary, vol. 4, 25 Dec. 1860 and 12 Jan. 1861, entries, James Gwyn Papers, SHC.

50. J.G. de Roulhac Hamilton, "Secession in North Carolina," in Daniel H. Hill, *North Carolina in the War Between the States*, vol. 1: *Bethel to Sharpsburg*, pp. 1–46 (Raleigh, N.C.: Edwards and Broughton, 1926), 33n.

51. William John Brown to Jno. Evans Brown, 21 Mar. 1861, Theodore Davidson Morrison Papers, SHC.

52. Vance, "To the Citizens of the Eighth District," 1.

53. Ibid., 2; Vance to William Dickson, 11 Dec. 1860, in Johnston, *Papers of Vance*, 71.

54. C. C. Jones to Vance, 4 Feb. 1861, in Johnston, *Papers of Vance*, 71.

55. "A Farmer" to the Editors, letter dated 7 Feb. 1861, *Raleigh Register*, 23 Feb. 1861. See ch. 2 of this book for reference to the dispute most likely referred to in the letter.

56. C.D. Smith to D.W. Siler, 17 Dec. 1860, Jacob Siler Papers, SHC.

57. T. Farrow to S.F. Patterson, 12 Feb. 1861, Jones and Patterson Family Papers, SHC.

58. Broadside, "To the People of Buncombe County," 18 Feb. 1861, Civil War Papers, Pack. The "hewers of wood and drawers of water" phrase is a quote from William L. Brownlow, in his *Knoxville Whig*, 26 Jan. 1861.

59. W.W. Lenoir to Vance, 7 Jan. 1861, in Johnston, *Papers of Vance*, 80.

60. "To the People of Buncombe County," 18 Feb. 1861, Civil War Papers, Pack.

61. "Siler to Fellow Citizens of Macon County," 4 Mar. 1861, Mary Gash Papers, NCDAH; William John Brown to Jno. Evans Brown, 21 Mar. 1861, Theodore Davidson Morrison Papers, SHC. For a more detailed analysis of the projected tax burden under the Confederacy, based on South Carolina's financial hardships only a month after it seceded, see Vance, "To the Citizens of the Eighth District," 3–4.

62. Vance, "To the Citizens of the Eighth District," 5.

63. Calvin J. Cowles to unknown person, 11 Dec. 1860, Calvin J. Cowles Papers, NCDAH; P.W. Hennessey to William Walker, 23 Feb. 1861, William Walker Papers, WCU.

64. "To the People of Buncombe County"; A.T. Davidson to his wife, 4 Apr. 1861, Allen Turner Davidson Papers, SHC.

65. See William C. Wright, *The Secession Movement in the Middle Atlantic States* (Rutherford, N.J.: Fairleigh Dickinson Univ. Press, 1973), 30–38, 46–52, 59–61, 113–21; and Mary E.R. Campbell, *The Attitude of Tennesseans Toward the Union, 1846–1861* (New York: Vantage, 1961), 149–50, for variations of this idea in other states. According to Wright, Maryland and New Jersey leaders produced the most developed plan and pushed hardest for it. Significantly, it was only in the mountains of East Tennessee that the proposal was ever seriously considered in that state.

66. Vance to W.W. Lenoir, 16 Dec. 1860, in Johnston, *Papers of Vance*, 78.

67. W.W. Lenoir to Vance, 7 Jan. 1861, in Johnston, *Papers of Vance*, 80.

68. Ibid., 78. Vance's final reference is to Sen. Charles Sumner, the outspoken Massachusetts abolitionist who fell victim to Preston Brooks' cane on the Senate floor in 1856.

69. Sitterson, *Secession Movement*, 199–200; W.W. Lenoir to Vance, 7 Jan. 1861, in Johnston, *Papers of Vance* , 80.

70. *Brownlow's Knoxville Whig*, 28 Jan. 1861; A.W. Howard to T.A.R. Nelson, 17 Apr. 1861, both quoted in Mary Campbell, *Attitude of Tennesseans*, 175, 192–93.

71. W.W. Lenoir to Vance, 5 Feb. 1861, in Johnston, *Papers of Vance*, 98.

72. Alexander H. Jones, *Knocking at the Door* (Washington, D.C.: McGill and Witherow, 1866), 14.

73. T.P. Siler to David W. Siler, 18 Dec. 1860, Jacob Siler Papers, SHC.

74. Vance, "To the Citizens of the Eighth District," 3.

75. Cotton, "Appalachian North Carolina," 81.

76. William John Brown to Jno. Evans Brown, 15 Apr. 1861, Theodore Davidson Morrison Papers, SHC.

77. Vance speech, 30 Nov. 1860, quoted in the *Fayetteville* (N.C.) *Observer*, 3 Dec. 1860.

78. W.G. Brownlow, *Sketches of the Rise, Progress, and Decline of Secession* (Philadelphia: George W. Childs, 1862), 109.

79. J.P. Eller to Vance, 28 Jan. 1861, Zebulon B. Vance Papers, NCDAH.

80. W.W. Lenoir to Zebulon Vance, 29 Nov. 1860, Lenoir Family Papers, SHC; and W.W. Lenoir to Vance, 7 Jan. 1861, in Johnston, *Papers of Vance*, 80.

81. A.T. Davidson to Theodore Davidson, 7 Apr. 1861, Allen Turner Davidson Papers, SHC.

82. Vance, "To the Citizens of the Eighth District," 7.

83. Of the mountain counties that held such meetings, only Jackson County unionists drew up resolutions unequivocally opposed to secession. This is ironic considering that it was the home county of secessionist William Holland Thomas, and that it voted overwhelmingly for a convention to consider secession on 28 Feb. See *Raleigh Register*, 5 Jan. 1861. For reports on other county meetings, see *North Carolina Standard*, 26 Dec. 1860; 2, 9, 16, 23 Jan. 1861.

84. *Raleigh Register*, 2 and 9 Jan. 1861.

85. Ibid., 2 Jan. 1861.

86. G.W. Moore to D.W. Siler, 21 Dec. 1860, Jacob Siler Papers, SHC. For a similar opinion, see B.F. Eller to Vance, 17 Dec. 1860, in Johnston, *Papers of Vance*, 74.

87. Robert B. Vance to Zebulon Vance, 21 Jan. 1861, in Johnston, *Papers of Vance*, 89.

88. J.C.L. Gudger to Vance, 27 Jan. 1861, in Johnston, *Papers of Vance*, 91. See also Robert G. Twitty to Vance, 16 Jan. 1861, Johnston, *Papers of Vance*, 87.

89. Calvin J. Cowles to S.W. Roosevelt, 10 Dec. 1860, Cowles Papers, NCDAH; C.C. Jones to Vance, 4 Feb. 1861, Johnston, *Papers of Vance*.

90. For estimates of Union strength prior to 28 Feb. see: L.S. Gash to D.W. Siler, n.d., Jacob Siler Papers, SHC; James W. Patton to William A. Patton, 14 Feb. 1861, James W. Patton Papers, SHC; Jarvis Buxton to Ralph A. Buxton, 14 Feb. 1861, Ralph A. Buxton Papers, SHC; and Zebulon B. Vance to C.C. Jones, 11 Feb. 1861, Zebulon B. Vance Papers, SHC; Also see S.O. Deaver to Vance, 28 Jan. 1861, J.P. Eller to Vance, 28 Jan. 1861, C.C. Jones to Vance, 4 Feb. 1861—all in Johnston, *Papers of Vance*, 91–95; "A Farmer" to the Editors, *Raleigh Register*, 23 Feb. 1861.

91. Examples of this prediction can be found in P.W. Hennessey to William Walker, WCU; Robert Henry Diary, 19 Jan. 1861, Robert Henry Manuscript Collection, Pack; William Holland Thomas to Jackson County Constituents, *Raleigh Register*, 23 Feb. 1861; William L. Love to Vance, in Johnston, *Papers of Vance*, 94, 96; Tod R. Caldwell to William A. Graham, 11 Feb. 1861, in Hamilton and Williams, *Papers of William A. Graham*, vol. 5, 233. For a more balanced county-by-county prediction, see Burgess Gaither to William A. Graham, 12 Feb. 1861, in Hamilton and Williams, *Papers of William A. Graham*, 234–235.

92. S.O. Deaver to Vance, 28 Jan. 1861, in Johnston, *Papers of Vance*, 92. See also B.F. Eller to Vance, 27 Dec. 1860, in Johnston, *Papers of Vance*, 74, in which Eller says that nearly all Wilkes County Democrats are secessionists.

93. J.M. Hamilton to Vance, 14 Jan. 1861, Zebulon B. Vance Papers, NCDAH; William L. Love to Vance, 1 Feb. 1861, in Johnston, *Papers of Vance*, 94.

94. S.O. Deaver to Vance, 28 Jan. 1861, in Johnston, *Papers of Vance*, 92; J.P. Eller to Vance, 28 Jan. 1861, Vance Papers, NCDAH.

95. John Ammons, *Outlines of History of French Broad Association and Mars Hill College* (Raleigh, N.C.: Edwards and Broughton, n.d.), 28–29.

96. Vance to Thomas George Walton, 19 and 22 Jan. 1861, Thomas George Walton Papers, SHC; Vance to C.C. Jones, 11 Feb. 1861, Zebulon B. Vance Papers, SHC; Kruman, *Parties and Politics*, 206; Sitterson, *Secession Movement*, 222; Daniel W. Crofts, *Reluctant Confederates: Upper South Unionists in the Secession Crisis* (Chapel Hill: Univ. of North Carolina Press, 1988).

97. Compare totals for both elections in tables 9.1 and 9.2. See Crofts, *Reluctant Confederates*, ch. 6, for comprehensive analysis of voter turnout in the two elections.

98. Vance to G.N. Folk, 9 Jan. 1861, in Johnston, *Papers of Vance*, 82.

99. Sitterson, *Secession Movement*, 206; S.F. Patterson to his son, 16 Mar. 1861, Jones and Patterson Family Papers, SHC.

100. The three secessionist delegates were elected from Burke, Jackson and Haywood counties. Burke County elected Clarke Moulton Avery, who defeated William C. Erwin by only 36 votes. Erwin, though running as a Unionist, the previous December had expressed strong reservations about the wisdom of remaining in the Union. Moulton Avery was the younger brother of the region's most prominent secessionist, William Waightstill Avery, and the son of Isaac T. Avery. See Phifer, "Saga of a Burke County Family," pt. 3, *North Carolina Historical Review* 39 (1962):315–24; Phifer, *Burke*, 319; and "Clarke Moulton Avery," biographical entry in Powell, *Dictionary of North Carolina Biography*, vol. 1, 67–68.

There was at the time, and there continues to be, some confusion, due to the closeness of the vote and due to mistaken early reports (see *Raleigh Register*, 23 Feb. and 6 Mar. 1861) as to which candidates were elected in the latter two counties. For confirmation of the fact that secessionists would have represented Jackson and Haywood, see the secessionist papers, *Asheville News*, 1 Mar. 1861, and Charlotte's *Western Democrat*, 12 Mar. 1861; and the unionist *North Carolina Standard*, 20 Mar. 1861; Sitterson, *Secession Movement*, 224, 228.

It is not clear how Sitterson made the distinctions he did between conditional and unconditional unionists. But in at least four of the counties he showed as having chosen unconditional unionist delegates, statements by or about the delegates made before the election indicate that they were clearly conditional unionists. These include Montreville Patton of Buncombe County, J.J. Gudger of Madison, Edmund W. Jones of Caldwell, and Allen T. Davidson of Cherokee. "To the People of Buncombe County," 18 Feb. 1861, Civil War Papers, Pack. J.C.L. Gudger to Vance, 27 Jan. 1861, in Johnston, *Papers of Vance*, 91; Tod R. Caldwell to William A. Graham, 11 Feb. 1861, in Hamilton and Williams, *Papers of William A. Graham*, vol. 5, 223; Allen T. Davidson to Theodore Davidson, 7 Apr. 1861, Allen T. Davidson Papers, SHC.

101. Sitterson, *Secession Movement*, 219. Of the ten delegates whose views at this time are known, all were conditional rather than unconditional unionists (see n. 100). I have not been able to determine the views of the delegates of the four northernmost counties (Ashe, Alleghany, Wilkes, and Watauga). Sitterson labels them unconditional unionists, which is plausible, particularly in Wilkes County.

102. Compare the county voting returns in tables 9.1 and 9.2.

103. Both Mark Kruman and Daniel Crofts make strong cases for a close correlation between a county's Whig or Democrat tendencies and its vote in the Feb. election. Elsewhere in the state, Whigs and unionist sentiment were closely associated, as were Democrats and secessionist feeling, but enough of the mountain counties proved exceptions to the statewide pattern to render any correlation there negligible. Kruman, *Parties and Politics*, 212–13; Crofts, *Reluctant Confederates*, tables 37–41.

104. Henderson County, with almost as strong a Whig voting record, was almost evenly divided in the Feb. election.

105. For references to each of these men as slaveholders, see ch. 3, and appendix. In at least one instance, those northern contacts won a convert to secession. A Wilkes County man returned from New York early in January and reported that he was "strong for disunion," since he had found "the Northerners are getting more and more for dissolving the Union." E. Jones to S.F. Patterson, 6 Jan. 1861, Jones and Patterson Family Papers, SHC.

106. See James Gwyn to Rufus T. Lenoir, 11 Mar. 1861, Lenoir Family Papers; William J. Brown to Jno. Evans Brown, 21 Mar. 1861, Theodore Davidson Morrison Papers; and Zebulon B. Vance to C.C. Jones, 11 Feb. 1861, Zebulon B. Vance Papers—all SHC. See also D.W. Siler to Fellow Citizens of Macon County, Mary Gash and Family Papers, NCDAH.

107. On 4 Feb., Virginians elected to their convention 122 unionist delegates and only 30 secessionist delegates. David M. Potter, *Lincoln and His Party in the Secession Crisis* (New Haven: Yale Univ. Press, 1942), 309.

108. On East Tennessee's prewar Unionism, the most basic works include Mary Campbell, *Attitude of Tennesseans*; Oliver P. Temple, *East Tennessee and the Civil War* (Freeport, N.Y.: Books for Libraries Press, rpt. ed., 1971; orig. ed., 1899); Thomas W. Humes, *The Loyal Mountaineers of East Tennessee* (Knoxville: Ogden Bros., 1888); Vernon M. Queener, "East Tennessee Sentiment and the Secession Movement, November 1860–June 1861," *East Tennessee Historical Society's Publications* 20 (1948):64; and J. Reuben Sheeler, "The Development of Unionism in East Tennessee," *Journal of Negro History* 29 (Apr. 1944):182–84. For one explanation of the different sectional attitudes of the two states' mountain regions, see John C. Inscoe, "Mountain Unionism, Secession, and Regional Self-Image: The Contrasting Cases of Western North Carolina and East Tennessee," in *Looking South: Chapters in the Story of an American Region*, ed. Winifred B. Moore and Joseph Tripp (Greenwood, 1989).

109. "David W. Siler to Fellow Citizens of Macon County," 4 Mar. 1861, Mary Gash and Family Papers, NCDAH; Sitterson, *Secession Movement*, 230–31; James Gwyn to Rufus T. Lenoir, 11 Mar. 1861, Lenoir Family Papers, SHC. For

a thorough account of the peace conference, see Dumond, *Secession Movement*, 239–66.

110. Gwyn to Lenoir, 11 Mar. 1861, Lenoir Family Papers, SHC; J.R. Siler to D.L. Swain, 19 Mar. 1861, Walter Clark Papers, NCDAH. For other reactions to Lincoln's inaugural, see *Raleigh Register*, 9 and 13 Mar. 1861.

111. Clingman, "On President Lincoln's Inaugural, Delivered in the United States Senate, March 7, 1861," in *Speeches and Writings*, 557. See also Clingman, "On the War Policy of the Administration, Delivered in the United States Senate, March 19, 1851," in *Speeches and Writings*, 558–63.

112. James Gwyn to Rufus T. Lenoir, 11 Mar. 1861, Lenoir Family Papers, SHC. For a similar sentiment by a former unionist, see S.F. Patterson to his son, 16 Mar. 1861, Jones and Patterson Family Papers, SHC.

113. William Holland Thomas to his wife, 5 June 1861, William Holland Thoms Papers, Duke.

114. Clingman, *Speeches and Writings*, 564.

115. "David W. Siler to Fellow Citizens of Macon County, 4 Mar. 1861, Mary Gash and Family Papers, NCDAH.

116. A letter from Samuel McDowell Tate in Morganton to Edmund W. Jones, on 13 Apr. 1861, Jones and Patterson Family Papers, SHC, indicates that he not only anticipated the attack there, but also expected Confederate troops to attack Washington within a day or two.

117. "Siler to Fellow Citizens of Macon County," 4 Mar. 1861, Mary Gash and Family Papers, NCDAH.

118. Charles Manly to David L. Swain, 22 Apr. 1861, David L. Swain Papers, NCDAH.

119. Clement Dowd, *The Life of Zebulon B. Vance* (Charlotte, N.C.: Observer, 1897), 441.

120. Josiah Cowles to Calvin J. Cowles, 3 June 1861; Calvin J. Cowles to S.W. Roosevelt, 6 May 1861, both in Cowles Papers, NCDAH.

121. N. Collin Hughes, *Hendersonville in Civil War Times* (Hendersonville, N.C.:Privately published, 1936), 10. Phifer, *Burke*, 320; Theodore F. Davidson, *Reminiscences and Traditions of Western North Carolina* (Asheville: Service Printing, 1928), 23–24.

122. Robert B. Vance et al. to John W. Ellis, 18 Apr. 1861, John W. Ellis Governor's Papers, NCDAH.

123. William J. Brown to Jno. Evans Brown, 15 Apr. 1861, Theodore Davidson Morrison Papers, SHC. (Brown began this letter on 15 Apr., but, in reporting the unfolding events to his son in Australia, continued adding to it over the next few days.)

124. Russell, "William Holland Thomas," 336. For a detailed account of the subsequent experiences of Thomas and the Cherokees, see Vernon H. Crow, *Storm in the Mountains: Thomas' Confederate Legion of Cherokee Indians and Mountaineers* (Cherokee, N.C.: Press of the Museum of the Cherokee Indian, 1982).

125. James Harper Diaries, vol. 1, 27 Apr. 1861 (typescript, 15), SHC; George F.W. Harper Diaries, 27–30 Apr. 1861, SHC; Alexander, *Here Will I Dwell*, 127.

126. James Gwyn's Diary, vol. 4, 1 May 1861, James Gwyn Papers, and James Gwyn to Rufus T. Lenoir, 2 May 1861, Lenoir Family Papers, both SHC; Francis B. Dedmond, "Harvey Davis's Unpublished Civil War "Diary" and the Story of Company D of the First North Carolina Cavalry," *Appalachian Journal* 13 (Summer 1986):379.

127. N.W. Woodfin, "To the Voters of Buncombe County," 9 May 1861, Civil War Papers, Pack.

128. Other early secessionists elected included William Holland Thomas (Jackson County), William Hicks (Haywood), Joel E. Foster (Ashe and Alleghany), John C. McDowell (Burke), James Councill (Watauga), James H. Greenlee (McDowell), and Milton Penland (Yancey). James G. McCormick, *Personnel of the Convention of 1861*, James Sprunt Historical Monograph, no. 1 (Chapel Hill: Univ. of North Carolina, 1900).

Former conditional unionists elected include Edmund W. Jones (Caldwell County), Allen T. Davidson (Cherokee), William M. Shipp (Henderson), Peter Eller (Wilkes), and James A. McDowell (Madison), a brother of secessionist John C. McDowell of Burke. Ibid.

129. Sitterson, *Secession Movement*, 245n; Jones, *Knocking at the Door*, 4–5.

130. For detailed accounts of the incident, see Elizabeth G. McPherson, ed., "Letters from North Carolina to Andrew Johnson," *North Carolina Historical Review* 28 (Oct. 1951):504–505, and 29 (Apr. 1952):264–268; Dykeman, *French Broad*, 129–31; Paludan, *Victims*, 57–58.

131. Sadie Smathers Patton, *The Story of Henderson County* (Asheville, N.C.: Miller Printing, 1947), 126; B.M. Edney to John W. Ellis, 20 May 1861, John W. Ellis Governor's Papers, NCDAH.

132. Jones, *Knocking at the Door*, 5; Hughes, *Hendersonville in Civil War Times*, 10.

133. See, e.g., a letter from a Haywood County farmer, *Raleigh Register*, 23 Feb. 1861.

134. Sheppard, *Cabins in the Laurel*, 65.

Epilogue

1. Taylor, *Alleghania*, v, 15–16, 1–2.

2. Ibid., 17.

3. Ibid., 17–18. In fairness, he did have and did use many more tangible signs of early disaffection and potential "counterrevolution" in East Tennessee and what would become West Virginia.

4. Paul D. Escott's latest works provide perhaps the most thorough and best documented treatment of disaffection in both North Carolina and the Confederacy. See Escott, *After Secession: Jefferson Davis and the Failure of Confederate Nationalism* (Baton Rouge: Louisiana State Univ. Press, 1978), esp. ch. 4; Escott, "The Failure of Confederate Nationalism: The Old South's Class System in the Crucible of War," in *The Old South in the Crucible of War*, ed. Harry P. Owens and James J. Cooke (Jackson: Univ. Press of Mississippi, 1983), 15–28;

Escott, "The Moral Economy of the Crowd in Confederate North Carolina," *Maryland Historian* 13 (Spring/Summer 1982): 1–17; and Escott, *Many Excellent People*, chs. 2 and 3. See also Georgia Lee Tatum, *Disloyalty in the Confederacy* (Chapel Hill: Univ. of North Carolina Press, 1934).

5. James Whitaker to unknown person, 3 June 1861, James Whitaker Papers, Duke.

6. Samuel A'Court Ashe, *History of North Carolina*, vol. 2 (Raleigh, N.C.: Edwards and Broughton, 1925), 661.

7. Griffin, *History of Old Tryon and Rutherford Counties*, 250–51.

8. Cotton, "Appalachian North Carolina," 86.

9. Russell, "William Holland Thomas," 337; William Enloe and J. Ramsey Dills to John Ellis, 28 June 1861, in Tolbert, *Ellis Papers*, vol. 2, 874.

10. *Rutherfordton Press*, 5 June 1861, quoted in Griffin, *History of Old Tryon and Rutherford Counties*, 251.

11. Davidson, "Carolina Mountaineer," 84–85.

12. For a biographical sketch of Allen T. Davidson, see Sondley, *Asheville and Buncombe County*, vol. 2, pp. 742–43.

Bibliography

I. Primary Sources

A. MANUSCRIPTS

Duke University Manuscript Collection:

Daniel M. Barringer Papers	Samuel Finley Patterson Papers
Daniel W. Bell Papers	Charles W. Reese Papers
Tod R. Caldwell Papers	John W. Reese Papers
Thomas L. Clingman Papers	Charles Rothrock Papers
Corpening Family Papers	William L. Scott Papers
William C. Daily Journal	Samuel P. Sherrill Account Books
George W. Hendrix Papers	William Holland Thomas Papers
Johnson W. King Diary	Bryan Tyson Papers
Thomas Lenoir Papers	James Whitaker Papers
Matthew N. Love Papers	

North Carolina Department of Archives and History:

Avery Family Papers	Gash Family Papers
W. Vance Brown Papers	Mary Gash & Family Papers
Joseph Cathey Papers	James Gordon Hackett Collection
Walter Clark Papers	Willie P. Mangum Papers
Katherine Clark Pendleton Conway Collection	David S. Reid—Governor's Papers
	Dr. John Scott Papers
County Slave Records: Ashe, Buncombe, Burke, Caldwell, Henderson, McDowell, Wilkes	David L. Swain Papers
	Zebulon B. Vance—Governor's Papers
Calvin J. Cowles Papers	Calvin H. Wiley Papers
Allen T. Davidson and Theodore F. Davidson Papers	

[315]

Southern Historical Collection, University of North Carolina at Chapel Hill:

Hamilton Brown Papers
Ralph P. Buxton Papers
David F. Caldwell Papers
Tod R. Caldwell Papers
Clingman-Puryear Papers
Calvin J. Cowles Papers
George Phifer Erwin Papers
William C. Erwin Account Book
William Glenny French's
    Recollection of Valle Crucis
William Gaston Papers
Gudger-Love Papers
James Gwyn Books
George F.P. Harper Diaries
James Harper Diaries
John Hewitt Memoir
Hoke Papers
Thomas D. Johnston Papers
Jones and Patterson Family Papers

Edmund Walter Jones Papers
Lenoir Family Papers
Lyle-Siler Family Papers
Ezekiel Henry McClure Papers
Thomas David Smith McDowell
    Papers
Miscellaneous Letters
Elisha Mitchell Papers
Theodore Davidson Morrison
    Papers
James W. Patton Papers
Thomas Settle Papers
John McKee Sharpe Papers
Jacob Siler Papers
Jesse R. Siler Papers
David L. Swain Papers
Col. Thomas George Walton Papers
James Watson Collection

Special Collections, Western Carolina University:

Beal-Siler Family Papers
Penland Family Papers
William W. Stringfield Papers

James W. Terrell Papers
William Walker Papers

Others:

Avery Family Letters, Owned by Priscilla Schoenen, Morganton, N.C.
Isaac Avery Letters, Owned by Mrs. Cliff Avery, Morganton, N.C.
Civil War Papers, Pack Memorial Library, Asheville, N.C.
James Logan Greenlee Letters, Davidsoniana Collection, Davidson College,
    Davidson, N.C.
Robert Henry Manuscript Collection, Pack Memorial Library, Asheville,
    N.C.
David L. Swain Epistolary Correspondence, North Carolina Collection,
    University of North Carolina at Chapel Hill

B. PUBLISHED

Avery, Myron H. and Kenneth S. Boardman, eds. "Arnold Guyot's Notes
    on the Geography of the Mountain District of Western North Carolina."
    North Carolina Historical Review 15 (July 1938): 251–318.
Bailey, Lloyd, ed. *News from Yancey: Articles from Area Newspapers, 1840–1900.*
    Burnsville, N.C.: Yancey Graphics, 1983.
Battle, Kemp P. *Memories of an Old-Time Tar Heel.*Edited by William J. Battle.
    Chapel Hill: Univ. of North Carolina Press, 1945.

Beveridge, Charles E., ed. *The Papers of Frederick Law Olmsted*. Vol. 2: *Slavery and the South, 1852–1857*. Baltimore: Johns Hopkins Univ. Press, 1981.

Brownlow, William G. *Sketches of the Rise, Progress, and Decline of Secession*. Philadelphia: George W. Childs, 1862.

Buckingham, James S. *The Slave States of America*. Vol. 2. London and Paris: Fisher, Son & Co., 1842.

Burson, William. *A Race For Liberty; or My Capture, Imprisonment and Escape*. Wellsville, Ohio: W.G. Forester, 1867.

Catterall, Helen T., ed. *Judicial Cases Concerning Slavery and the Negro*. Vol. 2. Washington: Carnegie Institution, 1929.

Clingman, Thomas L. *Selections from the Speeches and Writings of Hon. Thomas L. Clingman of North Carolina*. Raleigh, N.C.: John Nichols, 1844.

Colton, Henry E. *Guidebook to the Scenery of Western North Carolina*. Asheville: Western Advocate Office, 1860.

————. *Mountain Scenery: The Scenery of the Mountains of Western North Carolina and Northwestern South Carolina*. Philadelphia: Hayes and Zell, 1859.

————. "Picturesque America: On the French Broad River, North Carolina." *Appleton's Journal* 4 (17 Dec. 1870).

Cooper, Susan Fenimore, ed. *William West Skiles: A Sketch of Missionary Life at Valle Crucis, 1840–1862*. New York: Pott, 1890.

Crayon, Porte. *The Old South Illustrated*. Edited by Cecil D. Eby, Jr. Chapel Hill: Univ. of North Carolina Press, 1959.

Davidson, Allen T. "Reminiscences of Western North Carolina." *Lyceum* 1 (Jan. 1891).

Davis, Rebecca Harding. "By-Paths in the Mountains." *Harper's New Monthly Magazine* 61 (July, Aug., Sept. 1880).

Disturnell, John. *Springs, Waterfalls, Sea-bathing Resorts and Mountain Scenery: Of the United States and Canada*. New York: J. Disturnell, 1855.

Drake, J. Madison. *Fast and Loose in Dixie*. New York: Author's Publishing Co., 1880.

Dunmond, Dwight L., ed. *Southern Editorials on Secession*. New York: Century, 1931.

Featherstonhaugh, George W. *A Canoe Voyage Up the Minnay Sotor*. Vol. 2. London: R. Bentley, 1847.

Goe, J.S. "Sheep and the Mountains of North Carolina." *North Carolina Planter* 3 (Mar. 1860):90.

Hamilton, J.G. de Roulhac, ed. *The Papers of Randolph Abbott Shotwell*. Vols. 1 and 2. Raleigh: North Carolina Historical Commission, 1929–1931.

————, ed. *The Papers of Thomas Ruffin*. Vol. 2. Raleigh: Edwards and Broughton, 1920.

Hamilton, J.G. de Roulhac, and Williams, Max R., eds. *The Papers of William Alexander Graham*. 5 vols. Raleigh: North Carolina Dept. of Archives and History, 1973.

Harvey, Will Wallace. "A Strange Land and Peculiar People." *Lippincott's Magazine* 12 (Oct. 1873):429–38.

Hesseltine, William B., ed. *Three Against Lincoln: Murat Halstead Reports the Caucuses of 1860*. Baton Rouge: Louisiana State Univ. Press, 1960.

Hickerson, Thomas Felix, ed. *Echoes of Happy Valley: Letters and Diaries, Family Life in the South, Civil War History*. Chapel Hill, N.C.: Privately published, 1962.

_____, ed. *Happy Valley History and Geneology*. Chapel Hill, N.C.: Privately published, 1940.

Johnston, Frontis W., ed. *The Papers of Zebulon Baird Vance*. Vol. 1: *1843–1862*. Raleigh: North Carolina Dept. of Archives and History, 1963.

Jones, Alexander H. *Knocking at the Door*. Washington, D.C.: McGill and Witherow, 1866.

Lanman, Charles., *Letters From the Alleghany Mountains*. New York: G.P. Putnam, 1849.

Malet, William W., *An Errand to the South in the Summer of 1862*. London: R. Bentley, 1863.

Michaux, Francois André. *Travels to the Westward of the Alleghany Mountains* (London: Richard Phillips, 1805). Reprinted in *Early Western Travels, 1748–1846*, edited by Reuben G. Thwaite. Cleveland, Ohio: Arthur H. Clark, 1904.

Newsome, A.R., ed. "A.S. Merrimon Journal, 1853–54." *North Carolina Historical Review* 8 (July 1931): 300–330.

Olmsted, Frederick Law. *The Cotton Kingdom*. New York: Mason Bros., 1861.

_____. *A Journey in the Back Country in the Winter of 1853–54*. New York: Mason Bros., 1860. Rpt. ed., G.P. Putnam, 1907.

_____. *A Journey in the Seaboard Slave States*. New York: Dix & Edwards, 1856.

Olsen, Otto H., and Ellen Z. McGrew, eds. "Prelude to Reconstruction: The Correspondence of State Senator Leander Sams Gash, 1866–67," pt. 1. *North Carolina Historical Review* 60 (Jan. 1983): 37–88.

Ralph, Julian. *Dixie: Or Southern Scenes and Sketches*. New York: Harper and Bros., 1896.

Rawick, George P., ed. *The American Slave: A Composite Autobiography*. Vol. 14: *North Carolina Narratives*, pt. 1. Westport, Conn.: Greenwood, 1972.

Ray, James M. "Reminiscences of Forty Years Ago." *Lyceum* 1 (Dec. 1890).

Richardson, Albert D. *The Secret Service, the Field, the Dungeon, and the Escape*. Hartford, Conn.: American, 1865.

Scott, W.L. "The Black Mountain and Its Surroundings." In *Sterling's Southern Fifth Reader*, edited by Richard Sterling. New York: Owens and Agar, 1866.

Shanks, Henry T., ed. *The Papers of Willie Person Mangum*. Vols. 4–6. Raleigh: North Carolina Dept. of Archives and History, 1956.

Steiner, Bernard C., ed. "The South Atlantic States in 1833, As Seen by a New Englander [Henry Barnard]." *Maryland Historical Magazine* 13 (Sept. 1918): 267–94.

Steward, Austin. *Twenty-two Years a Slave and Forty Years a Freeman*. Rochester, N.Y.: Allings & Cory, 1859.

Taylor, James W. *Alleghania: A Geographical and Statistical Memoir*. St. Paul, Minn.: James Davenport, 1862.

Tolbert, Noble J., ed. *The Papers of John Willis Ellis*. Vol. 1: *1841–1859*. Raleigh: North Carolina Dept. of Archives and History, 1964.

Wagstaff, H.M., ed. *Minutes of the N.C. Manumission Society, 1816–1834*. James Sprunt Historical Studies, vol. 22, nos. 1–2. Chapel Hill: Univ. of North Carolina Press, 1934.

Warner, Charles D. *On Horseback: A Tour in Virginia, North Carolina and Tennessee*. Boston: Houghton Mifflin, 1888.

Wheeler, John H. *Historical Sketches of North Carolina from 1584 to 1851*. Vol. 1. Philadelphia: Lippincott, Grambo, 1851.

Woodward, C. Vann, ed. *Mary Chesnut's Civil War*. New Haven: Yale Univ. Press, 1981.

Yearns, W. Buck, and John G. Barrett, eds. *North Carolina War Documentary*. Chapel Hill: Univ. of North Carolina Press, 1980.

Zeigler, Wilbur G., and Ben S. Grosscup. *The Heart of the Alleghanies or Western North Carolina*. Raleigh: Alfred Williams, 1883.

C. NEWSPAPERS AND JOURNALS
Asheville News
Asheville Spectator
Asheville Weekly Citizen
Carolina Watchman (Salisbury)
Franklin Observer
Highland Messenger (Asheville)
Hillsborough Recorder
Knoxville Whig
North Carolina Standard (Raleigh)
North Carolina Planter
Raleigh Register
Raleigh Standard
Western Carolinian (Salisbury)

II. Secondary Sources

A. BOOKS
Alexander, Nancy. *Here Will I Dwell: The Story of Caldwell County*. Salisbury, N.C.: Rowan Printing, 1956.

Allen, W.C. *Annals of Haywood County*. Spartanburg, S.C.: Reprint Co., 1935, rptd. 1977.

Ammons, John. *Outlines of History of the French Broad Association and Mars Hill College*. Raleigh, N.C.: Edwards and Broughton, n.d.

Arthur, John P. *A History of Watauga County, North Carolina, with Sketches of Prominent Families.* Richmond: Everett Waddey, 1915.

_____. *Western North Carolina: A History From 1730 to 1913.* Raleigh: Edwards and Broughton, 1914.

Ashe, Samuel D'Court. *History of North Carolina.* Vol. 2. Raleigh, N.C.: Edwards and Broughton, 1925.

Atherton, Lewis E. *The Southern Country Store, 1800–1860.* Baton Rouge: Louisiana State Univ. Press, 1949.

Bailey, Fred A. *Class and Tennessee's Confederate Generation.* Chapel Hill: Univ. of North Carolina Press, 1987.

Bailyn, Bernard. *The Ideological Origins of the American Revolution.* Cambridge, Mass.: Harvard Univ. Press, 1967.

Barney, William L. *The Road to Secession: A New Perspective On the Old South.* New York: Praeger, 1972.

_____. *The Secessionist Impulse: Alabama and Mississippi in 1860.* Princeton, N.J.: Princeton Univ. Press, 1974.

Barrett, John G., *The Civil War in North Carolina.* Chapel Hill: Univ. of North Carolina Press, 1963.

_____, *North Carolina as a Civil War Battleground, 1861–1865.* Raleigh: North Carolina Dept. of Archives and History, 1980.

Bassett, John Spencer. *The Congressional Career of Thomas L. Clingman.* Trinity College Historical Papers, ser. 4. Durham, N.C.: Trinity College Historical Society, 1900.

Beaver, Patricia D. *Rural Community in the Appalachian South.* Lexington: Univ. Press of Kentucky, 1986.

Bergeron, Paul H. *Antebellum Politics in Tennessee.* Lexington: Univ. Press of Kentucky, 1982.

Berlin, Ira. *Slaves Without Masters: The Free Negro in the Antebellum South.* New York: Random House, 1974.

Billings, Dwight B., Jr. *Planters and the Making of a "New South": Class, Politics and Development in North Carolina, 1865–1900.* Chapel Hill: Univ. of North Carolina Press, 1979.

Blackmun, Ora. *Western North Carolina: Its Mountains and Its People to 1880.* Boone, N.C.: Appalachian Consortium Press, 1977.

Blethen, H. Tyler, and Curtis Wood. *From Ulster to Carolina: The Migration of the Scotch-Irish to Southwestern North Carolina.* Cullowhee, N.C.: Mountain Heritage Center, Western Carolina Univ., 1983.

Boles, John B. *Black Southerners, 1619–1869.* Lexington: Univ. Press of Kentucky, 1984.

Boney, F.N. *Southerners All.* Macon, Ga.: Mercer Univ.Press, 1984.

Boyd, William K. *The History of North Carolina: The Federal Period.* Chicago: Lewis Publishing Co, 1919.

Boykin, James H. *North Carolina in 1861.* New York: Bookman Assoc., 1961.

Brock, William R. *Conflict and Transformation: The United States, 1844–1877.* (Kingsport, Tenn.: Kingsport Press, 1973.)

Browder, Nathaniel C. *The Cherokee Indians and Those Who Came After: Notes for a History of Cherokee County, North Carolina, 1835–1860*. Hayesville, N.C.: Privately published, 1973.

Brown, Cecil K. *The State Highway System of North Carolina: Its Evolution and Present Status*. Chapel Hill: Univ. of North Carolina Press, 1931.

_____. *A State Movement in Railroad Development: The Story of North Carolina's First Effort to Establish an East and West Trunk Line Railroad*. Chapel Hill: Univ. of North Carolina Press, 1928.

Burnett, Fred M. *This Was My Valley*. Ridgecrest, N.C.: Heritage Printers, 1960.

Burnham, W. Dean. *Presidental Ballots, 1836–1892*. Baltimore: Johns Hopkins Univ. Press, 1955.

Burton, Orville Vernon. *In My Father's House Are Many Mansions: Family and Community in Edgefield, South Carolina*. Chapel Hill: Univ. of North Carolina Press, 1985.

Burton, Orville V., and Robert C. McMath, Jr., eds.. *Toward a New South: Studies in Post-Civil War Southern Communities*. Westport, Conn.: Greenwood, 1982.

Campbell, John C. *The Southern Highlander and His Homeland*. New York: Russell Sage Foundation, 1921.

Campbell, Mary E.R. *The Attitude of Tennesseans Toward the Union, 1847–1861*. New York: Vantage,1961.

Cash, W. J. *The Mind of the South*. New York: Knopf, 1941.

Cathey, Cornelius O. *Agricultural Developments in North Carolina, 1783–1860*. Chapel Hill: Univ. of North Carolina Press, 1956.

_____. *Agriculture in North Carolina Before the Civil War*. Raleigh: North Carolina Dept. of Archives and History, 1974.

Caudill, Harry M. *Night Comes to the Cumberlands: A Biography of a Depressed Region*. Boston: Little, Brown, 1962.

Censer, Jane T. *North Carolina Planters and Their Children 1800–1860*. Baton Rouge: Louisiana State Univ. Press, 1984.

Chambers, Joseph Lenoir. *The Breed and the Pasture*. Charlotte, N.C.: Stone and Barringer, 1910.

Channing, Steven A. *Crisis of Fear: Secession in South Carolina*. New York: Simon and Schuster, 1970.

Clark, Thomas D., ed. *Travels in The Old South: A Bibliography. Vol. 3*. Norman: Univ. of Oklahoma Press, 1959.

Cochran, Weimer. *Nantahala People and Events*. Berea, Ky.: Berea College Appalachian Center, 1987.

Collins, Bruce. *White Society in the Antebellum South*. London: Longman, 1985.

Connor, R.D.W., ed. *A Manual of North Carolina*. Raleigh: E.M. Uzzell, 1913.

_____. *North Carolina: Rebuilding An Ancient Common-wealth: 1584–1925. Vol. 2*. Chicago: American Historical Society, 1929.

Cooper, Horton. *History of Avery County, North Carolina*. Asheville, N.C.: Biltmore Press, 1964.

Cooper, William J., Jr. *Liberty and Slavery: Southern Politics to 1860*. New York: Knopf, 1983.

————. *The South and the Politics of Slavery, 1828–1856*. Baton Rouge: Louisiana Univ. Press, 1978.

Corbitt, David L. *The Formation of the North Carolina Counties, 1663–1943*. Raleigh: North Carolina Dept. of Archives and History, 1950.

Coulter, E. Merton. *William G. Brownlow: Fighting Parson of the Southern Highlands*. Chapel Hill: Univ. of North Carolina Press, 1937.

Craven, Avery O. *The Growth of Southern Nationalism, 1848–1861*. Baton Rouge: Louisiana State Univ. Press, 1953.

Crenshaw, Ollinger. *The Slave States in the Presidential Election of 1860*. Johns Hopkins Univ. Studies in Historical and Political Science, ser. 63, no. 3. Baltimore: Johns Hopkins Univ. Press, 1945.

Crofts, Daniel W. *Reluctant Confederates: Upper South Unionists in the Secession Crisis*. Chapel Hill: Univ. of North Carolina Press, 1989.

Crow, Vernon H. *Storm in the Mountains: Thomas' Confederate Legion of Cherokee Indians and Mountaineers*. Cherokee, N.C.: Press of the Museum of the Cherokee Indian, 1982.

Davidson, Theodore F., *Reminiscences and Traditions of Western North Carolina*. Asheville: Service Printing, 1928.

Degler, Carl N. *The Other South: Southern Dissenters in the Nineteenth Century*. Boston: Northeastern Univ. Press, 1982.

————. *Place Over Time: The Continuity of Southern Distinctiveness*. Baton Rouge: Louisiana State Univ. Press, 1977.

Donald, David. *Looking Homeward: A Life of Thomas Wolfe*. Boston: Little, Brown, 1987.

Dowd, Clement. *The Life of Zebulon B. Vance*. Charlotte, N.C.: Observer Printing and Publishing, 1897.

Drake, Richard B. *Mountaineers and Americans*. Berea, Ky.: Berea College Press, 1976.

Duggar, Shepherd M. *War Trails of the Blue Ridge*. Banner Elk, N.C.: Puddingstone Press, 1932, rptd. 1974.

Dumond, Dwight L. *The Secession Movement, 1860–1861*. New York: Macmillan, 1931.

Dykeman, Wilma. *The French Broad*. New York: Rinehart, 1955.

Eller, Ronald D. *Miners, Millhands and Mountaineers: Industrialization of the Appalachian South, 1880–1930*. Knoxville: Univ. of Tennessee Press, 1982.

Escott, Paul D. *After Secession: Jefferson Davis and the Failure of Confederate Nationalism*. Baton Rouge: Louisiana State Univ. Press, 1978.

————. *Many Excellent People: Power and Privilege in North Carolina, 1850–1900*. Chapel Hill: Univ. of North Carolina Press, 1985.

Fain, James T., Jr. *A Partial History of Henderson County*. New York: Arno, 1980.

Faust, Drew Gilpin, ed., *The Ideology of Slavery: Proslavery Thought in the Antebellum South, 1830–1860*. Baton Rouge: Louisiana State Univ. Press, 1981.

Fehrenbacher, Don E. *The Dred Scott Case: Its Significance in American Law and Politics.* New York: Oxford Univ. Press, 1978.

————. *The South and Three Sectional Crises.* Baton Rouge: Louisiana State Univ. Press, 1980.

Finkelman, Paul. *Slavery in the Courtroom: An Annotated Bibliography of American Cases.* Washington, D.C.: Library of Congress, 1985.

Fletcher, Arthur L. *Ashe County: A History.* Jefferson, N.C.: Ashe County Research Association, 1963.

Foner, Eric. *Free Soil, Free Labor, Free Men: The Ideology of the Republican Party before the Civil War.* New York: Oxford Univ. Press, 1970.

Ford, Thomas R., ed.. *The Southern Appalachian Region: A Survey.* Lexington: Univ. Press of Kentucky, 1962.

Fossett, Mildred B. *History of McDowell County.* Marion, N.C.: McDowell County American Revolution Bicentennial Commission Heritage Committee, 1976.

Fox, John, Jr., *Blue-Grass and Rhododendron: Out-doors in Kentucky.* London: Archibald Constable, 1905.

Franklin, John H. *The Free Negro in North Carolina, 1790–1860.* Chapel Hill: Univ. of North Carolina Press, 1943.

Fredrickson, George. *The Black Image in the White Mind: The Debate on Afro-American Character and Destiny, 1817–1914.* New York: Harper and Row, 1971.

Freel, Margaret Walker. *Our Heritage: The People of Cherokee County, North Carolina, 1540–1955.* Asheville: Miller Printing, 1956.

————. *Unto the Hills.* Andrews, N.C.: Privately published, 1976.

Genovese, Eugene D. *The Political Economy of Slavery: Studies in the Economy and Society of the Slave South.* New York: Pantheon, 1965.

————. *Roll, Jordan, Roll: The World the Slaves Made.* New York: Pantheon, 1974.

Ginns, Patsy Moore. *Rough Weather Makes Good Timber: Carolinians Recall.* Chapel Hill: Univ. of North Carolina Press, 1977.

Gray, Lewis C. *History of Agriculture in the Southern United States to 1860.* Vol. 1. Washington, D.C.: Carnegie Institution, 1933.

Gray, Sam, ed., *The Many Faces of Appalachia: Exploring a Region's Diversity.* Boone, N.C.: Appalachian Consortium Press, 1985.

Greenberg, Kenneth S. *Masters and Statesmen: The Political Culture of American Slavery.* Baltimore: Johns Hopkins Univ. Press, 1985.

Griffin, Clarence W. *The History of Old Tryon and Rutherford Counties, 1730–1930.* Asheville, N.C.: Miller Printing, 1937.

Hahn, Steven. *The Roots of Southern Populism: Yeomen Farmers and the Transformation of the Georgia Backcountry, 1850–1900.* New York: Oxford Univ. Press, 1983.

Hamilton, Holman. *Prologue to Conflict: The Crisis and Compromise of 1850.* Lexington: Univ. of Kentucky Press, 1964.

Hamilton, J.G. de Roulhac. *Party Politics in North Carolina, 1835–1860*. James Sprunt Historical Publications, vol. 15, nos. 1 and 2. Chapel Hill: Univ. of North Carolina, 1916.

Harper, Margaret E. *Fort Defiance and the General*. Hickory, N.C.: Clay Printing, 1976.

Harris, J. William. *Plain Folk and Gentry in a Slave Society: White Liberty and Black Slavery in Augusta's Hinterlands*. Middleton, Conn.: Wesleyan Univ. Press, 1985.

Hayes, Johnson J. *The Land of Wilkes*. Wilkesboro, N.C.: Wilkes County Historical Society, 1962.

Hicks, George L. *Appalachian Valley*. New York: Holt, Rinehart and Winston, 1976.

Higgins, Jody, ed.. *Common Times: A Written and Pictorial History of Yancey County*. Burnsville, N.C.: Yancey Graphics, 1981.

Higgs, Robert J., ed. *Voices from the Hills: Selected Readings on Southern Appalachia*. New York: Unger, 1975.

Hill, Daniel H. *North Carolina in the War Between the States*. Vol. 1: *Bethel to Sharpsburg*. Raleigh: Edwards and Broughton, 1926.

Hilliard, Sam B. *Hog Meat and Hoecake: Food Supply in the Old South, 1840–1860*. Carbondale: Southern Illinois Univ. Press, 1972.

Holt, Michael F. *The Political Crisis of the 1850s*. New York: Norton, 1978.

Hughes, N. Collin. *Hendersonville in Civil War Times*. Hendersonville, N.C.: Privately published, 1936.

Humes, Thomas W. *The Loyal Mountaineers of Tennessee*. Knoxville: Ogden Bros., 1888.

Johnson, Guion G. *Ante-Bellum North Carolina: A Social History*. Chapel Hill: Univ. of North Carolina Press, 1937.

Johnson, Michael P. *Toward a Patriarchal Republic: The Secession of Georgia*. Baton Rouge: Louisiana State Univ. Press, 1977.

Kenzer, Robert C. *Kinship and Neighborhood in a Southern Community: Orange County, North Carolina, 1849–1881*. Knoxville: Univ. of Tennessee Press, 1988.

Kephart, Horace. *Our Southern Highlanders*. New York: Macmillan, 1913; rev. ed., 1941.

Konkle, Burton A. *John Motley Morehead and the Development of North Carolina, 1796–1866*. Philadelphia: William J. Campbell, 1922.

Kruman, Marc W. *Parties and Politics in North Carolina, 1836–1865*. Baton Rouge: Louisiana State Univ. Press, 1983.

Lefler, Hugh T. *North Carolina History Told By Contemporaries*. Chapel Hill: Univ. of North Carolina Press, 1948.

Lewis, Ronald L. *Black Coal Miners in America: Race, Class, and Community Conflict*. Lexington: Univ. Press of Kentucky, 1987.

————. *Coal, Iron, and Slaves: Industrial Slavery in Maryland and Virginia, 1715–1865*. Westport, Conn.: Greenwood, 1979.

Lovin, Clifford R., ed. *Our Mountain Heritage: Essays on the Natural and Cul-*

tural History of Western North Carolina. Cullowhee, N.C.: Mountain Heritage Center, Western Carolina Univ., 1979.

Marsh, Blanche. *Historic Flat Rock*. Asheville: Biltmore Press, 1961.

McCormick, James G. *Personnel of the Convention of 1861*. James Sprunt Historical Monograph, no. 1. Chapel Hill: Univ. of North Carolina, 1900.

McFarland, Betty. *Sketches of Early Watauga*. Boone N.C.: The Branch, 1973.

McKinney, Gordon B. *Southern Mountain Republicans, 1865–1900: Politics and the Appalachian Community*. Chapel Hill: Univ. of North Carolina Press, 1978.

McLeod, John Angus. *From These Stones: Mars Hill College, 1856–1968*. Mars Hill, N.C.: Mars Hill College, 1968.

Medford, W. Clark. *The Early History of Haywood County*. Asheville: Miller Printing, 1961.

Mitchell, Broadus. *Frederick Law Olmsted: A Critic of the Old South*. Johns Hopkins Univ. Studies in History and Political Science, vol. 42. Baltimore: Johns Hopkins Univ. Press, 1924.

Mitchell, Robert D. *Commercialism and Frontier: Perspectives on the Early Shenandoah Valley*. Charlottesville: Univ. Press of Virginia, 1977.

Morley, Margaret W. *The Carolina Mountains*. Boston: Houghton Mifflin, 1913.

Norton, Clarence C. *The Democratic Party in Ante-Bellum North Carolina, 1835–1861*. Chapel Hill: Univ. of North Carolina Press, 1930.

Oakes, James. *The Ruling Race: A History of American Slaveholders*. New York: Knopf, 1982.

Owsley, Frank Lawrence. *Plain Folk of the Old South*. Baton Rouge: Louisiana State Univ. Press, 1949.

Paludan, Phillip S. *Victims: A True Story of the Civil War*. Knoxville: Univ. of Tennessee Press, 1981.

Patton, Sadie Smathers. *The Story of Henderson County*. Asheville: Miller Printing, 1947.

Pearsall, Marion. *Little Smoky Ridge: The Natural History of a Southern Appalachian Neighborhood*. University, Ala.: Univ. of Alabama Press, 1959.

Pegg, Herbert D. *The Whig Party in North Carolina*. Chapel Hill: Colonial Press, 1968.

Phifer, Edward W., Jr. *Burke: The History of a North Carolina County, 1777–1920, with a Glimpse Beyond*. Morganton, N.C.: Privately published, 1977.

Phillips, Robert B. *One of God's Children in Toe River Valley*. Bakersville, N.C.: Privately published, 1983.

Phillips, Ulrich Bonnell. *Life and Labor in the Old South*. Boston: Little, Brown, 1929; rptd. 1963.

Potter, David M. *The Impending Crisis, 1848–1861*. New York: Harper and Row, 1976.

_____. *Lincoln and His Party in the Secession Crisis*. New Haven: Yale Univ. Press, 1942.

Powers, Elizabeth D. and Mark E. Hannah. *Cataloochee: Lost Settlement of the Smokies*. Charleston, S.C.: Powers-Hannah Publishers, 1982.

Raine, James W. *The Land of Saddle-bags: A Study of the Mountain People of Appalachia*. New York: Council of Women for Home Missions and Missionary Education Movement of the U.S. and Canada, 1924.

Ready, Milton. *Asheville, Land of the Sky: An Illustrated History*. Northridge, Cal.: Windsor Publications, 1986.

Reid, Paul A. *Gubernatorial Campaigns and Administrations of David S. Reid, 1848–1854*. Cullowhee, N.C.: Western Carolina College, 1953.

Roberts, Derrill C. *Joseph E. Brown and the Politics of Reconstruction*. University, Ala.: Univ. of Alabama Press, 1973.

Rogers, Lou. *Tar Heel Women*. Raleigh, N.C.: Edward and Broughton, 1949.

Roper, Laura Wood. *FLO: A Biography of Frederick Law Olmsted*. Baltimore: Johns Hopkins Univ. Press, 1973.

Schwarzkopf, S. Kent. *A History of Mt. Mitchell and the Black Mountains: Exploration, Development, and Preservation*. Raleigh: North Carolina Division of Archives and History, 1985.

Shackelford, Laurel, and Bill Weinberg, eds. *Our Appalachia: An Oral History*. New York: Hill and Wang, 1977.

Shapiro, Henry D. *Appalachia on our Mind: The Southern Mountains and Mountaineers in the American Consciousness*. Chapel Hill: Univ. of North Carolina Press, 1978.

Shepherd, Ruth W., ed. *The Heritage of Ashe County, North Carolina*. Winston-Salem, N.C.: Hunter Printing, 1984.

Sheppard, Muriel E., *Cabins in the Laurel*. Chapel Hill: Univ. of North Carolina Press, 1935.

Shields, Joanna Nicol. *The Line of Duty: Maverick Congressmen and the Development of American Political Culture, 1836–1860*. Westport, Conn.: Greenwood Press, 1985.

Shore, Laurence. *Southern Capitalists: The Ideological Leadership of an Elite, 1832–1885*. Chapel Hill: Univ. of North Carolina Press, 1986.

Sitterson, J. Carlyle. *The Secession Movement in North Carolina*. James Sprunt Studies in History and Political Science, vol. 23, no. 2. Chapel Hill: Univ. of North Carolina Press, 1939.

Smith, C.D., *A Brief History of Macon County, North Carolina*. Franklin, N.C.: Franklin Press, 1891.

Soltow, Lee. *Men and Wealth in the United States, 1850–1870*. New Haven, Conn.: Yale Univ. Press, 1975.

Sondley, F.A., *Asheville and Buncombe County*. 2 vols. Asheville, N.C.: Citizen Co., 1922.

Stampp, Kenneth. *The Peculiar Institution: Slavery in the Ante-Bellum South*. New York: Random House, 1956.

Starobin, Robert S., *Industrial Slavery in the Old South*. New York: Oxford Univ. Press, 1970.

Stephenson, John B. *Shiloh: A Mountain Community*. Lexington: Univ. Press of Kentucky, 1968.

Stowe, Steven M. *Intimacy and Power in the Old South: Ritual in the Lives of the Planters*. Baltimore: Johns Hopkins Univ. Press, 1987.

Swaim, Douglas. *Cabins and Castles: The History of Architecture of Buncombe*

County, North Carolina. Raleigh, N.C.: North Carolina Division of Archives and History, 1981.

Taylor, Rosser H., *Slaveholding in North Carolina: An Economic View*. James Sprunt Historical Publications, vol. 18. Chapel Hill: Univ. of North Carolina Press, 1926.

Temple, Oliver P. *East Tennessee and the Civil War*. Freeport, N.Y.: Books for Libraries Press, 1899, rptd. 1971.

Thornton, J. Mills, III. *Power and Politics in a Slave Society: Alabama, 1800–1860*. Baton Rouge: Louisiana State Univ. Press, 1978.

Todd, John Emerson. *Frederick Law Olmsted*. Boston: Twayne, 1982.

Tucker, Glenn. *Zeb Vance: Champion of Personal Freedom*. Indianapolis: Bobbs-Merrill, 1965.

Turner, William H., and Edward J. Cabbell, eds. *Blacks in Appalachia*. Lexington: Univ. Press of Kentucky, 1985.

Van Noppen, Ina W., and John J. Van Noppen. *Western North Carolina Since the Civil War*. Boone, N.C.: Appalachian Consortium Press, 1973.

Vance, Rupert B. *Human Geography of the South: A Study in Regional Resources and Human Adequacy*. Chapel Hill: Univ. of North Carolina Press, 1932.

Wade, Richard C. *Slavery in the Cities: The South, 1820–1860*. New York: Oxford Univ. Press, 1964.

Wagstaff, Henry G. *States Rights and Political Parties in North Carolina, 1776–1861*. Johns Hopkins Univ. Studies in Historical and Political Science. Baltimore: Johns Hopkins Univ. Press, 1906.

Ward, Doris Cline, ed. *The Heritage of Old Buncombe County*. vol. 1. Winston-Salem, N.C.: Hunter Publishing, 1981.

Watson, Harry L. *Jacksonian Politics and Community Conflict: The Emergence of the Second American Party System in Cumberland County, North Carolina*. Baton Rouge: Louisiana State Univ. Press, 1981.

Weaver, Charles Clinton. *Internal Improvements in North Carolina Prior to 1860*. Series 21, Historical and Political Science. Baltimore: Johns Hopkins Univ. Press, 1903.

Weller, Jack E. *Yesterday's People: Life in Contemporary Appalachia*. Lexington: Univ. of Kentucky Press, 1965.

Wellman, Manly Wade. *The Kingdom of Madison: A Southern Mountain Fastness and Its People*. Chapel Hill: Univ. of North Carolina Press, 1973.

Whitaker, Walter C. *The Southern Highlands and Highlanders*. Hartford, Conn.: Church Missions Publications, 1916.

Wiebe, Robert H. *The Opening of American Society From the Adoption of the Constitution to the Eve of Disunion*. New York: Vintage, 1984, rptd. 1985.

Wiener, Jonathan M. *Social Origins of the New South: Alabama, 1860–1885*. Baton Rouge: Louisiana State Univ. Press, 1978.

Williamson, J.W., ed. *An Appalachian Symposium*. Boone, N.C.: Appalachian Consortium Press, 1977.

Wilson, Samuel Tyndale. *The Southern Mountaineers*. New York: J.J. Little and Ives, 1914.

Wolfe, Thomas. *The Hills Beyond*. New York: New American Library, 1935, rptd. 1982.

Wood, Gordon S. *The Creation of the American Republic, 1776–1787*. Chapel Hill: Univ. of North Carolina Press, 1969.

Wooster, Ralph A. *The People in Power: Courthouse and Statehouse in the Lower South, 1850–1860*. Knoxville: Univ. of Tennessee Press, 1969.

————. *Politicians, Planters and Plain Folk: Courthouse and Statehouse in the Upper South, 1850–1860*. Knoxville: Univ. of Tennessee Press, 1975.

————. *The Secession Conventions of the South*. Princeton, N.J.: Princeton Univ. Press, 1962.

Wright, Gavin. *The Political Economy of the Cotton South: Households, Markets, and Wealth in the Nineteenth Century*. New York: Norton, 1978.

Wright, William C. *The Secession Movement in the Middle Atlantic States*. Rutherford, N.J.: Fairleigh Dickinson Univ. Press, 1973.

Wyatt-Brown, Bertram. *Southern Honor: Ethics and Behavior in the Old South*. New York: Oxford Univ. Press, 1982.

Yates, Richard E. *The Confederacy and Zeb Vance*. Tuscaloosa, Ala.: Confederate Publishing, 1958.

B. ARTICLES AND PAPERS

"The Age of the Drovers." *The State* 27 (25 July 1959): 11–12.

Arensberg, Conrad M. "American Communities." *American Anthropologist* 57 (Dec. 1955): 1143–62.

Bailey, Fred A. "Class and Tennessee's Confederate Generation." *Journal of Southern History* 51 (Feb. 1985): 31–60.

Barney, William L. "Toward the Civil War: The Dynamics of Change in a Black Belt Country." In *Class, Conflict, and Consensus: Antebellum Southern Community Studies,* edited by Orville V. Burton and Robert C. McMath, Jr., pp. 146–71. Westport, Conn.: Greenwood, 1982.

Baron, Hal Seth. "A Case for Appalachian Demographic History." *Appalachian Journal* 4 (Spring-Summer 1977), 208–15.

Beck, John J. "Building the New South: A Revolution from Above in a Piedmont County." *Journal of Southern History* 53 (Aug. 1987): 441–470.

Billings, Dwight, Kathleen Blee, and Louis Swanson. "Culture, Family, and Community in Preindustrial Appalachia." *Appalachian Journal* 13 (Winter 1986), 154–70.

Blaser, Kent. "North Carolina and John Brown's Raid." *Civil War History* 24 (Dec. 1978): 295–320.

Blethen, H. Tyler, and Curtis Wood. "Land and Family in the Tuckaseigee Valley, 1800–1850." Paper Delivered at Ninth Appalachian Studies Conference, Boone, N.C., Mar. 1986.

————. "A Trader on the Western Carolina Frontier: James Patton, 1783–1845," unpublished manuscript.

Blosser, Susan S. "Calvin J. Cowles's Gap Creek Mine: A Case Study of Mine Speculation in the Gilded Age." *North Carolina Historical Review* 51 (Oct. 1974): 379–400.

Brinkman, Leonard W. "Home Manufacturers as an Indication of an Emerging Appalachian Subculture, 1840–1870." *West Georgia College Studies in the Social Sciences* 12 (June 1973): 50–58.

Burnett, Edmund C. "Hog Raising and Hog Driving in the Region of the French Broad River." *Agricultural History* 20 (Apr. 1946): 86–103.

Butts, Donald C. "The 'Irrepressible Conflict': Slave Taxation and North Carolina's Gubernatorial Election of 1860." *North Carolina Historical Review* 58 (Jan. 1981): 44–66.

Cabbell, Edward J. "Black Diamonds: The Search for Blacks in Appalachian Literature and Writing." *Now and Then* 3 (Winter 1986): 11–13.

_____. "Black Invisibility and Racism in Appalachia." *Appalachian Journal* 8 (Autumn 1980): 48–54.

_____. "History Uncovers the Role of Black Appalachian Women." *Now and Then* 3 (Winter 1986): 13–15.

Campbell, Mrs. John C. "Flame of New Future for the Highlands." *Mountain Life and Work* 1 (Apr. 1925).

Carr, John W., Jr. "The Manhood Suffrage Movement in North Carolina." *Trinity College Historical Society Papers*, ser. 11 (1915).

Clark, Ernest James, Jr. "Aspects of the North Carolina Slave Code, 1815–1869." *North Carolina Historical Review* 39 (Spring 1962): 148–64.

Crawford, Martin. "Slaveholding and Power in the New River Valley: Ashe County, North Carolina, in 1860." In *Proceedings of the New River Symposium, May 1982*. Wheeling: National Park Service and West Virginia Dept. of Archives and History, 1983: 30–35.

Crofts, Daniel W. "The Union Party of 1861 and the Secession Crisis." *Perspectives in American History* 11 (1977–78): 327–76.

Dabbs, James M. "Beyond the Appalachians." *Appalachian Journal* 2 (Winter 1975): 86–96.

Davidson, Theodore F., "The Carolina Mountaineer: The Highest Type of American Character." *First Annual Transactions of the Pen and Plate Club of Asheville, N.C.* Asheville: Hackney and Mole, 1905.

Dedmond, Francis B. "Harvey Davis's Unpublished Civil War 'Diary' and the Story of Company D of the First North Carolina Cavalry." *Appalachian Journal* 13 (Summer 1986): 368–407.

Deyton, Jason Basil. "The Toe River Valley to 1865." *North Carolina Historical Review* 24 (Oct. 1947): 423–66.

Dickerson, Lynn. "Thomas Sutpen: Mountain Stereotypes in *Absalom, Absalom!*" *Appalachian Heritage* 12 (Spring 1984): 73–78.

Donnelly, William J. "Conspiracy or Popular Movement? The Historiography of Southern Support for Secession." *North Carolina Historical Review* 42 (Jan. 1965): 70–84.

Drake, Richard B. "Slavery and Antislavery in Appalachia." *Appalachian Heritage* 14 (Winter 1986): 25–33.

Dunbar, Gary S. "Silas McDowell and the Early Botanical Exploration of Western North Carolina." *North Carolina Historical Review* 41 (Autumn 1964): 425–35.

Durrill, Wayne K. "Producing Poverty: Local Government and Economic Development in a New South County, 1874–1884." *Journal of American History* 71 (Mar. 1985): 764–81.

Dykeman, Wilma. "Appalachia in Context," In *An Appalachian Symposium*, edited by J.W. Williamson. Boone, N.C.: Appalachian Consortium Press, 1977.

Eller, Ronald D. "Appalachian Oral History: New Directions for Regional Research." In *An Appalachian Symposium*, edited by J.W. Williamson. Boone, N.C.: Appalachian Consortium Press, 1977.

————. "Land and Family: An Historical View of Preindustrial Appalachia." *Appalachian Journal* 6 (Winter 1979): 83–110.

————. "The Search for Community in Appalachia." Keynote Address, Ninth Annual Appalachian Studies Conference, Boone, N.C., 21 Mar. 1986.

Elliott, Robert N. "The Nat Turner Insurrection as Reported in the North Carolina Press." *North Carolina Historical Review* 38 (Jan. 1961): 1–18.

Escott, Paul D. "The Failure of Confederate Nationalism: The Old South's Class System in the Crucible of War." In *The Old South in the Crucible of War*, edited by Harry P. Owens and James J. Cooke, pp. 15–28. Jackson: Univ. of Mississippi Press, 1983.

————. "Moral Economy of the Crowd in Confederate North Carolina." *Maryland Historian* 13 (Spring/Summer 1982): 1–17.

Finnie, Gordon E. "The Anti-Slavery Movement in the Upper South Prior to 1840." *Journal of Southern History* 35 (Aug. 1969): 329–30.

Ford, Lacy K. "Rednecks and Merchants: Economic Development and Social Tensions in the South Carolina Upcountry, 1865–1890." *Journal of American History* 71 (Sept. 1984): 294–318.

Franklin, John Hope. "The Free Negro in the Economic Life of Ante-Bellum North Carolina." *North Carolina Historical Review* 14 (July and Oct. 1942): 239–59, 359–75.

Frost, William G. "Our Contemporary Ancestors in the Southern Mountains." *Atlantic Monthly* 83 (Mar. 1899): 311–19.

Gallaher, Art, Jr. "The Community As a Setting for Change in Southern Appalachia." In *The Public University in Its Second Century*, edited by Lloyd Davis. Public Affairs Series, no. 5. Morgantown: West Virginia Center for Appalachian Studies and Development, 1967.

Gallman, Robert E. "Self-Sufficiency in the Cotton Economy of the Antebellum South." *Agricultural History* 44 (Jan. 1970): 5–23.

Gass, W. Conrad. "The Misfortunes of a High-Minded and Honorable Gentleman: W.W. Avery and the Southern Code of Honor." *North Carolina Historical Review* 56 (July 1979): 278–97.

Genovese, Eugene D. "Yeomen Farmers in a Slaveholders' Democracy." *Agricultural History* 49 (Apr. 1975): 331–42.

Gifford, James M. "Our Pioneer Heritage." In *Our Mountain Heritage*, edited by Clifford R. Lovin. Cullowhee, N.C.: Mountain Heritage Center, Western Carolina Univ., 1979.

Green, Fletcher M. "Democracy in the Old South." *Journal of Southern History* 12 (1946): 117–92.

————. "Gold Mining: A Forgotten Industry in Antebellum N.C." *North Carolina Historical Review* 14 (Jan. and April 1937): 1–19, 135–55.

Hahn, Steven. "The Yeomanry of the Nonplantation South: Upper Piedmont Georgia, 1850–1860." In *Class, Conflict, and Consensus: Antebellum Southern Community Studies*, edited by Orville V. Burton and Robert C. McMath, pp. 29–56. Wesport, Conn.: Greenwood, 1982.

Hamilton, J.G. de Roulhac. "Secession in North Carolina." In Daniel H. Hill, *North Carolina in the War Between the States*, vol. 1: *Bethel to Sharpsburg*, pp. 1–46. Raleigh: Edwards and Broughton, 1926.

Horton, Laurel. "Nineteenth Century Quilts in Macon County, North Carolina." In *The Many Faces of Appalachia: Exploring a Region's Diversity*, edited by Sam Gray, pp. 11–23. Boone, N.C.: Appalachian Consortium Press, 1985.

Howard, Victor B. "John Brown's Raid at Harper's Ferry and the Sectional Crisis in North Carolina." *North Carolina Historical Review* 55 (Oct. 1978): 396–420.

Inscoe, John C. "Faulkner, Race, and Appalachia." *South Atlantic Quarterly* 86 (Summer 1987): 244–53.

————. "Mountain Masters: Slaveholding in Western North Carolina." *North Carolina Historical Review* 61 (Apr. 1984): 143–73.

————. "Mountain Unionism, Secession, and Regional Self-Image: The Contrasting Cases of Western North Carolina and East Tennessee." In *Looking South: Chapters in the Story of an American Region*, edited by Winifred B. Moore and Joseph Tripp. Westport, Conn.: Greenwood, 1989.

————. "Olmsted in Appalachia: A Connecticut Yankee Encounters Slavery and Racism in the Southern Highlands, 1854." *Slavery & Abolition* 9 (Dec. 1988).

————. "Thomas Clingman, Mountain Whiggery, and the Southern Cause." *Civil War History* 33 (Mar. 1987): 42–62.

Jeffrey, Thomas E. "Beyond 'Free Suffrage': North Carolina Parties and the Convention Movement of the 1850s." *North Carolina Historical Review* 62 (Oct. 1985): 387–419.

————. "Internal Improvement and Political Parties in Antebellum North Carolina, 1836–1860." *North Carolina Historical Review* 55 (Apr. 1978): 111–56.

————. "National Issues, Local Interests, and the Transformation of Antebellum North Carolina Politics." *Journal of Southern History* 50 (Feb. 1984): 43–74.

————. "Thomas Lanier Clingman and the Invention of the Electric Light: A Forgotten Episode." *Carolina Comments* 32 (May 1984): 71–82.

————. " 'Thunder from the Mountains': Thomas Lanier Clingman and the End of Whig Supremacy in North Carolina." *North Carolina Historical Review* 56 (Oct. 1979): 366–95.

Jones, Loyal. "Appalachian Values," In *Voices from the Hills: Selected Readings of Southern Appalachia*, edited by Robert J. Higgs, pp. 507–17. New York: Ungar, 1975.

Johnson, Clifton H. "Abolitionist Missionary Activities in North Carolina." *North Carolina Historical Review* 40 (Jan. 1963): 295–320.

Johnson, Guion Griffis. "The Ante-Bellum Town in North Carolina." *North Carolina Historical Review* 5 (Oct. 1928): 372–89.

Johnson, Michael P. "Work, Culture, and the Slave Community: Slave Occupations in the Cotton Belt in 1860." *Labor History* 27 (Summer 1986): 325–49.

Johnston, Frontis W. "The Courtship of Zeb Vance." *North Carolina Historical Review* 31 (Apr. 1954): 222–39.

Kelly, James C. "William Gannaway Brownlow," pts. 1 and 2. *Tennessee Historical Quarterly* 43 (1984): 25–43, 155–72.

Klotter, James C. "The Black South and White Appalachia." *Journal of American History* 66 (Mar. 1980): 832–49.

Kruman, Marc W. "Thomas L. Clingman and the Whig Party: A Reconsideration." *North Carolina Historical Review* 64 (Jan. 1987): 1–18.

Lambert, Robert S. "The Oconaluftee Valley, 1800–1860: A Study of the Sources for Mountain History." *North Carolina Historical Review* 35 (Oct. 1958): 415–26.

London, Lawrence F. "George Edmund Badger and the Compromise of 1850." *North Carolina Historical Review* 15 (Jan. 1938): 1–22.

Mann, Ralph. "Isolation and the Social Economy of an Appalachian Community: Burkes Garden, Virginia, in the 1840s and 1850s." Paper Delivered at Fifth Citadel Conference on the South, Charleston, S.C., Apr. 1987.

————. "Master and Slave in the Other South." Paper Delivered at Conference for Carl Degler, Stanford Univ., May 1987.

McDonald, Forrest, and Grady McWhiney. "The Antebellum Southern Herdsman: A Reinterpretation." *Journal of Southern History* 41 (May 1975): 147–66.

McKinney, Gordon B. "Southern Mountain Republicans and the Negro, 1865–1900." *Journal of Southern History* 41 (Nov. 1975): 493–516.

McWhiney, Grady, and Forrest McDonald. "Celtic Origins of Southern Herding Practices." *Journal of Southern History* 51 (May 1985): 165–200.

Moore, James Tice. "Secession and the States: A Review Essay." *Virginia Magazine of History and Biography* 94 (Jan. 1986): 60–76.

Morrill, James R. "The Presidential Election of 1852: Death Knell of the Whig Party of North Carolina." *North Carolina Historical Review* 44 (Oct. 1967): 342–59.

Morrow, Ralph E. "The Proslavery Argument Revisited." *Mississippi Valley Historical Review* 48 (June 1961): 79–94.

Murphy, James B. "Slavery and Freedom in Appalachia: Kentucky as a Demographic Case Study." *Register of the Kentucky Historical Society* 80 (Spring 1982): 151–69.

"Narrative of Col. John Stuart of Greenbriar." *William and Mary Quarterly* 22 (Apr. 1914): 229–34.

Nelson, B.H. "Some Aspects of Negro Life in North Carolina During the Civil War." *North Carolina Historical Review* 25 (Apr. 1948): 143–66.

Newsome, A.R. "Twelve North Carolina Counties in 1810–1811." *North Carolina Historical Review* 5 (Oct. 1928): 413–46.

Olsen, Otto. "Historians and the Extent of Slave Ownership in the Southern United States." *Civil War History* 18 (June 1971): 101–16.

Opie, John. "Where American History Began: Appalachia and the Small Independent Family Farm." In *Appalachia/America: Proceedings of the 1980 Appalachian Studies Conference*, edited by Wilson Somerville, 58–67. Boone, N.C.: Appalachian Consortium Press, 1981.

Otto, John Solomon. " 'Hillbilly Culture': The Appalachian Mountain Folk in History and Popular Culture." *Southern Quarterly* 24 (Spring 1986): 25–34.

———. "Southern 'Plain Folk' Agriculture: A Reconsideration." *Plantation Society in the Americas* 2 (Apr. 1983): 29–36.

Parish, Peter. "The Edges of Slavery in the Old South: Or, Do Exceptions Prove Rules?" *Slavery & Abolition* 4 (Sept. 1983): 106–25.

Patton, Sadie. "Fame of WNC as Major Health Resort Dates from 18th Century." *Asheville Citizen*, 26 Mar. 1950.

Pearsall, Marion. "Cultures of the South." *Anthropological Quarterly* 39 (Apr. 1966): 128–41.

Pearson, Alden B., Jr., "The Tragic Dilemma of a Border State Moderate: The Rev. George E. Eagleton's Views on Slavery and Secession." *Tennessee Historical Quarterly* 32 (Winter 1973): 360–73.

Pessen, Edward. "How Different from Each Other Were the Antebellum North and South?" *American Historical Review* 85 (Dec. 1980): 1146–47.

Peterson, Owen M. "W.W. Avery in the Democratic National Convention of 1860." *North Carolina Historical Review* 31 (Oct. 1954): 463–78.

Phifer, Edward W. "Champagne at Brindletown: The Story of the Burke County Gold Rush, 1829–1833." *North Carolina Historical Review* 40 (Oct. 1963): 489–500.

———. "Money, Banking, and Burke County in the Ante-Bellum Era." *North Carolina Historical Review* 37 (Jan. 1960): 22–37.

———. "Saga of a Burke County Family." *North Carolina Historical Review* 39 (Winter, Spring, and Summer, 1962). 1–17, 140–47, 315–24.

———. "Slavery in Microcosm: Burke County, North Carolina." *Journal of Southern History* 28 (May 1962): 137–65.

Queener, Vernon M. "East Tennessee Sentiment and the Secession Movement, November 1860–June 1861." *East Tennessee Historical Society's Publications* 20 (1948): 59–83.

Ralph, Julian. "Our Appalachian Americans." *Harper's Monthly Magazine* 107 (June 1903): 32–41.

Rothstein, Morton. "The Antebellum South as a Dual Economy: A Tentative Hypothesis." *Agricultural History* 41 (1967): 373–82.

Rubin, Julius. "The Limits of Agricultural Progress in the Nineteenth Century South." *Agricultural History* 49 (Apr. 1975): 362–73.

Schlotterbeck, John T. "The 'Social Economy' of an Upper South Community: Orange and Greene Counties, Virginia, 1815–1860." In *Class, Conflict and Consensus: Antebellum Southern Community Studies*, edited by Orville V. Burton and Robert C. McMath, Jr., pp. 3–28. Westport, Conn.: Greenwood, 1982.

Shalhope, Robert. "Toward a Republican Synthesis: The Emergence of an Understanding of Republicanism in American Historiography." *William and Mary Quarterly* 34 (1982): 334–56.

Sheeler, J. Reuben. "The Development of Unionism in East Tennessee." *Journal of Negro History* 29 (Apr. 1944): 166–203.

Sitterson, Joseph Carlyle. "Economic Sectionalism in Ante-Bellum North Carolina." *North Carolina Historical Review* 16 (Apr. 1939): 134–56.

Stealey, John Edmund, III. "Slavery and the Western Virginia Salt Industry." *Journal of Negro History* 59 (Apr. 1974): 105–31.

Stuckert, Robert P. "Black Populations of the Southern Appalachian Mountains." *Phylon* 48 (June 1987): 141–51.

Sutch, Richard. "The Profitability of Antebellum Slavery—Revisited." *Southern Economic Journal* 31 (Apr. 1965): 365–77.

Tennent, Gaillard S. "Medicine in Buncombe County Down to 1885: Historical and Biographical Sketches." Pamphlet rptd. from *The Charlotte Medical*, 1906.

Trelease, Allen W. "The Passive Voice: The State and the North Carolina Railroad, 1849–1871." *North Carolina Historical Review* 61 (Apr. 1984): 174–204.

Vipperman, Carl J. "Civic Virtue, Country Ideology, and the Machiavellian Moment in Southern History." In *Citta e Campagna Nell'Eta Dorata: Gli stati Uniti Tra Utopia e Reforma*, edited by Valeria G. Lerda. Rome: Bulzoni Editore, 1986.

Wallace, Carolyn A. "David Lowry Swain, The First Whig Governor of North Carolina." In *Studies in Southern History*, edited by J. Carlyle Sitterson. James Sprunt Studies in History and Political Science, vol. 39. Chapel Hill: Univ. of North Carolina Press, 1957.

Walton, Brian G. "Elections to the United States Senate in North Carolina, 1835–1861." *North Carolina Historical Review* 53 (Apr. 1976): 168–92.

Watson, Harry L. "Conflict and Collaboration: Yeomen, Slaveholders, and Politics in the Antebellum South." *Social History* 10 (Oct. 1985): 273–98.

————. "Squire Oldway and His Friends: Opposition to Internal Improvements in Antebellum North Carolina." *North Carolina Historical Review* 54 (Apr. 1977): 105–19.

Wilhelm, Gene Jr. "Appalachian Isolation: Fact or Fiction?" In *An Appalachian Symposium*, edited by J.W. Williamson, pp. 77–91. Boone, N.C.: Appalachian Consortium Press, 1977.

————. "Folk Culture History of the Blue Ridge Mountains." *Appalachian Journal* 2 (Spring 1975): 192–222.

————. "Folk Settlements in the Blue Ridge Mountains." *Appalachian Journal* 5 (Winter 1978): 204–45.

Williams, Cratis D. "The Southern Mountaineer in Fact and Fiction," *Appalachian Journal* 3 (Autumn 1975 and Winter 1976): 8–61, 100–62.

Williams, Max R. "The Foundations of the Whig Party in North Carolina." *North Carolina Historical Review* 47 (Spring 1970): 115–29.

————. "William A. Graham and The Election of 1844: A Study in North Carolina Politics." *North Carolina Historical Review* 45 (Jan. 1968): 23–46.

Woodson, Carter G. "Freedom and Slavery in Appalachian America." *Journal of Negro History* 1 (Apr. 1916): 132–50.

C. THESIS AND DISSERTATIONS

Abrams, William J., Jr. "The Western North Carolina Railroad, 1855–1894." Master's thesis, Western Carolina Univ., 1976.

Burton, William Franklin, Jr. "The Issue of *Ad Valorem* Taxation in Ante-Bellum North Carolina." Master's thesis, Univ. of North Carolina, Chapel Hill, 1940.

Butts, Donald C. "A Challenge to Planter Rule: The Controversy over the Ad Valorem Taxation of Slaves in North Carolina, 1858–1862." Ph.D. diss., Duke Univ., 1978.

Censer, Jane T. "North Carolina Planters and Their Children." Ph.D. diss., Johns Hopkins Univ., 1982.

Cotton, William D. "Appalachian North Carolina: A Political Study, 1860–1899." Ph.D. diss., Univ. of North Carolina, Chapel Hill, 1954.

Daniel, Carolyn A. "David Lowery Swain, 1801–1835." Ph.D. diss., Univ. of North Carolina, Chapel Hill, 1954.

Dunn, Durwood C. "Cades Cove During the Nineteenth Century." Ph.D. diss., Univ. of Tennessee, Knoxville, 1976.

Ford, Lacy K., Jr. "Social Origins of a New South Carolina: The Upcountry in the Early Nineteenth Century." Ph.D. diss., Univ. of South Carolina, 1983.

Gilbert, Clarence N. "The Public Career of Thomas L. Clingman." Master's thesis, Univ. of North Carolina, Chapel Hill, 1946.

Glass, Brent D. "King Midas and Old Rip: The Gold Hill District of North Carolina." Ph.D. diss., Univ. of North Carolina, Chapel Hill, 1980.

Hartman, Vladimir E. "A Cultural Study of a Mountain Community in Western North Carolina." Ph.D. diss., Univ. of North Carolina, Chapel Hill, 1957.

Heath, Raymond A., Jr. "The North Carolina Militia on the Eve of the Civil War." Master's thesis, Univ. of North Carolina, 1974.

Horton, Frazier Robert. "Negro Life in Watauga County, North Carolina." Bachelor's thesis, Agricultural and Technical College of North Carolina (Appalachian State Univ.), 1942.

Jeffrey, Thomas E. "The Second Party System in North Carolina, 1836–1860." Ph.D. diss., Catholic Univ. of America, Washington, D.C., 1976.

Kenzer, Robert C. "Portrait of a Southern Community, 1849–1881: Family, Kinship, and Neighborhood in Orange County, N.C." Ph.D. diss., Harvard Univ., 1982.

Leath, Thomas H. "The Know-Nothing Party in North Carolina." Master's thesis, Univ. of North Carolina, Chapel Hill, 1929.

Russell, Mattie. "William Holland Thomas, White Chief of the North Carolina Cherokees." Ph.D. diss., Duke Univ., 1956.

Schlotterbeck, John T. "Plantation and Farm: Social and Economic Change in Orange and Greene Counties, Virginia, 1716 to 1860." Ph.D. diss., Johns Hopkins Univ., 1980.

Shay, John M. "The Anti-Slavery Movement in North Carolina." Ph.D. diss., Princeton Univ., 1970.

Shinoda, Yasuko I. "Land and Slaves in North Carolina in 1860." Ph.D. diss., Univ. of North Carolina, Chapel Hill, 1971.

Shirley, Franklin R. "The Rhetoric of Zebulon B. Vance: Tar Heel Spokesman." Ph.D. diss., Univ. of Florida, 1985.

Shrader, Richard A. "William Lenoir, 1751–1839." Ph.D. diss., Univ. of North Carolina, Chapel Hill, 1978.

Siegmann, Marlene D. "Thomas Lanier Clingman, Political Pilgrim, 1843–1852." Master's thesis, Wake Forest Univ., 1964.

Taylor, Robert Love. "Mainstreams of Mountain Thought: Attitudes of Selected Figures in the Heart of the Appalachian South, 1877–1903." Ph.D. diss., Univ. of Tennessee, Knoxville, 1971.

Walther, Eric H. "The Fire-Eaters, the South, and Secession." Ph.D. diss., Louisiana State Univ., 1988.

Wieman, David F. "Petty Commodity Production on the Cotton South: Upcountry Farmers in the Georgia Cotton Economy, 1840 to 1880." Ph.D. diss., Stanford Univ., 1983.

Williams, Cratis D. "The Southern Mountaineer in Fact and Fiction." Ph.D. diss., New York Univ., 1961.

Index

*Mountain Masters, Slavery, and the Sectional Crisis in Western
North Carolina* was designed by Dariel Mayer, composed by
Bruce Graphics, Inc., printed by Cushing-Malloy, Inc.,
and bound by John H. Dekker & Sons, Inc. The book is set
in Palatino. Text stock is 60-lb. Glatfelter Antique, B-16.